Roads to Social Capitalism

Theory, Evidence, and Policy

Peter Flaschel
Professor of Economics
Bielefeld University, Germany

Sigrid Luchtenberg
Professor of Education
Duisburg-Essen University, Germany

Edward Elgar
Cheltenham, UK • Northampton, MA, USA

Published by
Edward Elgar Publishing Limited
The Lypiatts
15 Lansdown Road
Cheltenham
Glos GL50 2JA
UK

Edward Elgar Publishing, Inc.
William Pratt House
9 Dewey Court
Northampton
Massachusetts 01060
USA

A catalogue record for this book
is available from the British Library

Library of Congress Control Number: 2012930618

FSC
www.fsc.org
MIX
Paper from
responsible sources
FSC® C018575

ISBN 978 1 78100 287 2

Printed and bound by MPG Books Group, UK

Contents

Part II The Forces to Cope With: Effective Demand, Finance and Innovation

About the Authors

Peter Flaschel is Professor Emeritus at Bielefeld University, Germany. He holds a PhD degree in Mathematics and a Habilitation degree in Economics. He has extensively published on Classical Economics and Heterodox Macrodynamical Model Building. He was on numerous occasions visiting professor at the University of Technology, Sydney and was invited in 2006 as Theodor Heuss Professor to the New School for Social Research, New York. He received an Opus Magnum Grant from the Fritz Thyssen / Volkswagen Foundations in 2007/08.

Sigrid Luchtenberg is Professor of Education at Duisburg-Essen University, Germany. She holds a PhD degree in German Linguistics and Literature and a Habilitation degree in Multicultural Education. Her interests in multicultural and comparative education have been the basis for various international contacts, as a returning visiting professor at the University of Sydney in particular. Her work on Human Rights and Citizenship Education has led her into topics of social sciences in general. Her numerous publications include work on Applied Linguistics, Migration, Multicultural Education, Media, and Social Structures of Capitalist Economies.

Foreword

In the midst of the double crisis of the Economy and of Economic Theory, we need innovative ideas. These ideas have to be soundly based on analytical foundations as well as on an appreciation of the limits of political economy. Flaschel and Luchtenberg have written a book which will be read deeply and for a long time. Exploring the ideas of Marx, Keynes and Schumpeter, they range across modern capitalist economies including the USA, China and the EU. They ask why unregulated Capitalism is in the doldrums and provide a theoretically sound answer to that question. They visit the Eurozone crisis and examine the choices open for Greece. They look for hopeful signs of reconstructing Capitalism along socially responsible lines in the many concrete policies being put forward in policy initiatives around the world. How the modern capitalist economy can continue to invest and innovate, maintain free labour markets and yet provide flexibility combined with security to its population, how financial markets can be better regulated, and how banks can be made more stable and less prone to violent speculation are some of the issues explored here. Social Capitalism is the future if we are to have a sustainable, humane society. The approach is rigourous yet politically nuanced. Here is a book which many should read, including even those readers for whom mathematics is a foreign territory. The substantial discussions are very rich and rewarding for students, researchers, policy makers and anyone who cares about a better future.

London, February 12, 2012 *Meghnad Desai*

Preface

This book is on roads to a kind of capitalism which eventually can be considered 'social' in nature. It approaches this task from the perspective of theory, evidence and policy from a positive as well as a normative point of view. In the latter case its approach may also be characterised by the triple: ideal, status quo and compromise, where our stress is on 'ideal' as the necessary prerequisite for formulating compromises in view of the status quo of actual societies.

The theoretical framework of the book attempts a synthesis of the work of Marx, Keynes and Schumpeter on ruthless capitalism, regulated capitalism and in the case of Schumpeter also competitive socialism. The current crisis in the financialization of capitalism and its repercussions on the viability of whole countries severely questions the achievements of mainstream economics and its disregard of Keynes's theory of effective demand and finance. Moreover, the neglect of Marx's work on the conflict between capital and labour in mainstream economics is obvious, while Schumpeter has become part of their story through its theory of economic development. The MKS approach of this book shows however that Marx, Keynes and Schumpeter can be synthesised in fruitful ways, which are yet far from being exhausted.

Applications of this approach will concern work regulations and labour market institutions, demand management problems, banking and financial markets as well as technological innovation processes. We add to this environmental issues accompanying the process of capital accumulation and an investigation of the national fiscal crises in the Southern part of the Euro Area, where we focus on the case of Greece and the – in our view – too restrictive IMF type measures used to consolidate the budget of the Greek government. In the final chapter we use these various aspects of the process of capital accumulation in order to develop our conception of the architecture of 'Social Capitalism' where in contrast to most types of socialism we insist on the relevance of the profit-seeking motive for the economic evolution of advanced Western societies. However, this motive is to be incorporated into a well-designed river bed of social and democratic regulations, since capitalism per se is neither economically viable nor socially responsible as history has shown and continues to show.

A number of professional colleagues, in particular Carl Chiarella, Reiner Franke and Gangolf Groh, have contributed kindly to the present project through stimulating discussions on various aspects of the subject matter of this book. We are also grateful for comments and criticisms we have received from participants at presentations of aspects of the material of this book at international conferences and research seminars. We moreover wish to thank Uwe Köller for his excellent editorial work. Finally we would like to thank Matthew Pitman of Edward Elgar for all he has done to make the publication process go as smoothly as it has.

Bielefeld and Essen, February 6, 2012

Peter Flaschel
Sigrid Luchtenberg

Acknowledgement

Peter Flaschel acknowledges support through an Opus Magnum Research Grant from the Fritz Thyssen/Volkswagen Stiftungen which allowed him to focus exclusively on this and other research projects during the academic year 2007/8.

General Introduction

In this chapter we will sketch one approach to the macroeconomic analysis of the dynamics of capitalist economies which we believe is principally in line with what we observe in reality, be it on the level of historical facts or on the level of rigorous macro-econometric analysis. These statements however do not mean that this theoretical approach is already well-established in the details of its formulation or beyond any doubt, but like capitalism itself it is – though imperfect – currently without genuine alternative, as far as an understanding of disequilibrium adjustment processes which constitute the restless dynamics of capitalism is concerned. This opinion may not be shared by many macro-economists, in particular by those working in the highly sophisticated and prestigious areas of current New Classical or New Keynesian macro-dynamical model building. On the basis of this theoretical prejudice, we will then discuss in highly stylised form the three most important varieties of current capitalism, as represented by the United States of America, the European Union and as an exceptional case the People's Republic of China. Our primary interest in this discussion is to see how close the political leadership of these economies are to a proper understanding and – on this basis – a proper institutional design and further social advancement of the parts of the world economy they are responsible for.

Against this background we will then briefly define our conceptualisation of 'social capitalism', a concept recently used in various ways in the academic and public debate.[1] Our interest in this concept is the degree of precision which can be associated with these compound words, in its understanding of both the words 'capitalism' (characterising the forces of production) and 'social' (representing the mode of production). We here would be neither content with approaches that understand nearly all capitalist economies with a social design as a specification of 'social capitalism', as for example the meanwhile questionable concept of a 'Social Market Economy' for the German welfare state of the so-called Freiburg School. Nor would we accept the removal of 'capital' from 'social capitalism' and regard the resulting shortcut expression of 'Socialism' as a theoretical fruitful step, since a proper model of non-profit seeking socialist forces of production as a competitive alternative to the profit-seeking capitalist forces of production[2] has not yet been provided in the academic literature on 'Socialism'.[3] In the individual chapters of the book we will move instead through various stages in the evolution of capitalism before we will arrive at our conceptualisation and analysis of 'social capitalism' and the inseparable nature these compound words should exhibit in future discussions on the evolution of the capitalist mode of production.

Goodwin's MKS system

The core piece of Marx's work appeared in 1867, *Capital*, Vol. I, where Marx laid the foundations for his labour theory of value on which he then built his theory of surplus value, his central tool for the investigation of the capitalist way of the exploitation of workers. Within the macroeconomic one-good world of the present as well as other macroeconomic books, the tools Marx used for his theory of exploitation are very simple to define and to apply, though this already changes when two-sector economies, producing a consumption-good as distinct from an investment-good, are considered. In such a case however not only Marxian topics have to be reconsidered, but also Neoclassical and Keynesian ones then need reinvestigation. This is however not the topic of this book which is concentrated on macroeconomic issues solely.

In 1967, 100 years after the publication of Marx's *Capital*, Richard Goodwin published his formalisation of another important topic in Marx's *Capital*, Vol. I, his theory of the reserve army mechanism the driving force behind the capitalist process of capital accumulation, in short, the Marxian theory of the distributive cycle. This growth cycle model has since then become the workhorse for many approaches to cyclical capital accumulation and this book is no exception in this regard.[4] Various other laws of motion in Marx's theory of capitalism concern however secular (quasi-monotonic) tendencies and these tendencies have not really be confirmed by history, like the tendency of the general rate of profit to fall, for example.

Marx died in 1883, the year in which two important later opponents of his theory were born, John Maynard Keynes and Joseph Alois Schumpeter. Keynes (1936) considered all theory before his own as but a special case of it, while Schumpeter, according to Goodwin

(1989, ch.8), not only was very critical of Marx, the prophet, the sociologist, and the economist, but also completely refuted Keynes's *General Theory* as being much too narrow. Goodwin (1989, ch.6) however views the contributions of these great economists as being not only compatible with each other, but he also demanded their urgent integration. In our view this is indeed a compelling need, since Keynes added effective goods demand in its interaction with financial markets to the conflict-driven production and distribution theory of Marx, while Schumpeter (1939) came up with a much more refined theory of cyclical capital accumulation, of – at his time – three long-waves in the evolution of capitalism, much more than it was possible for Marx to foresee in 1867. It is our view that the MKS system proposed by Goodwin (1989) as a fruitful analytical framework is indeed the best point of departure for the understanding and the theorising of the evolution of capitalism in Marx's times, in Keynes's and in Schumpeter's times as well as in our times now.

We do not deny that the integration of the work of these three great economists is not without contradictions and that it is partly still in its state of infancy, with some parts already being quite developed, like the theory of demand-driven distributive cycles, see here Chapter 4. In contrast, other parts are quite underdeveloped, like the analysis of credit-driven capital accumulation and innovation, or speculation-driven financial markets as in the current financial crisis of commercial banking, on the markets for financial assets and indeed within entire economies.

The working hypothesis of this book is that the MKS system is the best theory we have at our disposal to approach an understanding of such issues or, to put it differently, the more we depart from the essential insights of these great economists the farther away we are from understanding what has happened and is currently happening in the world economy and what we might expect to happen in it in the future. Mainstream economists have done everything they could to discredit the theory of Keynes, even if they used his name in their modelling approaches. But as the recent financial crisis has shown, there are many things that his theory would have been able to predict, in contrast to the currently fashionable general equilibrium theories of the New Classical and the New Keynesian variety.

Schumpeter did not face the same difficulties in getting accepted by mainstream economics (though not right from the start), since his views on the potential failures of capitalism were not so obvious and since his work on a Western type of socialism was largely ignored by economists. Things concerning Marx were however of quite the opposite type and in his case neither orthodox nor non-orthodox model-oriented theory has taken his theory of exploitation in production and in the distribution of the national product very seriously, the exceptions being contributions from the perspective of Analytical Marxism on the one hand (where there is currently some revival through rigorously trained young economists) and from a Goodwinian perspective on the other hand (where there has been a steady, though small, flow of contributions since 1967).

Marx, Keynes and Schumpeter also considered the capitalist world from the social and the philosophical point of view (ranging from harsh critique to sceptical challenge), views which are normally either neglected in the literature or discredited by (questionable) associations with the actual evolution of socialism in the East. In this respect our point of departure – originally underlying the gestation of this book – was in fact not so much a Marxian theory of Socialism, where nothing too specific has been published by Marx and Engels, based on their approach to the understanding of capitalism using historical materialism. It may be that capitalism was just not yet developed enough to clearly describe an alternative to it as Schumpeter (1942) did it in detail in his book. In Schumpeter's approach Socialism is not conceived as the product of the (r)evolutions in the Eastern part of Europe, but as the result of the activities of the great dynasties in the Western part of the world through the visible hand they created in the planning of large national and international companies. Such 'social' planning of (large-scale) investment, trying to cope with the dark forces of the future, is also part of Keynes's philosophy of how to regulate the future evolution of capitalism.

Judging from the perspective of the history of economic thought leads us to the question what we can consider as an alternative to the MKS system as described above. The Classical authors Smith, Ricardo and Mill are not really in contradiction with the views of an MKS-system, though there may be aspects, like Smith's invisible hand that are meanwhile acknowledged as clearly not being part of the world we are living in. As Neoclassical authors we would name in this respect Walras, Hayek and Wicksell (related respectively to RBC theory, New Classical theory and New Keynesian theory). In our view it is however not possible to build a reasonably complete theory of the dynamics of capitalism on such a set of authors from the Neoclassical world, one that can really compete with an MKS analysis of the periodically failing interaction of the goods markets with the labour markets on the one hand and the financial markets on the other hand. As pronounced above, we will now look at three typical and central forms of capitalism as to be found in the United States, in the People's Republic of China, and in Europe from the perspective of an MKS-based theory. We here point already to the fact that capitalism per se needs not be associated with democratic political structures, but can also be associated with 'plutocratic' ones or be at work under the rule of one party.

The United States of America

From the perspective of the preceding section, the biggest problem for the conduct of the economy and society of the United States of America lies in the fact that its fundamental understanding of its capitalist forces of production is not of the MKS variety, but more of a Walrasian laissez-faire type as far as academic teaching and reasoning is concerned. This reasoning is of course made more suggestive and popularised by the media and the politicians. Its basic credo is that everybody is responsible for his or her own life and basically has to care about her/himself. A European-type welfare state is therefore hard to justify and to realise in the United States and must be redefined and extended by the educational system, which is not a typical welfare state issue, in order to push the US into the role of a leader – instead of a laggard – in comparison to other welfare states, see Garfinkel, Rainwater and Smeeding (2010).

But in a world of MKS type, we have demand-driven distributive cycles with recurrent mass unemployment, we have unregulated Schumpeterian processes of creative destruction and we have financial markets and banking systems which tend to act like casinos with an ever increasing range of speculative objectives. It is therefore an unacceptable conclusion that the ordinary (worker) household is solely responsible for its fate in such a system if the mass unemployment created through insufficient effective demand is caused by speculation-driven financial markets and the implied rationed investment behaviour. Of course, as far as the Marxian reserve army mechanism is concerned, workers are partly involved in and responsible for its historical occurrences. This is also acknowledged by Marx in the discussion of this mechanism, but he also made clear that – at least at his time – workers are much too weak to really change this reserve army mechanism in significant ways.

This may no longer be true in general in the varieties of capitalism that now exist, but it is certainly still true in the case of the US economy where unions are weak and where corporatist regimes between firms and workers do not show ways out of the profit- and subsequent wage-squeeze processes which characterise the working of such unregulated capitalism. The basic insight of an MKS approach is that capitalism without state intervention is not a viable construction. This was obvious in 19th century British type capitalism which ruined the health of worker families to such an extent that the military began to complain about the state of its soldiers. Chancellor Bismarck in Germany was one of the first who realised that capitalism without a social network for workers would become a failure on socio-political grounds. Beveridge (1945) with his book 'Full Employment in a Free Society' designed the foundations of the welfare state in the UK, including the realisation of basically full employment within the capitalist forces of production.

But after the fall of the Iron Curtain in the Eastern part of Europe – and partly already through Reaganomics and Thatcherism as a response to the Marxian profit-squeeze of the 1960s and 1970s (and its welfare state implications) – the ideas of Beveridge have lost most of their relevance. The Marxian theory that unregulated capitalism produces segmented labour markets, with pauperism down at the bottom, and the Keynesian theory that unregulated capitalism produces recurring severe booms and busts, including financial crisis, was simply not a topic that bothered both influential politicians and opinion makers on both sides of the Atlantic.

In the case of the US – and to a certain degree also in the UK – the influence of neoliberal thinking was and still is particularly deep rooted, with general equilibrium ideas of the New Classicals and the New Keynesians at the top of the hierarchy of these wrong conceptions of the working of capitalism and thus the world we are living in. Such theories are formulated with great rigour nowadays, but their relevance is often judged in the mainstream literature from a methodological standpoint solely, namely whether they are microfounded (from the perspective of a single agent, not from a more appropriate principal-agent point of view), of course, whether they assume continual market-clearing, and whether they are using 'rational expectations', i.e., expectations that make no systematic errors over the whole future of the economy. With such a theoretical core behind the economic and political debate in the USA on all levels of the society, the decisions that flow out of the debate will at best be contradictory, since they are orthodox in nature as long as there is room for the misconduct of the economy and they become by and large ad-hoc Keynesian in nature in times of severe economic and financial crisis, due to a lack of alternatives in such cases, i.e., in the case of a Hobson's choice.

In the case of the United States of America there is another political problem that is intervening with and amplifying the incommensurate state of socio-economic theory and practice. According to Schumpeter (1942) majority voting is designed to bring about governments that are capable of acting, since it – at least when Duverger's law holds[5] – tends to produce two party systems, as in the USA for example. However, the president of the United States is elected separately so that it may happen – as it is currently the case for President Obama – that he lacks a majority in the house of representatives. This means in the present situation of the USA that an expansionary Keynesian fiscal policy can be prevented by the Republican opposition, which has for the Republican party the three-fold advantage that it can stick to its neoliberal ideas (and enforce them via the House of Representatives) as in the current crisis of the US economy, that it can blame President Obama for the outcome of no economic recovery during the coming elections and that it can integrate the right-wing tea-party movement into its own election campaigns. The situation is as the one in Greece where the party that was indeed responsible for the turmoil in the real and the financial markets (in the USA due to its laissez-faire policy during the subprime crisis in particular) is trying as much as possible to tie the hands of the governing party in its handling of the crisis of the state. In a situation of severe economic and social crisis this must be considered as not only completely inefficient, but also as a highly undesirable outcome of democratic decision making (in this particular design).

The British majority voting system is in this respect significantly more coherent in its construction, since the Prime Minister is always elected by and leading a majority of the members of Parliament (at least generally, in the two-party outcomes of majority voting systems).[6] This does of course not mean that the ruling party always adopts the right policy measures in a state of crisis as the current one, but such an elected Prime Minister can of course be subject to a resolution of no confidence and thus be 'induced' to resign, like Tony Blair in 2007, if essential elements of his policy decisions turn out to be ineffective or detrimental or simply unacceptable. We consider it an open question here whether a proportional voting system, like the one in Germany, has more disadvantages or advantages over a properly designed majority voting system and also leave aside the questions about what improvements can indeed be designed for the

British system in order to increase its degree of effectiveness, its degree of representation and its social acceptance by the voting population.[7]

The People's Republic of China

There is one striking contrast between China and the United States of America that in fact speaks in favour of China from the purely economic perspective. It is given by our conjecture that it is not only much easier for China to adopt an integrated MKS framework for its economic policies, but that China has already done this successfully in the past, quite in contrast to the USA. Overall macroeconomic control is what China is in fact doing in a very strict manner. To relate Marx with Chinese economic and social policy is of course easy from an ideological point of view, since the People's Republic of China is ideologically seen based on Marx's (and his successors') views of the world. This does not mean that China is using Marx's theoretical insights in the gestation of its economic and social policy which some might claim is now more capitalist (and in Marx's categories: exploitive) than socialist in nature. This may indeed be a correct claim, but it in fact only implies a rereading of Marx's theory of *Capital*, Vol. I – III, and its continuation up to the present time, that implies that the forces of production of capitalism are (still) unrivalled in the world economy. Yet, the relations of production which surround the Chinese forces of production are, we believe, far from being acceptable from a socio-political Marxian point of view. This in particular concerns the creation of absolute and relative surplus value (as investigated in Marx's *Capital* Vol. I), where China's economy is clearly exploitive in nature, concerning labour productivity as well as income distribution. And in the political sphere the lack of human rights, division of power and freedom of opinion is obvious.

This judgement however does not question that China's 'Socialism' is best built on the progress achieved by the capitalist conduct of enterprises, the heritage of the Vanderbilts, the Rockefellers and the Carnegies as Schumpeter (1942) stated it in his theory of a competitive type of socialism. The Soviet Union – and with it the German Democratic Republic – failed, because they did not realise this and instead created economic production structures that were not capitalistically planned as in the Western world, but unprofessionally regulated ones with soft budget constraints throughout, because the adoption of Western type planning and financial control was beyond the ideological horizons of the Central Committees of the former Eastern socialist countries.

Gorbachev may have understood the need for such a change on the level of Soviet enterprises, but it may have been already too late for a controlled adoption of such economic reforms, so that he primarily induced political change, not based on any sound economic reasoning, which however is the foundation for political change in the longer run. The Soviet Union therefore collapsed from the top, before it had been built on more solid grounds at the bottom, which then became by and large the subject of an unregulated imposition of a capitalist system. The ideological barriers concerning the capitalist conduct of enterprises of former Eastern socialism were however successfully removed in China under Deng Xiaoping.[8] One may claim here that this was just the result of accepting the superiority of the capitalist forces of production as they were accepted by Marx at his time and praised by Schumpeter with his figure of the dynamic entrepreneur, in the form of the family dynasties and the large companies that in his views have shaped world capitalism thereafter.[9]

Schumpeter (1942) analysed that the capitalism of his time could fail nevertheless – due to growing hostility – and could be replaced by a Western type of socialism for which he investigated in detail the chances of being or becoming a democratic one. We here assert that China has indeed realised the vision of Schumpeter (1942) of a competitive (Western) type of socialism, but in fact one that comes from the Far-East, that is socially and politically still undetermined in its future, in particular in the extent of democratic decision making, not to speak of a constitution with a proper separation of power.[10] Schumpeter (1942) did not exclude the possibility that his type of competitive socialism could also be an authoritarian one in the longer run. We therefore now indeed have a factual example for his approach to socialism, which integrates the 'bourgeois element' on the level of business elites, the social and political future of which is however an open question.[11]

Coming back to the Marxian component in Chinese policy we assume that politicians in China are aware of the working of the Marxian reserve army mechanism, the second basic conflict between capital and labour, besides the one in production. We assume (or hope) that Chinese policy is far-sighted enough to not only regulate conflicts in production by law to such an extent that China's still 'ruthless' form of capitalism becomes a viable way of product and process gestation and innovation (including environmental issues), that moreover takes account of the wage–price spiral of the Marxian distributive cycle such that the rapid growth of the Chinese economy is not only serving the new capitalists, but also the working population.

To understand (intuitively) the Marxian approach to the conflict between capital and labour in production and in income distribution does not mean that one must use it in favour of the working class (as the example of Margaret Thatcher shows), but the Chinese government would only be wise if it would attempt to balance the interest of both classes (if it can recognise them as such) to a sufficient degree. To argue in this way does not mean, however, that the lack of a democratic constitution with a sound division of powers – which in our view is much more fundamental than the question of how many parties compete against or within each other under such a constitution – becomes acceptable, if a certain degree of social care about the employment and the income of the working population is realised. Finally, regarding Keynes's views on fiscal policy and financial market regulation, we interpret the behaviour of Chinese economic policy as being definitely of a Keynesian type. There should be no reservation in China against the Keynesian view of the need for state intervention, be it in the counter-cyclical conduct of fiscal policy, the partial control of the investment behaviour of firms or the exclusion of too much speculation in the financial management of the economy. The limits of laissez-faire thinking and of neoliberalism are certainly not a substantial intellectual barrier for Chinese economic thinking and their visible hand in the conduct of firms and in micro- and macro-economic policy making.

In closing this section, let us briefly compare this with the socio-economic situation in the United States of America. As we have explained, political actors there face great difficulties in understanding and applying the basic insights of an MKS-oriented view of the world. The current government is now almost incapable of acting even if it is assumed that it understands the causes and the cures of the current crisis. It is already facing the next electoral campaign, with its enormous consumption of campaigning efforts, money and repetitive arguments. And it is situated in a political environment where right-wing stupidities rule the roost in the public debate in place of rational arguments (in our view) of democrats about the best way for the future evolution of the United States. Can such a deeply split country with its plutocratic tendencies and their 'telecratic' amplifications really compete with a well-determined and from the purely economic perspective relatively insightful one-party rule of the Chinese type in the longer-run? We have doubts about that, though there is definitely also considerable innovative potential within the forces of production of the United States of America, concerning both high-tech capital and high-skilled labour, a situation which in our view could be significantly fostered if there were understanding of the real forces that shape capitalism in the USA and also more socio-philosophical reflection of the state of the US society.[12]

The European Union

In their book on *The Future of Europe* Alesina and Giavazzi (2006), themselves Europeans, arrive at the conclusion that Europe will lose its influential role in the world if it is not subject in the near future to an extensive economic-political reform with the aim of giving up its overprotected and overregulated socio-economic structures, i.e. in particular, its political influence on the economics of the European countries and the support of their welfare state regulations. In contrast to this reasoning of Alesina and Giavazzi (2006) this chapter, by and large, takes its point of departure – in comparison to the situation in the United States of America – from the basic insight (which need not be shared, of course) that the future of capitalism will depend very much on its capability to integrate its 'dynamic forces of production' with a truly 'social mode of production', a theoretical and societal project that proper Neoliberals will regard as not only superfluous, but also detrimental for the progress of free-market capitalism and that most neo-Marxists would probably consider as deeply contradictory, since they consider 'socialism' and 'capitalism' as being inherently antagonistic conceptualisations of human societies. Wolff (2002) however states:

> *For elements of communism are developing under capitalism, behind our backs. Engels, in particular, points out that a number of elements of advanced capitalism are either already models of communism, or ripe for takeover.*

Compared to the times of Engels we now know much more about the historical evolution of capitalism, and also of socialism and communism. Our objective with this book is to show that the above integration towards what we will call 'social capitalism' is however not a reconciliation of conceptualisations of 'socialism' with those of 'capitalism', but that capitalism itself can indeed be induced to develop the elements which make it a 'social' mode of production in a stable democratic environment.

Looking at the current situation in the European Union and the Eurozone from a welfare-state point of view one can – based on Esping-Andersen's (1990) famous work – nowadays distinguish at least four types of welfare states, two continental ones in the North and in the South, the Nordic countries and the United Kingdom as an exceptional case. The case of Ireland differs from the UK, despite at least some common Anglo-Saxon heritage, due to Ireland being part of the Eurozone and due to the relatively recent rise and fall of Ireland as a Celtic tiger. A similar classification regarding the OECD countries (in 1990) can be found in Pryor (2010, table 4.1), where we would however move the Netherlands into the set of Nordic countries now and Ireland and Switzerland out of his group of Anglo-Saxon economic systems into the continental north.[13] In this book we will not focus on exceptional profiles, as they may also be observed in the Baltic states which belong to those countries in the European Union which were part of the Soviet bloc before the fall of the Iron Curtain. In this book, we will also not consider the evolution of these latter countries, which came out of this bloc and its environment and joined the European Union.

Instead we look in specific ways at the performance of some welfare states in the 'continental north' (primarily Germany, but also Austria) where corporatist regimes between capital and labour, Hartz IV reforms[14] of the labour market of the German Social Market Economy and the establishment of networks of civic work are important characteristics or maybe future developments. In the 'continental south' we will focus in later parts of the book on the case of Greece as the most vulnerable country in the current southern danger-zone of possible state defaults. Both types of welfare states may be considered as 'ugly' ones, in the first case – in Germany – due to the invasion of its concept of a Social Market Economy by neoliberal ideas, which opened the watergate into temporary employment and low income work without a general minimum wage floor. In the case of Greece this label 'ugly' is appropriate due to the rampant debt-financed fiscal policy of its past governments which also had severe negative impact effects on the competitiveness of the Greek economy. In contrast to this, one can distinguish 'good' from 'bad' welfare states, where the first characterises the situation where it is basically accepted that 'good' welfare measures have their price in the form of high taxes and where 'bad' signifies the opposite, namely low welfare measures, but also low taxes as far as the provision of welfare programs is concerned.

It goes without saying that all actual examples exhibit much more detail than such a simple classification can show. Yet, the Danish flexicurity system with its high unemployment benefits and strictly activating labour market policy measures (as an example for the 'good' case) is clearly quite different from the workfare system in the UK, where little welfare is combined with only small contributions to the unemployed, in particular the young members of the workforce, though there are in fact general minimum wage regulations in the UK (and the USA) in contrast to Germany. Pryor (2010) concludes in his study of four types of economic and cultural systems that the differences are more in the social economic outcomes than in strictly economic ones. Astonishingly enough, Alesina and Giavazzi (2006) give a positive picture of the Scandinavian countries in spite of their general rejection of welfare states, high taxes and state influence.

The case of the European Union therefore clearly shows varieties of capitalism in operation, and this even more so if the new members of this union – and also Switzerland – are taken into account. Starting from Bismarck's social reforms and Beveridge's conceptualisation of the welfare state, we have an astonishing variety of forms attempting to cope with the 'natural' forces of production of capitalism within Europe, exhibiting specific changes in this variety in the prosperity phase after World War II, in the stagnant phase that followed (with Thatcherism at the one extreme and Mitterand's socialist experiments at the other), and with further changes in the decades after the fall of the Iron Curtain and the disappearance of Eastern type socialism. We conclude from all this that there exists a great potential of possibilities within Europe that allows us to learn from its various forms of capitalism, from the regimes of good, bad and ugly welfare states, from workfare systems, flexicurity approaches and from the performance of the democratic institutions and parties in these various European countries.

Flexicurity, the combination of flexibility with security, has become a seriously studied approach in the EU with the aim to improve the economic and social situation in the member states. The European Commission held consultations with relevant stakeholders, the outcomes of which were published as its Communication on Flexicurity in June 2007.[15] In November 2007, The European Council added 'Draft Council Conclusions Towards Common Principles of Flexicurity'[16] which shows the relevance the flexicurity model had gained in the EU. This is also related to the so-called Lisbon Strategy (see below). In 2008, a 'Mission for Flexicurity' was set up by the Commission which studied the possibility for flexicurity in different EU countries and underlined the positive role of a flexicurity model.[17] The question as to how flexicurity can be introduced in different countries is also a topic of European Flexicurity Pathways, as, for example, discussed by Bekker and Wilthagen (2008). The European Commission has underlined from the beginning that Member States should be encouraged to develop their own flexicurity strategies, depending on their national situation.

Flexicurity is supposed to create a more flexible workforce, but at the same time employment security for workers. There are also critical statements by organisations such as The Trade Union Confederation ETUC which fears that flexicurity will mainly support workers' flexibility. On the other hand, the employer organisation BusinessEurope regards flexicurity as an opportunity to modernise labour markets.[18] There are four policy components described by the EU-Commission 2007 which include flexible and reliable contractual arrangements through modern labour laws, collective agreements and work organisation, comprehensive lifelong learning (LLL) strategies, effective active labour market policies designed to especially reduce unemployment spells and to ease transitions into new jobs and also to create modern social security systems (adequate income support, employment encouragement, labour market mobility), including social protection provisions like unemployment benefits, pensions and healthcare.[19] The Commission also established principles, referred to as '*flexicurity* components'.[20] A main topic here is one of balancing, for example establishing a balance between rights and responsibilities within the labour market and also to produce balanced policy packages to promote climates of trust. This is not astonishing, since flexicurity can only develop if both sides – employees and employer – find a balance between their various claims.

In the autumn of 2006, the majority of EU citizens accepted the idea of a knowledge-based economy, that is, the importance of education, which also includes lifelong learning (Eurobarometer 66).[21] Nevertheless, the topic of education is still a fairly neglected issue in major countries of the EU like Germany and the United Kingdom. We view the direction of the political debate on labour market institutions (and indirectly on full employment) in the European Union as a very fruitful one, though there is always the danger that the proper balance between flexibility and security is not adequately established in the actual adoption of such labour market strategies. But the construction of an ideal flexicurity system as in Flaschel and Greiner (2011, 2012) may be one thing and the struggle for its most important ingredient, safe life-course perspectives for the employees within an actual flexicurity economy can be quite another issue and may demand very cumbersome social processes of the learning-by-doing type. In our view the European Union is however heading into the right direction in this matter, and thus also indirectly addressing the Marxian issue of the distributive cycle, though this topic is at present set aside to a certain degree due to the current preoccupation of European politicians with the financial and the fiscal crisis within the Eurozone.

Concerning such issues, the renaissance of Keynes's (1936) *General Theory of Employment, Interest and Money* has long been overdue and its relevance cannot be underestimated, even though many would also point to Minsky's (1982, 1986) work as far as the prediction of recurrent deep financial crisis on a worldwide scale is concerned. But Keynes (1936) was the founder of feedback-guided macroeconomics with financial markets at the top of the interacting feedback channels between the major markets of the macroeconomy. He already wrote in his *General Theory*:

> *The introduction of a substantial Government transfer tax on all transactions might prove the most serviceable reform available, with a view to mitigating the predominance of speculation over enterprise in the United States.* (Keynes 1936, 159-60)

Major contributions to his theoretical approach also came from Tobin, see for example Tobin (1980) on asset accumulation and economic activity. However, despite the renaissance of such Keynesian thinking about the role of the financial markets in the evolution of the real markets of the economy, international policy is still largely divided on how to react to the turmoil on financial markets, not to speak of their regulation, and also regulation of the banking sector. The topic of a financial transaction tax is still controversial, but the European Union intends to push for a decision on a financial transaction tax at the Cannes G20-Summit in 2011. European Commission president Jose Manuel Barroso wants to introduce a tax on financial transactions to curb excessive speculation in the markets and to create more revenue for debt-ridden governments. There is however significant resistance to such plans from within the EU (from the British, Dutch and Swedish government) as well as from within the G20 countries. It seems that the financial crisis needs first to become much worse, before the dysfunctional role of the financial sector for a proper evolution of the real economy becomes widely accepted as a central insight of Keynes's *General Theory*.

Concerning Schumpeter's insights the situation is quite a different one. There are important initiatives within the European Union which attempt to push them forward in particular from the viewpoint of European innovation-driven international competitiveness, but also from the viewpoint of labour market reforms and the input they need from the educational system. Most prominently among these initiatives is the so-called Lisbon Strategy. This Lisbon Strategy (or Agenda) was adopted by the European Council for a ten-year period in the year 2000 as the result of a special meeting in Lisbon, Portugal. The aims were to strengthen employment, economic reform and social cohesion as part of a knowledge-based economy, due to the effects of globalisation and the appearance of knowledge-driven economies, both of which were viewed as demanding transformations of the European economy. The ambitious aim was summarised in the goal to become the 'most dynamic competitive knowledge-based economy in the world', so that the 'knowledge triangle' – research, education and innovation – can be called a core factor in European efforts to meet the ambitious Lisbon goals (Lisbon European Council 23 and 24 March 2000).[22] Hartmann (2007a) points out that the Lisbon strategy – especially the renewed one from 2005 – is strongly influenced by Neo-Schumpeterian and Evolutionary Economics and by economists, such as Chris Freeman or Bengt-Ake-Lundvall who are working in these areas. This corresponds to the statement of Hanusch and Pyka (2007a) that the Lisbon Agenda is mainly based on innovation strategies in line with Neo-Schumpeterian Economics. In order to not only focus on industry dynamics, they suggest the approach of Comprehensive Neo-Schumpeterian Economics (CNSE) which is characterised by three pillars, that is, the industry sector, the financial sector and the public sector. An empirical study of 14 developed EU countries shows in their view that 'CNSE can be operationalised without major difficulties' and can combine the Lisbon Agenda with their three-pillar approach. Their study shows that country heterogeneity in Europe demands a 'sound, balanced and differentiated policy', but allows 'grouping countries with similar pillar compositions'. Such an analysis should contribute to the discussion of policy measures within the Lisbon Agenda.

The Lisbon Agenda certainly contains important aims and suggestions but in June 2009, shortly before Sweden took over the presidency of the Council of the European Union, Fredrik Reinfeldt, the then Swedish prime minister admitted its failure, which may be due to several reasons, one of which might have been its non-binding character, but probably also the financial crisis in 2008.[23] Yet, the imminent danger of a failure of the Lisbon strategy was already a topic in the Kok Report 2004 which accused the EU member states lacking commitment (Civitas 2007).[24] This led to the decision to relaunch the Lisbon strategy, so that in March 2005 a renewed strategy was published which also focused on more coordination and exchanges between the member states.[25] Hartmann (2007a, p.26) describes three aspects of renewal, intended to combine growth and jobs creation:

> *Making Europe a more attractive place to invest and work, foster knowledge and innovation for growth, and creating more and better jobs.*

According to Hartmann (2007a, p.26ff.), the original aspects of competition and socially oriented markets are underlying these points, but knowledge and innovation have clearly become the dominant issues. Nevertheless, innovation dynamics and the fostering of social cohesion are viewed as combined strategies. This corresponds to Hartmann's (2007a, p.36) conclusion that

> *Entrepreneurship and innovation are seen as key factors for growth and competitiveness, but while it is necessary to implement Schumpeter to achieve the forefront of technological and economic development in a fast changing, globalised world, the internal (European) system needs also certain socioeconomic stability and (re)compensation mechanisms to be socially viable and desirable. Thus, the question is how to achieve fertile creative destruction mechanisms but maintain social stability and justice, corresponding to the intrinsic values of the European Union, for example democracy, social cohesion and freedom of the actors.*

As we have already discussed above, the European Union focused on the flexicurity concept as a possible solution.

In March 2010 a new 10-year strategy was proposed by the European Commission with the aim of reviving the economies of the European Union. The targets of the Europe 2020 strategy concern: Employment, R&D innovation, Climate and Energy, Education and Poverty reduction. Meanwhile, all member states have adopted national targets in these fields according to the Commission[26] though there is also the criticism that the 2020 strategy 'treats all EU countries' economies as the same regardless of how they now operate' (Civitas 2007).[27] At least, the member states are asked for reports each year to show their activities for the Europe 2020 national targets. Furthermore, it is suggested that the 'civil society' – including businesses, trade unions, non-governmental organisations and individual citizens – has to integrate itself into the aims of Europe 2020. Again – as in the Lisbon Agenda, the five targets of Europe 2020 are ambitious, but they now differ between the member states. For instance, there is the general aim of employment for 75% of 20–64 year old citizens, but while

Germany is supposed to reach 77%, Denmark and the Netherlands intend to get 80%, but some member states also less than 75% as Greece 70%, Spain 74%, Ireland 69–71%, Italy 67–69%. There are also significant differences with regard to education which include two aspects: a reduced percentage of early school-leavers, and access to tertiary education. While the EU expects 10% of early school-leaving, Greece should get 8.7%, Spain 15%, Ireland 8%, and Italy 15–16%. Not unrelatedly, with regard to tertiary education, Italy exhibits with 26–27% a very low rate, similar to Greece with only 32%, while Spain is with 44% above the EU target of 40% and Ireland has with 60% the highest rate. These rates are not set by the EU, but are set by the member states.[28]

Both educational targets can be understood to contribute to several aims which are the decisive factors of Europe 2020: the reduction of school drop-out rates will not only most likely raise the EU employment rate, but should also contribute significantly to a reduction of poverty in Europe and thus also to social cohesion. A higher number of students who leave schools with a certificate also adds to an improvement of production as does a higher amount of tertiary education.[29]

The aim of the Lisbon Agenda to create a dynamic competitive knowledge-based economy can also be found in Europe 2020, where, for example an investment of 3% of GDP in Research and Development (R&D) is set as an objective. Since investment in R&D was only in some parts of the European Union a relevant issue, the necessity to include this task in Europe 2020 was high, especially in view of the higher R&D expenditures in China and the developing Asian economies. The economic growth in these latter countries indeed allows for such increases in their R&D expenditures. Until 2010, there were four member states (Germany, France, the United Kingdom and Italy) who exhibited two thirds of R&D expenditures in EU-27, which made a R&D target in Europe 2020 a necessity, since R&D is closely related to economic growth.[30]

Among the five targets for Europe 2020, 'climate and energy' has to be understood as a target for sustainable growth with the aim of a competitive, but low-carbon economy, the development of new green technologies and production methods, and the improvement of the business environment. Thus, 'climate and energy' targets are part of an economic competitiveness strategy (also with regard to small manufacturing firms), aiming at a reduction of dependence on fossil fuels, but also supporting the environment and thus the lifestyle of the European citizens.[31] Europe 2020 is still in its starting phase so that possible results or failures are not yet stated in the media. The aim of a 'smart, sustainable and inclusive economy' can be found among its targets, though there is certainly also a competitive goal to be found.[32]

The three growth objectives – smart, sustainable and inclusive growth – provide a résumé of seven, so-called flagship initiatives. Thus smart growth includes 'a digital agenda for Europe – fast/ultrafast internet and interoperable applications – innovation Union – for example, refocusing R&D – and youth on the move – different measures to improve students' skills, better studying possibilities etc', while the 'resource efficient Europe and an industrial policy for the globalisation era' section calls for sustainable growth with flagship initiatives like reducing CO^2 emissions, or the development of industrial policy for the globalisation era. Inclusive growth contains 'an agenda for new skills and jobs as well as a European platform against poverty', where ensuring economic, social and territorial cohesion are viewed as a help against poverty as well as improving employment. All flagship initiatives deal with competitive economic developments and a focus on skilled employees.[33]

In view of the economic and financial crisis in the world economy with their iterant, erratically behaving stock markets we do not view the European Union to be in a more comfortable position than the United States of America, though the profile of European problems has become quite different from that of the USA as was shown above. In contrast to Alesina and Giavazzi (2006), (see the characterisation of their book at the beginning of this section), we would however – with the crisis in hindsight – conclude that capitalism demands more, not less, regulation in order to counteract its sometimes very severe social segmentation processes,[34] its creation of private media with a poor value-based orientation, its creation of financial market structures that are driven by short-sighted gamblers instead of serving long-run investment strategies and – in the political area – by forcing presidential candidates to depend more and more on huge amounts of money and in particular on the TV media in the curtailment of the contents of their presidential campaigns.

Plan of the Book

We have discussed in this chapter in stylised form three varieties of capitalism which are normally not viewed in this way. We considered first the US economy and its 'free to lose' type of capitalism, then the Chinese economy with which we have associated the realisation of a

Schumpeterian type of competitive socialism and finally the European Union with its multi-layered social structures and its attempts to reform labour market institutions, implement regulative policy measures and induce competitiveness and innovation, three areas of economic and social policy with which we associated the theoretical system discussed at the beginning of this chapter.

In the remainder of this book we will continue to elaborate and to build on such a theoretical framework. In Part I we study Marx's distributive cycle with homogeneous labour as well as with segmented labour markets. We discuss policy measures intended to mitigate the consequences of Marx's reserve army mechanism and the overshooting income claims of capital and labour it implies. We supplement this factual approach to capital accumulation and the policy measures it may call for with a normative one where full employment is constructed within an ideal circular flow of income and transfers and a work-wage management system which guarantees the stability of the economy on the macro-level.The resulting flexicurity model is to be contrasted of course with the actual debate on flexicurity in the EU and its realisation in Denmark in particular.

Part II provides partial models of what we consider as MKS theory. We investigate in its three chapters the Marxian distributive cycle in its interaction with Keynesian goods market dynamics and also the latter dynamics in its interaction with financial markets and commercial banking. Here we again introduce a normative model for commercial banking as defined by a narrow banking system with a Fisherian 100% reserve ratio. In a third chapter we finally study Schumpeterian innovation waves and the dynamic patterns they can give rise to.

In Part III we turn to the investigation of further major current problems which question short-run economic stability or long-run social viability on a worldwide scale. In Chapter 7 we study environmental decay as a further problem of unrestricted capitalism in association with the working of Marx's reserve army mechanism which further questions the long-run viability of this mechanism. We then again introduce a normative framework (based on a flexicurity system), where environmental rehabilitation takes place and leads to a sustainable type of capital accumulation. Chapter 8 considers the case of rampant fiscal policies of the government of single countries, a situation which is currently endangering the Euro and which has raised the question of whether the Eurozone will survive the current financial crisis. We consider the policy of the IMF in practice and in theory in the case of Greece and then again an ideal policy with a longer-run strategy for the evolution of such countries that have been subject to rampant fiscal policy, like in Greece.

In Chapter 9 we finally discuss against the background of an unleashed capitalist economy the variety of welfare, workfare and flexicurity systems discussed and implemented in various countries in the EU. In contrast to this, we then introduce a new social structure of capital accumulation which we call 'social capitalism'. We intend with this composite concept to be more precise than what is called a 'Social Market Economy' in Germany, by stressing that the forces of production of the economy are capitalist in nature while the mode of production is a social one. We stress that this concept is also directed against all tendencies to define the socialism of the 21st century without an integration of the progress (in the conduct of firms) which has been achieved through the capitalist forces of production. Schumpeter's concept of competitive socialism may however constitute a (less pleasant) alternative to our conceptualisation of social capitalism as the discussion of China's current evolution intended to indicate.

We do not think that our concept of 'social capitalism' is already fully articulated and sufficiently implemented in the academic or public discussion.[35] Instead it is intended to serve as a precise point of departure for further scientific discussion and investigation. It is our conviction however that the future of ruthless capitalism is a finite or even gloomy one and that capitalism will either become social in nature (through theory-guided policy actions) or fail – at least in its democratic design. We can learn from Marx in this respect that capitalism must be subject to well-designed factory laws (now of twenty-first century type of course) and solid labour market institutions (see part I of the book). Keynes laid the theoretical foundations for macroeconomic overall control (including financial markets) and Schumpeter the foundations for technological progress and product innovation theory where the observed long waves in economic activity however need to be regulated from the social point of view.

The figure I.1[36] summarises to a certain extent the skeleton of the reasoning in this book. Its left hand side is more associated with the contents of Chapters 1,2,4,5 and 6 while its right hand side finds more expression in Chapters 3,5,7,8 and 9. Positive approaches deal with issues such as mass unemployment, segmented labour markets, effective demand problems and excessive banking. Normative approaches concern full employment, narrow banking, environmental protection and sound fiscal policies. All this finally leads us to the construction of 'social capitalism' which is stable from the viewpoint of

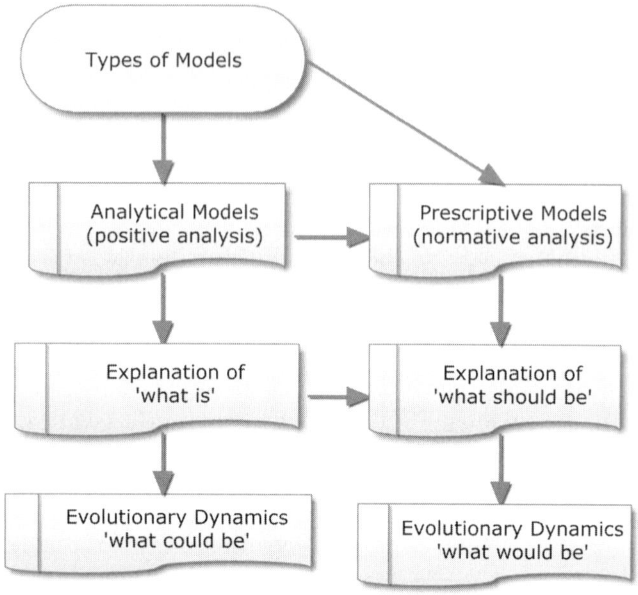

Figure I.1 Methodology of the book

a Marxian work-wage management system, from the viewpoint of the conduct of Keynesian fiscal and monetary policy and competitive from a Schumpeterian perspective of creative destruction and innovation policies.

Summing up, and in view of what we have just discussed, we would define 'Social Capitalism' as being founded on the MKS approach to an understanding of the nature of capitalism, as far as the forces of production are concerned. Yet it must then be embedded in social relations of production which – on the level that EU type capitalism has now partly reached – should be progressively extended to establish safe life-course perspectives of households, an up-to-date comprehensive all-day schooling system and finally the coordination of activities on all levels of business administration as well as in public adminstration by democratically elected and controlled elites, at least in all areas where such coordination decisions concern a significant number of workers or citizens. Instead of a society perceived as being led by an invisible hand on apparently independently acting markets or being subject to neoliberal laissez-faire policies, we observe a visible hand in business as well as public adminstration activities, where – as under the existing advanced capitalism – coordination and incentive problems have to be solved and further developed in professional ways. This is not a third way between the neoliberal and the socialist views of the world (which are both misleading), but the application of a social philosophy which can be derived from a proper understanding of MKS-based theory of the evolution of capitalism in place of hypothetical Walrasian theories of market capitalism or market socialism. The only real alternative may be Chinese type competitive socialism, the social philosophy of which still remains undecided and one that is currently definitely questionable from a Marxian perspective, concerning the exploitation of labour power in factories as well as on the labour market and also the short-sighted cost-oriented exploitation of nature. Factory laws and labour market regulations as we discuss them in Chapter 1 may be – among other measures of social legislation – essential steps in the further evolution of the Chinese society.

Notes

[1] See Kersbergen (1995), Chan (2002) and Corfe (2008) in particular and here Chapter 9 for details.

[2] See Cockshott, Cottrell and Dieterich (2010) for a recent attempt in this direction.

[3] This in fact also holds for Schumpeter's (1942) theory of socialism, where his description of the execution of 'socialist blueprints' (even when enriched – as is proposed by him – with the directive of 'ex-bourgeois elements') is too close to static Walrasian-type Market Socialism to be convincing, and this also from today's potential of computability capacities.

[4] See Flaschel (2009) for a detailed discussion of the Marxian origins of the Goodwin growth cycle model and Flaschel and Landesmann (2006, 2008) for the 'legacy of Richard Goodwin'.

[5] See Grofman, Blais and Bowler (2009).

[6] This was however not the case in the UK general elections of 2010 where a so-called hung parliament resulted due to the lack of an absolute majority for the Conservative party which then formed a coalition government with the Liberal Democrats. Such a coalition is however still much more able to act than is the case for the hostile interactions of Republicans and Democrats in the USA.

[7] See Alonso, Keane and Merkel (2011) for a variety of contributions on the future of representative democracy.

[8] See McGregor (2010, ch.7). The history of the People's Republic of China and its political leadership is reflected in detail in Kissinger (2011).

[9] One may argue that societies like China win when it comes to copying the initial successes of societies like the American one, but will always lack the innovative capacity of the US economy. An example is the iPad, where a society such as China could never have come up with such an idea, but the iPads of the future will surely be produced in China and also improved on. The closed nature of the Chinese society however will prevent the rise of a truly innovative class of Schumpeterian type. Here the Americans, for all their other problems, will continue to dominate.

[10] See here however Z. Yongnian's article: 'China and democracy: Not a contradiction in terms' in Wong and Bo (2010).

[11] Schumpeter's (1942) leadership model of democracy and theories that can be built on this approach, not however his model of a competitive type of socialism, are discussed in detail in Brooker (2010).

[12] For the evolution of the relationships between corporate governance and democracy from the historical and the theoretical point of view see Gomez and Korine (2010).

[13] Pryor's (2010) book provides a detailed study of his classification scheme, in particular regarding comparisons with the cultural systems he identifies.

[14] See Chapter 2 for a detailed discussion.

[15] See http://eur-lex.europa.eu/LexUriServ/LexUriServ.do?uri=CELEX:52007DC0359:EN:NOT

[16] See http://register.consilium.europa.eu/pdf/en/07/st15/st15497.en07.pdf

[17] See European Commission (2008)

[18] See http://www.eurofound.europa.eu/eiro/2007/07articles/eu0707069i.htm

[19] See European Commission (2008a).

[20] See http://www.eurofound.europa.eu/eiro/2007/07/articles/eu0707069i.htm

[21] See Eurobarometer 66, 'Public opinion in the European union', European Commission Fieldwork: October-November 2006, http://ec.europa.eu/public_opinion/archives/eb/eb66/eb66_en.pdf

[22] See http://www.europarl.europa.eu/summits/lis1_en.htm, http://cordis.europa.eu/fp7/understand_en.html and http://www.euractiv.com/en/future-eu/lisbon-agenda/article-117510

[23] See http://www.euractiv.com/en/priorities/sweden-admits-lisbon-agenda-failure/article-182797

[24] See http://civitas.org.uk/eufacts/FSECON/EC12.htm and http://ec.europa.eu/information_society/tl/essentials/reports/kok/index_en.htm

[25] See http://www.euractiv.com/en/innovation/growth-jobs-relaunch-lisbon-strategy/article-131891

[26] See http://ec.europa.eu/europe2020/index_en.htm

[27] See http://civitas.org.uk/eufacts/FSECON/EC12.htm

[28] See Europe 2020 targets (http://ec.europa.eu/europe2020/pdf/targets_en.pdf)

[29] See http://ec.europa.eu/europe2020/index_en.htm and http://civitas.org.uk/eufacts/FSECON/EC12.htm

[30] See http://ec.europa.eu/research/innovation-union/pdf/competitiveness-report/2011/part_1.pdf

[31] See http://ec.europa.eu/europe2020/index_en.htm

[32] See http://ec.europa.eu/europe2020/index_en.htm and http://europa.eu/press_room/pdf/complet_en_barroso____007_-_europe_2020_-_en_version.pdf

[33] See http://ec.europa.eu/europe2020/tools/flagship-initiatives/index_en.htm

[34] Like the ones one can observe in large US cities like Baltimore for example.

[35] See Kersbergen (1995), Chan (2004) and Corfe (2008) for its propagation.

[36] We have to thank Aloys Prinz for allowing us to use this figure from one of his comments on our work.

PART I

Failing Capitalism: Baseline Scenarios and Social Reforms

1. Capital Accumulation and the Marxian Reserve Army

... a rise in the price of labour resulting from accumulation of capital implies the following alternative: Either ... Or, on the other hand, accumulation slackens in consequence of the rise in the price of labour, because the stimulus of gain is blunted. The rate of accumulation lessens; but with its lessening, the primary cause of that lessening vanishes, i.e., the disproportion between capital and exploitable labour-power. The mechanism of the process of capitalist production removes the very obstacles that it temporarily creates. The price of labour falls again to a level corresponding with the needs of the self-expansion of capital, whether the level be below, the same as, or above the one which was normal before the rise of wages took place. (Marx 1954, p.580)

1.1 Introduction

In the recent past, unregulated financial markets appeared to be the big threat for the proper working of advanced capitalism. Starting from a subprime mortgage crisis, to which US policy makers at first paid not much attention to, due to the belief that markets do regulate themselves, the banking system came close to a systemic banking crisis, with stock markets collapsing, and with now a threatening fiscal crisis and government insolvency in particular in the 'PIGS' of Southern Europe (Portugal, Italy, Greece, Spain) and maybe further countries.

There is fear that the Eurozone may collapse and there are proposals to throw countries like Greece out of the Eurozone, since they have systematically violated the conditions of the EU growth and stability pact. So far the worst case has been prevented by massive policy interventions, but the situation is still far from being rectified. This holds in particular for banking where the scheduled banking regulations (Basel III and more) are not of a very far reaching type. For example a return to narrow banking, an idea initially proposed by Irving Fisher

(1935) in the aftermath of the Great Depression of the 1930s, is not really a topic in the banking regulation debate, a Tobin tax on financial transactions (in our view also on capital gains) is not considered seriously, since the Casino function of modern capitalism is still believed to be the efficient way to channel savings into investment or to back up endogenous credit by endogenous money creation.

Uncontrolled financial innovations, like securitization and credit default swaps, will however continue to happen in the future and will continue to create financial crises in the way it is described (and predicted for the current crisis) in Minsky's work, see Minsky (1982) in particular. But in the light of the above quotation from Marx's *Capital*, Vol. I, we will substantiate in this book that there is a more fundamental contradiction in the capitalist mode of production, clearly visible in the ruthless form it is working now in Russia and similar countries, but less visible in the advanced Western capitalist economies, namely the recurrent phenomenon of mass unemployment and the social degradation of the workforce it implies. It is our view that these processes will undermine the working of democracy in the long-run and thus question in a more fundamental way the values on which Western democracies are based. Tendencies towards such a development exist in the USA which is on the way to a plutocratic society, and also in Italy, there in particular supported by the TV media, in a kind of 'telecracy'.

And quite in general there is the evolution of Western democracies towards segmented societal structures with a significant segment of low income population and with age poverty as one of its consequences and as another: low educated children, who have no real life perspectives. Such tendencies are clearly visible in Germany where school education is far from being a coherent whole, but where teachers suffer from burnout syndromes and where youth violence is becoming more and more a severe problem.

It is the intention of this book to investigate this development, building on Marx's analysis of the fundamental conflict in capitalism, the conflict between capital and labour not only over income distribution, but also within the process of capitalistic production. We however believe that this conflict can be transformed into a social system in which (regulated) profit-seeking behaviour can be made compatible with social evolution, based on human rights and democratic decision processes. It is therefore our intention to not only investigate the Marxian reserve army mechanism in its working and its social implications, but also to demonstrate to the reader in a sequential manner that there is an increasing structure of societal reforms at our disposal where the end-result can be a type of full employment capitalism, where profit-seeking is not in contradiction with a rational, well educated structuring of the societies we are living in. The present chapter will start this investigation by beginning with a model where the Marxian reserve army mechanism works as described in the above quotation, producing not only recurrent mass unemployment, but also low income work and a dead segment in the labour market. In subsequent chapters we then modify this approach by institutional changes which show that the described conflict between capital and labour can be attenuated in a stepwise fashion.

Capitalism may be viewed and valued from different perspectives, depending on its economic and political appearance, and especially on personal experience and knowledge. The influence of historical time can clearly be seen in the work of Marx, Keynes and Schumpeter. Can or should capitalism be described as failing from their perspective?

In the following we will show from a Marxian perspective on capitalist production and income distribution between capital and labour that a politically unregulated (and therefore unleashed) capitalist economy tends to an extreme splitting of the society in a rich and influential group, and a majority of poor and underprivileged persons. Such a development can in turn lead to civil disturbances, protests and even revolutions, as in particular the German Chancellor Bismarck as one of the first realised. We too suggest in this chapter that an unregulated capitalism will become a failing one from the social and the political perspective and needs definite state intervention, as it most of the time has indeed been necessary from its very beginning up to the present times.

1.2 Marx's General Law of Capitalist Accumulation: The Basic Case

In this section, we consider Marx's 'general law of capitalist accumulation' in the basic form he used as a starting point, in his words, see Marx (1954, ch.XXV.1), when the composition of capital remains the same, which in our simple model is given by the assumption of a fixed proportions technology (with Harrod neutral technical change, see below). We consider against this background the model of Goodwin (1967) of the distributive growth cycle and the reserve army mechanism in a suitably extended form in order to provide somewhat broader foundations for a discussion of the working of such a mechanism in descriptive form.

An Extended Goodwin Growth Cycle Model

The state variables of the Goodwin's (1967) growth cycle model are: $v = \omega L^d/Y$ (labour's share in national income, with $\omega = w/p$ the real wage) and $e = L^d/L$ (the employment rate). By definition these two variables must fulfill the following two identities: $\hat{v} = \hat{\omega} - \hat{z}, \hat{e} = \hat{K} - \hat{L} - \hat{z}$, where K denotes the capital stock, L the stock of workers and $m = \hat{z}$ the given growth rate of labour productivity: $z = Y/L^d$, L^d labour demand. Here, $\hat{x}$ is used to denote the growth rate of a variable x. Goodwin's model thus assumes a Leontief technology with Harrod neutral technical change, with the fixed potential output to capital ratio given by $y = Y/K$ and with labour productivity denoted by $z = L^d/L$, which is growing at a constant rate m. Capital stock depreciation is represented by a constant rate δ.

On this basis we consider the following generalisation of Wolfstetter's (1977, pp.147 ff.) reformulation of Goodwin's model (where a constant mark-up a on unit wage costs $\frac{wL^d}{pY}$ is assumed).

$$\begin{aligned}\hat{\omega} &= \hat{w} - \hat{p} = f(e) + \eta\hat{p} - \hat{p} \\ &= f(e) + (\eta - 1)\beta_p(\frac{(1+a)wL^d}{pY} - 1),\ f' > 0, \qquad (1.1)\\ \hat{K} &= s(v)(1-v)Y/K - \delta. \qquad (1.2)\end{aligned}$$

Eq. (1.1) is Goodwin's real wage Phillips curve, now in general nonlinear form and augmented by a term which characterises the inflation targeting of workers: $\eta\hat{p}$, that is, workers actually receive a real wage increase which is lower for $\eta < 1$ (higher for $\eta > 1$) than the inflation-adjusted rate of growth of workers' real wage: $\hat{\omega} = f(e)$. The marked up cost-term $\frac{(1+a)\omega L^d}{Y}$ in the function $\beta_p(\frac{(1+a)wL^d}{pY} - 1)$ that provides the theory of price inflation of the model, represents the desired price level capitalist firms are adjusting to, with β_p as the speed of adjustment chosen by firms. The other law of motion (1.2) simply represents Goodwin's accumulation formula $\hat{K} = s(v)(1-v)y - \delta$, with a flexible savings rate of capitalists $s(v) \leq 1$ (while workers do not save). Both equations are discussed and explored in detail in Wolfstetter (1977), there in linearised form and for $\eta \leq 1$ solely.

We assume that the system (1.1) – (1.2) exhibits a sufficient degree of differentiability and that it has an economically meaningful steady state solution, representing a balanced growth path of the economy, $0 < v_o, e_o < 1$, which is uniquely determined by the equations (1.3) – (1.4) provided below. In fact, as we shall see below, the second equation determines the steady state wage share v_o independently from the other law of motion, while the first law of motion provides on this basis the steady state rate of employment (given by $f(e_o) = 0$ if $1 + a = v_o^{-1}$ holds).

Transformed to the state variables v, e, the wage share and the employment rate, the above dynamical system reads:

$$\hat{v} = f(e) + (\eta - 1)\beta_p((1 + a)v - 1) - m = f(e) + (\eta - 1)g(v), \quad (1.3)$$
$$\hat{e} = s(v)(1 - v)y - \delta - (n + m). \quad (1.4)$$

To explore the dynamics of this η–parametrized family of differential equations (1.3), (1.4), a slightly modified version of Olech's Stability Theorem which directly applies to a system formulated in rates of growth[1] and not in terms of time derivatives is now very comfortable:

Proposition 1: *Assume that the Jacobian* $J = (J_{ik})$ *of system (1.3), (1.4) fulfills: trace* $J < 0$, $\det J > 0$ *and* $J_{12}, J_{21} \neq 0$ *everywhere in* $\Re^2_+$. *Then, the equilibrium* v_o, e_o *of system (1.3), (1.4) is asymptotically stable in the large, that is, each trajectory which starts in* $\Re^2_+$ *will approach the equilibrium point* (v_o, e_o) *without hitting the boundary of* R^2_+.

Proof: By means of the diffeomorphism $D : \Re^2 \rightarrow \Re^2_+$ defined by $D(x, y) = (e^x, e^y)$ we get the following equivalent parameterised system of differential equations on $\Re^2$:

$$\dot{x} = \tilde{f}(e^x, e^y, \eta), \quad \dot{y} = \tilde{s}(e^x). \quad (1.5)$$

The linear part or the Jacobian of this system reads

$$J(x, y) = \begin{pmatrix} J_{11}e^x & J_{12}e^y \\ J_{21}e^x & 0 \end{pmatrix}$$

and it fulfills the same conditions as were postulated with regard to J. The above transformed system (1.5) consequently allows the application of Olech's original theorem, see Flaschel (2009, Ch.4), that is, it – and therefore also system (1.3), (1.4) – is asymptotically stable in the large.

Corollary: *The systems* $\tilde{f}, \tilde{s}$ *and* $-\tilde{f}, -\tilde{s}$ *fulfill the assumptions of the above proposition for* $\eta < 1$ *and* $\eta > 1$*, respectively.*

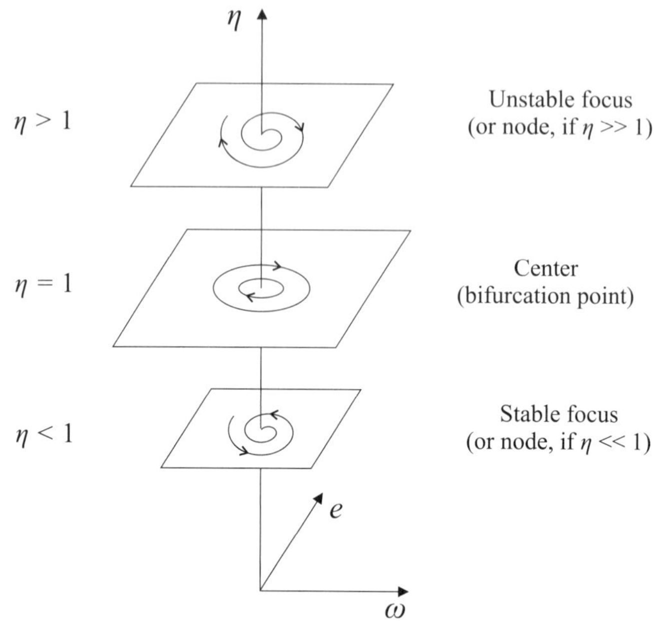

Figure 1.1 The Goodwin growth cycle as a degenerate Hopf bifurcation of the extended distributive cycle model

The interaction between the share of wages v and the employment rate e will thus always lead to or away from[2] the steady state equilibrium depending on what type of inflation targeting prevails in the economy. Figure 1.1 summarises these two results together with an obvious conjecture on what will happen in the limit case $\eta = 1$, that is, the Goodwin case. This diagram shows that the Goodwin case $\eta = 1$ cannot be structurally stable, since the topological properties of its dynamics are not preserved if this system is slightly disturbed by the inflation target term $\eta\hat{p}$.

By definition of the variables v, e it is, of course, desirable to point to some basic additional mechanisms which ensure that any trajectory which starts in the interval $(0, 1) \times (0, 1]$ cannot leave this subset of $\Re^2_+$. A possibility to obtain such a behaviour is given by the following modification of system (1.3), (1.4):

$$\hat{v} = f(e, v) - (\eta - 1)g(v) - m, \quad \eta \geq 1 \tag{1.6}$$

$$\hat{e} = s(v, e)(1 - v)y - \delta - (n + m), \quad s(v, e) = 0 \text{ for } e \approx 1 \tag{1.7}$$

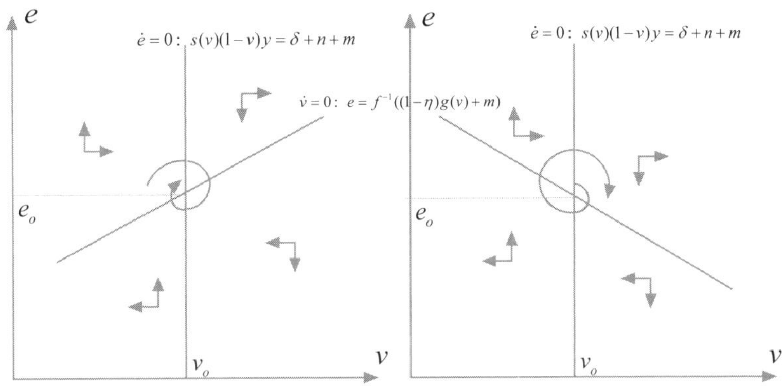

Figure 1.2 The distributive cycle: Attracting and repelling balanced growth configurations

where the modified function f is assumed to depend on v if and only if v is close to unity, in which case it is assumed that the conflict over income distribution implies that $f(e, v) \leq 0$ is fulfilled. The dynamical system (1.6), (1.7) is thereby perturbated in such a way that it points inward at the right hand side of $(0, 1) \times (0, 1]$ in the explosive case $\eta \geq 1$. And eq. (1.7) implies that $e \approx 1$ now acts as an upper ceiling on capital accumulation, that is, the implied cycles cannot hit the upper boundary of $(0, 1) \times (0, 1]$. Hence, eq.s (1.6), (1.7) indicate how economically meaningless values $v \geq 1, u > 1$ can be avoided for cycles which start in the economic part of the phase space $(0, 1) \times (0, 1]$. The result is that a limit cycle, representing persistent fluctuations in employment and income distribution, will be generated in the economic part of the phase space. This can be proved by way of the so-called Poincaré-Bendixson Theorem which in simple words states that this will always happen when for example a unique locally unstable steady state is surrounded by forces that keep the dynamics bounded.

The findings of this subsection can be used to provide the following baseline scenario. It is likely that close to the steady state of the model (where unemployment is of a type that is considered as normal) workers will base their negotiations on a target that is higher than just the inflation rate (which is close to zero if $1 + a = 1/v_o$ holds true). The steady state will therefore be repelling and the economy will move away from it. Figure 1.2 shows this situation in detail. This argument can be extended to all situations of abnormally high employment rates and may then demand upper ceilings as discussed above. In simpler terms one can just impose the side condition $e = 1$ once full employment is reached and let the wage share continue to rise until it has reached a level where investment is insufficient to further maintain the full employment level. The wage share may still continue to rise, creating a situation known as stagflation from the early 1970s, but there will come a point where no further increases of it will be accepted by firms (or by the 'government' as in the wage price freeze under the Nixon administration in the US economy). This will create the basis for a limit cycle situation, that is, persistent fluctuations in the rate of employment and the wage share, which can only (partially) be avoided if workers do no longer target for inflationary compensation. In the depressed state of the economy where both the rate of employment and the wage share are below their normal (average) levels this may then create forces that tend to bring the economy back to its balanced growth path (from below). These forces may however disappear again when the economy has returned to larger than normal employment levels, in particular if there has been a considerable wage squeeze during the downturn of this distributive cycle. Thereafter the described situation of a profit squeeze is reappearing again leading from a prosperity phase back – through a reoccurring phase of stagflation – into a new depression.

This is the basic form of the Marxian 'General Law of Capital Accumulation' based on the conflict between capital and labour about income distribution. It envisages a conflicting income demand process that is overshooting in four ways when one of its state variables, wage share and employment rate, has reached its normal level. The employment rate overshoots in the boom phase as well as in the bust as does the wage share, following the evolution of the employment rate with a quarterly phase delay. This overshooting distributive cycle is generated here through a centrifugal wage–price dynamics around its balanced growth path, which when they have become sufficiently pronounced generate a wage–price spiral in the boom which will generate a profit squeeze below or latest at full employment after which the reserve army of unemployed will be filled up again to such a degree that the wage share starts falling again. This happens to such an extent that capital accumulation will become abnormally high whereby the whole process is repeating itself.

In Figure 1.3 we provide an empirical example for the kind of phase diagram dynamics associated with the Marxian overshooting distributive cycle, see Figure 1.2 for its theoretical representation:

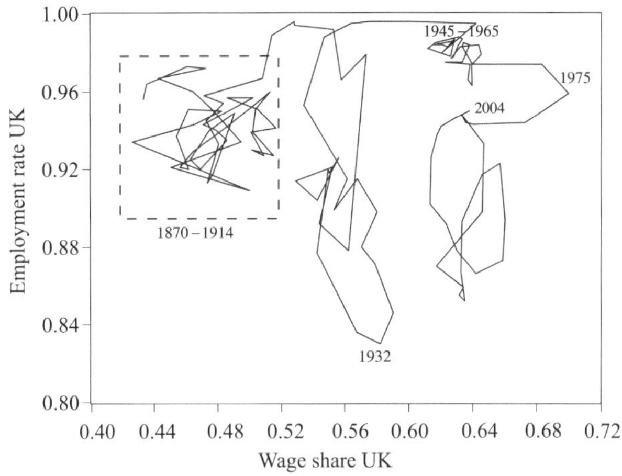

Figure 1.3 The distributive cycle: UK 1870–2004

We observe that the clockwise orientation of the Goodwin distributive cycle is mirrored by the shown UK data after World War I. Moreover, the impact of Magaret Thatcher (Prime Minister from 1979–1990) and Thatcherism is clearly visible in this phase plot. It appears as if Margaret Thatcher very well understood the Marxian reserve army mechanism and the overshooting wage claims it implies. One may however object that Friedman (1968) provided an alternative theory for this with the at his time so-called natural rate of unemployment and the cyclical movements around this equilibrium rate. His influential approach may provide an explanation of the policy change that happened under Margaret Thatcher in Great Britain and Ronald Reagan in the USA. Yet, the Walrasian underpinning, with its perfectly competitive markets, of the Friedman approach is in our view way off the point however, since this approach only allows for frictional unemployment by and large.

Some Marxian Aspects behind the Goodwin Growth Cycle Model

The situation of conflict between capital and labour we have investigated in the preceding section concerns the distribution of income between these two classes (with the government still being only in the background of the model). This however is a conflict on a second stage of the capitalist process of production, concerning the distribution of the result Y of this process. An equally important conflict between these two classes however is the one within and surrounding the production process itself. The components of this conflict are here hidden in the parameters of the model and also behind its state variables. They concern:

- the enforcement of the productivity level z, that is, in particular the number of hours worked by each worker. The details of the struggle about the length of the working day in the 19th century are described and analysed in detail in Marx's (1954) *Capital*, Volume I.X.
- the lack of any unemployment or health insurance, including at Marx's times also the lack of any occupational health and safety measures,
- the lack of any employment protection. Here the Goodwin model is in fact assuming free hiring and firing, since overtime and undertime work are immediately realised by employing new workers or by setting them free again, respectively,
- the possibility to lower the average real wage accruing to the workforce by increasing the rate of productivity growth m.

Marx (1954) analysed all these issues on the basis of the labour theory of value which we view as providing a Marxian System of National Accounts, see Flaschel (2010, part I), not as a theory that is meant to provide a price theory or an approximation for it, though of course the total labour costs (direct labour and the one incorporated in the means of production) constitute a significant component in price formation. Such empirical issues are however bypassed here and are in fact not a problem in a one-sectoral macromodel of the type here considered. Here, Marxian labour values are simply defined by:

$$\nu Y = L^d + \nu\delta K, \quad \text{or} \quad \nu = \frac{L^d}{Y}(1 - \delta K/Y)^{-1},$$

since indirect labour is only present in the form of the fixed capital goods that are used up in production. Making use of the consumption basket of workers per day worked: $c_w = C_w/L^d$, Marx then defined the rate of exploitation and the value rate of profit by the expressions:

$$\epsilon = \frac{1 - \nu c_w}{\nu c_w} = \frac{1 - \xi}{\xi}, \quad \rho = \frac{\nu(Y - \delta K) - \xi L^d}{\nu K},$$

where he called the magnitude $\xi = \nu c_w$ the value of manpower. The rate of exploitation was then described as representing the ratio between surplus labour to the labour time needed for reproducing the means of living of the workforce (per worker), the so-called necessary labour time. The rate ϵ therefore measures ratio between surplus and necessary labour or as rate of surplus value the division of the workday into the part where the worker works for his own reproduction and the part where he works in order to create surplus for the capitalist firm.

It is obvious that there holds

$$r = (1 - v)y - \delta = \frac{Y - \delta K - c_w L^d}{K} = \rho, \quad i.e.,$$

the value rate of profit is equal to the price rate of profit in such a one-sectoral framework. Moreover we have for the value rate of profit the factorisation

$$\rho = \frac{\nu(Y - \delta K) - \xi L^d}{\nu K} = \frac{L^d - \xi L^d}{\nu K} = \epsilon \frac{\xi L^d}{\nu K},$$

since the labour value of net output $\nu(Y - \delta K)$ is equal to the total labour time (measured here in work-days) performed by the workers, l^d. The fraction $\Omega = \frac{C}{V} = \frac{\nu K}{\xi L^d}$ is called by Marx the organic composition of capital or the ratio of constant to variable capital, in distinction from the technical composition $\frac{K}{L^d} = \frac{K}{Y}\frac{Y}{L^d}$. The latter ratio is rising in our model at the rate m, just as $c_w = \omega$, while labour values ν are falling at the rate $-m$, since $(1 - \delta K/Y)^{-1}$ is a given magnitude. This implies that the value of labour power ξ is constant over time in the steady state and thus also the rate of exploitation, and of course the rate of profit.[3]

It is often suggested that Marx's labour theory of value is redundant, since everything – in particular in the present section can be better presented and analysed in terms of prices of production which are just given by the price level p in this one sectoral framework. The advocates of this statement consequently suggest only to consider the expression $r = (1 - v)y - \delta$, the price rate of profit of the economy. They therefore only look at income distribution in this context. Yet, Marx did dig deeper and decomposed the rate of profit into

$$r = \epsilon \frac{\nu c_w L^d}{\nu K},$$

as was shown above. This decomposition shows that strategies that can raise the rate of profit r are not only given by a consideration of income distribution, but also by an increase in labour productivity as measured by the inverse of labour values, in Marx (1954, p.48) as well as in the

UN's System of National Accounts of 1968, see Flaschel (2010, part I). Technical change of this type, a reduction in the workers consumption basket, c_w, and an increase of the subdivision of the working day into unpaid labour time, (in terms of labour values) and paid labour time thus represent three different ways to pull up the rate of profit r and these tendencies have expressed themselves in capital-using labour-saving technical change as the typical form of the capitalist type of technical progress, in the reoccurring reduction of the real wage and thus consumption of the workforce (as described here by the distributive cycle) and the struggle about the length and the intensity of the working day (as analysed by Marx under the headings 'absolute and relative surplus-value').

These issues are inherently dynamic ones, that cannot be properly analysed with a uniform and given rate of profit, the point of departure of the Neo-Ricardian theory and its comparative static exercises. Instead we can reformulate the Goodwin model by way of a Marxian variable transformation which expresses the wage share v as follows:

$$v = \frac{\omega L^d}{Y} = \frac{\nu\omega L^d}{\nu Y} = \frac{\xi L^d}{\nu K}\frac{K}{Y} = \xi\frac{L^d}{\nu K}\frac{K}{Y}$$

where both fractions on the right hand side are given magnitudes in the model of this section and where ξ is the product of labour values and the consumption basket of workers. On the basis of such a decomposition Marx concludes:

> *The rise of wages therefore is confined within limits that not only leave intact the foundations of the capitalist system, but also secure its reproduction on a progressive scale. The law of capitalistic accumulation, metamorphosed by economists into pretended law of nature, in reality merely states that the very nature of accumulation excludes every diminution in the degree of exploitation of labour, and every rise in the price of labour, which could seriously imperil the continual reproduction, on an ever-enlarging scale, of the capitalistic relation. It cannot be otherwise in a mode of production in which the labourer exists to satisfy the needs of self-expansion of existing values, instead of, on the contrary, material wealth existing to satisfy the needs of development on the part of the labourer. As, in religion, man is governed by the products of his own brain, so in capitalistic production, he is governed by the products of his own hand.* (Marx 1954, *Capital*, Volume I, p.582)

1.3 Factory Acts, Hiring and Firing, Migration and a Real Wage Barrier

In this section, we will first consider briefly forms of work regulation from an historic viewpoint, concentrating on what Marx experienced in the United Kingdom of his times.

Already in 1802, the British government passed the first act to improve the working conditions in factories which should be followed by many further acts, known as the factory acts, subsequently approved by the Parliament of the United Kingdom. The main intention was to limit the working time of women and children.

Thus, for example the Factory Act of 1850[4] made it no longer possible for employers to decide on the work time but they had to accept limited hours per day and per week for children and women. So children as well as women could only work from 6 a.m. to 6 p.m. in the summer and 7 a.m. to 7 p.m. in the winter. Furthermore, all work would end on Saturday at 2 p.m. Yet, 60 hours work was still permitted per week.

In 1878, all the previous 15 acts were put together in one Factory Act. To its important results belongs the fact that the Act now applied to all trades and did no longer allow children under 10 to work at all.[5]

While the Factory Acts were mainly dealing with the working time of women and children, the discussion about working time nowadays is more concerned with overtime hours, short-timework and the like. Against this background, we now consider in this section an alternative set of extensions of the basic Goodwin growth cycle model (of the case where $\eta = 1$ holds). We on the one hand integrate the fact that the working day became normalised at the times when Marx wrote and published *Capital*, Volume I so that we now have to distinguish between the normal working day (say of 8 hours) and the over- and undertime work that occurred due to the existence of business cycles. The number $L^d = (y/z)K$ now represents the number of hours worked (demanded by firms), while we denote by L^w now the number of workers employed by firms (their workforce). The ratio $u^w = L^d/L^w$ thus denotes the utilisation rate of the workforce of firms which therefore no longer are allowed to hire and fire on a daily basis (if they considered this as profitable at all). Instead, we now assume that firms (have to) change their workforce in delayed form according to the law of motion

$$\dot{L}^w = \beta_e(L^d - \bar{u}^w L^w) + nL^w, i.e., \quad \hat{L}^w = \beta_e(u^w - \bar{u}^w) + n.$$

Per unit of capital, that is, in intensive form, this gives rise to:

$$\hat{l}^w = \beta_e(u^w - \bar{u}^w) + n - \hat{K}, i.e., \hat{l}^w = \beta_e(\frac{y/z}{l^w} - \bar{u}^w) + n - (s(v)(1-v)y - \delta),$$

where the natural rate n is considered as a measure of trend growth for the economy. We are thus postulating that there is a lag (caused by legislation, but partly also due to profit calculations, frictions etc.) of size $1/\beta_e$ between current over- or undertime work and the return to a normal rate of workforce utilisation. The workday is thus not only normalised by legislation, with paid over-time or unpaid under-time work being allowed, and the rate of hiring and firing that can be realised by firms is now also a regulated one.

Note that the above formulation has already more recent legislation in mind where the workday is now restricted to say 8 hours of work and where therefore there is now enough excess capacity of workers to go significantly beyond this limit by means of paid overtime work. In Germany, for instance, the Working Time Act (Arbeitszeitgesetz) declares 8 hours as the regular daily working time, which can be extended up to 10 hours under certain conditions. Further regulations are given with regard to breaks, work on Sunday and so forth.[6] We assume in the following – in order to avoid the use of differential inequalities – that workers are paid per hour actually worked (with no reduced hours compensation paid by the government) and that there is enough overhead capacity such that no upper limit on hours worked applies. Of course, episodes where this does not hold (where legislation was less strict as described by the above factory acts) can be modelled in similar ways with not much change in the results obtained below. The conflict about the length of the working day, analysed in great detail in Marx (1954, ch.XVII), is no longer in existence in this form, since workers were paid per workday under these circumstances so that extra work was unpaid work, creating in Marx's terms absolute surplus value and thus pure extra profits to firms.

But capital also works on the supply side of the labour market, in addition to the demand $L^d = y/zK$ the full employment of the capital stock generates (Keynesian demand problems are treated in later chapters here). We assume that the capitalist economy is surrounded by subsistence economies, people living in peripheries or in rural outside economies like at Marx's time in Ireland with respect to the UK (where however pangs of hunger often forced working class people to emigrate to the United States of America). If the rate of employment e has become sufficiently high due to the working of the above recruitment or dismissal mechanism for the workforce of firms, firms start to seek for labourers outside the centres they are situated in. In the late 1950s and the 1960s in Germany, this was even done to a certain degree by more or less urging working class people from Southern Europe and Turkey – often after testing them extensively as to their physical potentials – to massively enter trains that brought them to Germany, where firms could engage them for two-five years due to the bilateral arrangements of Germany with the home countries of the work migrants. We model this fact by just assuming now that the rate of growth of the workforce n (which can also be done by changes in the participation rate, at Marx's time with respect to women and children), becomes now an increasing function of the employment rate e.

Finally, we also modify the real wage Phillips curve of the model and assume that there is an Robinsonian real wage barrier[7] present in it which implies that real wage increases are more pronounced if the real wage is below some critical value and vice versa. For reasons of simplicity we assume that this barrier is given by the steady state value of the real wage of the original Goodwin model.

In this section we therefore extend the Goodwin growth cycle model (the case $\eta = 1$) in a different way and do this as follows:

$$\hat{v} = f(e) + \alpha(\omega_o - \omega) - m = f(e) + g(v_o - v) - m, e = \frac{L^d}{L}, \tag{1.8}$$

$$\hat{u}^w = s(v)(1-v)y - (\delta + n(e) + m) - \beta_e(u^w - \bar{u}^w), u^w = \frac{yK}{zL^w}, \tag{1.9}$$

$$\hat{e} = \hat{L}^w - n = \beta_e(u^w - \bar{u}^w). \tag{1.10}$$

The linear part or the Jacobian of this system reads

$$J = \begin{pmatrix} -g'(e_o)v_o & 0 & f'(e_o)v_o \\ \sigma'(v_o)u_o^w & -\beta_e u_o^w & -n'(e_o)u_o^w \\ 0 & \beta_e e_o & 0 \end{pmatrix} = \begin{pmatrix} - & 0 & + \\ - & - & - \\ 0 & + & 0 \end{pmatrix}$$

where we have made use of the abbreviation $\sigma(v) = s(v)(1-v)y - (\delta + n(e) + m)$.

The Routh–Hurwitz conditions for local asymptotic stability and thus convergence to the state of the model, which is given by

$$v_o = \sigma^{-1}(\delta + n(e_o) + m), u_o^w = \bar{u}_o^w, e_o = f^{-1}(m),$$

are:

$$\begin{aligned}
a_1 &= -\text{trace} \quad J > 0, \\
a_2 &= \begin{pmatrix} J_{11} & J_{12} \\ J_{21} & J_{22} \end{pmatrix} + \begin{pmatrix} J_{11} & J_{13} \\ J_{31} & J_{33} \end{pmatrix} + \begin{pmatrix} J_{22} & J_{23} \\ J_{32} & J_{33} \end{pmatrix} > 0, \\
a_3 &= -\det J > 0, \\
b &= a_1 a_2 - a_3 > 0.
\end{aligned}$$

The first three conditions are obviously fulfilled. And with respect to b we get that it is fulfilled for all $f'(e_o)$ chosen sufficiently small, since the determinant is thereby made sufficiently small, while the expression $a_1 a_2$ remains bounded away from zero.

Since the slope of the Phillips curve, $f'(e_o)$, only appears in the determinant of J we also get that the condition $b > 0$ will be violated when this slope becomes sufficiently large. Flexible wages are therefore endangering the stability of the economy, while sufficiently sluggishly wage adjustment (with respect to the demand pressure on the labour market) are making the economy a viable one. This implies – in the context of the modelled economy – that neoliberal policies which suggest a flexible adjustment of wages with respect to demand and supply on the labour market may kill the 'patient' instead of curing him.

Moreover, since the term

$$|J_{11} J_{23} J_{32}| = |\beta_e e_o n'(e_o) u_o^w g'(e_o) v_o|$$

appears with opposite signs both in $a_1 a_2$ and a_3 (and thus cancels), we have that the remainder of b will depend in all remaining terms positively on both $g'(v_o)$ and $n'(e_o)$. We get, on the one hand, that faster migration processes are good for the stability of the economy (but not for those workers that are dispelled from the labour market in the bust) and, on the other hand, that stronger reactions to the real wage barrier are also good for the stability of the economy.

The effect of higher β_e values is however ambiguous, since it appears both in the determinant and in $a_1 a_2$, and only in the determinant in combination with the demand pressure term $f'(e_o)$. Increasing the speed of adjustment of the hiring and firing process of firms may therefore be dangerous in contrast to what laissez-faire oriented neoliberalism does suggest. The same holds true for the term $\sigma'(v_o)$ – and here without ambiguity – which, when increased, increases the determinant, while not changing $a_1 a_2$. The more sensitive capital accumulation becomes with respect to income distribution between capital and labour, the more likely it becomes that the balanced growth path of the economy becomes an unstable one. This changes however when insiders (the workforce of firms) and their degree of utilisation u^w enters the wage-bargaining process (of course in a positive way), making the term J_{12} positive, which increases a_2, but leaves a_1, a_3 unchanged. Adding insider influences to the outside effect of the rate of unemployment thus makes the economy more stable and thus mitigates the role of income distribution on the rate of accumulation that drives the economy.

One can transform the considered macrodynamics again into a two-dimensional one, by assuming $\beta_e = \infty$ in which case $u^w = \bar{u}^w$ holds. In this case one has to investigate the system:

$$\hat{v} = f(e) + g(v_o - v) - m, \tag{1.11}$$

$$\hat{e} = s(v)(1 - v)y - (\delta + n(e) + m). \tag{1.12}$$

The Jacobian of this system is characterised by

$$\begin{pmatrix} - & + \\ - & - \end{pmatrix}$$

This allows again for the application of Olech's theorem and thus for a global stability result as in the preceding section. The intuition behind this result is simple. Since $a_1 a_2$ depends on the parameter β_e in a quadratic way and the determinant only in a linear way, the term $a_1 a_2$ will dominate the a_3 term if the considered parameter becomes sufficiently large. It is however questionable whether such a situation will hold in reality, since there are restrictions to hiring and firing by legislature and also from the profit maximising perspective of firms. The three dimensional case may therefore be the more relevant one from the empirical perspective.

1.4 Social Legislation under Bismarck

We conclude from what is shown in Figure 1.3 and in the analysis accompanying it that the unrestricted working of the distributive cycle is not the way an advanced capitalist economy can reproduce itself that is viable in the long-run. The first person who became fully aware of this fundamental problem of capitalism on the side of the ruling classes was definitely Otto von Bismarck, Prime Minister in Prussia (appointed in 1862), and later on Chancellor in the German Empire which was founded in 1871 with Wilhelm I as first German emperor (and king of Prussia). When the last German emperor – Wilhelm II – came into power in 1888, the time of Bismarck as politically influential German chancellor was soon over, since Wilhelm II intended to make his own type of in fact internationally and nationally unbalanced policy. Bismarck thus resigned from his chancellorship in 1890.

The social legislation initiated by Bismarck was by no means an act of humanism, but a reflected strategic reaction to the social movements which the conflict between capital and labour in the sphere of production and about income distribution had created. A similar observation may hold for the Cold War period after World War II, while the opposite happened after the fall of the Iron Curtain in the 1990s, which was preceded however by Reaganomics and Thatcherism in the 1980s in the Anglo–Saxon world as a reaction to the stagflation of the 1970s. These latter deregulation policies did not at all pay attention to the social consequences they caused (compared to the prosperity phase after WWII). The implied social degradation processes of the workforce will be considered in the next chapter.

Otto von Bismarck was born as a member of the Prussian landed aristocracy and after his education soon became part of the Prussian Parliament as a Conservative. As chancellor of the new Empire, Bismarck soon started to deal with social legislation though his first domestic measures were aimed at the role of the Catholic Church and its influence. These actions are known as 'Kulturkampf' and can be regarded as part of secularisation though this was not the aim. A main success was the introduction of 'civil marriage' but the results of the 'Kulturkampf' were not generally successful with regard to the influence of political parties. One of Bismarck's aims had been to reduce the influence of the Catholic-oriented parties, such as the German Centre party. Therefore he even cooperated with the liberal parties in spite of significant areas of disagreement.

The failed revolution of 1848 as well as the social situation of the working class had raised the interest in the population of the German states in social issues, although the 1848 revolution was mainly part of a civil movement with the aim of a German unification. But after 1848, the first worker unions were established and social parties were founded, partly related to the ideas of Karl Marx. Thus, an important working class movement could develop with social parties, unions, and other working class organisations with the intention to improve the economic and social situation of the workers. Bismarck succeeded in 1878 to implement an 'antisocialist law' with the help of conservative and national-liberal parties, but the socialist movement nevertheless grew stronger so that the law was not renewed in 1890. Bismarck's best known and certainly most important decisions were the implementation of the world's first social legislations which are supposed to be established not only due to the insight in the necessity of interference of the state to improve the burdensome lot of workers, but also due to the fact of the increasing influence of the social-democratic party, which Bismarck hoped to reduce by introducing several social laws. These mainly were insurance bills so that the workers of the economy were not left unprotected.[8] Bismarck was aware of the bad working conditions and willing to improve them, but wanted at the same time to avoid regulations that could harm the economy.

Three areas of risk were regulated starting with the Health Insurance for part of the workers in 1883 which was transferred into Health Insurance Act for most of the workers. This is the starting point of Medical Care in Germany. The Health Insurance was financed by contributions of employees (two-thirds of the sum) and employers (one-third of the sum). In 1884, The Accident Insurance Act followed which was of high relevance especially for workers in particulary dangerous establishments. This insurance was paid by employers who otherwise had to pay for workers who suffered an accident. The Law of Invalidity and Old Age Insurance for workers, journeymen and apprentices was the third social law in 1889 which was the starting point of a general old age pension insurance. Employers and employees had to pay each half of the costs which was also subsidised by the state.[9] Thus, the social security legislation which was implemented by Bismarck can without doubt be regarded as a first step towards a welfare state though the situation of working families remained difficult in the 19th century.

It was criticised as 'Staatssozialismus' especially by the liberals but in 1881 Bismarck even made a prediction:

> *It is possible that our policy may be reversed at some future time when I am dead; but State Socialism will make its way.* (Busch 1898)

There are also reasons for the remaining bad situation of workers to be found in Bismarck's social laws themselves, since, for example, not all workers were included in the three laws and not all possible cases were considered, at least not in the beginning. Other critical points are related to the fact that the Old Age Program allowed only payment after 30 years of work and not before the age of 70 though the average age expectation was below 50 at that time. As David Khoudour-Casteras (2008) shows, there was a notable positive effect of the social legislation with regard to the German emigration (mainly to the United

States) since many Germans now decided to abandon their migration plans.

1.5 Social Legislation in the Context of the Distributive Cycle

The above provides a prominent example that capitalism without legislation would not be a socially viable system. Chancellor Bismarck was fully aware of this fact and acted accordingly. In the present section we briefly show how the model of the preceding one can be modified to take account of such social legislation, in fact with no effects on the dynamics of the considered model if external effects on the productivity of firms are not considered. Workers' demand for higher wages may however be significantly modified, as (neo-)liberals claim. As shown, emigration of workers from Prussia was certainly reduced by Bismarck's social legislation. These effects can be associated with the employed model, but are here only mentioned in passing.

Unemployment insurance had not yet been introduced under Bismarck, but only in 1927. Furthermore, the social insurances introduced in the 19th century had to be improved and expanded. We now consider as an example a pay-as-you-go type of unemployment insurance which is modelled as follows:

$$\dot{B} = \tau_b \omega L^d - \alpha_b \omega (1-e)L, \quad i.e., \tag{1.13}$$

$$\dot{b} = \tau_b v y - \alpha_b \omega (1-e)l - \sigma(v)b, \quad b = B/K \tag{1.14}$$

due to $\dot{b} = \hat{B}b - \hat{K}b$. The funds for unemployment benefits are therefore depleted by such payments $\alpha_b \omega(1-e)L$ and are raised by the pay-as-you-go contributions of the employed workers based on the wage income they currently receive. We have formulated the rule for the unemployment benefits such that it stays in proportion to the evolution of the real wage of the employed. Note we implicitly assume in the above rule for unemployment benefits that not only the employed, but also the unemployed are uniform in their characteristics, that is, in their work profiles. Besides uniform skills we thus in particular assume that the unemployed are not yet classified according to their duration of being unemployed. In reality there is of course a microstructure present in the reserve army. A first step into such a direction will be the subject of the next chapter.

The considered system is thus based on worker's solidarity with no contribution from the side of firms. It just redistributes consumption between employed and unemployed workers with no effect on total consumption demand, that is, the laws of motion of the economy remain completely unaffected through this modification of the distribution of wage income.

Replacing the stock for unemployment benefits B by a stock for pension payments the same holds true for a Bismarckian system of Old Age and Disability Insurance Bill if it is also formulated as a pay-as-you-go system just as in the case of unemployment benefits. The letters B, b have just to be replaced by P, p in order to describe this old age system in formal terms. Of course the contribution now goes to a different part of the population which we propose to model as $R = \alpha_p L$, and thus as being proportional to the total workforce, but not a portion of it anymore.

With respect to the Health Insurance Bill (of 1883) we follow the above proposal and assume that workers pay only a portion h_w while firms contribute the remainder out of their profits (net of depreciation). We again assume for pensioners that their number is proportional to the labour supply and given by $\alpha_p L$. Finally h is the portion of adults who need medical treatment and μ is the cost of it in real terms (again all individual characteristic are ignored on this macro-level). This gives:

$$\dot{H} = \alpha_h \tau_h \omega L^d + (1 - \alpha_h)(1 - v)Y - \delta K - \mu\eta(1 + \alpha_p)L, \ i.e., \quad (1.15)$$

$$\dot{h} = \alpha_h \tau_b v y + (1 - \alpha_h)(1 - v)y - \delta - \mu\eta(1 + \alpha_p)l - \sigma(v)h, \ h = \frac{H}{K} \quad (1.16)$$

where health care expenditures are simply proportional to the size of the adult population.

In this situation the growth law for the capital stock is reduced by the term $(1-\alpha_h)\hat{K}$ which changes the term $\sigma(v)$ to $\alpha_h\sigma(v)$ as the only change of the model. The qualitative dynamic properties of the economy are thus again unchanged, though the pace of capital accumulation is somewhat reduced now in quantitative terms. It goes without saying that the size of the contributions to unemployment, pension and health insurances are to be tailored such that they are compatible with the level of real wages (which is however growing with rate m in our economy).

We conjecture that such social legislations will improve the performance of the economy, in particular the state and the growth rate of labour productivity, since safe life-course perspectives provide a stimulus to the members of the workforce. However, they must understand that such a social system with basic welfare structures is to be protected against excessive real wage claims, here modelled by way of a real wage barrier in the bust, which in the boom period acts as an inflation break. It has moreover been shown in Flaschel and Greiner (2009) that the introduction of maximum real wages into the Goodwin (1967) framework (and also minimum real wages, as they are now discussed in Germany, but refuted by laissez-faire oriented politicians), defined in proportion to labour productivity z, can reduce the fluctuations of the distributive cycle significantly, since they are acting as ceilings and floors concerning the dynamics of the wage share. In our view, the German unions, in the late 1960s and the early 1970s, did not pay sufficient attention to such issues[10] and thus were contributing to the end of the prosperity phase and the process of stagflation, which led the German economy into a long depression, partially also caused by the distributive effects of the oil price shocks, but attributed to them in an exaggerated way, since these were price shocks, but not per se the continual source of inflationary pressure.

1.6 Conclusions and Outlook

We have considered in this chapter the interaction of income distribution with capital accumulation from a Marxian perspective. The description of this cyclical process is provided in the baseline case of a constant composition of capital by the Goodwin (1967) growth cycle model. Here we abstract from Keynesian goods market problems and focus solely on the labour market. We have modified this baseline model of cyclical growth in various ways and provided thereby several scenarios where the conservative distributive cycles of the Goodwin case turned into damped oscillations (and eventually also monotonic adjustment processes when some adjustment speeds become sufficiently high). As Marx we however consider the working of the reserve army mechanism in the present framework as a relatively smooth process. Marx (1954, XXV,p.2ff.) considers various extensions of the reserve army dynamics, among others the case of a rising composition of capital and of segmented labour markets. His latter approach will be the subject of the next chapter.

Concerning the first issue, the rising organic composition of capital and the tendency of the profit rate to fall that is associated with it in the literature we only briefly remark here in view of what has been discussed in Section 1.3 that such monotonic tendencies are not easy to prove from the theoretical and the empirical perspective if one adopts a secular perspective, maybe even from the process of industrialisation up to now. In Section 1.3 we have considered the following decomposition of the rate of profit r :

$$r = \rho = \epsilon \frac{\omega L^d}{Y} \frac{Y}{K}.$$

From the perspective of Schumpeter's (1939) analysis of long waves in the evolution of capitalism we can conclude that so-called capital productivity Y/K has risen in the prosperity phase of these waves and fallen in the subsequent depressions so that its movement is long-wave like, but not falling throughout the evolution of capitalism, which can be related to the Kaldorian stylised fact of no secular tendency in this ratio. The wage share $\omega L^d/Y$ and also the profit share have behaved in a similar way and in fact in a Goodwin (1967) distributive cycle fashion, see Figure 4.10 in this book, also representing a long phased cycle that is not unrelated to the Schumpeterian industrial cycle of waves of innovations and their diffusion and their petering out. And with respect to Marx's rate of exploitation ϵ the same conclusion holds, since this ratio (surplus value $S = \nu(Y - \delta K) - \xi L^d = (1 - \xi)L^d$ to necessary labour time $V = \xi L^d$) is in Marx's view if at all rising, but not falling from a secular perspective, due to technical changes which lower the time needed to produce the consumption basket of the workforce families. Though an important topic in Marx's (1954, ch.XXV) analysis of monotonic tendencies in the evolution of capitalism, we will not go any deeper into a discussion of the law of a falling rate of profit in this chapter.

From the viewpoint of the labour theory of value, the more important topic in our view is given by Marx's detailed analysis of the production of absolute and relative surplus value S which is underlying the fight about the variable ξ, the value of labour power. This variable is of great help in understanding the evolution from Smithian manufacturing (and its tendencies to a very specific division of labour) via the industrial revolution through Fordism up to the information technology revolution of our times.

From the perspective of Schumpeter's (1939) microbased investigations, one could add stochastic terms to the models of this chapter, concerning the ratios y and z, in the latter case around a rising trend and in the former case (and maybe also with respect to z) around a long wave of about fifty years. Yet, the microeconomic analysis of the processes behind such exogenous forces driving the interaction of capital accumulation with income distribution must here remain a subject for future research due to the macroeconomic orientation of this book, see however the companion to Neo-Schumpeterian Economics by Hanusch and Pyka (2007) as an encompassing survey on the microeconomic issues treated in the Neo-Schumpeterian literature.

We have considered in this chapter a variable savings rate of capitalists $s(v)$, coupled with the assumption that capitalists invest their savings directly into capital goods (in order to have the validity of Say's Law. This guarantees that the goods supply create an equal amount of goods demand (no Keynesian demand rationing).[11] The function of such financial markets (including commercial banking) then is (or should be) to transmit these savings into the financing of investment by firms. Yet, these activities concern a monetary economy and it was shown by Keynes (1936) that such an economy may then suffer from a lack of effective goods demand and thus excess capacities not only on the labour market, but also with respect to the utilisation of the capital stock of firms.

We already stress here our view that capitalism without significant regulation and state legislation is not a viable economic system, but tends to destroy the fundament on which it is built, the existence of a properly working labour market and the quality of the supply of labour by the working population. At Marx's times (and nowadays still in the periphery of Western capitalism) this was an obvious fact concerning all members of the working household who were physically able to do some work, but such mechanisms are also present in a somewhat more hidden form in advanced Western economies, not only in the neoliberal Anglo–Saxon world, but also in modern welfare states like Germany. This chapter has however shown that legislation that introduces baseline features of a welfare state is possible under capitalism without depriving it of its productive forces, despite this change in the relations of production. The Bismarckian reforms in such a direction may have been a reaction to the socialist movements of his time, but were certainly also understood as being a necessity for the creation of a modern and viable capitalist economy.

Notes

[1] This fact and the direction of motion of the variables v, e (see Figure 1.1) imply that the v, e–axes of $\Re^2_+$, the positive orthant in the phase plane, are trajectories of (1.3), (1.4) which cannot be approached by the trajectories which start in positive part of the phase plane $\Re^2_+$.

Our restricted consideration of the invariant set $\Re^2_+$, which excludes the singular point $(0,0)$, consequently is legitimate.

[2] $\eta > 1$ implies a totally unstable system, since the trajectories of this system – when running them backwards: $(u(-t), v(-t)), t \to \infty$ – are globally asymptotically stable.

[3] This provides a counterexample to the Marxian analysis of a secular tendency of the rate of profit to fall, where the proponents of this tendency in this particular case confuse the fact that the technical capital composition K/L^d is rising with the fact that the organic composition of capital is constant in the case here considered, where this rate and also the rate of exploitation are given magnitudes in the steady state (the latter is of course varying along the distributive cycle).

[4] See also Marx (1954), p.229f.

[5] See Historyhome.co.uk (2010) and Cornish and Clark (1989)

[6] See BMAS (2010)

[7] or inflation barrier, see Marglin (1984), Ch.5 for details on such concepts.

[8] See Eurofound (2009) and van Meerhaeghe (2006)

[9] See Holborn (1969)

[10] Their behaviour can be related to the case $\eta > 1$ we have investigated in section 1.2.

[11] In a later chapter we will however consider financial markets and the allocation of the savings of asset holding capitalists to equities, bonds and checkable and saving deposits.

2. Segmented Labour and an Employer of Last Resort

> *The folly is now patent of the economic wisdom that preaches to the labourers the accommodation of their number to the requirements of capital. The mechanism of capitalist production and accumulation constantly effects this adjustment. The first word of this adaptation is the creation of a relative surplus population, or industrial reserve army. Its last word is the misery of constantly extending strata of the active army of labour, and the dead weight of pauperism.* (Marx 1954, p.603)

Chapter 1 has provided insights into a period of capitalism where nearly no hindrances existed for the exploitation of the working population so that capitalism could be described as failing with regard to the development of a society in which all members are able to live in an acceptable way. As we have shown, social legislation began in Europe (in Germany under Bismarck) at a time when many workers (including children) were suffering from too much work and little income with no social insurances. It lasted until the 1920s before unemployment insurances were established in European countries.

The question now is whether the present situation of the working population can be considered as acceptable or whether we see again a failing capitalism at work which needs urgent changes. If we look at the case of Germany, for example, we find a larger portion of the active working population in a situation which can be compared with the Marxian reserve army of the preceding chapter: Low income work, atypical work, 'part-time' jobs, temporary employment, etc. Such jobs function as potential threat to those workers who still have a regular job. Even employment insurance has meanwhile become a threat to regular workers, since after a year of unemployment a worker in Germany gets into the Hartz IV regulations which not only means a very low income, but also degrading controls and also quite often social exclusion. These facts show that capitalism still has a failing character from the social perspective, leading to a split of the society which endangers the advances in its social and political structure that have taken place in its prosperity phase after World War II.

2.1 Segmented Labour Markets in Marx's and in our Times

In this chapter[1] we consider the Marxian theory of segmented labour markets which he introduced in conjunction with his discussion of the general law of capitalist accumulation. Reconsidering the Marxian trichotomy of floating (fluid), latent and stagnant segments of the labour market made in his Chapter XXV, Section 4,[2] where the last segment – the stagnant one – can also be described as a dead segment, we can easily discover similarities on the level of well-being (not in absolute income of course) to the situation of employees in the German economy of the 21st century. We have normal occupations, the floating segment, atypical employment in the low income sector (part-time workers, temporary work organised by special leasing firms and low paid, so-called mini jobs, in the latent segment, and unemployed persons receiving unemployment benefits (for one year, elderly people for 18–24 months) and long-term unemployed persons, with only marginal chances of a return to proper work, in the dead segment of the labour market.

Germany had a regulation for unemployed persons until 2005 which consisted of two forms of unemployment support, a maximum of two years unemployment benefits, and thereafter 'Sozialhilfe' (social help) with a smaller sum of money. In general, the length of payment and some other decisions were dependent on the length of working time before becoming unemployed and thus on the amount of payment into the unemployment insurance which was – and is – obligatory in Germany.[3]

In 2005, a radical labour market 'reform' took place against which protests have never stopped. It is named 'Hartz IV' because one of the main persons involved in the creation was Peter Hartz, a former German CEO, among others at the Volkswagen enterprise. A reason for the new regulation was the high increase of unemployed persons at the end of the 20th and beginning of the 21st century so that a commission was founded, the Hartz Commission, which intended to reduce the number of more than four million unemployed persons to less than half of it within four years, which however never happened. The new regulations have reduced the payment of unemployment benefits to one year, and put together 'Sozialhilfe' (social help) and a new unemployment benefit system II, better known in Germany under the name Hartz IV. The number IV can be explained by the following development from 2002 on:[4]

- Hartz I (implemented 2003) made reforms of the restrictive legislation on temporary work and work leasing, both of which were eased. Stricter rules with regard to registering as unemployed and accepting offered work were made
- Hartz II (also implemented 2003) has renewed the possibilities of founding a one-person business (Ich-AG) and made a reform of the mini-jobs (income up to 400 Euro) which do only demand (small) social securities payment from the employer, but not from the employee
- Hartz III (implemented 2004) includes a reorganisation of the employment agency and special rules of cutting benefits if an offered work is not accepted without understandable reasons
- Hartz IV (implemented 2005) has merged Sozialhilfe (social help) and unemployment benefit to unemployment benefit II which is at present fixed on Euro 364 per month (plus payment of rents etc). For children there exist further standard rates.

While the – in 2004 renewed – Federal Institute for Employment has to deal with unemployed persons, try to find jobs for them and to organise the Hartz IV-payment, the underlying laws are to be found in the German Social Security Codes II and III which regulate the work of the Federal Institute for Employment. Both codes have been updated in recent years. While the main topics in Social Security Code II deal with basic social care as well as employment promotion, the dominant aspects in Social Security Code III refer to job-creating-measures and job training. Hartz IV recipients are mainly part of Security Code II, while unemployed persons who receive unemployment benefits for one year (about 60% of their former income), are dealt with in Security Code III though some tasks are mixed. Persons who earn only little in a job can receive an additional support within the Hartz IV regulations. A basic tenor in both codes is the orientation towards work-fare in contrast to welfare, which means that unemployed persons are supposed to engage themselves in skill enhancement and intensive job finding (Eurofound, 2009).

In 2009, there were 43 million persons in the active part of the German labour force, but nearly five million persons had only a minijob (Federal Statistical Office 2011). Since the 1990s the number of low wage jobs has significantly increased by up to 20% of all employees.[5] Additionally, the German government refuses an all-embracing minimum wage but has only accepted it in a few sectors so far. Solow (2008, 12ff.) discusses several possible reasons for the German downward development in labour market regulations, among which the growth of the service sector (in contrast to the manufacturing sector), gradual weakening of union power, intensified competition through incoming workers, for example from Eastern Europe, and relics of the Bismarckian organisation of the German welfare state (especially the 'male breadwinner household') are underlined as possible negative influences. He – as well as Bosch and Weinkopf (2008) and Bosch and Kalina (2008) – argues that the introduction of minimum wages might be a first step away from this downward development.

In 2010, there were 3 244 000 unemployed persons, following the information of the Federal Institute for Employment, which is a significant fall compared to 2009. Altogether, around 6 million employable persons received in 2010 benefits due to the Social Security Codes II and III, which means a reduction of 2% with regard to the preceding year, mainly with regard to those who received unemployment benefits. There were on the other hand one and a half million persons involved in a measure of labour market policy, mainly a form of skill training, which was nearly 15% less than a year ago, which means reduced support in finding a new job.

The data of long-term unemployed persons (Hartz IV receivers) show more than 20% of more than 24 months unemployed in total unemployment (Bundesagentur für Arbeit, 2010), but many Hartz IV receivers are in this system for more than five years, and more than 10 years even. This problem is related to the question of sufficient qualifications which are often missing. Therefore, so-called Hartz IV people are often linked to so-called problem-groups, which include migrants without any professional or even educational qualifications, single parent households, unskilled persons in general and early school leavers.

While the data from the Federal Statistical Office seem to suggest not only lots of different supports for unemployed persons, but also a decreasing number of unemployed persons (of both types) the situation of these parts of the society is far from being satisfactory (Bundesagentur für Arbeit, 2010).

The situation of Hartz IV receivers is not only close to poverty – a fact which is especially difficult for children and juveniles, but it also contains many degrading situations since persons who apply for Hartz IV have not only to reveal the details of their financial situation (savings, properties etc) and their living conditions (family, friends etc.), but they are forced to change their living place when they have too many rooms or pay a high rent (which will be overtaken by the agency). Furthermore they have to apply for all extra expenses, including clothing, birthday presents, travelling to a sick relative and so on.

Another degrading aspect is the often low support in finding a new job or even getting new qualifications which gives a feeling of being no longer part of the workforce. Furthermore, the public opinion on idle workforce members who are viewed as refusing work, can be, and is, also degrading. It has also to be taken into consideration that many long-term unemployed persons who live from Hartz IV will get into a difficult situation when they are old, because their retirement pension can be very low so that they will depend on the paid basic social help for aged persons.

Therefore, it is correct to compare Hartz IV with the stagnant (dead) segment of Marx's classification as described above. Of course, their situation is not comparable to the situation of the dead segment on the labour market at his times, but in a cross-sectional comparison they are nevertheless in a comparable position concerning life perspectives, neighbourhood problems, tendencies to drug consumption and inclination towards violence.

Moreover, there are certainly many difficult atypical working conditions in Germany that can be related to the Marxian latent segment though these workers have a chance to move up into the floating segment like skilled and well trained unemployed persons who may find a new job after some months. On the other hand, there are many persons in this segment who can also easily drop into the stagnant segment when, for example, part-time occupied workers lose their job, or temporary work organised by special leasing firms is so low paid that the comparison with regular workers is discriminating. These types of workers are indeed also supported through the Hartz IV program to a significant degree (around 3/4 of the Hartz IV receivers).

Unemployment is, of course, the root of all these problems. In this chapter we will therefore – among other questions – also deal with proposed solutions to solve this problem such as Basic Income Guarantees (BIG)[6] or an Employer of Last Resort (ELR). The importance of such programs cannot be underestimated, since the increase in child poverty that is accompanying mass unemployment is indeed of the type of a ticking time bomb (in Germany social help supplied to children increased from 130000 children in 1965 to 1.7 million children in 2010. To have approximately 10% of workers in the new classification system 'Hartz IV families' who are by and large chronically unemployed with no hope for improvement of their lot, represents a situation in a democracy that can only be considered as fatal. This chapter will provide against such a background a model of Marx's segmented labour market analysis and a reform proposal, that tries to cure such a situation.

Goodwin's (1967) Marxian growth cycle model is one of the truly baseline models of macroeconomic theory, comparable to the orthodox Solow (1956) model in its simplicity, but totally different in its implications from the latter type of growth theory. This has indeed also been acknowledged by Solow himself, see Solow (1990), and has led to numerous publications on modifications and extensions of this approach to a distributive cycle. Barbosa-Filho and Taylor (2006) have characterised this cycle mechanism, see also Taylor (2004, ch.9) in this regard. Recently, in 2006, there has been a special issue in the Journal *Structural Change and Economic Dynamics* on Goodwin's legacy and its continuation as well as an edited volume on this subject, see Flaschel and Landesmann (2008). There has also been recent empirical work on this distributive cycle by Harvie (2000), Mohun and Veneziani (2008), Franke et al. (2006) and others. This indicates that the model of the reserve army mechanism designed by Goodwin (1967, 1972) on the basis of Marx's analysis of this mechanism is still attracting numerous studies of its further development and its empirical evaluation.

From this perspective, this chapter extends – from a different angle compared to what has been presented in Chapter 1 – the growth cycle of Goodwin (1967) to incorporate the various forms of unemployment first pointed out by Marx in *Capital* Vol.I, Chapter 25.[7] In that chapter, Marx identifies three types of unemployment: the floating, the latent and the stagnant one. In Goodwin's model, only the floating type of unemployment is considered. We extend Goodwin's model by postulating an interaction between the above three labour market segments and show that, in the presence of a benefit system that is undertaken by government as an employer-of-last-resort, the dead segment of the labour market can be eliminated, whilst preserving the macro-stability of the economy.

The chapter therefore shows that Goodwin's model, which is characterised by the unrestricted operation of the 'law of capitalist accumulation', can be reformulated in such a way as to produce socio-economic outcomes that are socially and politically acceptable. We should however mention that in our formulation of reformed capitalism that is presented here, the role of changes in the composition of capital remains to be explored. In his detailed exposition of the operation of capitalist accumulation, Marx places great emphasis on the rise in the organic composition of capital as a principal force behind the increase in structural unemployment. We do not pursue this matter in this chapter. Our main focus is to integrate the three segments of the labour market under the assumption of a given capital intensity (constant labour productivity) and to show, on this basis, that active labour market policy can generate an outcome that eliminates the stagnant portion of unemployment.

The rest of the chapter is structured as follows. Section 2.2 deals with the segmented labour market, in which the different types of unemployment interact on the basis of rates of employment and unemployment. Section 2.3 provides a steady state analysis of the model, and shows that the steady state rates of employment in the latent and dead segments depend on the speeds with which workers are pushed into or out of these segments. Section 2.4 investigates the stability properties of the extended Goodwin model. We find that adding the latent and dead portions of the labour market in this model generates potentially destabilising forces, despite the fact that there is a stabilising inflation barrier term in our Phillips curve formulation. In Section 2.5 we briefly review the debate on an Employer of Last Resort (ELR) and the affordability, manageability and stability features of this policy proposal, where stability primarily concerns price stability, but also the problems discussed by Kalecki (1943) in his article on the 'The political aspects of full employment'. Section 2.6 introduces an active labour market policy into the extended Goodwin model of this chapter where government acts as an employer-of-last-resort thereby eliminating the stagnant portion of the labour market, whilst erecting a benefit system that sustains the incomes of workers that move from the floating labour market into the latent one. We show that this policy guarantees the macro-stability of the economy's growth path. Section 2.7 takes a look at the development and present situation in Austria as a neighbouring country of Germany and considers the possibilities and problems of introducing an Employer of Last Resort (or even civic work) system into this economy. Section 2.8 concludes.

2.2 Divided Labour and the Distributive Cycle

The model of the distributive cycle we have considered in Chapter 1 by and large described a viable situation for a capitalist economy. However, there is one serious neglect in such a scenario of the conflict between capital and labour about income distribution as it was provided so far, where mass unemployment is occurring without any social consequences for the household structure of the working class. This neglect concerns the social implications of mass unemployment, namely the creation of degraded work this implies. In Marx's (1867, ch.IIV) description of the reserve army mechanism this however is taken note of and it is even claimed there that the distributive cycle will necessarily imply a hierarchy of three segments in the labour market which are unavoidable under an unrestricted evolution of the capitalist mode of production.

We consider the Marxian growth cycle model as it was formulated by Goodwin (1967), that is, we restrict the analysis to the case $\eta = 1$ again, but add as in Marx (1867, ch.25.4) to what he calls the floating labour market (the labour market as it is considered by the Goodwin (1967) model), his consideration of the evolution of latent and stagnant portions within the labour markets. The growth cycle dynamics for the floating labour market can then be formulated (if the other segments of the labour market are still ignored):

$$\hat{\omega} = \beta_w(\frac{\bar{y}/\bar{z}}{l^s} - \bar{e}), \quad l^s = \frac{L^s}{K}, \tag{2.1}$$

$$\hat{l}^s = n - \bar{y}(1 - \omega/\bar{z}), \quad \omega = w/p. \tag{2.2}$$

Adding the other two segments of the labour market we assume now for the floating part of it (indexed by 1) as law of motion for their real wage:

$$\hat{\omega}_1 = \beta_{we_1}(\frac{\bar{y}/\bar{z}_1}{l_1^s} - \bar{e}_1) + \beta_{we_2}e_2 - \beta_{wd}\frac{D}{L^s} + \beta_{w\omega_1}(\omega_1^o - \omega_1), \tag{2.3}$$

$$\hat{l}^s = n - \bar{y}(1 - \omega_1/\bar{z}_1 - \bar{\omega}_2/\bar{z}_2). \tag{2.4}$$

The real wage Phillips curve in the first labour market remains based on the demand pressure term in the first labour market $\frac{\bar{y}/\bar{z}_1}{l_1^s} - \bar{e}_1$, and is now augmented by the positive influence of the second labour market on the first one, through an increasing rate of employment $e_2 = \frac{\bar{y}/\bar{z}_2}{l_2^s}$

in the atypical (second) labour market, and by a negative influence from the third segment of the labour market where there is in our model no employment at all and which we therefore consider as the 'dead' segment of the labour market. The extent of this dead segment is measured by D/L^s and is related to what Marx considers as pauperism in his ch.25.4.

The law of motion for labour intensity is the same as before, but now refers to the whole of labour supply per unit of capital. This is again driven by the rate of profit, where the given real wage per unit of capital has now to be deducted. We assume in this chapter that the real wage in the latent segment of the labour market is a given subsistence wage, while there are no wages paid at all in the sphere of pauperism. Note that the given magnitudes $\bar{z}_1, \bar{z}_2$ of output per unit of employed labour have now to be interpreted in inverted form as employment coefficients since they are used here to calculate employment on the two active labour markets on the basis of a given output–capital ratio $\bar{y}$.

Note also that we have, by definition, the identity $L^s = L_1^s + L_2^s + D$ where total labour supply grows at the natural rate n. The split of this labour supply into a floating, a latent and a dead segment must now be formulated in order to complete the model. We further assume that there are upward and downward movements between the floating and the latent segments of the labour market. We denote the floating and latent segments as type 1 and type 2 employment respectively. The unemployment rate in the floating segment is an indicator of the percentage of type 1 workers that are compelled to move into the latent segment and the employment rate of the latent segment is an indicator of the percentage of people who get the chance to move back into the first labour market. This gives the laws of motion:

$$\hat{L}_2^s = \gamma_1^d(1 - e_1) - \gamma_1^u e_1 + n, \quad (2.5)$$

$$\hat{D} = \gamma_2^d(1 - e_2) - \gamma_2^u e_2 + n. \quad (2.6)$$

We have already added here a similar law of motion for the movement in and out of the dead segment of the labour market which therefore also assumes that there are ways to leave the sphere of pauperism. Yet the downward leading coefficients γ_1^d, γ_2^d will be significantly larger than the upward leading ones γ_1^u, γ_2^d. This is briefly exemplified for the first labour market as follows. In the steady state we will have

$$\gamma_1^d(1-e_1)-\gamma_1^u e_1=0, \quad i.e., \quad e_1=\frac{\gamma_1^d}{\gamma_1^d+\gamma_1^u}=\frac{1}{1+\gamma_1^u/\gamma_1^d}$$

This suggests that for plausible values of e_1, say values greater than 50%, the parameter γ_1^u must be significantly less than γ_2^d. Taken together we have as laws of motion for this economy with three labour market segments the differential equations (where everything is expressed per unit of capital and denoted in lowercase letters):

$$\hat{\omega}_1 =\beta_{we}(\frac{\bar{y}/\bar{z}_1}{l_1^s}-\bar{e}_1)+\beta_{we_2}\frac{\bar{y}/\bar{z}_2}{l_2^s}-\beta_{wd}d/l^s+\beta_{w\omega_1}(\omega_1^o-\omega_1), \quad (2.7)$$

$$\hat{l}^s =n-\bar{y}(1-\omega_1/\bar{z}_1-\bar{\omega}_2/\bar{z}_2), \quad (2.8)$$

$$\hat{l}_2^s =\gamma_1^d-(\gamma_1^d+\gamma_1^u)\frac{\bar{y}/\bar{z}_1}{l_1^s}+n-\bar{y}(1-\omega_1/\bar{z}_1-\bar{\omega}_2/\bar{z}_2), \quad (2.9)$$

$$\hat{d} =\gamma_2^d-(\gamma_2^d+\gamma_2^u)\frac{\bar{y}/\bar{z}_2}{l_2^s}+n-\bar{y}(1-\omega_1/\bar{z}_1-\bar{\omega}_2/\bar{z}_2). \quad (2.10)$$

Here the statically endogenous variable l_1^s is given by $l_1^s=l^s-l_2^s-d$. This represents a description of the Marxian reserve army mechanism with the three segments of the labour market he assumed as typical for its working under the capitalism of his time.

We summarise the structure of the considered economy by way of Figure 2.1.

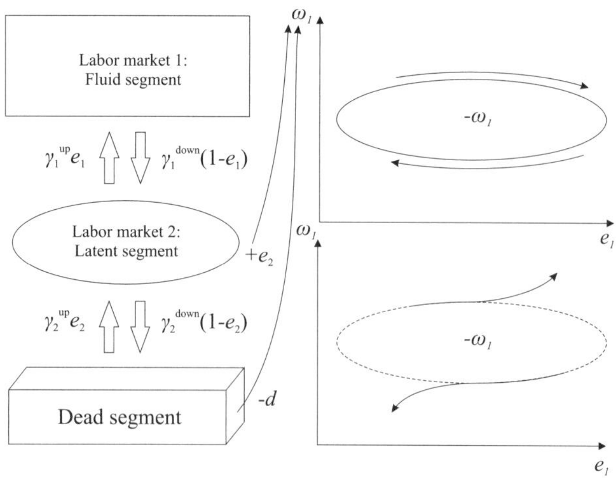

Figure 2.1 The flow of workers between the segments of the labour market

Figure 2.1 shows on its left hand side the flows occurring between the segments of the labour market which are therefore not completely separated from each other, but segmented to a degree that is mirrored through the size of the γ parameters. The figure at top right shows an example of a Goodwin type distributive cycle which will be modified to a convergent dynamics if the real wage barrier we considered in the preceding chapter is added to it, here simply visualised by the term $-\omega_1$ in the centre of it, the real wage of the workers in the fluid part of the labour market. The arrows in the middle indicate the forces that impact the fluid labour market because of the presence of the other two labour markets, namely the state of employment in the latent part of the labour market as measures by the employment rate e_1 and the size of the dead segment of the labour market, d, here measured relative to the size of the capital stock. The size of the first variable has a positive impact on the wage claims made in the fluid labour market while the size of the second one has a negative effect on the wage negotiations.

The analysis of the model in subsequent sections will show that these feedbacks arising from the lower labour markets onto the dynamics in the first one will add destabilising forces to the distributive cycle generated in the fluid part of the labour market, as indicated in the figure at bottom right.

2.3 Steady State Analysis

In the steady state, where time derivatives are zero, the system can be expressed as follows:

$$0 = \beta_{we_1}(\frac{\bar{y}/\bar{z}_1}{l_1^s} - \bar{e}_1) + \beta_{we_2}\frac{\bar{y}/\bar{z}_2}{l_2^s} - \beta_{wd}d/l^s + \beta_{w\omega_1}(\omega_1^o - \omega_1), \quad (2.11)$$

$$0 = n - \bar{y}(1 - \omega_1/\bar{z}_1 - \bar{\omega}_2/\bar{z}_2), \quad (2.12)$$

$$0 = \gamma_1^d - (\gamma_1^d + \gamma_1^u)\frac{\bar{y}/\bar{z}_1}{l_1^s} + n - \bar{y}(1 - \omega_1/\bar{z}_1 - \bar{\omega}_2/\bar{z}_2), \quad (2.13)$$

$$0 = \gamma_2^d - (\gamma_2^d + \gamma_2^u)\frac{\bar{y}/\bar{z}_2}{l_2^s} + n - \bar{y}(1 - \omega_1/\bar{z}_1 - \bar{\omega}_2/\bar{z}_2), \quad (2.14)$$

which gives for the determination of the steady state the equations

$$0 = \beta_{we}(\frac{\bar{y}/\bar{z}_1}{l_1^s} - \bar{e}_1) + \beta_{we_2}\frac{\bar{y}/\bar{z}_2}{l_2^s} - \beta_{wd}d/l^s, \tag{2.15}$$

$$0 = n - \bar{y}(1 - \omega_1/\bar{z}_1 - \bar{\omega}_2/\bar{z}_2) \rightarrow \omega_1^o = \frac{\bar{y}(1 - \bar{\omega}_2/\bar{z}_2) - n}{\bar{y}\bar{z}_1)} > 0, \tag{2.16}$$

$$0 = \gamma_1^d - (\gamma_1^d + \gamma_1^u)e_1, \quad e_{1o} = \frac{\gamma_1^d}{\gamma_1^d + \gamma_1^u} \tag{2.17}$$

$$0 = \gamma_2^d - (\gamma_2^d + \gamma_2^u)e_2, \quad e_{2o} = \frac{\gamma_2^d}{\gamma_2^d + \gamma_2^u}. \tag{2.18}$$

Substituting the steady state expressions for e_1 and e_2 into these equations gives the following system:

$$0 = \beta_{we_1}(\frac{\gamma_1^d}{\gamma_1^d + \gamma_1^u} - \bar{e}_1) + \beta_{we_2}\frac{\gamma_2^d}{\gamma_2^d + \gamma_2^u} - \beta_{wd}d^o/l^{so}, \tag{2.19}$$

$$0 = n - \bar{y}(1 - \omega_1/\bar{z}_1 - \bar{\omega}_2/\bar{z}_2) \rightarrow \omega_1^o > 0, \tag{2.20}$$

$$0 = \gamma_1^d - (\gamma_1^d + \gamma_1^u)\frac{\bar{y}/\bar{z}_1}{l_1^s} \rightarrow l_1^{so} = \frac{\gamma_1^d + \gamma_1^u}{\gamma_1^d}\frac{\bar{y}}{\bar{z}_1} \tag{2.21}$$

$$\rightarrow l_1^{so} = l^{so} - l_2^{so} - d^o > 0, \tag{2.22}$$

$$0 = \gamma_2^d - (\gamma_2^d + \gamma_2^u)\frac{\bar{y}/\bar{z}_2}{l_2^s} \rightarrow l_2^{so} = \frac{\gamma_2^d + \gamma_2^u}{\gamma_2^d}\frac{\bar{y}}{\bar{z}_2} > 0. \tag{2.23}$$

This further gives, for the determination of the steady state values of d, l^s, the two equations:

$$d^o = [\beta_{we_1}(\frac{\gamma_1^d}{\gamma_1^d + \gamma_1^u} - \bar{e}_1) + \beta_{we_2}\frac{\gamma_2^d}{\gamma_2^d + \gamma_2^u}]l^{so}/\beta_{wd} \tag{2.24}$$

$$d^o = l^{so} - [\frac{\gamma_1^d + \gamma_1^u}{\gamma_1^d}\frac{\bar{y}}{\bar{z}_1} + \frac{\gamma_2^d + \gamma_2^u}{\gamma_2^d}\frac{\bar{y}}{\bar{z}_2}] \tag{2.25}$$

We assume that the term in the square bracket in eq. (2.24) provides a value between zero and one so that this linear curve is positively sloped and flatter than the other straight line, given by eq. (2.25). It is then obvious that these two equations have a positive intersection and this solution automatically fulfills $d^o/l^{so} < 1$, that is, $D/L^s < 1$ as it should be the case. We note that the slope of this curve depends on the speeds of adjustment in the first labour market, in the form of ratios with β_{wd} in the denominator. The adjustment parameters β_{we_1} and β_{we_2} must therefore be sufficiently small relative to β_{wd} in order to allow for a positive steady state solution. In other words, a system where the influence of β_{wd} onto the fluid labour market is too weak is therefore problematic even from the viewpoint of steady states, independently of the stability features of this steady state.

Note again that the steady state rates of employment in the first and the second labour market are given by

$$e_1^o = \frac{\gamma_1^d}{\gamma_1^d + \gamma_1^u}, \quad e_2^o = \frac{\gamma_2^d}{\gamma_2^d + \gamma_2^u}$$

The rate e_1^o is thus different from what is usually considered as the NAIRU employment rate $\bar{e}_1$ and it increases with γ_x^d, the speed by which workers are pushed into a lower segment of the labour market, and it decreases with γ_x^u, the speed by which workers can climb up again into the higher segment of the labour market. Though there is social segmentation through this labour market structure, it is nevertheless possible to overcome the barriers created by the workings of unrestricted capitalism to a certain degree. We summarise the steady state analysis by way of what is shown in Figure 2.2.

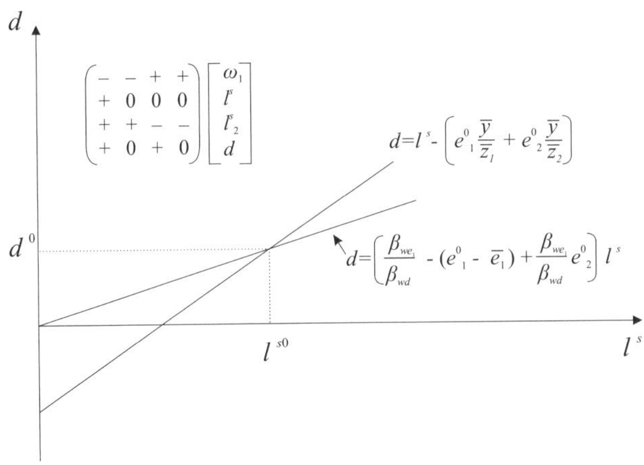

Figure 2.2 Steady state employment rates and the determination of l^{so}, d^o

Top left we show the feedback structure of the dynamics as it is represented by the signs of the entries in the Jacobian matrix of the model at the steady state. The slopes of the two isoclines that determine through their intersection the steady state values l^{so}, d^o is such that indeed positive values for these two ratios exist and are uniquely determined. We for example get from Figure 2.2 that increasing output to factor employment ratios z_i[8] will reduce the dead segment of the labour market on average – or if the model is convergent – in the long-run. This is a very astonishing result, since the impact effect of an increase in the $z_i's$ is to lower labour demand in the corresponding markets.

2.4 Stability of Balanced Growth?

In this section we investigate the stability properties of the Marxian growth cycle model with the segmented labour markets we have formulated above. We consider the 4D autonomous system given by:

$$\hat{\omega}_1 = \beta_{we_1}(\frac{\bar{y}/\bar{z}_1}{l^s - l_2^s - d} - \bar{e}_1) + \beta_{we_2}\frac{\bar{y}/\bar{z}_2}{l_2^s} - \beta_{wd}d/l^s \quad (2.26)$$

$$+ \beta_{w\omega_1}(\omega_1^o - \omega_1) \quad (2.27)$$

$$\hat{l^s} = n - \bar{y}(1 - \omega_1/\bar{z}_1 - \bar{\omega}_2/\bar{z}_2) \quad (2.28)$$

$$\hat{l}_2^s = \gamma_1^d - (\gamma_1^d + \gamma_1^u)\frac{\bar{y}/\bar{z}_1}{l^s - l_2^s - d} + n - \bar{y}(1 - \omega_1/\bar{z}_1 - \bar{\omega}_2/\bar{z}_2) \quad (2.29)$$

$$\hat{d} = \gamma_2^d - (\gamma_2^d + \gamma_2^u)\frac{\bar{y}/\bar{z}_2}{l_2^s} + n - \bar{y}(1 - \omega_1/\bar{z}_1 - \bar{\omega}_2/\bar{z}_2) \quad (2.30)$$

Since linear dependent expressions cancel in the calculation of the determinant of the Jacobian of this system at the steady position, we can simplify the right hand side of these equations as follows, without changing the sign of the determinant of this Jacobian:

$$\hat{\omega}_1 = \beta_{we_1}(\frac{\bar{y}/\bar{z}_1}{l^s - l_2^s - d} - \bar{e}_1) + \beta_{we_2}\frac{\bar{y}/\bar{z}_2}{l_2^s} - \beta_{wd}d/l^s \quad (2.31)$$

$$\hat{l^s} = \omega_1 \quad (2.32)$$

$$\hat{l}_2^s = -(\gamma_1^d + \gamma_1^u)\frac{\bar{y}/\bar{z}_1}{l^s - l_2^s - d} \quad (2.33)$$

$$\hat{d} = -(\gamma_2^d + \gamma_2^u)\frac{\bar{y}/\bar{z}_2}{l_2^s} \quad (2.34)$$

After further reductions we arrive at a reduced form Jacobian for this system, which reads:

$$J_o = \begin{pmatrix} 0 & d/(l^s)^2 & 0 & -1/l^s \\ 1 & 0 & 0 & 0 \\ 0 & 1/(l^s-d)^2 & 0 & -1/(l^s-d)^2 \\ 0 & 0 & 1/(l^s)^2 & 0 \end{pmatrix}$$

This gives for the determinant of this Jacobian the expression:

$$J_o = (-d/l^s + 1)/[(l^s)^3(l^s-d)^2] = (1-d/l^s)/[(l^s)^3(l^s-d)^2] > 0$$

since $d < l^s$ holds at the steady state.

With respect to the other stability conditions we have to consider the sign distribution within the Jacobian of the dynamical system:

$$\hat{\omega}_1 = \beta_{we_1}\left(\frac{\bar{y}/\bar{z}_1}{l^s - l_2^s - d} - \bar{e}_1\right) + \beta_{we_2}\frac{\bar{y}/\bar{z}_2}{l_2^s} - \beta_{wd} d/l^s + \beta_{w\omega_1}(\omega_1^o - \omega_1) \tag{2.35}$$

$$\hat{l}^s = n - \bar{y}(1 - \omega_1/\bar{z}_1 - \bar{\omega}_2/\bar{z}_2) \tag{2.36}$$

$$\hat{l}_2^s = \gamma_1^d - (\gamma_1^d + \gamma_1^u)\frac{\bar{y}/\bar{z}_1}{l^s - l_2^s - d} + n - \bar{y}(1 - \omega_1/\bar{z}_1 - \bar{\omega}_2/\bar{z}_2) \tag{2.37}$$

$$\hat{d} = \gamma_2^d - (\gamma_2^d + \gamma_2^u)\frac{\bar{y}/\bar{z}_2}{l_2^s} + n - \bar{y}(1 - \omega_1/\bar{z}_1 - \bar{\omega}_2/\bar{z}_2) \tag{2.38}$$

which is given by

$$J_o = \begin{pmatrix} - & ? & ? & ? \\ + & 0 & 0 & 0 \\ + & + & - & - \\ + & 0 & + & 0 \end{pmatrix}$$

If the first term in the Phillips curve is dominating the second and the third one with respect to the state variable l^s, l_2^s, d[9] so that the floating part dynamics of the model is in particular of the type of a Goodwin cycle $J_{12} < 0$ (with damped oscillations however), we in particular get[10]

$$J_o = \begin{pmatrix} - & - & + & + \\ + & 0 & 0 & 0 \\ + & + & - & - \\ + & 0 & + & 0 \end{pmatrix}$$

In addition to the stability result obtained above we see further stabilising feedback channels at work. In the Goodwin subdynamics, that is, the interaction of the state variables ω_1, l^s, we have again the result of the distributive cycle without segmented labour markets. And in the lower two segments we have also a stable, partial interaction of the state variables l_2^s, d (see the 2D submatrix at the bottom to the right).

There are however also destabilising feedback chains at work now. There is first the cumulative interaction of d, ω_1 in the laws of motion of real wages and of the dead segment of the labour market. And secondly, there is the cumulative interaction between the state variables l_2^s, ω_1 in the laws of motion for real wages and the latent segment of the labour market. These positive feedback loops are represented in the Jacobian matrix shown in Figure 2.2 by the enlarged plus signs.

Of course all these statements are made from a partial perspective concerning the principal minors of order 2 of the Jacobian J solely. There are no destabilising adjustment processes in the trace of J. We however conclude from these observations that the stable Goodwin growth cycle within the floating element of the labour market is plagued by some positive feedback chains caused by the existence of the latent and the dead part of the labour market and their interaction with the real wage dynamics in particular. Should these feedback chains make the overall dynamics unstable this will occur by way of a Hopf bifurcation, through the death or birth of unstable or stable limit cycles, since the determinant of the system cannot change its sign, that is, the roots of the Jacobian can only enter the positive part of the complex plane of complex numbers by becoming complex at the bifurcation point. The loss of stability therefore necessarily occurs in the presence of business fluctuations of the distributive cycle type.

2.5 The Debate on an Employer of Last Resort

In this section we primarily review the concept of an Employer of Last Resort, or briefly ELR, as it is discussed in the literature. We then provide in the next section a model of the Marxian reserve army cycle with a social structure of capital accumulation which at its bottom contains a portion of the working class where an ELR approach is urgently needed. This holds true from the perspective of human rights, of Social-democrats, but also for example from the viewpoint of the German concept of a 'social market economy'. We have studied the characteristics of the reserve army mechanism with such unregulated labour markets in earlier sections, and thus now enter the stage where we can ask what an ELR can achieve in such a segmented economy.

Although unemployment must be regarded as a major economic as well as social problem, it is often discussed as being functional for capitalism, a discussion which is focusing on the idea of the compelling need for a reserve army of unemployed for the proper functioning of capitalism (with Marx being the first to take note of this, see the preceding chapter). While the Human Rights Declaration (1948) underlines the right to a job, unemployment has been a severe challenge within the capitalist system to date.

In a capitalist society the normal way to earn money in order to live properly is to offer work on the labour market if one is not a member of the group of employers or the group of wealthy persons. When, on the other hand, full employment is rarely occurring and even regarded as objectionable, the question has to be answered how unemployed persons can be enabled to lead a satisfying life.

Since Minsky (1986) the concept of an 'Employer of Last Resort' (ELR) has been discussed, rejected and further developed. There exist different conceptions of an ELR system which can also be seen when such an ELR system is compared with related programs like the 'Basic Income Guarantee' (BIG) or workfare program (see Wray and Tcherneva, 2005).

In the 19th century some first insurances were implemented as part of a basic welfare concept, such as health insurance (see Chapter 1). In Germany, the concept of unemployment insurance was only introduced in 1927. Other countries followed pushed by the world-wide economic crises while especially in the Nordic countries the Ghent system – a trade union organised unemployment insurance – was already introduced in the early 1900s.[11] The name refers to the Belgian city where it was first implemented. It was then adopted by Scandinavian states and partly in Belgium. As the development since then has shown, unemployment insurances cannot in general cope with high unemployment rates.

The general aim of such an insurance as well as of BIG and of ELR systems can be described as an intention to allow workers to live a decent life in contrast to the problematic life of an unemployed person who may undergo social degradation through long-term unemployment and personal losses. The buffer stock principle of an ELR system must of course take account of the actual situations on the labour markets of given capitalist economies. But models which try to find compromises solely with their starting point in the actual capitalist economies (like the USA) will not be able to reflect the situation in more comprehensive ways.

Therefore we will show in Chapter 3, how an Employer of First Resort (EFR) added to our models of this and the preceding chapters can provide employment guarantees, not Job Guarantees (JGs), to skilled or even high-skilled persons, since in our ideal architecture of an advanced capitalist economy the educational system will allow that there are no unskilled workers (but only part-time unskilled work). This approach can therefore be characterised as an abstract modelling of a full employment economy. It represents an ideal economy to be compared with the status quo of actual developed capitalist economies only later on.

In this section, we will however discuss the BIG and ELR systems in more detail in order to demonstrate the possibilities and limits of these approaches in view of economic reality.

BIG is defined by van Parijs (2001) as an 'income paid by a government to each adult member of society'[12] with the aim to improve societal justice and individual freedom even if the paid sums are mainly supposed to be around the poverty line.[13] There are similar approaches like the concept of the 'free activity society with a basic income as a society of culture' which is described by Blaschke (2010) and is based on the assumption that capitalist surplus production will lead to serious economic and financial crisis. Dahrendorf (1990) also suggests a basic income guarantee to fight poverty and points out that the sum paid need not be competitive with normal wages.[14] Another approach by Lawn (2009) is to combine environmental problems with basic income needs.

Tcherneva and Wray (2005) describe an inevitable inflationary trap as the main problem of a BIG system, which makes the – in their view nevertheless closely related – model of an ELR superior.[15] In contrast to BIG, ELR is characterised by work requirement and thus it is not aiming solely at a reduction of the prevailing poverty among the inactive population. Its aim is described 'to promote full employment and price stability'.[16] Jobs are offered to anyone 'who is ready, willing and able to work' which will be paid by a 'single, uniform wage'.[17] Furthermore, benefits like healthcare and child care insurances are also intended. Price stability is regarded as dependent from the fact that 'ELR operates as a buffer stock'.[18] ELR-jobs, it is supposed, have to be carefully chosen, partly combined with training courses, since the main goal still is finding a non-ELR-job, since ELR-jobs are in general paid only a basic wage income (though at a living-standard level) and are mainly provided by non-profit community organisations. The necessity of working is supposed to improve the employability of ELR-workers in possible private-sector activities.[19]

Tcherneva and Wray (2005) summarise the advantages of ELR – shown to be related to the 'Jefes de Hogar'-Plan in Argentina[20] – as follows:

- ELR is universal and purely voluntary (no punitive conditionality criteria or demeaning means-tests)
- ELR jobs give income and socially valuable goods and services
- ELR jobs serve many societal needs (like, for example environmental cleanup or care for the young, sick or elderly)
- ELR jobs support social cohesion and advanced citizenship due to their work programs which are important for the society
- The minimum guaranteed wage for ERL jobs can also improve the chances to be taken back into private sector jobs for marginally higher wages
- ELR is supposed to increase efficiency due to training and constant working obligations.

There are, of course, opposite points of view present in the economic and social sciences literature. One critical commentator – Malcolm Sawyer (2005) – argues that

- The availability of ELR jobs leads to the abolition of unemployment benefits
- The jobs which are provided would typically be low-skilled ones (p.3) which causes problems for unemployed skilled workers
- There will be ELR jobs similar to regular jobs but lower paid
- Many jobs, like care for the elderly, cannot be offered solely through ERL jobs, so that in fact only few jobs are really applicable as ELR

jobs, especially since these jobs are supposed to be non-competitive with regular jobs

- The ELR jobs have to be available rather quickly for demanding unemployed persons because they receive no unemployment benefit, but they have at the same time to be of a kind where it does not matter when they are done only for some time (p.8)
- It is unclear whether all offered jobs have to be taken by the unemployed persons
- The term 'unemployed' is not clearly defined: are retired persons or students or underemployed persons included?
- The necessity of suitability checks is not clarified, for example for jobs taking care of children.
- There is a danger for wages concerning similar jobs in the regular public sector.
- It is not clarified how ELR will cope with sudden increases in numbers of unemployed persons.

Further critical questions are related to financing and funding as well as structural issues.[21]

Tcherneva and Wray (2005) have dealt with some of the mentioned critical questions and argue that[22]

- ELR systems will carefully screen the suitability of possible employees and find alternatives for those who are unsuitable for certain jobs
- All ELR workers are free to give up the job but also the employers have the right to dismiss ELR workers
- The cyclical swing in the ELR job demands will not be extreme in booms or busts
- The fact that the ELR wage is kept constant will be a stabilising force.

There are still further questions to discuss with regard to BIG and ELR, especially with regard to the various models of the welfare state. This concerns unemployment insurance as well as the demand for proper jobs instead of just ELR type ones. In European welfare states like, for example, Germany, employed people have an unemployment insurance for which they have to pay 1.5% of their income with a similar contribution by their employers. There will be paid about 60% of the last income for one year after which a so-called Hartz IV transfer system replaces unemployment benefits (see Section 2.7).

Important in comparison with an ELR system is the alternative that unemployed persons are supposed to find new low-income or regular jobs with the help of the public organisations or private agencies so that an ELR would be dispensable in such a situation. In the Northern countries of Europe this system is characterised by an even much stricter structure which offers new jobs but which also demands that unemployed workers accept them by and large. The questions which arise in these welfare structures are whether their relatively generous unemployment insurance with activating job-finding procedures can be regarded as superior to the BIG or the ELR proposal and whether they therefore provide the better solution at least in countries of primarily 'Nordic' type.

The main problem here – as with the other proposals – remains, of course, that there is no full employment, as we will construct it in the flexicurity model of the next chapter, where also the stability of such a situation will be investigated.

2.6 Active Labour Market Policy and an Employer of Last Resort

We have so far considered an economic system with three labour markets, a fluid one, a latent one and a dead one, where people are imagined of only casually doing some work, but primarily live on the individual charity of the other members of the workforce.[23] We have indeed assumed implicitly that people in the 'dead' segment of the labour market live on charity received from the other members of the working class, thereby redistributing part of the latter's consumption demand. Moreover, this segment is not totally a 'dead' one, since the parameter γ_2^u provided the extent that they can return to the latent segment of the labour market, depending on the rate of employment in this market. Workers employed in this second, latent portion of the labour market receive a given (minimum) real wage, while the fluid labour market works in the way it is assumed to work in the context of models of the distributive cycle. We have abstracted in the extension of the Goodwin model to this new situation from the social legislation we have discussed in Chapter 1 and thus assume again that a part of the unemployed in the two active labour markets are living on the basis of the incomes of larger families they are belonging to, as is, for example, often the case in Spain with its larger family structures.

Yet, in the present section we return to an unemployment benefit system in the two active labour markets of the model and assume that this addition makes then secure in the downward direction, that is, the massive generation of a totally degraded workforce is thereby no longer possible. Of course, there may exist disabled people of various kinds, but this is not a problem a macro-model has to deal with so that we now can simply assume that $\gamma_2^d = 0$ is established through a social network for the unemployed. Moreover we are assuming an active labour market policy, attempting to moderate the operation of the Marxian distributive cycle, now within the context of a dual structure of segmented labour markets, here in particular through an activation program that tries to counteract the flow of workers dismissed from the first labour market into the latent one, which we now consider to be more of the type of a low income sector, representing 'atypical employment'. Last, but not least, we postulate that the public sector can demand services from the unemployed (who are all receiving unemployment benefits). The organisation of these (social) services demands of course microeconomic coordination and also incentives and sanctions.

We thus assume now the existence of a public Employer of Last Resort who organises the sector of those workers who are not employed by capitalist firms. The classic, but not the best example for such a task are military services, for instance in the USA, which may be supplemented by the alternative of civilian service and the like. The public sector thus now takes care of a better working of the fluid labour market, tries to reduce the extent of the second one, the low income sector as much as possible, and administers the funds (received from the employed) for the unemployed, in combination with which the government also conducts a system of social services supplied by the 'unemployed' (including skill preservation processes).

In order to do this, we start again from the 4D model of unrestricted capitalism:

$$\hat{\omega}_1 = \beta_{we_1}(e_1 - \bar{e}_1) + \beta_{we_2}e_2 - \beta_{wd}d/l^s + \beta_{w\omega_1}(\omega_1^o - \omega_1) \tag{2.39}$$

$$\hat{l}^s = n - \bar{y}(1 - \omega_1/\bar{z}_1 - \bar{\omega}_2/\bar{z}_2) \tag{2.40}$$

$$\hat{l}_2^s = \gamma_1^d - (\gamma_1^d + \gamma_1^u)e_1 + n - \bar{y}(1 - \omega_1/\bar{z}_1 - \bar{\omega}_2/\bar{z}_2) \tag{2.41}$$

$$\hat{d} = \gamma_2^d - (\gamma_2^d + \gamma_2^u)e_2 + n - \bar{y}(1 - \omega_1/\bar{z}_1 - \bar{\omega}_2/\bar{z}_2) \tag{2.42}$$

We now modify these laws of motion for real wages and the three labour markets as follows:

$$\begin{aligned}
\hat{\omega}_1 =& \beta_{we_1}(e_1 - \bar{e}_1) + \beta_{we_2}(e_2 - \bar{e}_2) + \beta_{w\omega_1}(\omega_1^o - \omega_1) && (2.43)\\
\hat{l}^s =& n - \bar{y}(1 - \omega_1/\bar{z}_1 - \bar{\omega}_2/\bar{z}_2) && (2.44)\\
\hat{l}_2^s =& \gamma_1^d - (\gamma_1^d + \gamma_1^u)e_1 + n - \bar{y}(1 - \omega_1/\bar{z}_1 - \bar{\omega}_2/\bar{z}_2) - \\
& \phi(\bar{e}_2 - e_2) && (2.45)
\end{aligned}$$

with

$$e_1 = \frac{\bar{y}/\bar{z}_1}{l^s - l_2^s}, \quad e_2 = \frac{\bar{y}/\bar{z}_2}{l_2^s}, \quad \bar{e}_1 = \frac{\gamma_1^d}{\gamma_1^d + \gamma_1^u}, \quad \bar{e}_2 = \frac{\gamma_2^d}{\gamma_2^d + \gamma_2^u}.$$

By the choice of the benchmark levels of the employment rates we have adjusted the steady state of the model to the one of the model of unrestricted capitalism. Moreover we assume that the size of the γ value is in an adequate range in this model with an active labour market policy, that is, they are assumed to be manipulated by policy such that the normal rates of employment are around 95 percent.

Policy now avoids the establishment of a dead segment on the labour market by erecting an unemployment benefit system with reserves B as follows:

$$\begin{aligned}
\dot{B} &= \tau_b\omega_1 L_1^d - \bar{\omega}_2(L_1^s - L_1^d) - \alpha\bar{\omega}_2(L_2^s - L_2^d) && (2.46)\\
&= \tau_b\omega_1 e_1 L_1^s - \bar{\omega}_2(1 - e_1)L_1^s - \alpha\bar{\omega}_2(1 - e_2)L_2^s && (2.47)
\end{aligned}$$

Workers employed in the first labour market are now taxed with rate τ_b in order to create inflows into the reserves of an unemployment benefit system. The outflow goes to unemployed workers of type 1 who receive the wage of the employed workers of type 2 as unemployment benefits. Unemployed workers of type 2 receive only a portion α of this wage however, yet they have income now and their decline into a dead segment of the labour market (which now no longer exists and which is no longer established in the course of time) is prevented by an active labour market policy.

This policy at least guarantees skill preservation for workers of type 1 and 2, by employing the $(1-e_1)L_1^s + (1-e_2)L_2^s$ workers as an Employer of Last Resort in public institutions, which provide social services and more, yet work that is not in competition with the activities occurring in the private sector of the economy. This amount of unemployment therefore is kept intact as suppliers of work of at least type 2. Moreover, active labour market policy also demands that government or private institutions attempt to channel back workers of type 2 into the first labour market. This gives rise to the $-\phi(\bar{e}_2 - e_2)$ expression in the law of motion that increases or decreases the extent of the second labour market.

A labour market reform along these lines thus eliminates the existence of a dead segment on the labour market and increases the flow back into the first labour market. Nevertheless, we still consider this as very basic reforms of the labour market institutions. Note that all workers still consume all of their income so that the redistribution of income between the employed and the unemployed does not question the validity of Say's law in such a Goodwin-type economy. Moreover we have for the variable $b = B/K$, the benefit funds per unit of capital, the law of motion

$$\hat{b} = \hat{B} - \hat{K} = \frac{\dot{B}}{K}\frac{K}{B} - \hat{K} \tag{2.48}$$

$$= \tau_b \omega_1 e_1 l_1^s - \bar{\omega}_2(1 - e_1)l_1^s - \alpha\bar{\omega}_2(1 - e_2)l_2^s - \bar{y}(1 - \omega_1/\bar{z}_1 - \bar{\omega}_2/\bar{z}_2) \tag{2.49}$$

with $e_1 = \frac{\bar{y}/\bar{z}_1}{l_1^s}, \quad e_2 = \frac{\bar{y}/\bar{z}_2}{l_2^s}$.

In the steady state this gives

$$\hat{b} = \tau_b \omega_1^o \frac{\gamma_1^d}{\gamma_1^d + \gamma_1^u} l_1^{so} - \bar{\omega}_2 \frac{\gamma_1^u}{\gamma_1^d + \gamma_1^u} l_1^{so} - \alpha\bar{\omega}_2 \frac{\gamma_2^u}{\gamma_2^d + \gamma_2^u} l_2^{so} - n \tag{2.50}$$

$$= 0$$

which when solved for the tax rate gives

$$\tau_b = \frac{\bar{\omega}_2\gamma_1^u}{\omega_1^o\gamma_1^d} + \frac{\alpha\bar{\omega}_2 \frac{\gamma_2^u}{\gamma_2^d + \gamma_2^u} l_2^{so} + n}{\frac{\gamma_1^d}{\gamma_1^d + \gamma_1^u} l_1^{so}} = \frac{\bar{\omega}_2\gamma_1^u}{\omega_1^o\gamma_1^d} + \frac{\alpha\bar{\omega}_2 \frac{\gamma_2^u}{\gamma_2^d}\frac{\bar{y}}{\bar{z}_2} + n}{\frac{\bar{y}}{\bar{z}_1}}$$

$$= \frac{\bar{\omega}_2\gamma_1^u}{\omega_1^o\gamma_1^d} + \alpha\bar{\omega}_2 \frac{\gamma_2^u}{\gamma_2^d}\frac{\bar{z}_1}{\bar{z}_2} + \frac{n\bar{z}_1}{\bar{y}} \tag{2.51}$$

This expression shows that the parameters of the model have to be determined with care such that the wage income after taxes of households of type 1 is of an appropriate size. Increasing movements from the second into the first labour market also decreases the tax rate of the employed workforce of type 1 as does a decrease in the downward direction. There is therefore a variety of ways (indeed still more) by which the tax rate on the income of those working in the first segment of the labour market can be decreased.

It is a bit surprising to get the result that an increasing value of the parameter α improves the income situation of the employed households of type 2, as does the real wage of workers employed in the second labour market as far as the tax rate is concerned. It lowers the value of ω_1^o however. Decreasing the downward movement of unemployed workers in the second labour market has also the side effect that workers of type 2 get more jobs in this market, since it is plausible to assume that workers of type 1 who enter the second labour market will have better chances to get a job there and will crowd out the type 2 workers who are looking for a job in their labour market.

For the Jacobian of the dynamics of our reform of capitalism towards one with an active and social labour market policy we get the sign distribution

$$J_o = \begin{pmatrix} - & - & - \\ + & 0 & 0 \\ + & + & - \end{pmatrix}$$

if we assume that adjustment term $\beta_{we_2}(e_2 - \bar{e}_2)$ is sufficiently strong. We then have that the coefficients $a_1, i = 1, .., 3$ in the Routh–Hurwitz polynomial are all positive (a positive J_{13} that is sufficiently small is already sufficient for this). In fact the determinant of J can be shown to be negative under mild conditions, so that only one minor of order two is creating a positive feedback loop which can destabilise the economy. The final Routh–Hurwitz stability condition on the parameters of the characteristic polynomial of the considered Jacobian is $a_1a_2 - a_3 > 0$ and this condition can be fulfilled if the parameter ϕ is chosen sufficiently large, since its appearance in the determinant cancels against one of its appearances in the term a_1a_2.

The considered system can therefore be stabilised in an obvious way, and we expect that these sufficient conditions are not really yet exploiting the parameter combinations where the balanced growth path of the model with an active income and labour market policy is attracting.

Figure 2.3 summarises what we have discussed above and shows in particular the more robust and stable feedback structure of the ELR variant of the model of this chapter.

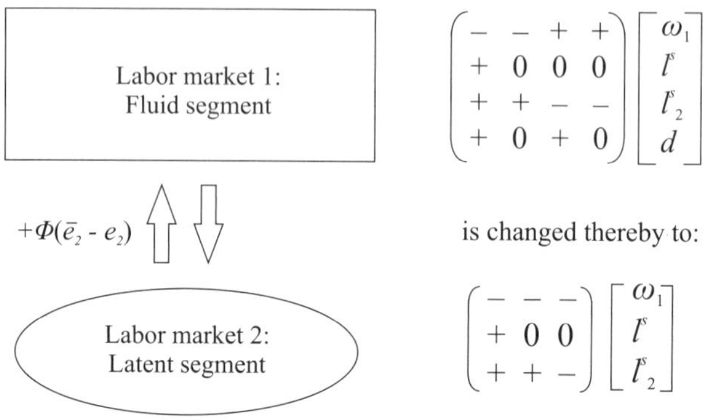

$$\dot{B} = \tau_b \omega_1 L_1^d - \bar{\omega}(L_1^s - L_1^d) - \alpha\bar{\omega}_2(L_2^s - L_2^d)$$

ELR – tasks: $\phi \uparrow, \gamma_1^{up} \uparrow, \tau_b, \bar{\omega}_2, \alpha$ adequate choice of parameters

Figure 2.3 The Marxian distributive cycle with an employer of last resort

The case of Germany after WWII provides an example where things went wrong due to a lack of cooperating corporatism between capital and labour primarily in the question of income distribution, though the concept of a social market economy was a success story in the prosperity phase after WWII. It was shown in Flaschel and Greiner (2008) that adding minimum real wages as well as maximum ones to the distributive cycle can reduce its amplitude significantly both in the prosperity phase and the depressed phase. The reserve army of unemployed is thereby reduced in the depression, and the social degradation of part of the workforce avoided. But in the prosperity phase, unions in Germany did not think in terms of Marx's reserve army mechanism and did not consider ceilings to their real wage claims. Chancellor Willy Brandt supported indirectly this behaviour when he proclaimed that full employment would now be maintained forever. But Marx's overshooting income claims mechanism worked in this context (leading first to stagflation and later on to stagnation without inflation). By contrast, minimum real wage legislation was not taken seriously after the Iron Curtain came down, neither by the social democrats who under Chancellor Schröder implemented the Hartz I – IV reforms, nor under Chancellor Merkel where the discussion about minimum wages was only conducted from a very microeconomic perspective. The result of such policies was the establishment of a progressively increasing low-income or part-time labour market segment and from there the flow of workers into Hartz IV which can by and large be considered a dead segment from the perspective of the social standards of the fluid segment of the labour markets in Germany.

These policies opened the watergate on the labour market into a downward direction and contributed significantly to a return of a labour market structure as investigated already by Marx (1954) in *Capital*, Vol. I and modelled in this chapter. Lacking insights into the Marxian reserve army mechanism on both sides of the conflict about income distribution (concerning agreements on both maximum and minimum real wages) as well as on both sides of the political spectrum in Germany (concerning resistance to processes of social degradation within the workforce) have now led in Germany to a situation where processes of social segmentation are difficult to stop or even overcome, even if policy would be willing to act accordingly.

The 1960s and early 1970s (where the Marxian insight into the working of capitalism and the reserve army mechanism was totally neglected)[24] can thus be considered as a time of lost chances, since maximum and minimum real wages are easier to negotiate and implement by private contracts or law in prosperity phases. To a certain degree the consequences of this failure was the disintegration of the concepts that constituted the German way to a 'Social Market Economy' into the direction of low income work, widespread poverty and their social consequences. The development of low-wage work in Germany shows – besides the Hartz IV system – a typical downward trend in the working of the labour market, also compared with other countries in Europe. Comparing Germany with the United Kingdom[25] and Denmark[26] points to three different approaches following the study by G. Esping-Andersen (1990) on welfare states, the social-democratic ones, the neoliberal ones and the conservative-corporatist types of welfare capitalism, in short: the good, the bad and the ugly.[27] With regard to low-wage work, Denmark had in 2005 with 8.5% a significantly smaller amount of employees in this sector than Germany with 20.8 % and the UK with 22.1%, although Denmark has no minimum wages, but a system of negotiations between employers' and employees' organisations.[28] Among the reasons mentioned to explain this fact the flexicurity model is the most popular one since it helps unemployed persons to return into the regular labour market, including a high rate of mobility out of the low wage jobs. In Germany, minimum wages might be a possible way to reduce the number of low-wage-workers and thus the danger that even more persons have to join the rather hopeless Hartz IV system.

In the following section we will have a look at Germany's neighbouring state, Austria, with a special interest in its achievement of relatively high employment coupled with moderate inflation outcomes and the way this is dealt with under Austrian Tripartism, that is, economic corporatism based on tripartite interactions between capital, labour, and state organisations.

2.7 Austria, Labour Market Outcomes and Civic Work

> *Researchers agree that Austria displays most of the basic characteristics of the ideal type of 'corporatism' that has been set up in the relevant literature (see, e.g., the corporatism index by Siaroff, 1999). First, in the sense of a formalised structure of the interest representation system that is characterised by a limited number of singular, compulsory, non-competitive, monopolised, centralised interest associations benefiting from various organisational and institutional privileges as classically defined by Schmitter (1979). Second, in the sense of a particular institutionalised process of policy-formation in which large interest organisations co-operate with each other and with state authorities, especially in the realm of wage and labour market policies. These two dimensions of corporatism are closely connected.* (Viebrock 2004, p.3)[29]

The Austrian economy exhibits about 8.4 million inhabitants of which 4148000 persons were gainfully employed according to the labour market statistics for the 3rd quarter of 2010; the participation rate of the inhabitants, aged between 15 and 64, was 72.6%. The overall unemployment rate of the workforce was about 4.4% (with roughly 25 % part-time work) and the long-term unemployment rate (unemployed for more than a year) was 1.1% (less than 50000 persons). These data show that the economic-financial crisis seems to be overcome, since in 2009 the unemployment rate was significantly higher (5.1%), though the data are somewhat difficult to compare due to an adjustment of the Austrian data to the Eurostat prescriptions.[30] The small number (1.1%) of long-term unemployed persons raises the question of how this rather small number can be explained, especially when compared with German data (where 57% of the unemployed persons were long-term unemployed ones).

The Austrian unemployment insurance includes several forms of payments to unemployed persons, such as unemployment benefits, unemployment assistance, advance pension payment, temporary assistance and transfer payment to elderly persons. Persons who apply for one of the unemployment payment schemes must be unemployed as well as able and willing to work. Furthermore, it is necessary that they have been in dependent contributory employment for a specified minimum duration. Thus, someone who has interrupted his/her working time for a longer period as well as school leavers have no right to receive unemployment benefits. Unemployed persons have to accept an offered job, otherwise their unemployment benefit is suspended. The extent of unemployment benefits is calculated on the basis of the previous income. The basic rate of the unemployment benefit payments usually equals 55% of the last net income, which is a bit smaller than in Germany. There are further regulations concerning whole families.

Unemployment benefit has a minimum duration of 20 weeks and can be paid – depending of the insurance paid during the time of employment – up to 52 weeks. The duration also depends on the age of the applicants. It is requested that job offers or schooling proposals are accepted. The regulations of unemployment benefits are similar to the German ones concerning unemployment benefits type I (Arbeitslosengeld I). While in Germany, persons who are unemployed for more than 52 weeks have to apply for the 'unemployment benefits type II' (Arbeitslosengeld II or Hartz IV) with its completely different regulation scheme compared to unemployment payments type I, in Austria an unemployment assistance follows the unemployment benefit payments, which is said to combine the principles of social insurance and welfare. Its rate is calculated on the basis of the formerly received unemployment benefit. It is up to 92% or 95% of the basic rate (95% for a basic rate of less than EURO 783.99). Furthermore, it is demanded that the applicants really need financial support, which mainly refers to the income of partners. The mentioned sums are much higher than under Hartz IV in Germany, but it is unclear whether additional payments concerning rent, etc. are paid. There are further limitations due to the duration of unemployment benefit payments. The fact that older unemployed persons have easier access to unemployment assistance could be taken as an indication that there are little or no chances for persons older than 55 to find a new job. Unemployment assistance can be paid without time limit if necessary, but Austria also has an activating labour market policy in the sense that unemployed persons with no chance to return to their original occupation can be given deviant work (Public Employment Service Austria (AMS) 2011).

In Austria, social welfare is based politically on a cross-party acceptance, a situation for which ÖKSA (the Österreichische Komitee für Soziale Arbeit) is the relevant institution. It was founded in 1956 as a bipartisan federal association and functions as an open platform for dialogue and coordination in governmental and non-governmental Austrian social politics. Melinz (2006) describes the Austrian welfare state as being of 'Bismarckian style', due to the underlying male breadwinner model. Furthermore, he argues that a Bismarckian Welfare System has to 'manage high levels of employment', since unemployment and 'atypical employment' are 'contributing to troubles in financing …'.[31] Another point is the 'status group oriented' welfare state which is oriented to and refers to different rules for workers, civil servants etc.[32]

As the European Commission (2010) emphasised, unemployment in Austria was measured in Spring 2010 at less than half of the European average. Nevertheless, unemployment had become a topic in Austria, too, so that the EU is supporting a range of projects through its European Social Fund. In particular older workers, people who have been out of work for a longer time, migrants, women, young people and those most at risk of social exclusion are at the centner of these projects.

There are further measures like minimum wages which are now around 1000 Euro in Austria. Yet, in general the (un-)employment situation in Austria is a 'mixed' one, since there are on the one hand low amounts of unemployed persons, especially long-term ones with rather high amounts of support, but on the other hand there exist specific groups like elderly persons who are in fairly uncomfortable situations. Furthermore, there are also forms of atypical work in Austria like short part-time and short fixed-time contracts, oral contracts, 'on-call work' and more.[33] There exists also labour leasing. This mixed situation in Austria demands further reflection on how to improve the situation without risking economic or financial problems.

Figure 2.4 summarises the performance of the Austrian economy against the labour market background we have just discussed. Compared to the German economy, see Figure 2.5, this is a significantly better performance of the labour market, while fluctuations in the inflation rate are by and large of the same magnitude in both countries.

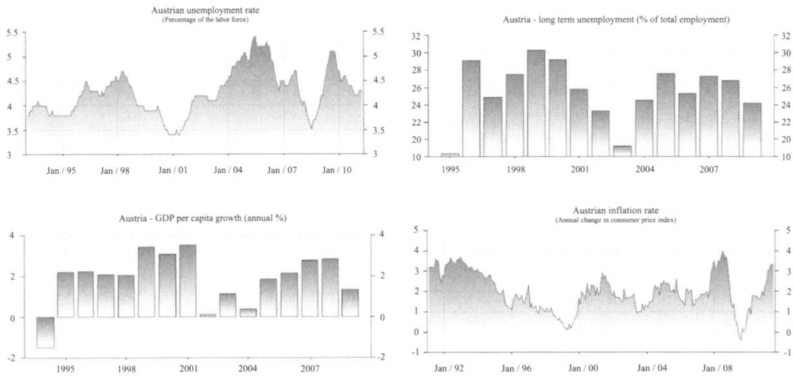

Figure 2.4 Austria 1993–2010: Total and long-term unemployment, price inflation and GDP per capita growth (Source: TradingEconomics.com; European Commission, 2010)

Figure 2.4 (as compared to Figure 2.5) shows that Austria's economic performance over the last 16–17 years was quite remarkable, though not yet based on a social policy of the ELR type as we have modelled it in the preceding section. The recorded labour force of Austria is approximately 4 million in size, which due to above figures roughly gives an average of 200000 officially unemployed people and approximately 50000 long-term unemployed workers (compared to 1.3 million in Germany in 2010).

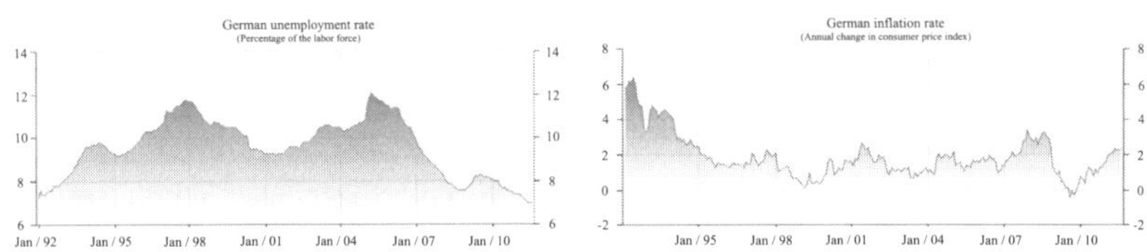

Figure 2.5 Germany 1992–2010: Total unemployment, CPI price inflation, respectively (Source: TradingEconomics.com; Deutsche Bundesbank, 2010)

The task of implementing an ELR system in Austria is thus from the quantitative macro-perspective not a formidable one. This may be different with respect to the coordination and incentive problems of this sector of the labour market, where detailed microeconomic judgements are certainly necessary and learning by doing processes are needed for acceptable outcomes.

Concerning moderate inflation dynamics, where the target of the central banks is around two percent, the Austrian economy thus performed quite well. Instead of conflicting income claims there is a corporatist regime working on the labour market, where the social partners are free to bargain in particular about money wages, and also minimum wages, but where there however should be some limits imposed by legislation concerning the role of minimum and maximum real wages (to be determined in view of the level of labour productivity).[34]

Within such bounds the outcome of the wage bargaining process may then depend on the current level of economic activity, where workers can improve their situation in the boom and may suffer some losses in the bust of the distributive cycle. However, it may well be that the processes of wage management, see Meade (1982) for prominent contribution in this area, will learn from history and theory to an extent that the distributive cycle, and the reserve army mechanism it is based on, is significantly reduced in its extent. A wage Phillips curve or relationship that integrates a real wage barrier into its operation, as in the model of this chapter, and which evaluates current (price) inflation properly ($\eta = 1$) may be a first step in such a direction.

In 2010, the German Federal Ministry of Labour and Social Affairs has taken steps to implement in an experimental phase so-called civic work (Bürgerarbeit) in certain regions of Germany. This activity is meant to provide a reasonable amount of income (900 Euro) for a given amount of weekly work (30 hours). The problem to be solved is primarily a microeconomic one: to determine socially valuable contributions to the work done in the private and the public sector that do not crowd out workers working in these two sectors of the economy. We view such attempts as going in the right direction and as directing – when applied to all unemployed workers after their first year financed through regular unemployment benefits (Arbeitslosengeld I) – towards an improvement of ELR principles, since this third type of work is characterised by and should realise in a better way the creation of a third type of labour market (besides private and public work) than just one of a last resort.

Types of work associated with the civic work program of the Federal Ministry of Labour and Social Affairs are named on the webpage of the ministry (Bundesministerium für Arbeit und Soziales, 2010). But, of course, this is only a partial and tentative approach for the moment, which may or may not face difficulties in implementation. From the macroeconomic point of view we would however demand that indeed all second stages of social aid (after one year of unemployment benefits, activated job search and further education and training) should be of the type of civic work, receiving civic income (which may depend on the skill level of the 1 year unemployed person). Of course, incentives and sanctions and learning by doing may be needed on the microeconomic level, and the implementation of networks in this sector which make it more transparent, more efficient and more acceptable from a social point of view. In any case the ELR perspective is just coming into existence in Germany, without any cross-reference to the ELR debate in the academic literature at present (in 2010).[35]

Nevertheless, the next steps in macroeconomic labour market policy could well be to implement principles of 'civic work and income' as follow-up to unemployment benefits, which then would become civic employment benefits in fact. The principle of giving and taking should indeed be taken much more seriously with respect to labour market reforms so that income transfers to the unemployed do in fact not fund unemployment = leisure (but active job search and training), and subsequently civic employment, that is, decent employment from a social point of view. There are currently approximately 700 000 so-called one Euro jobs in Germany, which might be considered ELR jobs, which is however too little in view of the 3 million people who are unemployed and too little from the perspective of civic work and civic income.

Programs in Germany (on a local and partial level still), where civic work financing and not 'leisure' financing is offered for about 900 Euro and 30 hours of work per week, represent in the case of Austria even on the macroeconomic level not a huge amount of money (in comparison to the amount of money that is currently spent on all forms of unemployment and social aid) in view of the 50 000 long-term unemployed workers and the billions that are currently spent in order to keep the banking system alive. Austria thus provides an example where private, public and civic work can generate a situation whereby the social problems of (long-term) unemployment can be significantly mitigated or even overcome. As with any reform of this type, however, it needs to be stressed that there is necessarily learning by doing involved concerning the selection of civic occupations (as distinct from private or public occupations), in organising the network of civic work (solving its coordination problems), in defining performance measures, providing incentives and sanctions to increase such performance, and in adjusting income transfers in view of what is happening on the fluid part of the labour market and its low-income counterpart.

In principle, however, there is nothing apparent in the Austrian situation that would severely question the stepwise implementation of such a refined ELR system in the economic and social structure of this country. Moreover, from a European perspective, it may even be worthwhile to support such reforms in the smaller countries of the EU, in order to learn what is (not) working well under such a regime change. The Austrian case is also a valid case for such a program, since Austrian inflation dynamics are to a larger degree controlled by the inflation rates in the German economy, due to the long tradition of having a strictly fixed exchange rate with respect to the Deutsche Mark (before the introduction of the Euro). The inflationary consequences of the above strategy for a full employment economy with a fixed base income should therefore be of a kind that does not endanger this private-public-civic workplace system, in particular if a corporatist bi- or tri-party system is capable of conducting a reasonable management of wage negotiations. Such a full employment economy thus needs not be characterised by centrifugal forces in its wage–price dynamics.

However, as we have seen in this chapter, the arguments of the critics of an ELR system not only point to the inflationary consequences of such labour market reforms, but – based on Kalecki (1943) – also to the definitely relevant possibility of firms losing control over production and innovation processes, since workers and their unions will implement more and more obstacles for a competitive and innovative behaviour of firms. As against this we would state that in a modern capitalist economy, there are already (high-tech) sectors where the cooperation and interaction of management and the employees of such organisations is performing well and where a lot is done in the provision of services to the employees with respect to their family life, well-being at the activity area, and the like.

However, in sectors with unpleasant work (piece-work, working under pressure, health hazards, etc.) and low income payments there will not be room for reasonable cooperation between capital and labour. But the evolution of such work, to be considered as atypical in a modern welfare state, is in fact social regress where primitive modes of production or the division of labour returns to a socio-economical structure that can endanger the further evolution of such societies. Technical progress under capitalism was labour-saving and capital-using, since wages were increasing and thus forcing firms to process innovations with more and more advanced techniques and more and more skilled labour (but as usual in economics not in a monotonic way, but through long-phased Schumpeterian innovation cycles).

In the current situation with significantly increasing rates of atypically employed workers and alienated work, there is of course no good reason why such workers will interact with their taskmasters in a reasonable and cooperative way. The current status quo in many advanced capitalist economies is therefore not a good basis for the envisaged labour market reforms. But does this imply that we should let things become even worse instead of attempting the proposed labour market reforms? We would not follow this type of reasoning, but believe that education and political debate have to be shaped such that the factual ideas and programs concerning civic work and income become more and more powerful and thus increasingly easier to implement and to be developed further. It is therefore a matter of social capital and its evolution over time that may render the Kalecki type negative implications of full employment less and less severe.

We believe that unions have learned such things to a certain degree from the long wave after World War II with its prosperity phase and its stagnant phase and now act accordingly. But it seems that neoliberal ideology prevents larger segments of capital from also acting in this way. There is thus urgent need for political debate on the implications of systems where a Marxian segmented labour market system has come back into the working of advanced capitalist systems and the long-term social regress this return implies. Of course, the message of Kalecki's (1943) essay on 'The political aspects of full employment' must be further reflected, such that neither the naive 'full employment promise' of the German Chancellor Brandt (having normal employment in mind) nor the view that some unemployment is 'natural' (as opposed to frictional unemployment) can be a sound strategy for the future.

2.8 Conclusions

In this chapter, we have extended a baseline version of the Goodwin (1967) model of the distributive cycle which describes the implications of the Marxian reserve army mechanism of capitalist economies. We added to this model segmented labour markets as described in Marx's *Capital*, Vol. I. The model exhibited a unique steady state solution which depends on the speeds with which workers are pushed into or out of the labour market segments. We investigated the stability properties of this model with segmented labour markets and found that, though there was a stabilising inflation barrier term in the assumed wage Phillips curve, the interaction with the latent and the dead portions of the labour market generated in this model potentially destabilising forces.

We then introduced an active labour market policy into it where government acts as employer-of-last-resort thereby eliminating the stagnant or dead portion of the labour market, whilst erecting an unemployment benefit system that sustains the incomes of workers that leave the floating or latent labour markets into unemployment to a certain extent. The ELR policy instruments concerned an activating labour market policy, attempting to bring people from the latent labour market back into the fluid one (from atypical employment back into normal employment) coupled with a minimum wage system in the latent (low income) segment of the labour market. We showed that these policy measures guarantee the macro-stability of the economy's growth path.

Instead of low wages in the latent segment of the labour market and the need for charity (Hartz IV from today's perspective in Germany) in its dead segment we have assumed in a revised version of the Goodwin model a pay-as-you-go BIG type unemployment benefit system in the now only dual labour market structure of the model and activating labour market policies that try to minimise the extent of the second labour market segment and an institutional system of ELR type where work skills are maintained and where there is a new network of social activities, instead of the waste and the significant economic and social costs that characterised the unrestricted capitalism of this chapter and the current situation in Germany. The affordability of such a structure needs however a certain level of real wages and thus should be embedded into a model where there is growth of labour productivity as considered in the preceding chapter.

Concerning inflation we have proposed a wage Phillips curve where elements of cautiousness are present, suggesting that more reflection is needed in order to design a corporatist wage management system that avoids strong inflationary pressure in the boom and the danger of deflation during busts. Such a system – not unrelated to the one existing in the Austrian economy – may then also be coupled with an – in the case of Austria – affordable civic work and income system which further improves the working of an ELR system as it is envisaged for the USA in particular. Such a labour market structure would eliminate the need for social aid and the social degradation the latter system usually implies.

We conclude from the above that a reformed type of capitalism is working much better as compared to the unrestricted working of it where labour market segmentation can represent a big economic and social problem. This can range from loss in social cohesion to class conflicts and more. There are a lot of parameter options in this reformulated model of capitalism that allow us to improve the situation even further, also concerning labour productivity through higher job satisfaction, a higher output–capital ratio and more.

As the model is formulated, we have however still the situation – as in Goodwin's original approach – that there is a free hiring and firing at work, a situation which may be made socially acceptable here (and in the now following chapter) to a certain degree by the income guarantees provided by the reformed labour market institutions and the more floating states in the two labour markets.

Notes

1 This chapter is partly based on Flaschel and Malikane (2011).

2 Where the above quotation has been taken from.

3 See Blien, Walwei and Werner (2002) for an overview of the situation of unemployed persons and German regulations before the so-called Hartz 'reforms'.

4 See Tompson (2009), 229ff.

5 See Bosch and Kalina (2008, 19ff.) for the development in the last twenty years.

6 The Hartz IV contributions of the state currently amount to roughly 500 Euro per head.

7 See Marx (1954).

8 Here no longer really measures of labour productivity in this partial form, since the model does not allow for isolated changes in the employment of the factors of production.

9 Such that the slope of the $\dot{\omega}_1$–isocline remains smaller than 1 (otherwise the model is per se not a viable one, see the discussion of its balanced growth path).

10 In order to get this result the conditions

$$\beta_{we_1}\frac{\bar{z}_2}{\bar{z}_1}(\frac{l_2^s}{l_1^s})^2 > \beta_{we_2}, \quad \beta_{we_1}\frac{\bar{y}}{z_1}(\frac{l^s}{l_1^s})^2, \beta_{we_1}\frac{\bar{y}}{z_1 l^s}(\frac{l^s}{l_1^s})^2 > \beta_{wd}$$

must hold. However, other cases with other stability properties are possible and thus make the outcome of this model of unrestricted capitalism somewhat ambiguous.

[11] See Bredgaard, Larsen and Madsen (2006, 65ff.).

[12] See van Parijs, P. (2001), 'A Basic Income for All', in: Cohen J. and J. Rogers (eds), *What's Wrong with a Free Lunch?*, Boston, MA: Veacon Press, quoted from Tcherneva, P. and Wray, L.R. (2005, p.129).

[13] See Tcherneva and Wray (2005, p.129ff.)

[14] See Dahrendorf (1990, p.177).

[15] See Tcherneva and Wray (2005, p.137).

[16] Tcherneva and Wray (2005, p.132).

[17] Tcherneva and Wray (2005, p.132).

[18] Tcherneva and Wray (2005, p.133).

[19] Tcherneva and Wray (2005, p.13ff.).

[20] Tcherneva and Wray (2005, p.138ff.).

[21] See Sawyer (2005, p.10ff.).

[22] Tcherneva and Wray (2005, p.134).

[23] In the extreme such people have been characterised in Marx 'The Eighteenth Brumaire of Louis Napoleon (1852)' as 'Lumpenproletariat', the 'refuse of all classes', including swindlers, confidence tricksters, brothel-keepers, rag-and-bone merchants, beggars, and other flotsam of society. We view the third segment of the labour market – when increasing – as being on the way to such a social structure, at Marx's times and today related to alcoholism, drug dealing and consuming, youth gang formation and racism.

[24] SeeWörgötter (1986) for an interesting interpretation of the Goodwin (1967) model that would have been of help in the public debate at that time.

[25] See Lloyd, Mason and Mayhew (2008).

[26] See Westergaard-Nielsen (2008).

[27] G. Esping-Andersen (1990, p.26ff.

[28] See Solow (2008).

[29] The quoted paper by Viebrock considers, on the basis of statements as the one shown above, the centralised mode of interest mediation within the Austrian system of 'corporatism' and the democratic deficit problem it entails. We do not go into such topics here, which however may be of great importance if the civic work system we are sketching in this section, as an alternative to the system of Austrian unemployment regulations, is put into operation.

[30] See Statistik Austria (2009) and Eurostat (2011c) for further details and comparisons.

[31] Melinz (2006, p.4).

[32] Melinz (2006, p.2).

[33] See Eurofound (2010)

[34] Neck (2009) provides a detailed graphical representation of the structure of the Austrian Social and Economic Partnership system including a discussion of the historical roots of this system. Moreover, we have to thank Reinhard Neck for providing useful comments on this section of the chapter and on the reasons why Austrian system of social partnership is losing ground, see also the paper by Viebrock (2004). Of course the usual caveats apply.

[35] There is currently also a debate in Austria about the German concept of civic work, but this debate does not really realise the potential of this concept, since it seems to focus on just augmenting the current social aid system by work obligations of those trapped in this social assistance system, instead of making it more attractive to really deliver civic work.

3. Full Employment Capitalism through an Employer of First Resort

3.1 Introduction

Flexicurity is a combination of flexibility and security in working arrangements. The concept is a response to the needs European labour markets are facing. On the one hand, the EU has to come to terms with changes in the world economy. ... Jobs change more quickly than before.

On the other hand, the EU needs to reinforce the European social models, which are committed to social protection, social cohesion and solidarity. Workers .... need good social protection in case a new job is not easily at hand or when employment is no longer a realistic option.

Flexicurity is an attempt to unite these two fundamental needs. It promotes a combination of flexible labour markets and adequate security. Flexicurity can also help provide an answer to the EU's dilemma on how to maintain and improve competitiveness whilst reinforcing the European social model.

Flexicurity does not mean 'hire and fire' .... . 'External flexicurity' attempts to offer safe moves for workers from one job into another, and good benefits to cover the time span, if needed.

Rather than job security, flexicurity focuses on 'employment security'. Employment security means staying in employment ... . The philosophy behind flexicurity is that workers are more prepared to make ... moves if there is a good safety net.

EU Member States have recognised that they need to develop innovative policies to help people stay in employment whilst ensuring that companies remain competitive on the global stage. .... The European Commission has, in response to this request, extensively researched possible solutions .... . (European Commission 2007).

3.2 A New Economic Structure for Capital Accumulation: Flexicurity Capitalism

We continue in this chapter[1] to argue that Goodwin's (1967) growth cycle model, portraying the Marxian reserve army mechanism, does not represent a process of social reproduction which can be considered an adequate socio-economic foundation for a democratic society in the long-run. The socio-economic reproduction process as depicted in that model depends on recurrent mass unemployment (sometimes also manipulated appropriately by policy) to remove the obstacles to capital accumulation erected by labour during the prosperity phase of such a conflict-driven cycle in income distribution, inflation and growth (as we have experienced it in the second half of the last century in the form of Reaganomics and Thatcherism in particular). We have seen in the preceding two chapters that social legislation and active labour market policy can however be used to mitigate the economic and social consequences of this process of the reestablishment of sufficient profitability for capitalist reproduction, but the segmentation of the workforce into normal and low income work is not really overcome thereby, even if Basic Income Requirements are met and are augmented by an Employer of Last Resort in order to keep workers in a job. We therefore now expand the latter concept into the direction of the flexicurity conceptualisation of labour market institutions – where we distinguish between a first (the private), a second (the public) and a third labour market (the Employer of First Resort, EFR), a labour market structure which is quite different from the ones we have discussed in the preceding chapter.

Our basic idea behind the concept of 'flexicurity' is not only income security, but also to implement activating labour market policies such that unemployment becomes basically of a frictional nature. From the microeconomic perspective, this means that labour market phenomena are studied by methods based on the U(nemployment)-V(acancy) approach, giving rise to the so-called UV or Beveridge curve. This curve can also be applied on the macroeconomic level, see Pissarides (1990) for a detailed study of this type. Frictional unemployment can have a geographical component as well as an occupational (skill-based) one and will exist in any capitalist economy that is subject to (Keynesian) fluctuating effective goods demand and (Schumpeterian) technical change. Subtracting this amount of unemployment from total unemployment basically leaves two alternatives: the Marxian one so far considered in this book (which is based on capital shortage) and the

Keynesian one (depressed levels of aggregate goods demand and income and thus underutilisation of both labour and capital).

We would follow here Friedman (1968) to a certain degree and consider the frictional component of unemployment (which he associated with disturbances of a hypothetical Walrasian economy), when equal to total unemployment, as full employment from a macroeconomic point of view (broadly speaking the situation in Germany in the 1960s, where vacancies were even outperforming the potential of non-employed people and led to strong migration processes, actively supported by firms). This unemployment rate should however not be confused – as Friedman (1968) did it – with the NAIRU rate of unemployment used in macroeconomics which can be considerably higher than just frictional unemployment (frictional unemployment was around 1% in the case of Germany in the 1960s). Our modelling of flexicurity will remove the Marx/Keynes types of unemployment surrounding the NAIRU level from the considered macroeconomy, while we simply abstract from frictional unemployment in this chapter, since we are considering this topic as being reserved for microeconomic research primarily.

Flexicurity is a new oxymoron, but the ideas comprising it can be traced back to indeed Beveridge (1942, 1945) already, the title of the latter work being: 'Full Employment in a Free Society'. And in the Beveridge Report he is stating the following:

> *There are some to whom pursuit of security appears to be a wrong aim. They think of security as something inconsistent with initiative, adventure, personal responsibility. That is not a just view of social security as planned in this Report. The plan is not one for giving to everybody something for nothing and without trouble... The plan is one to secure income for subsistence on condition of service and contribution and in order to make and keep men fit for service...* (Beveridge 1942)

Flexicurity was introduced on the political level in Denmark by the social democratic prime minister Poul Nyrup Rasmussen in the 1990s and it was introduced into the academic literature by Ton Wilthagen (1998).[2] The role of the flexicurity approach for the performance of the Danish economy is critically investigated in Andersen and Svarer (2007); for further critical assessments of the proposals for a flexicurity economy the reader is referred to recent contributions by Funk (2008) and Viebrock and Clasen (2009). We stress in this context that the approach to flexicurity taken in the present chapter is, however, an abstract and primarily macrotheoretic one that in particular abstracts from the difficulties of how to implement under flexicurity appropriate coordination and incentive principles on the microeconomic level.

Our approach to labour market institutions of the flexicurity type differs significantly from the Basic Income Guarantee (BIG) and Employer of Last Resort (ELR), though these approaches and our approach may have similar aims. Our approach can be characterised as an abstract representation of a full-employment economy, comparable in spirit to the Tableau Economique of Quesnay. It depicts an ideal economy to be compared with the status quo of actual developed capitalist economies. Such a comparison should then allow us to formulate compromises between the ideal and the status quo of actual economies, like the United States of America or Australia, as described in Tcherneva and Wray (2005) in the first case and in Quirk et al. (2006) with respect to Job Guarantee (JG) principles in the second case. We would, however, argue that these latter approaches in fact present compromises without really formulating an ideal on the basis of which these compromises can be discussed.

We do the opposite here and may therefore be considered as complementary to the ELR and JG approaches. However, the ideal world of our model contains no unskilled or low-skilled labour, since we assume that a well-designed schooling system would reduce unskilled labour to an insignificant portion of the population.[3] We thus have an Employer of First Resort (EFR) in our model who has to provide employment guarantees (not JGs) to skilled or even high-skilled persons, while the buffer stock principle of an ELR system must of course take account of the actual situations on the labour markets of given capitalist economies.

From a general point of view we however share the view of Tcherneva and Wray (2005) that the ELR procedures are superior to the BIG procedures, but we go on from there to an EFR modelling of the interaction of the labour markets in the private and the public sector. Moreover, we think that the design of an educational system is of decisive importance for the proper functioning of a flexicurity-based social structure of capital accumulation. Nevertheless, practical proposals for the JG system represent valuable inputs for the flexicurity modelling on our abstract macroeconomic level.[4]

3.3 Hallmark Denmark: Flexicurity, Denmark-style

Danish statistics show that the unemployment rate in Denmark (Statistics Denmark, 2011) went down from 3.8% in January 2007 to below 2% in June 2008, but then up to 4.3% in the first months of 2010. The number is again declining at the end of 2010. Even the numbers of 2010 are low in view of the worldwide crisis and compared to other countries in Europe. The highest unemployment rate was measured in 2004 and 2005 with more than 6%, but on the whole the period since 1993 is called a 'golden age' for the Danish labour market due to the generally high employment rates.[5] Such data underly our interest to study the Danish way to deal with the labour market and especially unemployment. As Bredgaard, Larsen and Madsen (2006, p.66) underline, the Danish flexicurity system is here of central importance for the positive developments on the Danish labour market since the early 1990s, but also 'a successful balancing of macroeconomic policy and trends in the international business cycle' as well as 'a new agenda for collective bargaining and wage formation' have helped the Danish 'miracle' of low unemployment and low inflation rates to happen (see Andersen and Mailand (2006) for further details of the collective bargaining system in Denmark).

The Danish flexicurity model exhibits several typical characteristics of the labour market with regard to (un)employment. Although the flexicurity model is a new political arrangement of the late 20th and early 21th century, there are some specific features with a long tradition such as unemployment benefit arrangements which are based on the Ghent system that was already started in the early 1900s, but was renewed in the late 1960s towards a primarily government-financed benefit system. It is, however, still organised primarily by the trade unions – through the formation of independent unemployment insurance funds.[6]

The Danish 'hiring and firing' system is even older in this regard, since it was already set up in 1899 as the Danish 'September Compromise' which initiated the self-regulation of the labour market by the labour market parties. The fact that the social partners could regulate most of the labour market problems among themselves with no intervention by the state is supposed to have created mutual trust even when significant conflicts had to be solved. These developments may also explain the cooperation between capital and labour in Denmark especially in contrast to other European countries. The Danish flexicurity model is described as a triangle: Flexible labour market (low job security), generous welfare schemes and an active labour market policy which originated in the labour market reform of 1993–1994, see Bredgaard, Larsen and Madsen (2006, p.64f.). The active labour market policy is even seen as 'high employment security', since the activating measures are supposed to help unemployed persons to find quickly a new job. Here, the difference between job and employment security is obvious. Social security can thus be regarded as a precondition for flexible labour markets and supports the willingness of Danish workers to practice job mobility. There is a rate of about 20% of workers who lose their job in a year, but most of them find a new one rather soon so that the long-term unemployment rate in Denmark is significantly smaller than in other OECD countries. It is the active labour market policy that especially deals with those workers who cannot find a new job within a shorter time period. The key words here are job training and education. This is part of CVT (continuing vocational training) policies which provide services and training for employed as well as unemployed persons. Both were implemented in the 1960s. Although the system is mainly financed by the government, the social partners are responsible for planning and administering this system.[7]

The Danish flexicurity system with its three interlinked parts of social security, flexible labour market and an activating labour market policy is in general positively evaluated. Nevertheless there exist also some difficulties and challenges, see Bredgaard, Larsen and Madsen (2006, p.71ff.): It is an open and debated question to what extent globalisation will affect jobs in a country like Denmark. A further issue is given by the question of how workers will live with repeated job failures and the demands from the activating labour market policy. Here the danger of sliding down into long-term unemployment and becoming a permanent welfare recipient has to be taken seriously into consideration even if Denmark has a high participation rate within its potential workforce. Long-term unemployment easily leads to social exclusion, a problem of immigrants in particular, especially from third-world countries.

'Atypical employment' is a topic too, which is of high importance in the unemployment discussions in most countries, but only seldomly mentioned in investigations about the Danish flexicurity model, since it is less important in Denmark than in other countries. There are predominantly women and low-educated persons working in the sector of atypical work. Bredgaard, Larsen, Madsen and Rasmussen (2009) discuss part-time employment, fixed-term contracts, temporary agency workers and self-employment as examples for atypical employment to be found in Denmark even under favourable labour market conditions. Part-time work is, however, not considered as 'atypical' in general and unemployed part-time workers have the same (relative) income protection as full-time workers, as is also the case for fixed-term employed persons. It seems that temporary agency workers are closest to questionable atypical work profiles in Denmark, though they have become a matter of collective agreements. Self-employment is also not characteristically atypical, and also rather seldom in Denmark. Bredgaard, Larsen, Madsen and Rasmussen (2009) describe one form of atypical work which was introduced as flex-jobs in 1998. 'Flex-jobbers' have a permanently reduced working ability, and it is more attractive for employers, flex-jobbers and municipalities to find suitable flex-jobs, because otherwise disability pensions have to be paid which is less attractive to the workers themselves as well as the paying institutions.

The development in atypical work can nevertheless become a danger within the Danish flexibility model. A problem in many European countries which is closely related to atypical work is low-wage work. Denmark's performance was with only 8.5% in 2005 clearly below those of other European countries, see Solow (2008a, p.6). Furthermore, low-wage workers in Denmark have good chances to leave this sector and gain a regularly paid job. This holds especially true for young employees, while the incidence of low-wage work is relatively high again for women and less educated workers, but also in hotels, restaurants and in retailing.[8]

A further problem listed in Bredgaard, Larsen and Madsen (2006, p.73f.) is the possible lack of incentives for an active job search, because of the high rate of income compensation for unemployed persons – especially those with a low income. Since income security is a necessary part of the Danish flexicurity model with its positive results for the economy, other forms of incentives and a strict demand for mobility and the acceptance of activation policies are the needed reactions. In general there seems to be a tendency to stress the need for incentives and motivation as well as sanctions in the Danish labour market policies. As the history of the Danish flexicurity model shows, it is, of course, subject to modifications, and each change in one of its three basic components can of course affect the other ones. So far the Danish flexicurity model has sustained its advantageous position which is mainly due to the three parts of the model, being of advantage for workers, unemployed persons and the firms. A main reason is certainly the cooperative attitude of the social partners in the labour market. Compared to other countries, we find a flexicurity model in operation which is forceful in supporting job flexibility where firms are profiting from as well as in providing income security which is supporting the life - course perspectives of workers who have thus no severe problem when losing their job, since they are not only supported financially but also in finding new employment with help with activating labour market measures.

Flexicurity is meanwhile intensively discussed in Europe as it seems to be very successful in Denmark. Bredgaard, Larsen and Madsen (2006, p.66ff.) show not only some essential changes that would become necessary when introducing such a system in other countries, but also point to the fact of a long development in Denmark with relatively stable institutions and class compromises. So it would be difficult to implement the cooperative trust between the Danish social partners and their tradition of regulating the labour market among themselves in other countries where this sort of behaviour does not belong to the 'social capital' of the country. Solow (2008a, p.14) also underlines such differences between other European countries and Denmark, where the government makes very little interventions in the labour market. The 'copy and paste' approach of transferring the Danish flexicurity policy is therefore rejected by Andersen and Svarer (2007, p.2f.) as being too naive although the occupation with the Danish model might at least lead to new insights, for example, with regard to balancing incentives, welfare provision and sanctions. Furthermore, there are aspects of the Danish approach such as the educational system and the health care system among others which are normally not related with economic issues, even in a flexicurity discussion, but which are nevertheless relevant for the success of the Danish model.[9]

As already mentioned, the discussion about flexicurity is of significant relevance for many European countries now, especially due to the high interest of EU institutions in this type of model, though there is not throughout the EU an acceptance of this approach, and also the existence of critical attitudes towards this new conceptualisation of the labour market. Both positions can be related to the two constituting components of flexicurity, the way flexibility and security – and especially their interaction – are evaluated through employers and employees, including social justice. These questions are also related to the discussion on job vs. employment security, see, for example, Keune and Jepsen (2007). There is moreover the problem that flexicurity is regarded as being misused as means of labour market deregulation, with only little security compensations, see, for example, Tangian (2007, p.554f). As the development in Denmark has already shown, the flexicurity system is less supportive for women (and migrants), so that its improvement regarding women is an important topic in its discussion, see, for example, Fredman (2004). Funk (2008) shows that European countries did react quite differently regarding flexicurity issues due to the peculiar conditions that exist in these countries, so that a European flexicurity model needs further reflection when applied within the member states.

There are also proposals for an improved flexicurity model like, for example, 'flexinsurance' – a contribution of the employers to social security proportional to the flexibility of a contract – combined with basic minimum income, see Tangian (2007, p.567ff.). Another option for renegotiating European flexicurity is opening the discussion for issues which do not deal solely with economic aspects, as, for example, 'Lifelong Learning' which describes a tendency to a more general type of social flexibility and security, see Vielle and Bonvin (2008). Flexicurity therefore remains an actual and highly relevant topic in the socio-economic debate in Europe.

Klammer (2004) discusses another aspect which is of importance for the development of flexicurity in Europe: The life - course perspective of the households of the economy where observed changing work biographies are a main reason to widen the flexicurity model. Such changes can be found with regard to work duration, work interruptions of women, part-time work, atypical work and unemployed workers. One of the questions here is how to deal with continuity as well as discontinuities during their working life which can be desired or involuntary in nature. It is also of importance to deal with the influence of job insecurity on a person's private life like family life. Lifelong learning is also a topic concerning life - course perspectives, especially with regard to access to the learning offers which are often not available for low qualified or older workers. Necessary or requested variations in working time due to different life situations like child raising or care for the elderly within families are further issues in the need to combine work and private demands.

As Klammer (2004, p.291f.) shows some models have been developed in Germany which tend in this direction like parental leave for child-raising. Work-time accounts can also be mentioned in this context. A general question here, however, is the role of the employees in such economic decision making processes and the need for financial support. Family-friendly working conditions remain therefore a topic for the modelling of a flexicurity economy. A further issue is re-entry into the labour market – representing a topic where solutions in the Danish flexicurity model have been found. The end of the working life at a provided age is a further economic question with relevance for the life - course perspectives of workers. In general, social demands embedded in a flexicurity system are deepened from such life-course perspectives. We will further deal with such life - course gestation issues in a broader context of 'social capitalism', see Chapter 9, where we will include issues of health care, care for the elderly and education in particular.

The Danish flexicurity discussion may provide a central example along the way to new labour market institutions, see for example the newsletter: *Future Watch, October 2006: Flexicurity – Denmark-Style* of the Center for Strategic and International Studies (CSIS). However, the discussion led so far lacks rigour and formal model building based on flexicurity principles and implied macroeconomic structures in order to investigate the implications of the institutions of a flexicurity structure when imposed on the process of capital accumulation.

To build a model, based on a reproduction scheme of a flexicurity economy, we need a presentation of its System of National Accounts and the behaviour of economic agents within such a structure. Moreover, the adjustment processes on the market for labour and for goods as well as the functioning of financial markets in such an economy needs detailed investigation. Analysis of this type is, however, at best in a state of infancy. The present chapter therefore intends to contribute to such an analysis and does so against the background of the models of capitalism we have developed in this book so far, in particular concerning Marx's general law of capitalist accumulation we considered in Chapter 1 and 2 for a single labour market and a system of segmented labour markets, respectively. In modelling a possible European future in this way, we hope to show that there is a type of capitalist economy which not only pays respect to the Human Rights, in particular their article 23,[10] but that is also compatible with the evolution of democracy and citizenship in the longer run.

By contrast, a neoliberal laissez-faire capitalist society that ruins family structures to a considerable degree (through alienated work, degrading unemployment and education- and value-decomposing visual media) cannot be made compatible with a democratic society in the long-run, since it produces disruptions ranging from social segmentation to class conflicts, racial clashes and more. Compared to this, we will argue in this chapter that stable balanced reproduction is possible under a socially-oriented regime of flexicurity capitalism which in addition is supported by reflected educational principles concerning skill formation, equal opportunity and citizenship education as essential pillars of a democratic society.

3.4 Labour Market Institutions under Flexicurity

The abstract vision of a new social reproduction scheme for capitalism as it is formulated in this chapter can be compared with work of Quesnay, Marx, Schumpeter and Keynes in this respect. It may be considered as radical and fundamental (but also as infeasible) as Quesnay's design of the Tableau Economique for the French economy in the 18th century, an ideal system where the productive sector was at the centre of interest and all taxes were paid out of rent (by the landlords). It may be compared with Marx's reproduction schemes, in *Capital* Volume II, for a capitalist economy of his times (schemes which were not considered feasible under capitalism by him). It may also be compared to Schumpeter's visions in his work on *Capitalism, Socialism and Democracy*, where he claimed that socialism would be the consequence of Western type capitalism (as it has been created by the Rockefellers and other industrial dynasties) and not as the result of the Eastern socialism that existed at his times. It may finally also be compared with the Social Philosophy of Keynes's General Theory and his discussion of the institutional means by which the trade cycle of conventional Western capitalism might be tamed. All these aspects may play a role in the understanding and the appraisal of the model of flexicurity capitalism that is now designed in this chapter.

In this section we consider first some basic features of a baseline macro-model of a flexicurity economy. Thereafter, the budget equations and their implications for economic behaviour are presented. We then investigate the stability of balanced growth paths of such an economy and also its sustainability concerning the generation of sufficient income and pension payments.

Fluctuating growth may be inevitable in any form of free market capitalism, but we believe it need not be accompanied by mass unemployment and the social degradation of part of the workforce through long-term unemployment, atypical employment or other forms of alienated work which in the longer run undermine family structures and social cohesion. We develop against this background a basic macrodynamic framework where this process of cyclical growth is overcome by an employer of 'first' (not last) resort which provides employment security but not job security, added to an economic reproduction process that is highly competitive (flexible). Such a flexicurity system is characterised by high labour and capital mobility, where fluctuations of employment in the private and the public sector are made socially acceptable through a third labour market where all remaining workers can find meaningful occupation and sufficient income. We show that such an economic reproduction process can be stable as well as sustainable.

In the model we only consider skilled work (based on an effective schooling system as for example in Finland). Note again that this does not mean that there is no unskilled work to do, but that part of the worktime of skilled workers must be devoted to unskilled activities. Workers can work in the private sector, in the public sector and, if dismissed from them, in the Employer of First Resort sector of the economy.

Basic Principles and Problems of a Flexicurity System

The flexicurity concept, primarily discussed with respect to the Nordic economies, intends to combine two labour market components which many economists would regard as difficult or impossible to reconcile, namely workplace flexibility in a very competitive environment, and income and employment (not job) security for workers. The problem is to find the appropriate mix between these two aspects of labour market institutions, in order to remedy the negative effects of flexibility without much security (free hiring and firing capitalism) and security without much flexibility (Soviet era socialism). The following aspects, questions and problems of the search for such a combination of flexibility with security need to be considered:[11]

1. How much flexibility do we wish to have in:
   - hiring, firing and employment discontinuities?
   - wage and price setting?
   - technical change and lifelong learning?
   - coping with the forces of globalisation and financialization?
   - work differentiation?
2. How much security do we think desirable in:
   - base income payments?
   - employment protection?
   - location of jobs (workplace mobility)?
   - skill preservation and the gestation of atypical employment?
   - Access to, and equal opportunity in, education at primary and secondary schools?

Moreover, in order to achieve social acceptance for such a combination of the needs of capital and the needs of labour, the following problems must also find a solution:

3. Basic aspects of social cohesion in a modern democratic market economy:
   - consent-based cooperation between capital and skilled labour
   - acceptance of job differentiation and status differences
   - proper citizenship education and democratic evolution
   - the accepted establishment of equal opportunity as well as differentiated labour profiles and processes of elite formation
   - reflected and controlled institutional evolution.

In this chapter we put forth a theoretical model which reconciles the flexibility issues relating to hiring, dismissal and wage and price setting with the security concerns relating to employment protection and basic income. The other aspects of the enumerated points will not be considered however. Moreover we shall simply assume here that the societal issues in the last block are developed to such an extent that the proposed model is not only transparent to the citizens of the society, but has indeed led to basic agreement on how the economy is to be organised and the society to be developed further.

Against this background we now design a theoretical alternative approach to the many current forms of capitalist economies with their income distribution driven cyclical processes of over-accumulation (in their prosperity phase) and mass unemployment (in the stagnant phase), as we have observed them after World War II, see Figures 1.3 and 4.1 and as formalised by Goodwin in 1967. We describe a capitalist economy with a private and a public sector that exhibits in addition a third labour market – in place of a reserve army of unemployed – which through its institutional setup guarantees full employment in its interaction with the private labour market, that is, the industrial sector, which is modelled here as highly flexible and competitive and a public labour market, where – to a certain degree more regulated – jobs are offered by the government.

Sectoral Accounts, Consumption and Investment under Flexicurity

In the basic accounting framework that follows, we are considering – for reasons of simplicity – an economy that exhibits a population and workforce which are growing with the natural rate n. We have three labour markets (private, public, EFR), where the second and third are considered in aggregate forms in general. The labour market in the private sector is not segmented from the other ones, since the latter – in particular the EFR market – represent basically a buffer stock for the first one. Workers are protected against discrimination concerning sex or race, but may be subject to discrimination with respect to age, due to the more intensive form of labour effort in the private sector. In view of what happens in actual economies it may well be that work in the private sector of the economy is primarily done by the younger members of the workforce, since work intensity is higher within firms, the workday is not normalised, and – in reality – the pace of technical change is higher in this sector than in the public one.

We reconsider first the sector of firms in such an economy which at first are accumulating physical capital solely on the basis of the profits they can realise:

Table 3.1 Firms: production and income account

Uses	Resources
δK	δK
$\omega_1 L_1^d,\ L_1^d = Y^p/z$	$C_1 + C_2 + C_r$
G	
$\Pi \quad (= Y^f)$	$I \quad (= Y^f)$
$\delta_1 R + \dot{R}$	S_1
Y^p	Y^p

This account is a very simple one. Firms use their capital stock (at full capacity utilisation) to employ the amount of labour (in hours): L_1^d, at the real wage ω_1, the law of motion which is to be determined in the next section from a model of the wage–price dynamics in the manufacturing sector. Workers L_1^w in the private sector of the economy do over- or under-time work, depending on the state of economic activity. The rate $u_w = L_1^d/L_1^w$ is the utilisation rate of the workforce in the first labour market, the industrial workers of the economy (all other employment comes from the working of households occupied in the public sector or through the EFR).

Firms produce full capacity output Y^p which is always fully sold, since goods demand is given by $C_1 + C_2 + C_r + I + \delta K + G + S_1 - \delta_1 R$, from the two types of consumers (and the retired households), the investing firms, the government and the net savings of households of type 1, since this savings is done in real terms. The demand side of the model is here such that the full capacity output can indeed be sold. Deducting from this output Y^p of firms their real wage payments to their workers (and depreciation) we get the profits of firms which are here assumed to be fully invested into capital stock growth $\dot{K} = I = \Pi$. We thus have Classical (direct) investment habits in this basic approach to a modelling of an employer of first resort. We assume a fixed proportions technology with $y^p = Y^p/K$ the potential output–capital ratio and with $z = Y^p/L_1^d$ the state of labour productivity (which determines the employment L_1^d of the workforce L_1^w of firms).

We next consider the households sector of our model which is composed of worker households working in the first labour market and the remaining ones that are all working in the second and the third labour market, given by L_2^w (the public sector and the EFR sector).

Table 3.2 Households 1 and 2 (primary and secondary labour market): income account

Worker Households 1:

Uses	Resources
$C_1 = c_1(1-\tau_1)\omega_1 L_1^d$	
$T = \tau_1\omega_1 L_1^d$	
$\omega_2(L - (L_1^d + L_g^d))$	
$\omega_2 L^r, L^r = \alpha_r L$	
S_1	$\omega_1 L_1^d$
$Y_1 = \omega_1 L_1^d$	$Y_1 = \omega_1 L_1^d$

Worker Households 2:

Uses	Resources
C_2	$\omega_2 L_2, L_2 = L - L_1^d, \quad \omega_2 = \alpha_\omega \omega_1$
Y_2	Y_2

Households of type 1 consume manufacturing goods of amount C_1. They pay all income taxes T and they pay in addition – via further tax transfers – all workers' income in the public sector and the 'third', the EFR labour market. Moreover, they pay the pensions of the retired households ($\omega_2 L^r$) and accumulate their remaining income S_1 in the form of a company pension into a fund R that is administrated by firms (with inflow S_1 and outflow $\delta_1 R$).

The transfer $\omega_2(L - (L_1^w + L_2^w))[= \omega_2 L_3^w]$ can be considered as 'solidarity' payments, since workers from the first labour market that lose their job will automatically be employed in the third labour market through which full employment is guaranteed by the government (as Employer of First Resort). We consider this employment as skill preserving, since it can be viewed as ordinary office or handicraft work (subject only to learning by doing when such workers return to the first labour market, that is, into employment in the production processes of private firms).

The second sector of households is here modelled in the simplest way that is available: Households regularly employed in the second and third labour market, that is, $L_2^w + L_3^w$ pay no taxes[12] and totally consume their income. We have thus Classical saving habits in this household sector, while households of type 1 may have positive or negative savings S_1 as residual from their income and expenditures. We here assume that they can accumulate these savings (or dissave in case of a negative S_1) from the stock of commodities they have accumulated as pension fund inventories in the past. The law of motion of pension funds is given by:

$$\dot{R} = S_1 - \delta_1 R$$

where δ_1 is the rate by which these funds are depreciated through company pension payments to the 'officially retired' workers L^r, assumed to be in constant proportion to the 'active' workforce $L^r = \alpha_r L$. These worker households are considered as not really inactive, but they can offer work according to their still existing capabilities as an addition to the supply of work organised by the government $L - L_1^w$, that is, the working potential of the officially retired persons remains an active and valuable addition to the work-hours that are supplied by the official workforce of the society. It is obvious that the proper allocation of the work hours in the public sector needs thorough reflection from the microeconomic and the social point of view, which however cannot be a topic in a chapter on the macroeconomics of such an economy.

As the income account of the retired households, given below, shows they receive pension payments equivalent to the income in the second labour market and they get in addition individual transfer income (company pensions) from the accumulated funds R in proportion to the time they have been active in the first labour market and as an aggregate household group of the total amount $\delta_1 R$ by which the pension funds R are reduced in each period.

Table 3.3 Retired households: income account

Uses	Resources
C_r	$\omega_2 L_r + \delta_p P_1/p, L_r = \alpha_r L$
Y_r	Y_r

There is finally the government sector which is also formulated in a very basic way. The government receives income taxes, the solidarity transfers (the substitute for unemployment benefits) for the third labour market, paid by workers in the first labour market, and old-age base pension payments. It uses its taxes proper to finance government goods demand G and the surplus of taxes over these government expenditures to actively employ the public servants in the government sector. In addition it employs the workers receiving EFR type 'unemployment benefits' from the households in first labour market, and it in fact also employs the 'retired' persons to the extent they are still willing to contribute to various social employment activities.

Table 3.4 The government: fiscal authority – employer of first resort

Uses	Resources
$G = \alpha_g T$	$T = \tau_h \omega_1 L_1^d$
$\omega_2 L_2^w = (1 - \alpha_g)T$	
$\omega_2(L - (L_1^w + L_2^w))$	$\omega_2 L_3^w$
$\omega_2 L^r$	$\omega_2 \alpha_r L$
Y^g	Y^g

In sum we get that workers are employed either in the first labour market and if not there then from their services in the government sector concerning public administration, infrastructure services, educational services or other public obligations and EFR type work (in addition there is potential labour supply $\alpha_r L$ from the retired households, who due to the long-life expectancy in modern societies can remain effective suppliers of specific work over a considerable span of time). In this way the whole workforce is always fully employed in this model of social growth (and the retired persons according to their willingness and capabilities) and thus does not suffer from human degradation in particular. Of course, there are a variety of issues concerning state organised work that point to problems in the organisation of such work, but all such problems exist also in actual industrialised market economies in one way or another.[13]

3.5 Flexicurity Growth: Full Capacity Adjustments towards Balanced Reproduction

The laws of motion which characterise our flexicurity economy concern the real wage in the private sector (of which the real wage in the public sector is a constant fraction), the employment policy of the firms in view of the labour force L_1^w they currently employ in the industrial sector and (as a secondary issue) the growth law of labour supply L. For the real wage dynamics, now restricted to the private sector of the economy, we use again the dynamic equation of the preceding chapters:

$$\hat{\omega}_1 = f(u^w - \bar{u}^w) + \alpha(\omega_{1o} - \omega_1), \quad f(0) = 0.$$

In this equation we denote by $u^w = \frac{Y^p/z}{L_1^w} = \frac{y^p/z}{l_1^w}$ the rate of utilisation of the labour force of the private sector, since there holds $L_1^d = Y^p/z$. We use the convention that lower case letters denote the extensive variable divided by the capital stock as its analogue on the intensive level. Real wages are adjusted more flexibly if the slope of the function f is increased.

The hiring and firing policy of firms is described by:

$$\hat{L}_1^w = \beta_{eu}(u^w - \bar{u}^w) + n,$$

which states that firms adjust their labour force around the natural rate of growth such that excess over- or under-utilisation rates of the workforce is counteracted, that is, they hire in the boom and fire in the recession, both measured relative to a normal rate of utilisation of their labour force and relative to the trend growth of the economy. Hiring and firing becomes more flexible when the parameter β_{eu} is increased.

We assume that the parameter ω_{1o} in the wage Phillips curve is determined such that there holds for the rate of profit at this level of the real wage:

$$r_o = r = \frac{Y^p - \omega_1 L_1^d - \delta K}{K} = y^p[1 - \frac{\omega_1}{z}] - \delta = n,$$

that is this real wage level allows the capital stock to grow in line with the natural rate of growth of the economy, since net investment equals profits by assumption. This is a necessary side condition to allow for a balanced growth path in this economy. Moreover, since the amount of total labour supply L is of no relevance for the private sector of the economy we get from this condition that the ratio $l = L/K$ will converge to a stationary value if the real wage converges to its normal level ω_{1o}.

Inserting the characteristics of this growth model into the two laws of motion which each make up its dynamics gives rise to the following 2D dynamics in the state variables $\omega_1, l_1^w = L_1^w/K$:

$$\hat{\omega}_1 = f(\frac{y^p}{zl_1^w} - \bar{u}^w) + \alpha(\omega_{1o} - \omega_1) \quad (3.1)$$

$$\hat{l}_1^w = \beta_{eu}(\frac{y^p}{zl_1^w} - \bar{u}^w) + n - r, \quad r = y^p[1 - \omega_1/z] - \delta \quad (3.2)$$

Based on this assumption we get for the interior steady state or balanced growth path of the social growth economy the equations ($\bar{u}_w = 1$ in the following for reasons of simplicity):

$$l_1^{wo} = y^p/z = l_1^{do} \quad (3.3)$$

$$\omega_1^o = \text{determined exogenously} < z \quad (3.4)$$

We have zero root hysteresis in the 3D system (when $\hat{l}$ is added to it), which allows us to treat and solve the first two equations independently of the third one which when appended can converge to any value of l, depending on shocks to labour supply, capital formation and the like. Note that this only applies if there is social consensus with respect to the steady state real wage ω_1^o as the benchmark for real wage negotiations in the first labour market.

Monotonic Convergence towards Balanced Growth

For the Jacobian of the core 2D dynamics evaluated at the steady state we get from the laws of motion:

$$J^o = \begin{pmatrix} -\alpha & -f'(0)/l_{1o}^w \\ y^p/z & -\beta_{eu}/l_{1o}^w \end{pmatrix} = \begin{pmatrix} - & - \\ + & - \end{pmatrix}$$

From the sign structure in this matrix it is obvious that we always have locally asymptotically stable dynamics (that is, trace $J^o < 0$, det $J^o >$ 0). Furthermore, the condition trace $J^o = 4 \det J^o$, i.e.,

$$(J^o_{11} + J^o_{22})^2 = 4(J^o_{11}J^o_{22} + J^o_{21}J^o_{12})$$

separates monotonic convergence (for parameters β_{eu} sufficiently large) from cyclical convergence (parameters β_{eu} sufficiently small). Reformulated, this condition reads:

$$|J^o_{22}| = |J^o_{11}| + 2\sqrt{|J^o_{21}J^o_{12}|}, \quad i.e., \quad \beta^H_{eu} = l^w_{1o}[|J^o_{11}| + 2\sqrt{|J^o_{21}J^o_{12}|}]$$

We thus get for the bifurcation value β^H_{eu} that separates monotonic from cyclical convergence:

$$\beta^H_{eu} = \alpha + 2\sqrt{f'(0)} \tag{3.5}$$

This critical parameter for the hiring and firing speed parameter in our growing economy is therefore in particular the larger, the larger there is the reaction of money wage inflation with respect to workforce utilisation. We thus get that economic fluctuations can be avoided in this type of economy if wages in the first labour market respond relatively sluggishly to demand pressure in this market (as measured by the utilisation rate of the insiders) and if hiring and firing is a sufficiently flexible process as envisaged by the concept of flexicurity capitalism. In a corporatist regime between capital and labour it can be expected that the slope of the function f at the steady state is relatively low so that relatively modest speeds of hiring and firing are already sufficient to make the economy converge to its balanced growth path without any cyclical adjustment patterns.

Global Stability

For an investigation of the global asymptotic stability of balanced growth we will now analyse the core dynamical system by means of so-called Liapunov functions. For this purpose we represent the 2D dynamics of the preceding subsection as follows.

$$\hat{\omega}_1 = G^1(\omega_1) + G^2(l^w_1), \quad G^{1'} < 0, G^{2'} < 0 \tag{3.6}$$

$$\hat{l}^w_1 = H^1(\omega_1) + H^2(l^w_1), \quad H^{1'} > 0, H^{2'} < 0 \tag{3.7}$$

The Liapunov function to be used in the stability proof then reads as follows:

$$V(\omega_1, l^w_1) = \int_{\omega^o_1}^{\omega_1} H^1(\tilde{\omega}_1)/\tilde{\omega}_1 d\tilde{\omega}_1 + \int_{l^{wo}_1}^{l^w_1} -G^2(\tilde{l}^w_1)/\tilde{l}^w_1 d\tilde{l}^w_1$$

This function describes by its graph a 3D sink with the steady state of the economy as its lowest point, since the above integrates two functions that are negative to the left of the steady state values and positive to their right. For the first derivative of the Liapunov function along the trajectories of the considered dynamical system we moreover get:

$$\begin{aligned}
\dot{V} &= dV(\omega_1(t), l_1^w(t))/dt = \left(H^1(\omega_1)/\omega_1\right)\dot{\omega}_1 - \left(G^2(l_1^w)/l_1^w\right)\dot{l}_1^w \\
&= H^1(\omega_1)\hat{\omega}_1 - G^2(l_1^w)\hat{l}_1^w \\
&= H^1(\omega_1)(G^1(\omega_1) + G^2(l_1^w)) - G^2(l_1^w)(H^1(\omega_1) + H^2(l_1^w)) \\
&= H^1(\omega_1)G^1(\omega_1) - G^2(l_1^w)H^2(l_1^w) \\
&= -H^1(\omega_1)(-G^1(\omega_1)) - (-G^2(l_1^w))(-H^2(l_1^w)) \\
&\leq 0 \qquad [= 0 \quad \text{if and only if} \quad \omega_1 = \omega_1^o, l_1^w = l_1^{wo}]
\end{aligned}$$

since the multiplied functions have the same sign to the right and to the left of their steady state values and thus lead to positive products with a minus sign in front of them (up to the situation where the economy is already sitting in the steady state). We thus have proved that there holds:

Proposition 1: *The interior steady state of the dynamics (with $r = y^p[1 - \omega_1/z] - \delta$):*

$$\hat{\omega}_1 = f\left(\frac{y^p}{zl_1^w} - \tilde{u}^w\right) + \alpha(\omega_{1o} - \omega_1), \quad \hat{l}_1^w = \beta_{eu}\left(\frac{y^p}{zl_1^w} - \tilde{u}^w\right) + n - r$$

is a global sink of the function V, defined on the positive orthant of the phase space, and is attracting in this domain, since the function V is strictly decreasing along the trajectories of the dynamics in the positive orthant of the phase space.

From the global perspective there may, however, occur supply bottlenecks in the first labour market. Here we assume that the economy is always working in a corridor around the steady state where the government as an employer of first resort still has a sufficient amount of workforce working in this range of activities organised by it. Due to the stability results obtained in the present and the preceding section this is not a very restrictive assumption under the normal working of the economy.

3.6 Company Pension Funds and Sustainability Levels

There is a further law of motion in the background of the model that needs to be considered in order to provide a statement on the full viability of the considered model of flexicurity capitalism. This law of motion describes the evolution of the pension fund per unit of the capital stock $\rho = \frac{R}{K}$ and is obtained from the defining equation $\dot{R} = S_1 - \delta_1 R$ as follows:

$$\begin{aligned}\hat{\rho} &= \hat{R} - \hat{K} = \frac{\dot{R}}{K}\frac{K}{R} - r = \frac{S_1 - \delta_1 R}{K}/\rho - r, \quad i.e.: \\ \dot{\rho} &= \frac{S_1}{K} - (\delta_1 + r)\rho = s_1 - (\delta_1 + r)\rho\end{aligned}$$

with savings of households of type 1 and profits of firms per unit of capital being given by:

$$s_1 = (1 - c_{h1}(1-\tau_h) - \tau_h)\omega_1 \frac{y^p}{z} - \alpha_\omega \omega_1 (l_3^w + l^r)$$

with $\quad l_3^w = l - (l_1^w + l_2^w), l^r = \alpha_r l$, i.e.,

$$s_1 = (1 - c_{h1}(1-\tau_h) - \alpha_g \tau_h)\omega_1 \frac{y^p}{z} - ((1+\alpha_r)l - l_1^w)\alpha_\omega \omega_1$$

For reasons of analytical simplicity we now assume that the government pursues an immigration policy that ensures for the total growth rate of the labour force the condition $n = \hat{K}$, that is, the total labour supply grows by this migration policy with the same rate as the capital stock. This keeps the ratio $l = L/K$ constant, a simplifying assumption that must be accompanied by the assumption that the actual l must be chosen in a certain neighbourhood of a base value l_o that is to be determined later on. Moreover, we assume for simplicity $\delta_1 = \delta$ for the depreciation rates of the capital stock and the stock of pension funds.

This gives for the law of motion of the pension fund to capital ratio the differential equation:

$$\begin{aligned}\dot{\rho} &= (1 - c_{h1}(1-\tau_h) - \alpha_g \tau_h)\omega_1 \frac{y^p}{z} - ((1+\alpha_r)l - l_1^w)\alpha_\omega \omega_1 - \\ &\quad y^p(1 - \frac{\omega_1}{z})\rho\end{aligned}$$

We thus get that the trajectory of the pension fund ratio ρ is driven by the autonomous evolution of the state variables ω_1, l_1^w that characterise the dynamics of the private sector of the economy and that have been shown to be convergent to the steady state values $\omega_{1o}, l_1^{wo} = \frac{y^p}{z}$. Assuming that these variables have reached their steady state positions then gives

$$\dot{\rho} = (1 - c_{h1}(1 - \tau_h) - \alpha_g \tau_h)\omega_{1o}\frac{y^p}{z} - ((1 + \alpha_r)l - l_1^{wo})\alpha_\omega\omega_{1o} - (\delta + r_o)\rho$$

which gives a single linear differential equation for the ratio ρ. This dynamic is globally asymptotically stable around its steady state position ($l_1^{wo} = \frac{y^p}{z}$):

$$\rho_o = \frac{(1 - c_{h1}(1 - \tau_h) - \alpha_g \tau_h)\omega_{1o}\frac{y^p}{z} - ((1 + \alpha_r)l - \frac{y^p}{z})\alpha_\omega\omega_{1o}}{\delta + r_o}$$

In this simple case we thus have monotonic adjustment of the pension-fund to capital ratio to its steady state position, while in general we have a non-autonomous adjustment of this ratio that is driven by the real wage and the employment dynamics in the first labour market. The steady state level of ρ is positive if there holds for the full employment labour intensity ratio:

$$l < \frac{(1 - c_{h1}(1 - \tau_h) - \alpha_g \tau_h)\frac{y^p}{z} + \frac{y^p}{z}\alpha_\omega}{(\delta + r_o)(1 + \alpha_r)\alpha_\omega}$$

We now assume moreover that the additional company pension payments to pensioners should add the percentage $100 \cdot \alpha_c$ to their base pension $\omega_2\alpha_r l$ per unit of capital. We thus have as further restriction on the steady state position of the economy, if there is a specific α_c target given:

$$\delta\rho_o = \alpha_c\omega_2^o\alpha_r l, \quad \omega_2^o = \alpha_\omega\omega_{1o}$$

Inserting the value for ρ_o then gives

$$\alpha_c = \delta\frac{(1 - c_{h1}(1 - \tau_h) - \alpha_g \tau_h)\frac{y^p}{z} - ((1 + \alpha_r)l - \frac{y^p}{z})\alpha_\omega}{(\delta + r_o)\alpha_\omega\alpha_r l}$$

We thus get that a target value for α_c demands a certain labour intensity ratio l and vice versa. For a given total labour intensity ratio there is a given percentage by which company pensions compare to base pension payments. This percentage is the larger the smaller the ratio l_1^{wo}/l due to the following reformulation of the α_c formula:

$$\alpha_c = \delta\frac{[1 - c_{h1}(1 - \tau_h) - \alpha_g \tau_h + \alpha_\omega]l_1^{wo}/l - (1 + \alpha_r)\alpha_\omega}{(\delta + r_o)\alpha_r\alpha_\omega} \qquad (3.8)$$

If this value of the total employment labour intensity ratio prevails in the considered economy (where it is of course as usually assumed that

$c_{h1}(1 - \tau_h) + \alpha_g \tau_h < 1$ holds) we have that core pension payments to pensioners are augmented by company pension payments by a percentage that is given by the parameter α_c and that these extra pension payments are distributed to pensioners in proportion to the time that they have worked in the private sector of the economy. There is thus a negative trade-off between the ratios l, α_c, as expressed by the eq. (3.8). This also shows that the total working population must have a certain ratio to the capital stock in order to allow for a given percentage of extra company pension payments.

Households of type 1 are by and large financing the second and the third labour market through taxes and EFR type 'unemployment benefits', besides their contribution to the base income of the retired people. Since firms have a positive rate of profit in the steady state, since the government budget is always balanced and since only households of type 1 save in this economy, we have thus now established the conditions under which such an economy accumulates to a sufficient degree not only capital, but also pension funds, under appropriate restrictions on labour supply.

3.7 Pension Funds and Credit-financed Investment

In this section we will investigate the implications of the situation where pension funds are used for real capital formation instead of remaining idle except for being used for company pension payments (of amount δR) at each point in time. The productive use of part of the pension fund R is here assumed to be rewarded at a given interest rate i applied to the debt level D accumulated by the firms in the private sector of the economy.

Accounting Relationships

The pension funds of workers are now considered as quasi commercial banks which give credit to firms out of their (real) funds and thus allow firms to invest in good times much beyond their retained earnings, which are profits net of interest payments on loans. The account of the sector of firms is thereby modified as follows:

Table 3.5 Firms: production and income account

Uses	Resources
δK	δK
$\omega_1 L_1^d = \omega_1 Y^p / z$	$C_1 + C_2 + C_r$
	G
iD	
Π	$I = (i_r(r - r_o) - i_d(d - d_o) + \bar{a})K$
$\delta R + \dot{R}$	S_1

The behaviour and financing of gross investment is shown in the next account.

Table 3.6 Firms: investment and credit

Uses	Resources
δK	δK
$I = (i_r(r - r_o) - i_d(d - d_o) + \bar{a})K$	Π
	$\dot{D} = I - \Pi$
I^g	I^g

We assume as investment behaviour of firms the functional relationship:

$$I/K = i_r(r - r_o) - i_d(d - d_o) + \bar{a}.$$

This investment schedule states that investment plans depend positively on the deviation of the profit rate from its steady state level and negatively on the deviation of the debt to capital ratio from its steady state value. The exogenous trend term in investment is $\bar{a}$ and it is assumed that it represents the influence of investing firms' 'animal spirits' on their investment activities.

Table 3.7 Firms' net worth

Assets	Liabilities
K	D
	Real Net Worth
K	K

In the management of pension funds we assume that a portion sR of them is held as minimum reserves and that a larger portion of them has been given as credit D to firms. The remaining amount are idle reserves D^s, not yet allocated to any interest bearing activity.

Table 3.8 Pension funds and credit (stocks)

Assets	Liabilities
R	sR
	D
	X excess reserves
R	R

Pension funds receive the savings of households of type 1 (the other households do not save) and they receive the interest payments of firms. They allocate this into required reserve increases, payments to pensioners, new credit demand of firms and the rest as an addition or substraction to their idle reserves.

Table 3.9 Pension funds and credit (flows)

Resources	Uses
S_1	$s\dot{R}$
rD	$\delta R + rD$
	$\dot{D} = I - \Pi$
	$\dot{X}$
$S_1 + rD$	$S_1 + rD$

The above representation of the flows of funds in the pension funds system implies for the time derivative of accumulated funds R the relationship

$$\dot{R} = S_1 - \delta R - (I - \Pi) = S_1 + \Pi - \delta R - I, \quad i.e.,$$

it is given by the excess of savings of households of type 1 over current company pension funds payments to retired households (now given by $\delta R + iD$) and the new credit that is given to firms to finance the excess of investment over retained profits.

Households in the first labour market consume with a constant marginal propensity out of their income after primary taxes. They pay the wages

Table 3.10 Households 1 (primary and secondary labour market): income account

Uses	Resources
$C_1 = c_{h1}(1 - \tau_h)Y_1^w$	
$T = \tau_h Y_1^w$	
$\omega_2(L - (L_1^w + L_2^w)) = \omega_2 L_3^w$	
$\omega_2 L^r$	
S_1	$\omega_1 L_1^d$
Y_1^w	Y_1^w

of the workers in the third (EFR-)labour market and they pay the common base rent of all pensioners (as intergenerational contribution). The remainder represents their contribution to the company pension scheme of the economy, from which they will receive the amount $\delta R + rD$ when retired (which of course is to be calculated then, while current pensioners receive the amount shown above at the current point in time).

Table 3.11 Households 2 (primary and secondary labour market): income account

Uses	Resources
C_2	$\omega_2(L_2^w + Lw_3)$
$Y_{2,3}^w$	$Y_{2,3}^w$

Table 3.12 Retired households: income account

Uses	Resources
C_r	$\omega_2 L^r + \delta R + iD$
Y^r	Y^r

Government gets taxes from households of type 1 and spends them on goods as well as services in the government sector. It administrates the common base rent payments as well as the payments of those not yet employed in the private and public sector of the economy. Its workforce consists of all workers that are not employed by firms as households of type 1 and also of all pensioners that are still capable and willing

Table 3.13 The government: income account – fiscal authority (employer of first resort)

Uses	Resources
$G = \alpha_g \tau_h Y_1^w$	$T = \tau_h Y_1^w$
$\omega_2 L_2^w = (1-\alpha_g)\tau_h Y_1^w$	
$\omega_2 L_3^w$	$\omega_2(L - (L_1^w + L_2^w))$
$\omega_2 L^r$	$\omega_2 L^r$
Y^g	Y^g

to work. The model therefore assumes not only that there is a work guarantee for all, but also a work obligation for all members in the workforce, with the addition of those that are retired but still available for work.

Investment and Credit Dynamics in Flexicurity Growth

As assumed above, we use the assumption that the government pursues an immigration policy that ensures for the growth rate of the labour force the condition $n = \hat{K}$, that is, the total labour supply grows by this migration policy with the same rate as the capital stock. This again keeps the ratio $l = L/K$ constant. Since we are therefore no longer able to determine the steady state value of the real wage ω_1 from the law of motion for l, we have to supply it again from the outside: as ω_1^o. This, however, no longer also provides us with the steady state value of the rate of profit, since profits are now to be determined net of interest payments: $r = y^p[1 - \frac{\omega_1}{z}] - \delta - id$, where $d = D/K$ denotes the indebtedness of firms per unit of capital. We assume as trend term in Okun's law the growth rate of the capital stock, that is, this part of the new hiring is just determined by the installation of new machines or whole plants (under the assumption of fixed proportions in production). The normal level of the rate of employment (utilisation rate) of the workforce employed by firms is again set equal to '1' for simplicity.

On the basis of these assumptions we get from what was formulated in the preceding subsection (where investment was assumed to be given now by $I/K = i_r(r - r_o) - i_d(d - d_o) + \bar{a} = n$):

$$\begin{aligned}
\hat{l}_1^w &= \beta_{eu}(\frac{y^p}{zl_1^w} - 1) \\
\hat{\omega}_1 &= f(\frac{y^p}{zl_1^w} - \bar{u}^w) + \alpha(\omega_{1o} - \omega_1) \\
\dot{d} &= [i_r(r - r_o) - i_d(d - d_o) + \bar{a}](1 - d) - r
\end{aligned}$$

The introduction of debt financing of firms thus makes the model more advanced in its economic structure, but not so much from the mathematical point of view, due to the recursive structure that characterises the dynamical system at this level of generality. We note that there is not yet an interest rate policy rule involved in these dynamics, but the assumption of an interest rate peg: $i = const.$ Note also that the law of motion for company pension funds is changed by the assumed change in pension funds behaviour. It does, however, not feed back into the above dynamics and is therefore not reconsidered here. Its qualitative features are, however, not changed under this new institutional setup.

We make use of the following abbreviation $r_{max} = y^p[1 - \omega_{1o}/z] - \delta$. We then have the following proposition:

Proposition 2: *The interior steady state of the considered dynamics is given by:*

$$l_1^{wo} = \frac{y^p}{z}, \ \omega_1^o,$$

where d_o, r_o have to be determined by solving the two equations

$$r_o = r_{max} - id_o, \quad r_o = \bar{a}(1 - d_o)$$

which gives for the steady state values of d, r the expressions:

$$d_o = \frac{\bar{a} - r_{max}}{\bar{a} - i}, \quad r_o = \bar{a}\frac{r_{max} - i}{\bar{a} - i}.$$

We assume that both the numerator and the denominator of the fraction that defines d_o are positive, that is, the trend term in investment is sufficiently strong (larger than the rate of profit before interest rate payments r_{max} and larger than the rate of interest i). Moreover, it is also assumed that $r_{max} > i$ holds so that all fractions shown above are in fact positive. In the case where $\bar{a} = r_{max} = y^p[1 - \omega_{1o}/z] - \delta$ holds we have $d_o = 0$ and $r_o = \bar{a}$ in which case the value of ρ_o is the same as in the sections on investment without debt financing. Nevertheless the dynamics around the steady state remain debt financed and are therefore different from the one of the preceding section. We thus can have a 'balanced budget' of firms in the steady state while investment remains driven by $I/K = i_r(r-r_o)-i_d(d-d_o)+\bar{a}$ outside the steady state position.

The Jacobian at the interior steady state of the considered 3D dynamics reads

$$J^o = \begin{pmatrix} 0 & -\beta_{eu}/l_{1o}^w & 0 \\ -\alpha & -f'(0)/l_{1o}^w & 0 \\ ? & ? & -(i_r + i_d)(1 - d_o) - (\bar{a} - r) \end{pmatrix}$$

This lower triangular form of the Jacobian immediately implies that the elements on the diagonal of the matrix J^o are just equal to the 3 eigenvalues of this matrix which are therefore all real and negative. This gives:

Proposition 3: *The interior steady state of the considered dynamics is locally asymptotically stable and is characterised by a strict hierarchy in the state variables of the dynamics.*

Due to the specific form of the considered laws of motion we conjecture that the steady state is also a global attractor in the economically relevant part of the 3D phase space. We then would get again monotonically convergent trajectories from any starting point of this part of the phase space and thus fairly simple adjustment processes also in the case where investment is jointly financed by profits (retained earnings) and credit.

The stability of the steady state is increased (that is, the eigenvalues of its Jacobian matrix become more negative) if the speed parameter characterising hiring and firing is increased, if the real wage barrier expression becomes more pronounced and if the parameters $i_r, i_d, \bar{a}$ in the investment function are increased.

Summing up, we thus can state that the adjustment processes and their stability properties remain very supportive for the working of our model of flexicurity type which can be made monotonically convergent to balanced growth with full capacity utilisation of both capital and labour with a sustainable distribution of income between firms, our three types of households and the government. We conclude that flexicurity capitalism may be a workable alternative to current forms of capitalism and can avoid in particular severe social deformations and human degradations caused by the reserve army mechanism and the mass unemployment it implies in certain stages of the long-phase distributive and welfare state cycle, which has been in the US and the UK more of a neoliberal cold turkey type and in Germany and in France more gradualistic in nature.

3.8 Schumpeterian 'Creative Destruction'

We now come to a brief discussion of the microeconomic problems for which a flexicurity economy should also offer solutions, namely the socially acceptable handling of exit and entry problems with respect to the formation of the real capital stock as well as labour supply of the economy.

The most remarkable feature of existing capitalism is definitely its property to revolutionise the technological foundations and the product frame of such market economies. The first indepth treatment of this fundamental tendency was given in Marx's (1954) *Capital*, Vol. I based on what he called the law of value. Schumpeter knew Marx's work very well, but developed his own vision of the microdynamics of capitalism which in place of some questionable monotonic tendencies asserted by Marx, with the exception of the secular law of increasing labour productivity, led him to the consideration of long waves in his work on business cycles (see Schumpeter, 1939). Marx, of course, had not lived long enough to become aware of long phased cyclical changes in the economic and social structure of capitalist economies, but was nevertheless able, on the basis of his value theory, to discuss the secular tendencies of the concentration and centralisation of capital and this even on a globalised scale.

Schumpeter's (1934) 'Theory of Economic Development' started from a quite different theoretical apparatus as compared to the classical theory of labour values and production prices, namely from the Walrasian concept of a perfectly competitive market economy which for him described the circular flow of economic life in given circumstances. To this he then added economic development and credit and most fundamentally the dynamic character of the entrepreneur who is initiating spontaneous and discontinuous changes in the routinised circular flow of economic activity which forever alter and displace the previously existing equilibrium state in fundamental ways.

> *These spontaneous and discontinuous changes in the channel of the circular flow and these disturbances in the center of equilibrium appear in the sphere of industrial and commercial life, not in the sphere of the wants of the consumer of final products* (Schumpeter 1934, p.65).

Concerning today's Walrasian theory of general equilibrium where production is but an appendix to consumption theory, this is a totally different perspective and this may also give one reason why Schumpeter (1942) later on used the theory of monopolistic competition as the starting point of his analysis of the dynamics of capitalism. Defining development as driven by the spontaneous action of the dynamic entrepreneur, Schumpeter (1934) then classifies the possibilities for such actions as follows:

> *Development in our sense is then defined by the carrying out of new combinations. This concept covers the following five cases: (1) The introduction of a new good — that is one with which consumers are not yet familiar — or of a new quality of a good. (2) The introduction of a new method of production, that is one not yet tested by experience in the branch of manufacture concerned, which need by no means be founded upon a discovery scientifically new, and can also exist in a new way of handling a commodity commercially. (3) The opening of a new market, that is a market into which the particular branch of manufacture of the country in question has not previously entered, whether or not this market has existed before. (4) The conquest of a new source of supply of raw materials or half-manufactured goods, again irrespective of whether this source already exists or whether it has first to be created. (5) The carrying out of the new organisation of any industry, like the creation of a monopoly position (for example through trustification) or the breaking up of a monopoly position.* (Schumpeter 1934, p.66)

To realise these various activities the role of credit is essential, since it allows entrepreneurs to start such projects with a degree of innovation, often created by new ideas of new entrants in certain markets. Credit helps to redirect labour and capital from old combinations to definitely new ones through process- or product-innovations and more, see the above list given by Schumpeter. It is therefore not just the use of idle resources of the economy, but the redirection of the employed resources towards new projects and the extra profits they can generate in comparison to their competitors. A typical example here is the railroadization discussed at length in Schumpeter (1939).

The innovative character of the Schumpeterian entrepreneurs thus alters the way the economy has been functioning so far and this the more rapidly the larger the scale on which such entrepreneurs enter the scene. Of course there are subsequent processes of the diffusion of the newly created technology or products which in the course of time reduce extra profits when the new projects have become routinised economic activities. Yet processes of innovation and diffusion may cluster in historical time and may thus lead to the long phased evolution of social structures of capital accumulation as they are described historically in Schumpeter (1939) as three Kondratieff waves (superimposed by shorter cycles in addition).

It is not our intention here to go into the details of Schumpeter's analysis of the forces that drive the evolution of capitalist economies. We refer the reader instead to the paper by Swedberg (1991) on Schumpeter's work and biography and to a voluminous edition on Schumpeter and Neo-Schumpeterian Economics edited by Hanusch and Pyka (2007). Our interest instead is to go on from Schumpeter's analysis of capitalism to his analysis of competitive socialism and the implications it may have for the model of flexicurity capitalism that is the subject of this chapter.

Questioning the sustainability of (at his time) existing Eastern type socialism from the viewpoint of immaturity, Schumpeter (1942) developed a concept of socialism for Western countries in the state of maturity. This concept can be characterised as providing a type of competitive socialism built on foundations erected unconsciously through the big enterprises created by the Rockefellers, the Vanderbilts and other famous dynasties in the Western industrialised countries. Schumpeter (1942) discusses the question of whether this type of socialism can work, what the corresponding socialist blueprints should look like and to what extent they will be superior to the capitalist mark II blueprints (of the mega-corporations). Schumpeter conceived the latter as having made obsolescent the entrepreneurial functioning of his view of capitalism, mark I, which was constructed around the figure a 'dynamic entrepreneur' and the process of creative destruction conducted by this leading form of an innovating economic agent.

Monopolistic practices, vanishing investment opportunities and growing hostility in the social structure of capitalism were part of the reasons that in Schumpeter's view characterised the decomposition of capitalism as he investigated it in 1942. Against this background he described the superiority of the socialist blueprint of Western competitive type, the transition to this form of social structure of accumulation and the comparative efficiency of such economies. In a separate chapter he discusses the human element in this type of economy, the problem of work organisation and the integration of bourgeois forms of management under capitalism into this type of socialism including the incentive problems concerning the behaviour of these economic agents. A typical statement with respect to the latter situation is:

> *It is not difficult however to insert the stock of bourgeois extraction into its proper place within that machine and to reshape its habits of work. ⋯ Rational treatments of the ex-bourgeois elements with a view to securing a maximum performance from them will then not require anything that is not just as necessary in the case of managerial personnel of any other extraction.* (Schumpeter 1942, p.65)

It may appear from today's perspective that his focused and provocative discussion of these points in section III of the chapter 'The Human Element' can be questioned to a certain degree. However, the managerial element in existing Western capitalism has become more and more the focus of public debate ranging from the salaries to the ethics the (top) managerial personnel should receive and adopt, respectively. Actual discussions on the behaviour of industrial management therefore are already preparing the ground for a situation where these persons may be granted an appropriate level of exclusiveness, that may however completely suffice to motivate their efforts to a sufficient degree with a problem-adequate perspective. We do not, however, claim here that such short characterisations suffice as considerations of the issue. On the contrary, detailed microeconomic and other investigations are absolutely necessary here to deal with such topics, yet, these issues have to be dealt with in actual capitalist management problems anyway. The important point in Schumpeter's arguments is that Western capitalism may transform itself automatically into some kind of competitive socialism on the basis of Western management principles. Such a statement can also be applied to the evolution of the Nordic European countries which may be en-route on a progress path towards a kind of social structure of capital accumulation we have modelled as flexicurity capitalism in this chapter.

With respect to the workforce of firms – in capitalism as well as in his type of socialism – Schumpeter (1942) states:

> *Second, closely allied to the necessity of incessant training of the normal is the necessity of dealing with the subnormal performer. This term does not refer to isolated pathological cases, but to a broad fringe of perhaps 25 % of the population. So far as subnormal performance is due to moral or volitional defects, it is perfectly unrealistic to expect that it will vanish with capitalism. The great problem and the great enemy of humanity, the subnormal, will be as much with us as he is now. He can hardly be dealt with by unaided group discipline alone - although of course the machinery of authoritarian discipline can be so constructed as to work, partly at least, through the group of which the subnormal is an element.* (Schumpeter 1942, p.213)

In view of our discussion of the working of Marx's general law of capital accumulation under today's conditions in Western type economies we would, however, point here to the fact that capitalism itself is in part responsible for the existence of the subnormal element as characterised in the above quote from Schumpeter's work. Mass unemployment, and its consequences for family life, alienation from human types of work organisation, degradation of part of the workforce as the 'unskilled' element in an otherwise flourishing economy, the rise and the fall of the welfare state and the latter's consequences for basic income needs, sufficient health care, sufficient care for the children and the elderly and adequate schooling systems are just some of the reasons why the 'subnormal' element in the population is a persistent fact of life. In this respect, we would claim that the social acceptance of a system of flexicurity capitalism would be one way to eliminate the 'subnormal' segment from the population gradually, but maybe not totally.

We therefore assert here that a system of flexicurity capitalism – based on the principles we have modelled in this chapter – would progressively tend towards social acceptance and social learning processes that put it on a progress path towards viable economic reproduction and sufficient income and – if security is well developed to cope with flexibility of a Schumpeterian kind (creative destruction) – that leads it into a situation where it can easily compete with societies that are still subject to the Marxian reserve army mechanism and the ruthless capitalism that derives from it.

The central message of Schumpeter's (1942) work on *Capitalism, Socialism and Democracy* – that socialism is created out of Western capitalist economies, and not on the basis of (the now past) Eastern type of socialism – thus can be carried over to the current debate on the possibility of flexicurity capitalism. Also this form of socio-economic reproduction may be organised through large production units and their efficient – though bureaucratic – management, a form of management that is developed out of the principles used under current capitalism in the efficient conduct of large (internationally oriented) enterprises. Equally well, as we currently experience it in the service sector (both for industrial production as well as for private consumption), there may still be sufficient room for the dynamic entrepreneur of Schumpeterian type, in particular through the flexible entry and exit conditions the flexicurity variant of capitalism should allow for.

It is certainly true that contemporaneous capitalism (often of the ruthless type, but in certain countries also of a socially acceptable kind) is not likely to be forced by evolution as such into a defensive position, at least in its performance on the goods and on the labour markets (though the current operation of financial markets have produced extremely undesirable results). Yet, the consciousness that ruthless, unrestricted capitalism is producing significant negative external social and environmental effects is increasing throughout the world economy and this gives the hope that an alternative form of capitalism – based on flexicurity principles – may be superior in its socio-economic performance, at least when approached in the state of maturity as it was already considered a necessity in Schumpeter's vision of a democratic society based on his type of competitive socialism.

To a certain degree this alternative variety of capitalism also is of a ruthless type, if Schumpeterian creative destruction processes are allowed for, but as in any democratic society there are of course more or less close limits to the choice of techniques (for example in bio-genetics) and the choice of products (for example in war-games), limits that are to be set by the elected political leadership of each country. Marx viewed the general law of capital accumulation and its perpetual reserve army mechanism as the element that not only allowed, but was also needed for the reproduction of capitalism. Schumpeter considered changes towards a competitive type of socialism as a possible alternative to the form of capitalism of his times. We think that there is now a chance for an alternative to current forms of ruthless capitalism which not only adopts some welfare principles, but that is founded on a coherently based socio-economic structure that is socially acceptable and is flexible enough to quickly adjust to the changing world market conditions. The foundations are the social acceptance of capitalism in an educated democratic society. The problems are given by the mastering of Keynesian types of business fluctuations and Schumpeterian types of creative process and product revolutions and

– of course – of the control of financial markets such that the real activities of an economy do not just become the side-product of a casino as it was already observed in Keynes's (1936) 'General Theory'.

The essential ingredients along the progress path towards a social structure of flexicurity type are not only a basic income guarantee of the workfare type (which includes the obligation to work), but also a reorganisation of the labour market towards an employer of first (not last) resort who organises in a decentralised way the work for all people not employed within privately run industries, but also the work of officially retired persons who are still willing to offer their human capital on the labour markets of the economy. The workability of the designed reproduction scheme of flexicurity type of course depends – in the same way as many other actual organisational problems – on detailed microeconomic analyses of the labour relations within large, medium-sized and small business firms as well as in the public sector. Such economic incentives (and sanctions) need to be coupled with an educational system that not only creates the basis for skill formation, but also provides the proper foundations for citizenship education in a democratic society, where citizens essentially approve the high degree of flexibility in the industrial part of the economy (and not only there) on the basis of the security aspects of the flexicurity concept.

Goodwin has proposed, see Flaschel (2009, the appendix to ch.10), to construct a M(arx)K(eynes)S(chumpeter) system for the analysis of the functioning and evolution of actual capitalism. We here in principle have proposed a similar solution with respect to ideal constructions by Marx (1954) and Schumpeter (1942), the so-called reproduction schemes of Marx and Schumpeter's vision of a competitive (Western, not Eastern) type of socialism. Both constructions have, however, to be confronted with Keynesian effective demand problems as the third component of Goodwin's MKS system. This system can be regarded as the attempt to introduce a social structure of capital accumulation which is not of the ruthless competitive type of factual capitalism, in particular of the form as we do observe it at present.

3.9 Conclusions

In this chapter, we have dealt with the flexicurity model in theory and in practice, the latter as it is investigated for the case of Denmark and comprehensively discussed in the European Union as well as in some of its member states. Our model of flexicurity which is to be regarded as an augmenting step in the discussion of active labour policies is characterised by three labour markets: a private and a public one and a third one that is organised by an Employer of First Resort. Thus, our approach noticeably differs from BIG and ELR approaches even if there are similar starting points and objectives.

A main part of this chapter concerned the development of a baseline macro-model of a flexicurity economy and a presentation of its accounting structure and the assumed economic behaviour of the sectors of the economy. We have investigated the stability of its balanced growth path, and also its sustainability from the perspective of income distribution. We have also included retired persons as part of the workforce (as long as they are willing to participate in social work and capable of doing so). An important question in the income generation performance of the labour market was the way pension funds were managed concerning the provision of additional company pension funds and their use as interest-bearing credit provisions to the firms of the economy. From the theoretical perspective we obtained the result that flexicurity capitalism is a stable and viable form of capitalism (if effective demand problems are set aside). Its important contribution is that the human degradations and social deformations which we experience in present forms of capitalism, due to the presence of high unemployment and the way this issue is handled by policy, can be – at least partly – avoided under the system of full-employment flexicurity capitalism. We have finally dealt with Schumpeterian processes of 'creative destruction'. Keynesian 'effective demand' problems will be dealt with in the following chapter.

Notes

[1] Foundations for this chapter have been laid in Flaschel (2009), Flaschel and Greiner (2011, 2012) and Flaschel, Greiner and Luchtenberg (2012).

[2] See also Wilthagen and Tros (2004).

[3] Of course, there are simple tasks to be done in the workplace; but this is part of the work of skilled and high-skilled workers.

[4] See, for example, Quirk et al. (2006).

[5] See Bredgaard, Larsen and Madsen (2006, p.62).

[6] See also Bredgaard, Larsen and Madsen (2006, p.65ff.) and Vandaele (2006) for more details about the Ghent system in Denmark.

[7] Bredgaard, Larsen and Madsen (2006, p.70)

[8] See also Solow (2008a, 13f.) and Westergaard-Nielsen (2008) for further details.

[9] See Bredgaard, Larsen and Madsen (2006, p.78f).

[10] See United Nations (1998), article 23: Universal Declaration of Human Rights, (http://www.un.org/Overview/rights.html)

[11] See also Keune and Jepsen (2007) and Tangian (2007, p.555f.).

[12] One could also assume that everything in the public sector is calculated net of taxation.

[13] EFR type work need not be organised by the government, but can also (partly) be organised by private firms, through subcontracted labour or temporary employment and the like, as we know it from advanced Western capitalist economies. It must, however, be subject to regulations which prevent associated exploitation mechanisms of the workforce as we have discussed in the preceding chapter.

PART II

The Forces to Cope With: Effective Demand, Finance and Innovation

4. Demand-Driven Distributive Cycles

In this chapter[1] we will discuss the central mechanisms by which output and income distribution are determined in a capitalist economy in the short as well as in the longer run. We thus and on the one hand now start to consider in detail Keynesian demand rationing on the market for goods and the problems this creates for the working of the economy. On the other hand, we introduce into these goods market dynamic and the implied labour market results an advanced type of wage–price spiral by which income distribution is determined in the longer run. We will find that the Marxian distributive cycle of Chapter 1 remains in place in such a framework, but is now interacting with effective goods demand which in turn depends on income distribution. We have to distinguish four possible scenarios as they are implied by the combinations of wage- and profit-led goods market regimes with goods- or labour-market dominance in the evolution of the real wage.

The main finding of this chapter is that the Marxian distributive cycle is no longer characterised by a single regime throughout. Instead we will still get the dominance of a profit-led demand regime, but now coupled with real wages that are led sometimes by the state of the goods market and sometimes by the state of the labour market. Data for the US economy after World War II seem to support these findings.

4.1 Introduction

Standard applied macro literature expresses labour market and goods market dynamics by a single Phillips curve, in which the cost pressure on the labour market is working on a single inflation rate. This reduced-form Phillips curve requires simple assumptions on markup pricing and Okun's law: prices have to be a constant mark-up on wages and the rate of utilisation of the workforce and the capital stock are always strictly positively correlated. Structuralist macro models, on the other hand, often consider two separate Phillips curves, one for the labour market and one for the goods market, in order to analyse the interacting dynamics of the adjustment processes on both markets, namely the wage–price spiral.

In this chapter, we introduce the results of a nonparametric estimate of the wage Phillips Curve,[2] showing a nonlinear relation between wage inflation and the employment rate, into a simplified version of the model by Flaschel and Krolzig (2006). This nonlinearity translates into a nonlinearity of the result of the wage–price spiral, the real wage dynamics, a dynamic equation in which the dependent variable is the wage share growth rate, and the predetermined variables are the employment rate, the capital stock utilisation rate and the inflationary climate of the economy.[3] Assuming an Okun's type law to hold, we can then derive a relation between the growth rate of the wage share and the capital utilisation rate. Equations of this kind are used in the related literature (for example, Taylor (2004)) to derive a distributive curve for the economy. The building block around which this chapter is organised is the study of how the estimated nonlinearity in the wage Phillips curve affects the distributive cycle we investigated in detail in Part I of this book.

In a structuralist fashion, we consider also the relation between the growth rate of capital stock utilisation and the wage share. Although, in the related literature, this so-called demand regime of an economy is a functional relation in which what matters are levels, we can characterise, without changing the story significantly, a negative dependence on the wage share of the growth rate of capital utilisation as profit-led demand regime, and a positive impact of the wage share on the capital utilisation growth rate as wage-led demand regime. Combining the nonlinear distributive schedule with such effective demand schedules, we analyse in depth the dynamic properties of the economy, with stress however on the empirically more relevant profit-led effective demand regimes.

The chapter is organised as follows. In Section 4.2, we review the baseline model we are considering. Then, in Section 4.3, we introduce the nonlinearity of the demand pressure term into the wage Phillips curve, and insert the demand regimes of the economy into an obtained reduced form of the baseline model, to derive in Section 4.4 a dynamic equation whose form will change according to whether the demand is profit-led or wage-led. After the characterisation of the properties of this single dynamic equation with its multiple steady states, we will build on it in Section 4.5 by adding a second dimension, namely the cross-relation between capital utilisation growth and the wage share level. This added dimension will lead to a 2D system in which the cross-dual interaction between the wage share and capital utilisation is investigated. In this case, however, the characterisation of the three equilibria of the model cannot be conclusive, since two of them are still of the structurally unstable type of the Goodwin (1967) growth cycle model. In Section 4.6, we will therefore consider both dual and cross-dual forces in the labour and the goods market.

Focusing on the profit-led case, which is the empirically relevant one for the US economy (at least in the long-run), we will show in Section 4.7 that this basically complete system will exhibit regions where convergence to boom or bust (depressed) steady states occurs, and regions where the economy either cycles around the basins of attraction of these two steady states or escapes from this situation by means of accelerating inflation or deflation. Section 4.8 provides an empirical comparison with phase plots of the US situation after World War II. Section 4.9 concludes.

Before we start with Section 4.2 we briefly provide a motivation for the result we obtain at the end of the chapter. Hirsch and Smale (1974), in a well-known book on dynamical systems, consider the set of possible limit sets of planar systems, which in the theorem they prove, can be steady states, closed orbits (like the one we considered in Chapter 1), or orbits that connect steady states. In 2D systems the set of limit sets of orbits is therefore very limited. This changes radically in dimension 3 where any number of strange attractors can occur. In the 2D case, these authors provide the following kind of graphical example that hurts the assumptions of the so-called Poincaré-Bendixson theorem:

> *In fact Figure B (here: Figure 4.1) is typical, in that one can show that a limit set other than a closed orbit or equilibrium is made up of equilibria and trajectories joining them. The Poincaré-Bendixson theorem says that if a compact limit set in the plane contains no equilibria it is a closed orbit.* (Hirsch and Smale 1974, p.240).

We claim on the basis of this quotation that the dynamics to be considered theoretically in this chapter are of the type shown in Figure 4.1 with the differences however that there is a further equilibrium at the origin of the phase plane and that the saddle arms do not enclose unstable equilibrium points (as in Hirsch and Smale's example), but stable ones. An empirical example which bears some relationship to the dynamics shown in Figure 4.1 has already – without noticing this on this level of the modelling of the distributive cycle[4] – been provided by the empirical phase plot in Figure 4.10 in this chapter. In the faltering boom in the 1970s we have despite high and increasing unemployment a rise of the wage share which we will explain in this chapter by a regime switch in relative wage and price flexibility. The same applies in 1990 where we see an increase in the wage share despite an unemployment level that is still high.

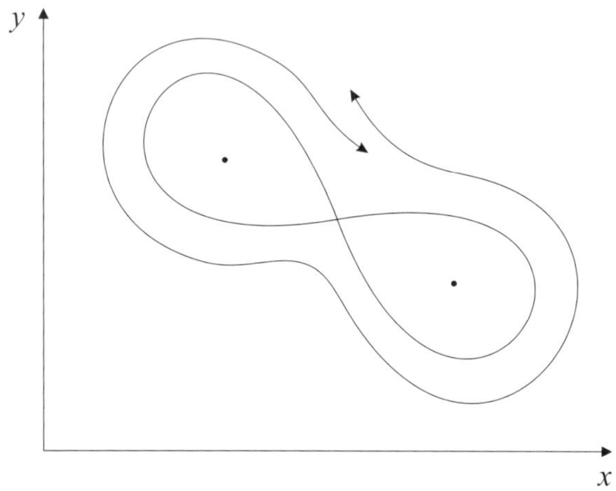

Figure 4.1 Limit sets in planar systems that are not closed orbits[5]

At the bottom and at the top of the long-phased cycle we have by contrast a normal working of the Marxian reserve army mechanism, but as said in the midrange of the employment data deviations from this normality. We will build in this chapter, based on a further empirical observation, a model that shows that the phase plot of Hirsch and Smale, as shown in Figure 4.1, can indeed be obtained from a macrodynamic theory which is fairly rich in structure, which can cope with any profile of labour productivity growth and which explains the cycle as we observe it in Figure 4.10.

4.2 Cross-over Wage–price Spirals

The starting point of this section is a simplified version of the model of the wage–price spiral estimated by Flaschel and Krolzig (2006), whose structural form is given by:[6]

$$\hat{w} = \beta_w(\bar{e} - e) + \kappa_w(\hat{p} + n_x(t)) + (1 - \kappa_w)(\pi^c + n_x(t)) \quad (4.1)$$

$$\hat{p} = \beta_{pu}(\bar{u} - u) + \kappa_p(\hat{w} - n_x(t)) + (1 - \kappa_p)\pi^c \quad (4.2)$$

where e is the rate of employment of labour, u the rate of employment of capital, the bars indicate NAIRU values of the two variables, $n_x(t)$ stands for the rate of Harrod-type technical change at time t, and where π^c is the inflationary climate. We define the real wage as $\omega = w/p$, so that the wage share is given by $v = (w/p)/x(t) = \omega/x(t)$.

In the wage equation we assume an ideal complete pass-through of actual labour productivity which must hold on a secular basis, but which will not happen at all moments of time, where busts may tend to lower this pass-through, while the opposite may be occurring in boom periods. In the cost push term of the wage equation we assume that it is on this basis given by a weighted average of myopically perfect price inflation anticipations and of our concept of an inflation climate. This climate term prevents agents from fully adjusting to inflationary shocks – which may be of a very temporary nature. Instead they reflect the climate, that is, surrounding current inflation, and put some weight on it in their wage negotiations. Due to the use of this climate expression in the price Phillips curve we only deduct labour productivity there from current wage inflation, since only this term is incorporating this productivity change. The parameter κ_p then measures the degree of markup pricing in price inflation, which is modified through the demand pressure term $u - \bar{u}$.

Note in the context of such a formulation of the wage–price spiral that we are assuming monetary adjustments in its background. Following the endogenous-money theory of the next chapter we will simply assume here that money does not influence this two-fold inflation dynamics in any significant way. Inflation is therefore a real phenomenon in this chapter and not a monetary one, as it is suggested by the monetarist approach to macrodynamics.

Rearranging terms, the two Phillips curves can then be rewritten in matrix form as follows:

$$\begin{pmatrix} 1 & -\kappa_w \\ -\kappa_p & 1 \end{pmatrix} \begin{pmatrix} \hat{w} - \pi^c - n_x \\ \hat{p} - \pi^c \end{pmatrix} = \begin{pmatrix} \beta_w(e - \bar{e}) \\ \beta_{pu}(u - \bar{u}) \end{pmatrix}$$

Defining $\kappa = (1 - \kappa_p \kappa_w)^{-1}$, the solution of this matrix equation yields:

$$\hat{w} - \pi^c - n_x = \kappa \left[\beta_w(e - \bar{e}) + \kappa_w \beta_{pu}(u - \bar{u})\right]$$
$$\hat{p} - \pi^c = \kappa \left[\kappa_p \beta_w(e - \bar{e}) + \beta_{pu}(u - \bar{u})\right]$$

Finally, using the definition of $\hat{v} = \hat{w} - \hat{p} - n_x$, in subtracting the second equation from the first one, we derive the following reduced-form law of motion for the wage share:

$$\hat{v} = \kappa \left[(1 - \kappa_p)\beta_w(e - \bar{e}) - (1 - \kappa_w)\beta_{pu}(u - \bar{u})\right] \tag{4.3}$$

The last equation shows that the wage share responds to both utilisation rates in labour input and capital, but to nothing else, not even labour productivity growth. Assuming for expositional simplicity the simplest form of an Okun's law,[7] $e = u$, $\bar{e} = \bar{u}$, we will then have that the real wage adjustment responds positively (negatively) to economic activity if

$$\alpha = (1 - \kappa_p)\beta_w - (1 - \kappa_w)\beta_{pu} > 0 \qquad \text{(respectively} < 0\text{)}.$$

Following Proaño et al. (2006), we denote the case of a positive response of $\hat{v}$ on economic activity ($\alpha > 0$) as labour-market led wage-adjustment process, whereas we will say that the wage-adjustment is goods-market led when $\alpha < 0$ holds.

On the other hand, it is common in structuralist macroeconomic modelling to consider also the way in which changes in the wage share affect the capital utilisation rate, to determine the so-called Effective Demand Regime of the economy. If the capital utilisation rate reacts positively to the wage share, the demand for goods is said to be wage-led, while if variations in the wage share cause changes in capital utilisation rate of opposite sign the demand regime is said to be profit-led.

As Flaschel and Krolzig (2006) pointed out, the sign of the parameter α, combined with the characteristics of the demand regime of the economy, determines whether real wage adjustments have stabilising or destabilising effects. Wage adjustments will have stabilising effects if the negative response of investment to changes in real wages outweighs the positive response of consumption, and if wages are more flexible to labour demand pressures than prices to goods market pressures (or both vice versa). Conversely, if investment reacts less than consumption to a change in real wages and wages remain more flexible than prices (each in terms of their own demand pressures), or both vice versa, then real wage adjustments will show destabilising effects. The four possible scenarios are presented in Table 4.1, taken from Proaño et al. (2006). It is not within the scopes of the present chapter to analyse in depth such type of effects, already broadly discussed in the quoted work. Yet, it should be obvious that the simple profit-squeeze mechanism of part I (where the economy was not demand led at all) has become quite advanced now by way of the two Phillips curves we have introduced in this section and by way of the Keynesian demand regimes that characterise the working of the economy.

Table 4.1 Four baseline real wage adjustment scenarios

	wage-led goods demand	profit-led goods demand
labour-market led	adverse	normal
goods-market led	normal	adverse
real wage adjustment	(convergent)	(divergent)

4.3 Nonlinearities in the Wage Demand-pressure Term

Let us now consider the first term in the square brackets in (4.3), describing how the wage share reacts to the employment rate level. Flaschel and Krolzig (2006) estimated a VAR for the US economy, assuming a linear relation between $\hat{v}$ and e. In what follows, we will consider instead a p-spline estimation of the money wage Phillips curve, where all parameters are now considered to be unknown, assumed to be a smooth function of their subsequent variable. This estimation gives rise to the nonlinear relationship between wage inflation and demand pressure on the labour market shown in Figure 4.2. The curve is increasing up to an employment rate of slightly more than 92%, then has an almost flat, slightly decreasing region, and eventually becomes again increasing for values of the employment rate smaller than 94%.

By looking at the plot of the first derivative of the function, we see that its curvature displays several changes. The first increasing portion is virtually linear; right after an employment rate of about 91%, the curve becomes concave, until an inflexion point around a 93.5% employment rate, after which the curve becomes increasing and convex again. Eventually, there is another inflexion point around an employment rate of 95.5% or so, and the final portion of the curve is increasing but concave. As seen in the bottom graph, the unconditional mean of the first derivative of β_w is around 0.6.

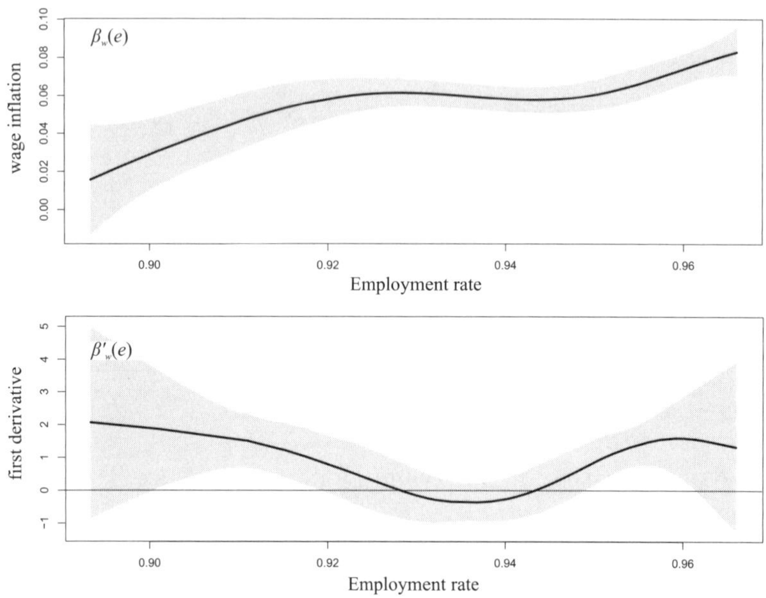

Figure 4.2 P-spline estimation of the wage inflation/employment rate dependence and its first derivative (with confidence intervals shown as gray areas)

Although the US labour market is not renowned worldwide for the strength of its labour unions, a standard economic intuition behind the behaviour of the curve could lie on a bargaining power argument relative to labour supply. For high levels of unemployment, the workers' bargaining power is small: they (or the labour union representing them) will be satisfied with only small increases or even decreases in the nominal wage in order to increase the employment rate. Corresponding to the centre of the curve, there is a flat region between bust and boom periods where labour is resisting wage inflation decreases at the given expected price inflation, a situation widely familiar through Keynes's discussion of it. Finally, as soon as the economic activity is above a NAIRU-type full employment rate,[8] workers will exercise their increased bargaining power in requiring significantly more than proportional increases in wage inflation (as compared to price inflation).

On the basis of the nonlinearity shown in Figure 4.2, assuming that price flexibility is higher than wage flexibility in the middle range of the money wage Phillips curve, we get for the assumed dynamics of the real wage the stylised situation shown in Figure 4.3. The opposite situation will hold in the cases where money wage inflation reacts strongly to the demand pressure in the labour market.

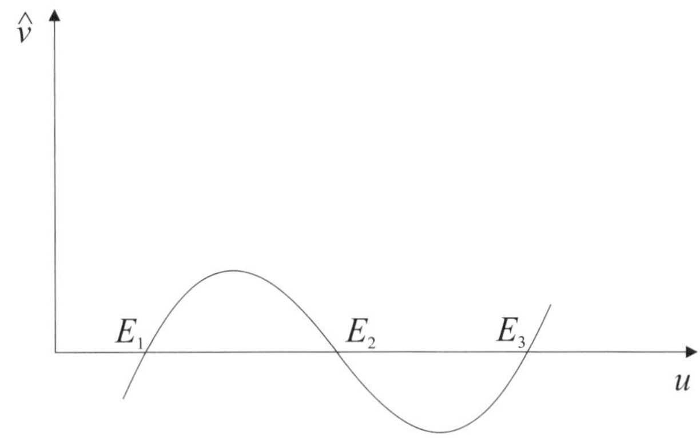

Figure 4.3 The reduced-form wage–price spiral under Okun's Law $e = u$

In view of such arguments, let us consider the term after the minus sign in (4.3) in more detail. To keep things simple, we still assume that the price flexibility parameter β_{pu} is a constant coefficient, so that the second term in square brackets in (4.3) is just a linear function. Assume also the simple Okun's Law $e = u$ to hold, to modify (4.3) as follows:[9]

$$\hat{v}(u) = \kappa\left[(1-\kappa_p)\beta_w(u-\bar{u}) - (1-\kappa_w)\beta_{pu}(u-\bar{u})\right] \tag{4.4}$$

Hence, $\hat{v}(u) > 0$ when $\beta_w^{'} > \frac{1-\kappa_w}{1-\kappa_p}\beta_{pu}$, $\hat{v}(u) < 0$ otherwise. The local maxima and minima of this composite function will lie where $\beta_w^{'} = \frac{1-\kappa_w}{1-\kappa_p}\beta_{pu}$. As for the other values of u in the domain, we will have that the growth rate of the wage share will increase when $\beta_w^{'} > \frac{1-\kappa_w}{1-\kappa_p}\beta_{pu}$, and decrease when the inequality is reversed. Loosely speaking, if the coefficient $\frac{1-\kappa_w}{1-\kappa_p}\beta_{pu}$ is positive but 'not too large' (less than, say, 1.5, according to Figure 4.2), plotting $\hat{v}$ against the capital utilisation rate will lead to the picture in Figure 4.3.[10]

The combination of data and the assumption on β_{pu} suggests a non-monotonic relation between wage share adjustment and the capital utilisation rate. In structuralist macro-textbooks the (long-run) relation between levels $v(u)$ is known as Distributive Curve. The sign of the first derivative of the function matters, in what $\frac{\partial v}{\partial u} > 0$ is interpreted saying that the economy is 'Marxist' or it exhibits 'profit-squeeze', given that an increase in capacity utilisation will result in a rising wage share and thus in a falling profit share. Conversely, $\frac{\partial v}{\partial u} < 0$ means that the economy exhibits 'forced saving' along Kaldorian lines (Taylor, 2004).

Note, however, that so far we have been dealing with log-derivatives and not levels on the y-axis. The adjustment process we are considering has already been described by saying the economy is labour-market led in correspondence to the steady states E_1 and E_3, whereas it is goods-market led in proximity of equilibrium E_2. Since a rising wage share will determine the profit share to fall, we can assimilate the labour-market led case with (a maybe cyclical) profit-squeeze and the goods-market led scenario with (a maybe cyclical) forced saving, but one should keep in mind here the long-run vs. short-run distinction.

Hence, some effort needs to be made in order to better characterise these dynamics, and reconcile the two points of view. Such an exercise is outside the scope of this chapter however. For what is compelling here, it is enough to say that, given the estimated nonlinearity of the wage Phillips curve with respect to the demand pressure term, and the assumption on the cost term in the reduced form (4.3), Figure 4.3 shows that a labour-market led distributive curve corresponds to the two unstable equilibria, while in the stable equilibrium the distributive curve is goods-market led.

The literature we are referring to considers also the long-run relation between levels $u(v)$, traditionally called Effective Demand Regimes. Again, the focus is on the sign of the first derivative of the function to determine whether the demand regime of the economy is wage-led $\frac{\partial u}{\partial v} > 0$ or profit-led $\frac{\partial u}{\partial v} < 0$. Combining the distributive curve with the demand regime of the economy, a 2D dynamical system of equations is then generally studied. The behaviour of the system depends on the slope of the two curves, which in Taylor (2004) are derived as isoclines in the phase space (u, v).

Traditionally, such systems are considered to be composed of linear equations. Given the results in Figure 4.3 as a prior, and the implied reduced form distributive curve, the dynamics of the model is now more involved than, for example, in Barbosa-Filho and Taylor (2006). In order to isolate the basic implications of the hypothesis made so far, we will start plugging the relation between the capital utilisation rate and the wage share into the curve $\hat{v}(u)$ derived from our empirical results. This substitution will allow us to analyse the relation between the wage share and its rate of growth.

This one-dimensional representation has the advantage of being very simple to analyse, but nevertheless already able to generate interesting dynamics, varying according to the assumed different demand regime scenarios.

4.4 The One-dimensional Baseline Dynamics

For the sake of simplicity, we assume for the time being $u(v)$ to be a linear function, as done, among others, in Barbosa-Filho and Taylor (2006). Plugging this simple equation for the demand regime into the distributive curve, we can derive a dynamic relation between the wage share adjustment process and its own level; the shape of this function will depend on the characteristics of the demand regime of the economy. The two possible cases, corresponding to a wage-led and a profit-led scenario respectively, are represented in Figures 4.4 and 4.5.

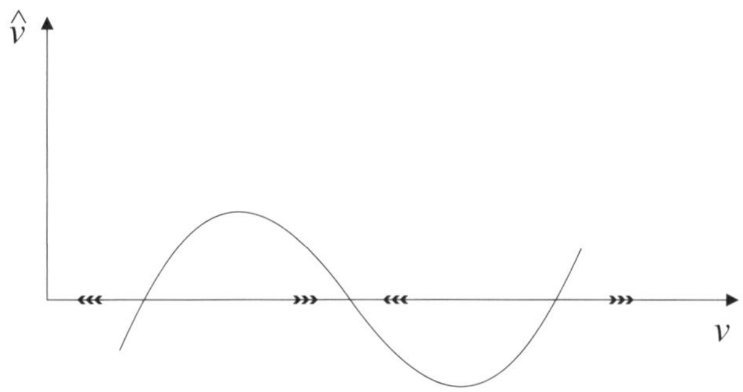

Figure 4.4 Real wage dynamics in a wage-led demand regime ($u_v > 0$): Corridor stability between booms and busts

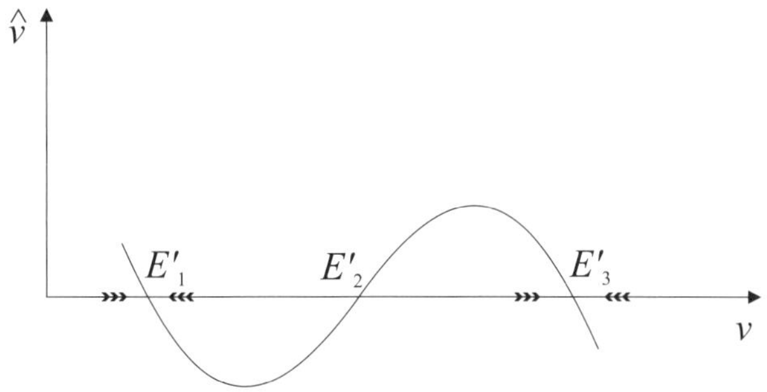

Figure 4.5 Real wage dynamics in a profit-led demand regime ($u_v < 0$) : Stable busts and stable booms

In these two simple one-dimensional plots, the analysis of the transitional dynamics is straightforward. The estimated nonlinearity in the demand-pressure term, combined with the assumed linear cost-pressure and demand regime, leads to three different values for v ensuring a constant wage share. It is clear, however, that the slope of the demand regime will play a crucial role in determining the stability of the points of rest of the equation we are studying.

In a wage-led scenario, the only stable equilibrium is E_2: as long as the wage-share lies within the open interval (E_1, E_3), we have a stable movement towards the steady state. Conversely, when the demand regime is profit-led, equilibrium E_2' is unstable and E_1', E_3' are stable. Hence, while a wage-led demand determines a corridor stability around an intermediate steady state, in the profit-led scenario we find two extreme equilibria, which we could call a stable bust (E_1') and stable boom (E_3').

It is worthwhile to notice, going back to Table 4.1, that the stable steady state in the wage-led scenario occurs for the goods-market led portion of the wage-adjustment curve, whereas the two stable equilibria in the profit-led demand regime correspond to the regions of the function $\hat{v}(u)$ where movements in wage inflation are labour-market led.

4.5 A Goodwin Cross-dual Extension of the Model

So far, we used the relation between the wage share adjustment process and the capital utilisation rate to derive a sketch of the basic dynamic properties of the wage–price spiral considered, under the nonlinear relation between the money wage adjustment process and the employment rate. A more complete analysis requires the consideration of how the adjustment process of capital utilisation rate is affected by variations in the wage share, or equivalently the effective demand regime adjustment process. To study this interaction, we need to add a dimension to the single equation system given by (4.3) under the assumed Okun's law. The simplest way to do so is to consider a linear relation:

$$\hat{u} = \beta_{uv}(v - v_o) \tag{4.5}$$

where v_o indicates a reference steady state level for the wage share, as it is shown in Figures 4.6 and 4.7. It is clear from the analysis above that a profit-led economy corresponds to the case in which $\beta_{uv} < 0$, and then (4.4) is an error-correction equation; a wage-led economy requires instead $\beta_{uv} > 0$. A steady state for the nonlinear relation (4.5) implies a horizontal isocline in the phase plane (u, v) corresponding to $v = v_o$. Considering Figure 4.2, we have now however 3 vertical isoclines for a zero wage share rate of growth, corresponding to capital utilisation rates of E_1, E_2, E_3 respectively.[11]

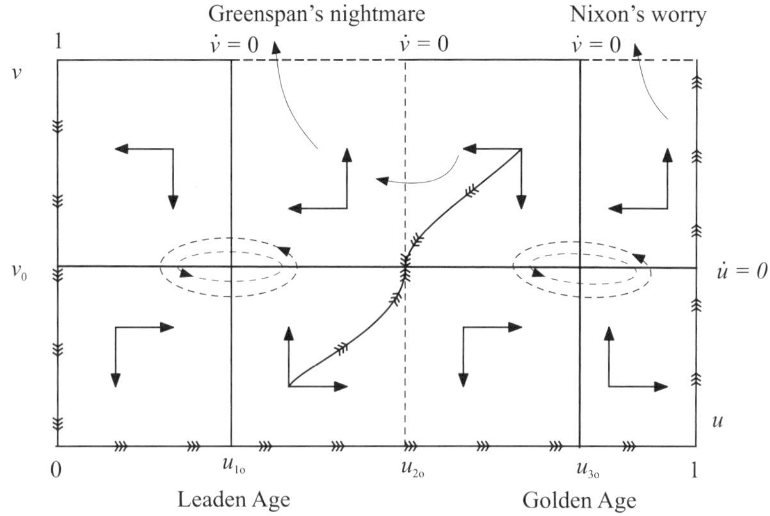

Figure 4.6 Phase diagram for the profit-led demand regime: $\hat{u}_v < 0$, with escape regions in the boom and the depressed situation due to wage and price inflation dominance, respectively

Let us now analyse qualitatively the dynamical properties of this system. In order to study the behaviour of the wage share relative to the capital stock utilisation rate, we have to consider all the several cases arising from the nonlinear functional form we are using. When $0 \leq u \leq u_1$ the wage share will decrease, given the positive slope of the function in that part of its domain. When $u_1 \leq u \leq u_2$, the wage share will rise. Before the curve reaches its local maximum, we have that $u \geq u_1$, and the positive slope of $\beta_w(\cdot)$ will produce an increase in v; when the curve starts to decrease, we have that $u < u_2$ and the negative slope of the function in that region will enable the wage share to keep on rising. The same lines of reasoning apply, *mutatis mutandis*, for $u_2 \leq u \leq u_3$: before the local minimum is achieved, the wage share will decrease because the capital utilisation rate is above the steady state level u_2; from that on, the new steady state level u_3 will lead the dynamics and, given the positive slope of the curve in that region, the wage share will keep decreasing. Finally, when $u_3 < u \leq 1$, the positive slope of the curve implies an increase in the wage share.

As for the dynamics of the capital utilisation rate, if the demand regime is wage-led, then $\beta_{uv} > 0$, and above the $\dot{u} = 0$ isocline the capital utilisation rate will increase; below the line u will fall. In the profit-led demand regime instead, given $\beta_{uv} < 0$, u will decrease above the $\dot{u} = 0$ isocline, whereas it will rise below the $\dot{u} = 0$ isocline.

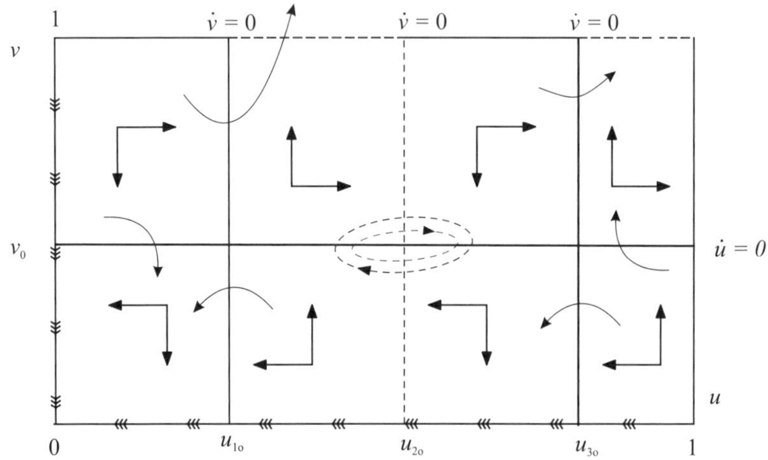

Figure 4.7 Phase diagram for the wage-led demand regime: $\hat{u}_v > 0$

The combinations of the two different demand regime scenarios with the dynamics of the wage share are presented in Figures 4.6 and 4.7. Note that we have here the wage share v on the vertical axis and the rate of employment on the horizontal one. This is done for expositional reasons, in particular of having the escape regions to be considered below at the top of the figures. The distributive cycle thereby gets the opposite orientation and is now turning counter-clockwise. The dashed lines indicate possible escape regions. Note that, because of the model's specification, in principle it is mathematically possible that at least the wage share goes above one. This is surely a weakness: in order to avoid it we should respecify the setup with the inclusion of additional nonlinearities able to ensure that the wage share is not allowed to exit the [0,1] interval. We will consider this issue further below. The Jacobian matrix, evaluated at one of the steady states (denoted by a_o), is:

$$J_o = \begin{pmatrix} 0 & \beta_{uv} u_o \\ \kappa[(1-\kappa_p)\beta_w^{'}(\cdot) - (1-\kappa_w)\beta_{pu}]v_o & 0 \end{pmatrix}$$

The trace of this matrix is equal to zero, its eigenvalues are thus purely imaginary (if the determinant is positive). On the other hand, the stability features of the different equilibria depend on whether the demand regime of the economy is wage-led or profit-led. If the economy is profit-led, then $\beta_{uv} < 0$. Looking at Figure 4.6, we see that for the steady state values u_1 and u_3, $(1-\kappa_p)\beta_w^{'} > (1-\kappa_w)\beta_{pu}$ holds, then the determinant of $J(u,v)$ (evaluated at the steady state) is positive and the two corresponding equilibria are stable, although not asymptotically stable. In fact – as shown in Figure 4.6 – these steady state positions are of the center type dynamics of the Goodwin (1967) growth cycle model in the ranges where the curve in Figure 4.6 is downward sloping. We thus have two local Goodwin growth cycle situations (see Figure 4.6), and in between a saddlepoint equilibrium where the separatrices may either wind around the shown persistent cycles or escape in the boom region or the depression region.[12]

If the separatrices that depart from the steady state in the middle of Figure 4.6 wind around the Goodwin center type dynamics and return to the saddle (see Figure 4.8 for a representation of this possibility), they enclose the two stability basins of the steady states left and right and they may attract movements that are situated outside the separatrices. We then have that the paths generated by the dynamics in this area oscillate around the depressions and the booms in a sequential manner. We thus may be trapped in a depressed region (a labour-market led Robinsonian 'leaden age', since wages are more flexible than prices) or in a boom region (a labour-market led Robinsonian 'golden age', again since wages are more flexible than prices) or may be thrown out of this situation and then oscillate between booms and depressions. Note here also that – due to our formulation of the wage and price Phillips curves – we have the fact that the shown cycles are completely independent from the evolution of labour productivity $z(t)$.

Suppose the initial condition to be, for example, in the top-right region in Figure 4.6: if the system does not escape out of the box, there is a movement towards north-west, until the isocline corresponding to u_3 is reached. Since we are above the isocline $\dot{u} = 0$, the system keeps moving to the left and then leaves the vertical isocline and starts going south-west. At that point, the dynamics might reach the saddle path, or move to the bottom part of the picture, or simply hit the isocline u_2, thus keeping going west. At that point, (if the north-west movement associated with this region does not cause the wage share to blow out), we will have again a movement to south-west. Not being able to determine at this stage of the analysis whether there is a basin of attraction somewhere in the top-left of the diagram, we can only suppose the system to keep moving in this direction until the isocline u_1 is hit. Then, the wage share falls until it reaches the value v_o. Then the system moves to the bottom, and again it might pass through all the bottom regions or reach the saddle path.

This is the situation where the dynamics stays in the unit square of the phase space. However, as pointed out above, there is the mathematical possibility that it escapes from it top right. If such a situation is approached, that is, if the wage share is moving towards E_1 on the right hand side (near the full capacity line $u = 1$), we have that wage inflation is outperforming price inflation: a situation that under the Nixon administration led to a wage and price stop in order to avoid accelerating wage–price inflation rates. In this way the economy may be stopped to produce outcomes that become non-viable and be forced to stay in the unit-square domain of the phase space. This instability of the private sector in a golden age may then lead the economy into the depressed part of the phase space from where it may recover after a while or not.

Yet the economy may also produce ever increasing wage shares in the left hand part of the figure, in the form of price inflation that is lower than wage inflation and thus leads to real wage increases. The cause of this possibility must be found in the wage level or the wage inflation rate to be still somewhat rigid in the downward direction. We have called this situation Greenspan's nightmare and associate this term with prices that are falling faster than wages. Yet such a situation may already come about when price disinflation is larger than wage disinflation and may thereby already lead to an adverse adjustment in the wage share (in the real wage in fact).

But these are the only possibilities where the economy may be endangered in its viability. The zero axes cannot be touched in such a growth rate dynamics, and the full capacity ceiling limits the dynamics on the right hand side of the (economically meaningful part of) the phase space. Therefore, at this level of generality the possible scenarios of the dynamical model are either bust or boom Goodwin cycles, or movements around these two situations or the two breakdown scenarios just discussed (as long as economic policy remains inactive in such a situation). Note that the Nixon problem is much easier to handle than the Greenspan problem, in particular if the latter is coupled with the occurrence of deflation and not just disinflation.

In Figure 4.7 we consider the same scenarios for the case of a wage-led economy. Given the positive value of β_{uv}, the dynamics of the capital utilisation rate are reversed. Thus, we find two saddle-point equilibria at E_1 and E_3, and an unstable one corresponding to E_2. Notice that, albeit the two external saddle points are compatible with the 1D analysis above, it is hard to find a parallel between the single dimension stability and the possibility of collapse that may now exist, either via hyperinflation to the right or hyperdeflation to the left. However, considering the own-level effects on the growth rates of both capital utilisation and wage share, will allow us to reconcile the 1D findings to the somewhat puzzling results of the present section. We do not go into the details here however, since the clockwise orientation (of this chapter) of the interior Goodwin cycles that this situation generates is counterfactual with empirical observations, at least for the US economy.[13]

Leaving this case we however briefly note that the rectangles top-right and bottom-left are definitely unstable regions leading the economy into hyperinflation[14] and economic breakdown, respectively. The situations below and above them, respectively, are not so obviously totally unstable, just as the areas adjacent to the rectangles to the left.

Let us finally point out that numerical simulations are generally needed in order to assess the size of the basins of stability of the stable steady states. Nonetheless, our qualitative analysis shows that the dynamics displayed by the system are already rich and more complex than just of a limit cycle type.[15]

4.6 Adding Keynesian Dual Forces

In thinking about the 2D system studied above, an econometrician's point of view would be of heavy criticism about the assumed and unnecessary restrictions on the influence of the levels of the two variables considered onto their respective rates of growth. Such influences should, in principle, not be denied to exist, and their empirical validity should be assessed using the available data. What we will try to do in the remaining part of the chapter is indeed to consider not only the cross-dual dynamics, but to introduce dependence of $\hat{u}, \hat{v}$ on their respective levels. This attempt can be seen as an effort to combine the model by Flaschel and Krolzig (2006) with the one by Barbosa-Filho and Taylor (2006) in the nonlinear setup of this chapter.

The first force to consider is the effect of the level of the wage share on its own rate of growth. In order to characterise this relation, affecting the reduced form of their model, Barbosa-Filho and Taylor (2006) use a combination of two arguments. The first one is based on an 'induced technical progress' relation between the level of the wage share and the rate of growth of labour productivity, known in the literature as Kaldor-Verdoorn equation. Generally, this effect is positive since higher wages to pay will induce firms to adopt more labour-saving techniques; however, the size of the parameter has to be estimated.

The second argument is that the bargaining power of the labour force increases with the wage share. Thus, the real wage rate of growth $\hat{\omega}$ should depend positively on the wage share. Assuming both relations to be linear, if the magnitude of the Verdoorn coefficient is higher than the constant value $\partial\hat{\omega}/\partial v$, or in other words, if the induced technical change effect is higher than the bargaining power effect on the real wage, then the function $\hat{v}(v)$ should have a negative slope.

A different story with the same ending is told in Flaschel and Krolzig (2006). They assume that an increasing wage share will dampen the evolution of wage inflation, building on Blanchard and Katz (1999) to 'microfound' this negative relation with a bargaining argument.

What about the dependence of the growth rate of capacity utilisation $\hat{u}$ on its own level u? Since the capacity utilisation rate is defined as $u = X/K$, where X is output and K is the installed capacity, its rate of growth is then given by $\hat{u} = \hat{X} - \hat{K}$. Barbosa-Filho and Taylor (2006) provide linear equations for the output growth rate and for capacity growth rate:

$$\hat{X} = \alpha_0 + \alpha_u u + \alpha_v v$$
$$\hat{K} = \beta_0 + \beta_u u + \beta_v v$$

There is a general consensus on the basic Keynesian stability condition $\partial\dot{X}/\partial X < 0$ to hold. Translated into the present framework this means $\alpha_u < 0$. One has, however, to consider also the effect of an increase in the capital utilisation rate on the productive capacity of the economy. Generally, capital formation responds positively to the level of economic activity (which can be interpreted as an acceleration principle). It follows immediately that the rate of growth of capacity is negatively affected by the level of capacity utilisation.[16] Equation (4.4) is then to be modified as follows:

$$\hat{u} = \beta_{uv}(v - \bar{v}) - \beta_{uu}(u - \bar{u}), \beta_{uu} > 0, \tag{4.6}$$

$$\text{with } \beta_{uv} \begin{cases} > 0 & \text{if the economy is wage-led} \\ < 0 & \text{if the economy is profit-led} \end{cases}$$

and is now interacting with an ODE that is augmented by a negative impact of the real wage on its rate of growth, represented by $-\beta_{vv}(v - \bar{v})$, in the dynamical analysis to be conducted below.

Defining $\bar{b} = \beta_{uu}\bar{u} - \beta_{uv}\bar{v} > 0$, the isocline $\dot{u} = 0$ will be of the form:

$$v = -\frac{\bar{b}}{\beta_{uv}} + \frac{\beta_{uu}\beta_{uv}}{u}$$

and it will have a positive intercept and negative slope in the plane (u, v) if the economy is profit-led, or a negative intercept and positive slope if the economy is wage-led. The other isocline is again given by:

$$\dot{v} = 0: \quad v = \bar{v} + \frac{\kappa\left[(1-\kappa_p)\beta_w(u-\bar{u}) - (1-\kappa_w)\beta_{pu}(u-\bar{u})\right]}{\beta_{vv}}$$

It is qualitatively seen identical to what is shown in Figure 4.6, but quantitatively rescaled by the parameters $\beta_{vv}, \bar{v}$, as shown above.

We stress again that the simple profit-squeeze phase plots of part I of the book (where the economy was not demand led at all) have become quite involved here by way of the assumption of two interacting Phillips curves and in particular due to the two different Keynesian demand regimes that now characterise the working of the economy.

4.7 Stability Analysis of the Full 2D System

We are now able to fully characterise the dynamics of the economy according to the features of the demand regime. The Jacobian matrix at the steady states is now given by:

$$J = \begin{pmatrix} -\beta_{uu}u_o & \beta_{uv}u_o \\ \kappa[(1-\kappa_p)\beta'_w(\cdot) - (1-\kappa_w)\beta_{pu}]v_o & -\beta_{vv}v_o \end{pmatrix}$$

in the profit-led case, $\beta_{uv} < 0$. Thus, when $(1-\kappa_p)\beta'_w(\cdot) > (1-\kappa_w)\beta_{pu}$, that is when the distributive curve has a positive slope, the determinant is positive. Given the negative trace, both real parts of eigenvalues of the matrix are negative, and an equilibrium corresponding to this situation is asymptotically stable. Conversely, when the slope of the locus $\dot{v} = 0$ is negative, the corresponding equilibrium will be a saddlepoint, as before. Figure 4.8 displays the phase diagram corresponding to a profit-led economy when the slope of the locus $\dot{u} = 0$ is such that the two curves intersect three times. As shown in the figure, the dynamics around the steady states E_1 and E_3 feature the same counterclockwise behaviour, although the negative trace of the Jacobian matrix ensures the convergence of these oscillations towards the steady states. As in Barbosa-Filho and Taylor (2006), this is due to the positive slope of the distributive curve in these regions, meaning, in their terminology, that there is a stabilising profit-squeeze effect. On the other hand, since at the intermediate equilibrium E_2 the distributive curve has a negative slope and intersects the demand regime 'from above', this steady state is a saddle point.[17]

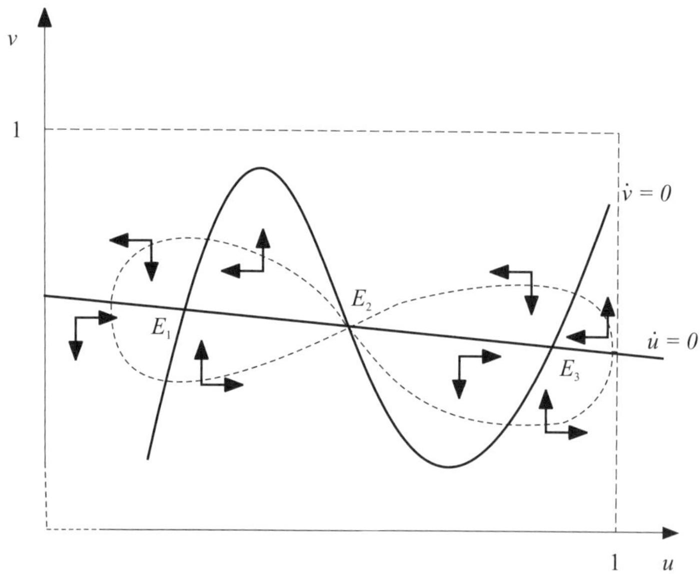

Figure 4.8 Phase diagram for the profit-led demand regime

The dynamics depicted in Figure 4.8 not only sheds further light on the corresponding 2D case, but also parallels closely enough the one-dimensional profit-led scenario. Imposing that both variables stay in the [0,1] interval, we have two areas in which the wage share and the capital utilisation rate will rotate counterclockwise around some equilibrium value, eventually converging to it, unless the system sits on the unique saddle path: in this case it will converge to the intermediate equilibrium E_2. Notice also that, since $\frac{\partial \hat{v}}{\partial v} = -\beta_{vv} < 0$, the equilibrium E_3 will correspond to the steady state 3 in Figure 4.3, whereas E_1 will be equivalent to equilibrium 1 in Figure 4.3. Figure 4.8 can be seen as somewhat combining the two cases discussed in Barbosa-Filho and Taylor (2006) with regard to the US economy (1948–2001):[18] the economy studied displays generally a stabilising profit squeeze effect, but in the period 1955–1970 the forced saving switch in the distributive curve determines an unstable equilibrium. However, while in their paper they found a demand regime steeper than the distributive curve, here the opposite is true. Thus, our intermediate equilibrium E_2 is only saddle path stable. Of course, the slope of the demand regime matters, in what determines how many equilibria we will find in our system.[19]

Given the negative slope of the demand regime in this case, we find a trade-off between short run growth and egalitarian distribution, which is a traditional feature of a profit-led economy:[20] in order to stimulate the economy towards a higher capital utilisation rate over the business cycle, a reduction in the wage share is needed. Note finally with respect to Figure 4.8 that there is of course a fourth steady state at the origin of the phase space (that cannot be reached from the positive orthant). Moreover, due to the existence of three interior steady state positions it is no longer clear how the NAIRU can be defined in such a framework.

We note again the possibility for hyperinflation processes top right (to be stopped by wage–price freezes among other possibilities) and the possibility for deflationary spirals top left in the phase diagram which may call for massive fiscal stimuli – like in Japan during its period of deflationary pressure which started in the early 1990s – but not for monetary policy within the context of this model.[21]

A wage-led demand regime leads to some complications. Since the locus $\dot{u} = 0$ has a negative intercept on the v-axis, an equilibrium with a very low rate of both capital utilisation and wage share could disappear, as is shown in Figure 4.9. According to the slope of the demand regime curve, there is even the possibility that the only surviving steady state is an intermediate one.

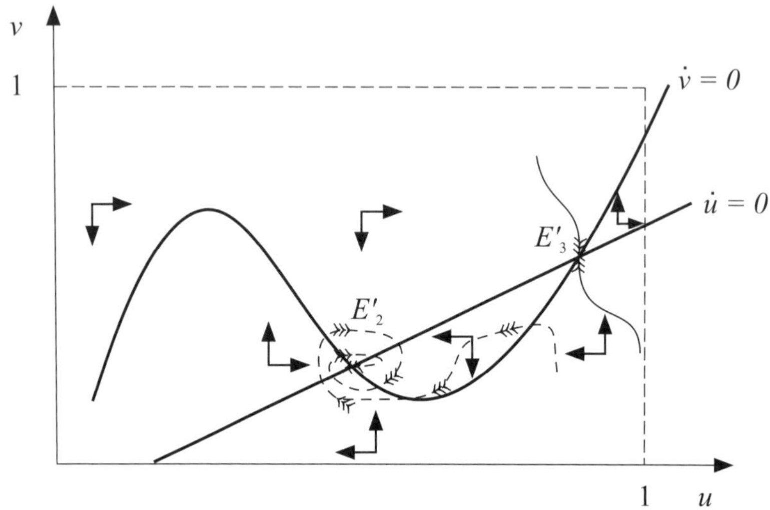

Figure 4.9 Phase diagram for the wage-led demand regime

Even this situation, however, matches our 1D findings in Figure 4.4: looking at the Jacobian matrix, given the positive value of β_{uv}, when the slope of the distributive curve is negative, the determinant will be positive, and the negative trace will ensure stability. Then, the clockwise oscillations around an intermediate equilibrium like E_2' will converge eventually to that steady state. Conversely, when $(1-\kappa_p)\beta_w'(\cdot) > (1-\kappa_w)\beta_{pu}$, the corresponding equilibrium will be a saddle. We observe again that the wage-led case is counterfactual to the empirical situation found to characterise the US economy after World War II: not only the long-phase cycle found to exist, but also most of the business cycles around it have a counterclockwise orientation.[22] On the basis of empirical observations about the economy we are studying, we therefore go no further in analysing a wage-led effective demand scenario.

Note also the difference between the two different scenarios in terms of policy implications. In a profit-led economy, starting from an equilibrium like E_1, a demand-based stimulus (restriction) to economic activity needs to be very strong to be effective. If this is the case, it will lead to a situation of the type E_3 (respectively E_1), but will pay a price in terms of distributive conflicts. Due to the stability features of both E_1 and E_3, if the strength of the policy measure is not enough, a demand shock can be ineffective in reaching the policy makers' *desiderata*. On the other hand, in a wage-led scenario, if the economy is in (or around) equilibrium, a further stimulus to the economic activity can have a very hard time in achieving the desired effects, because of the uniqueness of the stable saddle path ensuring convergence to an equilibrium like E_3. On the other hand, if policy makers acting in a wage-led economy deem it overheated at an equilibrium like E_3 they will find easy ways to sort the desired effects by adopting restrictive policy measures, but they will pay the price of a lower wage share.

The analysis of these two different kinds of asymmetry in the effectiveness of demand policy deserves further attention, and is left for future research here, together with deeper considerations about the mechanisms behind the agents' inflationary expectations.

4.8 The US Distributive Cycle after WWII

In the empirical phase plots shown in Figure 4.10, we depict an estimated long phase cycle as against the six business cycles that were observed in the considered time span in the US economy (bottom right and left). As shown in Kauermann et al. (2007) by specific measures, all business cycles have by and large the same counterclockwise orientation as the long-phase cycle. The bottom right figure seems to suggest that the depressed business cycles are at most two in number. In the figures top right and left we show in addition the time series (by dots) that was used in the estimations as well as in the long phase fluctuations and the business fluctuations around them.[23]

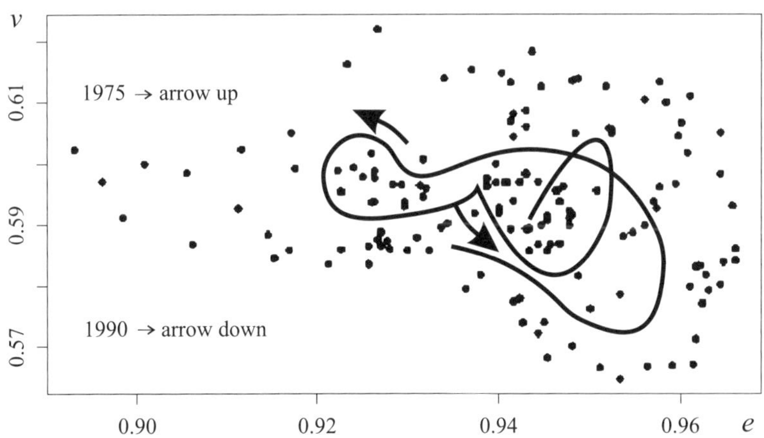

Figure 4.10 Long phase and business cycles in the US economy after World War II

Inspecting the measured long phase cycle for the US economy in more detail shows – in contradiction to the phase plots one relates with the Goodwin (1967) growth cycle model – that (top left in this figure) the wage share can increase again during phases of significant unemployment of both labour and capital, in fact after a Goodwin-like phase of decline due to the rise in unemployment (fall in the employment rate). This further Goodwin loop – which is not possible in the many conventional studies of Goodwin's growth cycle model – is perfectly in line with what we have derived in Figure 4.8 and it shows that the depressed area in this figure is indeed relevant for one episode in the evolution of the distributional conflict in the US economy.

We stress again that the situations depicted in Figure 4.10 reject the case of a wage-led economy, but support it in the just discussed form in the case of the intermediate occurrence of goods-market led regime.[24]

We conclude that this simple model of a wage–price spiral is already rich enough to allow for somewhat persistent periods of booms, and for considerably long depressions that may need economic policy interventions aimed at avoiding economic breakdown along the trajectories of the dynamics in certain parts of the phase space.

4.9 Conclusions

In this chapter, we studied the effects of a nonlinearity in the demand pressure term of a wage Phillips curve in a structuralist macro model considering the dynamic interaction between the distributive curve and the demand regime of an economy. To do so, we borrowed both from Flaschel and Krolzig (2006) and Barbosa-Filho and Taylor (2006). Considering a simplified 1D case in which a dynamic demand regime equation is inserted into the reduced form wage–price spiral, we found that:

i) in a profit-led scenario there are two stable extreme equilibria, corresponding respectively to a low level of the wage share and to a high one, and one unstable intermediate equilibrium;
ii) in a wage-led economy there is a single stable steady state for an intermediate level of the wage share and two saddle-path stable equilibria featuring respectively a low or a high level of the wage share which determine the corridor of viability of the economy.

The explicit consideration of the demand regime in a 2D system, featuring only the cross-dual interactions between v and u, led to a more complex characterisation of the dynamic properties of the economy. We found that, in the profit-led case, the two extreme, stable equilibria display counterclockwise dynamics, while the intermediate steady state is only saddle-path stable. In the wage-led case, the intermediate stable steady state features clockwise dynamics, the (one or two, depending on the slope of the demand regime) extreme one(s) being saddle point(s). However, in this case, considering only the cross-dual dynamics, it is not possible, in principle, to determine whether the Goodwin-style equilibria are attractors, because of the purely imaginary roots of the characteristic polynomial of the Jacobian matrix.

Finally, allowing not only the cross-dual effects but also own effects on the two variables, whose dynamic behaviour we have studied, permits us to better characterise otherwise somewhat foggy dynamics, and to better qualify and assess the findings of the simple 1D case we considered as a starting theoretical point of this chapter.

The synthesis of the Marxian distributive cycle with the Keynesian theory of effective demand we have presented in this chapter of course needs to be extended in the direction of the study of Keynesian fiscal policy rules of the type we will consider in Chapter 8,[25] here however with the state of the business cycle as its core argument in place of, or in addition to, the debt to capital ratio we use in this chapter. Interpreting the fixed-price bonds of Chapter 8 as money (which they from a broader perspective in fact are) then also allows us to integrate monetary policy in the demand-driven distributive cycle of this chapter. It may then be argued that Greenspan's low interest rate policy (easy money policy) to fight deflationary forces may not have been the right policy to pursue, since strong fiscal stimulus may have been the better (the Keynesian) choice in such a situation, which could also have helped to prevent the subprime crisis, caused by too much liquidity and too much carelessness in the economy, and the banking and state crises that followed.

Using a strongly countercyclical Keynesian fiscal policy was however not really an option from the viewpoint of mainstream economics before the advent of the current financial crises. In the case of our model it would in essence make the entry J_{11} in the Jacobian more negative and thus the $\dot{u}-$isocline shown in Figure 4.8 steeper. The figure shows that this would move the equilibria E_1, E_3 closer to each other in the horizontal direction and thus probably reduce the size of the fluctuations of the employment rate of both capital and labour. In the extreme case of a $\dot{u}-$isocline which has become steeper than the backward bending part of the $\dot{v}-$isocline the economy would no longer exhibit three equilibria, but then only a single and a stable one, where however some sort of intermediate NAIRU rate of employment becomes established. In such a situation, though the economy is still goods-market led, we have a Keynesian dynamic multiplier process that is of such a stable nature that it overcomes the centrifugal forces of the profit-led demand component.

It may however well be that relying on Keynesian demand management in the market for goods provides too little influence on an economy which is driven by a wage–price spiral and the distributive cycle in the long-run. Wage management in a corporatist setup may therefore be an unavoidable next step in the evolution of modern capitalist economies. The discussion of this chapter has hopefully shown that such income policies may be much more appropriate than the uncontrolled working of the distributive cycle we considered theoretically (and empirically: for the US economy after WWII) in this chapter.

Notes

[1] This chapter is based on Flaschel, P., Tavani, D., Taylor, L. and T. Teuber (2008).

[2] See also Flaschel, Kauermann and Semmler (2007) for a nonparametric estimation of the wage–price spiral and the PcGets estimate of this spiral in Flaschel and Krolzig (2006).

[3] As in Flaschel, Tavani, Taylor and Teuber (2008).

[4] The results of this chapter came indeed as a surprise, see Tavani, Flaschel and Taylor (2011) for their first publication.

[5] Adapted from Hirsch and Smale (1974, p.240)

[6] In their model, the authors consider, in both equations, error-corrections for the deviation of the wage share from a certain level v_0. For reasons of expositional simplicity, we do not analyse in this chapter the consequences of this augmentation in both the money wage and the price Phillips curve.

[7] See Okun (1970) for the original formulation.

[8] However, we will see later on that the NAIRU concept itself is made ambiguous by implications of this functional form.

[9] Note that we use the deviations $u - \bar{u}$ also in the nonlinear money wage Phillips curve as reference by simple variable substitution.

[10] In the terminology we used above, this curve shows that the economy is labour-market led around E_1 and E_3, but goods-market led around E_2. In the case of the 2D dynamics we will consider later on, the curve will be an isocline (in rescaled form).

[11] This is different from Rose's (1967) original situation of a single steady state (despite the presence of our nonlinear money wage Phillips curve in this early model of employment dynamics) and the difference is due

to the different type of wage–price spiral that is used in Rose's original contribution.

12 It is easily seen that the steady state corresponding to the intersection between the horizontal isocline $v = v_o$ and the vertical one $u = u_2$ is a saddle, because of the negative value of the determinant of the Jacobian evaluated at that point.

13 See Figure 4.10 and its discussion below.

14 A case resembling the situation in Germany in the late 1960s and early 1970s where full employment of the labour force was given and where wages were increasing significantly.

15 See the quotations from Hirsch and Smale (1974) in this matter.

16 Note that we have assumed $\dot{x} = 0$ in our model, meaning that a profit-led scenario will occur if $\beta_v > 0$ and a wage-led scenario if $\beta_v < 0$.

17 Note that in contrast to Figure 4.7 the equilibria E_1, E_3 in Figure 4.8 are attracting ones and that the cycles are here clockwise in orientation (and the saddlepaths are attracting outside, not inside trajectories.

18 Although in their paper, they have explicit time series thresholds for the change in slope. The explanation we provide is in terms of quantitative values of the two variables of interest.

19 Note however that the case in which the locus $\dot{u} = 0$ is so steep that there is only one intermediate equilibrium requires an intercept of the curve higher than 1, and this is a case we would like to rule out from the analysis. Naturally, the last word has to be said by the econometricians, but we proceed here assuming that the $\dot{u} = 0$-isocline is sufficiently flat.

20 See among others Naastepad (2006).

21 See Chapter 5 for the consideration of fiscal policy in the context of the Goodwin (1967) model.

22 See Proaño, C., Flaschel, P., Krolzig, H.-M. and M. B. Diallo (2011).

23 Note here that the cycle shown in Figure 4.10 has been derived by HP-filtering which reduces the volatility of the actual data (shown by circles) considerably.

24 It must however be noted, in this respect, that we used the employment rate in place of capacity utilisation. This is because the assumed one-to-one relation between the two variables assumed throughout has no parallel in actual data.

25 See also Chiarella and Flaschel (2000), Chiarella, Flaschel and Franke (2005) and Chiarella, Flaschel and Semmler (2012a,b) with respect to Keynesian approaches to macrodynamics which integrate the wage–price spiral.

5. Banking, Financial Markets and the Narrow Banking Idea

The recommendations in this report aim to create a more stable and competitive basis for UK banking in the longer term. That means much more than greater resilience against future financial crises and removing risks from banks to the public finances. It also means a banking system that is effective and efficient at providing the basic banking services of safeguarding retail deposits, operating secure payments systems, efficiently channelling savings to productive investments, and managing financial risk. To those ends there should be vigorous competition among banks to deliver the services required by well-informed customers. Independent Commission on Banking (2011, p.7)

5.1 Introduction

In this chapter[1] we model the problematic role of modern banking – besides their traditional role as credit institutions – when banks are also acting as investment banks, by concentrating specifically on their stock market activities as a possible substitute for credit creation. We show that such a mixed orientation of the activities of commercial banks is endangered by unstable feedback structures which can imply that the steady state of the economy becomes repelling, if 'Minsky Drifts' are at work which drive crucial financial parameters beyond certain critical values. In contrast to such a situation of broad banking we will then provide a model of narrow banking and of Fisher's (1935) 100% money idea where such tendencies towards real-financial market instability are eliminated through legal restraints. Moreover, this model will also show that such a narrow banking system (where trade in equities is excluded from the behaviour of commercial banks) is not only safe with respect to bank runs, but also dynamically stable and also efficient in the credit supply it generates or the credit demand it serves. The chapter therefore not only suggests to separate traditional banking from investment banking, but also to base credit on the creation of time deposits only, while checkable deposits are secured by very high (in the ideal 100%) reserves. With respect to checkable deposits commercial banks are therefore reduced to the role of depositary institutions and thus not allowed to create money and loans out of deposits for which they pay no interest. All perfectly liquid assets are therefore then under the full control of the central bank.

Over the last 25 years a great deal of research has demonstrated both theoretically and empirically how the financial markets, and especially the commercial banking sector amplify – through the financial accelerator mechanism put forward by Bernanke and Gertler (1989) – developments that originated in the real side of the economy. As pointed out by Bordo (2007), the prominent role of credit in the amplification of shocks has been acknowledged for a long time already. According to Kindleberger and Aliber (2005), it is the instability of credit that leads to macrofinancial instability, while for Minsky (1982, 1986) it is the way financing becomes de-linked from collateral which contributes to a downward spiral once large real or financial shocks occur. In recent times, however, the role and extent of commercial banking itself and the issue of whether it adds to macroeconomic instability has become the focus of a large body of literature, see Adrian, Moench and Shin (2010), Brunnermeier and Sannikov (2010), and Gorton (2009, 2010).

This is the more so the more the traditional banks have been turned into investment banks. As Gorton (2010) shows in earlier times loan losses and bank runs were usually the way crises were triggered, but in recent times banking crises seem to be strongly related to adverse shocks in asset prices. This is occurring when banks have significantly invested in capital assets. One might want to show how such asset accumulation of banks can lead to a channel through which some exacerbating or even destabilising effects on the macroeconomy can be generated.

In this chapter we pursue a rather traditional route and model in the first instance a broad banking system characterised by the non-separation of commercial and investment banking. Such a system was put in place by the partial repeal of the Glass-Steagall Act of 1933 and the Bank Holding Company Act of 1956 through the Gramm-Leach-Bliley Act of 1999.[2] Thereafter we contrast such a system with a narrow banking system, characterised by a Fisherian 100 percent reserve ratio for checkable deposits and the exclusion of trade in stocks and other assets from commercial bank activities. We use a minimal structure of financial assets to reconsider the issue of broad versus narrow banking: a risky asset (equities E) and two types of deposits, checkable and time (saving) deposits D_c and D_t, respectively, besides high powered money H supplied by the central bank. In particular we focus on the destabilising credit channel effect that comes into operation if commercial banks are strongly stock market oriented in their decision on new loan supplies.

In contrast, we then explore what it means for macroeconomic stability and loan supply efficiency if the banking sector of the economy is simply a narrowly defined depository institution with respect to pure money holdings and is primarily concerned with channelling the flow of savings (time deposits) into investment flows, where banks act as credit creators, generating endogenous credit, however not endogenous money. As we will show, such an economy is characterised by strong stability features. In our view this situation is to be preferred to that of broad or excessive banking, that is commercial bank money creation in combination with speculative stock market activities which may be more flexible with respect to large upturns in investment booms, but that may be dangerous in opposite situations, where risk management has failed to work, and in cases where large bankruptcy scenarios (banks, firms and also governments) can have dramatic chain effects on the working of the national and the world economy.

The remainder of this chapter is organised as follows: In the next section the general theoretical framework featuring a broad banking system is introduced by means of the discussion of the balance sheets and flow accounts of the different sectors of the economy. We there also introduce the share price dynamics and its interaction with the broad banking system of this section. In Section 5.3 the stability properties of a broad banking macro-financial system are discussed and compared with what happened under 'Excessive Banking' before and after the subprime crisis in the US economy. Thereafter, in Section 5.4 the model is modified towards a narrow banking system and its stability and efficiency properties are analysed. Finally, Section 5.5 concludes.

5.2 The Theoretical Framework

For the sake of expositional clarity we introduce the theoretical model by way of balance sheets and flow accounts for the four sectors of the economy: firms, commercial banks, households and the central bank. We do not consider goods price inflation and normalise the corresponding price level at 1. The only variable price of the model is the share price p_e.

We model the economy first with a completely passive central bank and commercial banks that create loans by selling equities on the stock market to the household sector (and vice versa with respect to credit reduction). Moreover they can create new deposits by providing loans through what we shall call 'ink stroke money', which they generate when loans reappear at first as checkable deposits in the household sector – possibly transferred into time-deposits thereafter. This latter process of credit creation will however only concern us in its details when the concept of a narrow banking system is introduced and compared with a broad banking system.

Firms

We assume that firms finance their investment into capital stock formation $\dot{K}$ through the issue of equities $\dot{E}^s$ and the additional use of new loans $\dot{\Lambda}$ as external sources. In the analysis of this chapter, however, we will abstract from the feedback effects of the accumulation of assets $\dot{E}$ and $\dot{K} = I$ (investment). Further, since the Metzlerian inventory adjustment process is not incorporated into the present framework, inventories $\mathcal{I}$ are just adjusted passively to the difference between aggregate supply and demand $Y - Y^d = \dot{\mathcal{I}}$, the former being determined by a dynamic multiplier process to be discussed later. These variables are summarised in Table 5.1.

Table 5.1 Balance sheet of the firms (f)

Assets	Liabilities
capital stock pK $[p = 1]$	loans Λ
inventories $\mathcal{I}$	equities $p_e E$
	net worth

Let us now consider the firms' production and investment behaviour in more detail. As usual, we assume that firms produce an output good Y using labour L and capital K (financed partly through loans Λ) as input factors. A specific formulation of such a production function is however not needed here: For our argument, it is sufficient to define the firms' profits (net of depreciation) as

$$\Pi_f = Y - wL - i_l\Lambda - r(Y)E - \delta K,$$

where w denotes the wage rate, L the level of employment (which is assumed to be a function of output with $L'(Y) > 0$). The symbol i_l

denotes the loan rate and δ the depreciation rate of the capital stock. We assume that the dividend rate r per unit of equity is a positive function of the level of output Y, such that

$$r = r(Y) \quad \text{with } r'(Y) > 0 \quad \text{holds.} \tag{5.1}$$

Retained profits Π_f are determined residually as shown above.

The direct transfer of income from firms to the household sector consists of labour compensation and dividend payments, that is

$$Y_{fh} = wL + rE_h, \tag{5.2}$$

where E_h is the stock of equities held by the household sector. Retained profits are calculated on the basis of output (not demand) as is customarily done in the literature.

As for net investment I, we assume that it depends positively on capacity utilisation and thus on Y and also positively on the state of confidence in the economy which we measure by the deviation of the share price p_e from its steady state value p_{eo}, and negatively on the firms' level of leverage, thus

$$I(Y, p_e, \Lambda) = \gamma_y Y + \gamma_e(p_e - p_{eo})E + \gamma_l(\Lambda_o - \Lambda) + \bar{I} \tag{5.3}$$

with $\gamma_y > 0$, $\gamma_e > 0$ and $\gamma_l > 0$.

The three sources for the financing of new investment are retained profits Π_f (which are assumed to be determined residually), new loans $\dot{\Lambda}$ and the issue of equities. Concerning the demand of firms for loans, we assume that it is determined by[3]

$$\dot{\Lambda}(Y, i_l) \;=\; \lambda_y (Y - Y_o) - \lambda_i(i_l - i_{lo}), \quad \lambda_y > 0, \lambda_i > 0, \tag{5.4}$$

where i_l is the loan rate (the determinants of which will be discussed below). We assume that this demand is fully served by the commercial banking sector. Table 5.2 summarises the flow account of the entrepreneurial sector.

Table 5.2 Flow account of the entrepreneurial sector

Uses	Resources
depreciation δK	
wage payments $wL > 0$	
loan payments $i_l \Lambda$	
dividends rE	
retained profits (or losses) Π_f	output Y

Commercial Banks

As previously mentioned, the term 'broad banking' characterises a financial system where the activities of commercial banks are not restrained to their classical role of interrelating households' real savings with the real investment of firms, but where the commercial banks also engage themselves in financial investment activities. As it was already acknowledged through the creation of the second Glass-Steagall Act of 1933, if the same entity (in this case, the commercial banks) is engaged in both lending (the granting of credit) and financial investment (the use of credit from the household sector), a conflict of interest is quite likely to occur. As was previously mentioned, the Glass-Steagall Act of 1933 greatly restricted the ability of banks to conduct such activities. Such a separation between commercial and investment banking institutions was however abolished by the Gramm-Leach-Bliley Act of 1999, see Barth et al. (2000).

In order to reflect such a broad banking system within our theoretical framework, we thus assume that commercial banks do not provide firms with new loans $\dot{\Lambda}$ out of checkable and time deposits D_c and D_t at a rate i_l (a rate which they set and control), but rather that they use their equities from the entrepreneurial sector $p_e E_b$, as illustrated in the balance sheet of the commercial banking sector, see Table 5.3. We thus consider primarily a process of asset substitution under broad banking and leave the generation of deposits that finance loans to later sections on narrow banking activities (which of course can also be present in the situation where broad banking is considered).

Table 5.3 Balance sheet of the commercial banking sector (b)

Assets	Liabilities
reserves $R\ (= H_b = \rho_b D_c)$	households' $c-$deposits D_c
loans Λ	households' $t-$deposits D_t
equities (from firms) $p_e E_b$	net worth

Apart from assuming that the loan rate set by commercial banks depends positively on the state of the business cycle, we model the conflict of interest of the commercial banks as arising from the non-separation between commercial and investment banking activities by assuming that, as the prospective returns in the equity markets increase, banks demand a higher interest rate on loans from firms to balance the profits of the two investment activities, and we write

$$i_l(Y, r_e^e) = i_{lo} + \mu_y (Y - Y_o) + \mu_e(r_e^e - r_{eo}^e) \tag{5.5}$$

where $\mu_y(> 0)$ represents the reaction of the loan rate with respect to the relative level of economic activity (measured by the difference between actual and steady state output) and where $\mu_e(> 0)$ reflects the extent of stock-market orientation of the commercial banks (r_e^e is the expected rate of return on equities to be defined below). The effect of such a specification of the loan rate is straightforward: if for example a stock market boom takes place, the commercial banks will increase the loan rate, which reduces the entrepreneurial sector demand for loans and thus the level of economic activity.[4]

To keep our model as parsimonious as possible we consider the interest rate on time deposits i_t as a given magnitude. Checkable deposits represent money endogenously generated by the commercial banking system through their loans (a process we will investigate in detail in a later section of the chapter). With respect to central bank money it is important to note that in the present framework the potential money multiplier is given by

$$M = D_c + H_h = \frac{1 + \rho_h}{\rho_b + \rho_h} H \equiv t_m H,$$

where $H(= H_h + R)$ denotes the high powered money issued by the central bank, and $H_h = \rho_h D_c$, and $R = \rho_b D_c$ represent the cash holdings of households and the reserve requirements of commercial banks, respectively (a positive reserve requirement ratio $\rho_b > 0$ is assumed on $c-$deposits, but none on $t-$deposits).

Finally, we assume that the profits

$$\Pi_{bh} = i_l \Lambda + r E_b - i_t D_t \tag{5.6}$$

made by the commercial banks remain positive in this chapter and are transferred to their owners, the household sector. The flow account of the commercial banking sector is shown in Table 5.4.

Table 5.4 Flow account of the commercial banking sector

Uses	Resources
interest rate payments $i_t D_t$	loan rate payments $i_l \Lambda$
reserve adjustment $\dot{R} = 0$	change in $c-$deposits $\dot{D}_c = 0, \quad \rho_{b1} > 0$
distributed profits Π_{bh}	dividends rE_b
loans (credit demand of firms) $\dot{\Lambda} = p_e \dot{E}_b^s + \dot{D}_t$	change in $t-$deposits $\dot{D}_t, \ \rho_{b2} = 0$

Households

The balance sheet of households is by and large self-explanatory and shown in Table 5.5.

Table 5.5 Balance sheet of the household sector

Assets	Liabilities
cash H_h	
$c-$deposits D_c	
$t-$deposits D_t	
Equities $p_e E_h$	

For simplicity we assume that private consumption is a linear function of households' income and thus of the activity level of the economy, and as in the investment function, of our measure of the state of confidence $(p_e - p_{eo})E$. Thus we write

$$C = \varsigma_y Y + \varsigma_e (p_e - p_{eo})E + \bar{C} \qquad (\varsigma_y > 0, \varsigma_e > 0). \qquad (5.7)$$

The flow account of the household sector (Table 5.6) mirrors these different activities and moreover shows again how loans are financed through the creation of time deposits. Due to these operations we assume that the savings of households go into the new equity supply of firms and the time deposits generated by the banking system. The aggregate income of households consists of wage income, dividend income and loan rate income (which includes income from time-deposit, but is reduced by defaulting loans).

Table 5.6 Flow account of the household sector

Uses	Resources
consumption C	wages wL
change in cash holdings $\dot{H}_h = 0$	interest on $t-$deposits $i_t D_t$
$c-$deposit change $\dot{D}_c = 0$	dividends $r(E_h + E_c)$
$t-$deposit change $\dot{D}_t$	banks' profit $\Pi_{bh} = i_l \Lambda + rE_b - i_t D_t$
households' equity demand $\dot{p}_e E_h^d$	
income Y_h	$wL + rE + i_l \Lambda$

Note that we simplify dividend distribution by assuming that all dividends are channelled back (one way or the other) into the household sector, that the savings of households are directed towards the demand of new equities solely and that their portfolio is modified by the loan-equity exchange of commercial banks. Finally, note also that dividends are paid per unit of equity and not per unit of value of the stocks and are thus independent of the occurrence of stock market rallies.

The Monetary Authority

It is currently assumed that the monetary authority is completely inactive, but has accumulated through its open market operations (which in this model can only concern the equity market) financial assets in the past. Table 5.7 shows the balance sheet of the central bank.

Table 5.7 Balance sheet of the central bank (c)

Assets	Liabilities
equities of firms $p_e E_c$	high powered money (cash) $H = H_h + R$
	net worth

Share Price Dynamics

Concerning the dynamics of equity prices we assume for simplicity that they are determined by the portfolio choice (desired portfolio readjustment) between money plus $t-$deposits $M + D_t$ and equities E

at the aggregate level.[5] Here we use a dynamic approach in place of a Tobinian equilibrium determination of the share price by assuming that a stock imbalance in the economy's gross portfolio, $p_eE^d - p_eE$, leads to a fractional flow demand for equities $\kappa_e(p_eE^d - p_eE)$, $\kappa_e \in (0,1)$,[6] which in turn generates a share price inflation (or deflation) according to

$$\hat{p}_e = \beta_e \kappa_e \left(\frac{p_eE^d - p_eE}{p_eE} \right), \tag{5.8}$$

with β_e the adjustment speed of share prices whereby equilibrium in the stock market is reestablished.

In the following we assume that the nominal demand for equities E^d is a function of the expected rate of return on this asset type, defined as

$$r_e^e = \frac{r(Y)}{p_eE} + \varepsilon_e, \tag{5.9}$$

where $r(Y)/(p_eE)$ denotes the dividend rate of return and ε_e the expected capital gains, that is

$$p_eE^d = f_e(r_e^e)E, \qquad f_e(r_{eo}^e)E = p_eE, \quad f_e^{'} > 0.$$

After inserting these expressions it can easily be seen that share price inflation (or deflation) is given by

$$\hat{p}_e = \beta_e \kappa_e \left(\frac{f_e(r_e^e)E - p_eE}{p_eE} \right)$$

or, by making use of (5.9) and the definition of $\hat{p}_e$, by

$$\dot{p}_e = \beta_e \kappa_e \left[f_e \left(\frac{r(Y)}{p_eE} + \varepsilon_e \right) - p_e \right]. \tag{5.10}$$

In order to model the trend-chasing feature of expected capital gains, observable in the real world, on the theoretical level one could use a scheme of nested adaptive expectations, as is done for instance in Flaschel et al. (2011), but we here simply use the conventional type of adaptive expectations formation

$$\dot{\varepsilon}_e \;=\; \beta_{\varepsilon_e}(\hat{p}_e - \varepsilon_e) = \beta_{\varepsilon_e} \left(\beta_e \kappa_e f_e \left(\frac{r(Y)}{p_e} + \varepsilon_e \right) - \varepsilon_e \right) \tag{5.11}$$

in order to not increase the dimension of the dynamics under consideration, without leading really to any increase in insight.

Viewed in isolation, the two laws of motion given by eqs. (5.10) and (5.11) – which show the dynamics of financial markets as primarily driven by the interaction between actual capital gains and expected ones – give rise to a two-dimensional system with the following Jacobian matrix (evaluated at the steady state)

$$J_o = \begin{pmatrix} \beta_e\kappa_e[-f_e'(\cdot)\frac{r(\cdot)}{p_e^2}]p_e & \beta_e\kappa_e f_e'(\cdot)p_e \\ \beta_{\varepsilon_e}\beta_e\kappa_e[-f_e'(\cdot)\frac{r(\cdot)}{p_e^2}] & \beta_{\varepsilon_e}[\beta_e\kappa_e f_e'(\cdot)-1] \end{pmatrix} = \begin{pmatrix} - & + \\ - & \pm \end{pmatrix}$$

Since the determinant of this matrix J is always positive, the local stability of this system depends solely on the trace of J. This gives rise to the critical stability condition

$$\beta_{\varepsilon_e}^H = \frac{\beta_e\kappa_e f_e'(\cdot)\frac{r(\cdot)}{p_e}}{\beta_e\kappa_e f_e'(\cdot)-1} > 0.$$

Asymptotic stability becomes lost at the Hopf-bifurcation point $\beta_{\varepsilon_e}^H$, where the system loses its stability in a cyclical fashion, in general through the disappearance of a stable corridor around the steady state or the birth of an attracting limit cycle (persistent fluctuations in share prices).

As discussed in Flaschel et al. (2011), by introducing a Tobin-like capital gains tax τ_e, or as other authors have proposed it: a transaction tax, with respect to the stock market, such instability features can however be suppressed. This modifies, in the case of a transactions tax, the second law of motion to

$$\dot{\varepsilon}_e = \beta_{\varepsilon_e}(\hat{p}_e - \varepsilon_e) = \beta_{\varepsilon_e}\left[\beta_e(1-\tau_e)\kappa_e f_e\left(\frac{r(Y)}{p_e} + \varepsilon_e\right) - \varepsilon_e\right]$$

and leads to

$$\beta_{\varepsilon_e}^H = \frac{\beta_e\kappa_e f_e'(\cdot)\frac{r(\cdot)}{p_e}}{\beta_e(1-\tau_e)\kappa_e f_e'(\cdot)-1} > 0$$

showing that the destabilising financial market accelerator can therefore always be tamed through the introduction of an appropriate level of Tobin taxation.[7] In the next section we analyse the feedback mechanisms and the stability properties of the theoretical model discussed above.

5.3 Feedback Mechanisms and Stability Properties under Broad Banking

The assumed major determinants of consumption and investment imply for the aggregate demand function the expression

$$Y^d = a_y Y + a_e(p_e - p_{eo})E - a_l(\Lambda - \Lambda_o) + \bar{A} \quad (a_y < 1), \qquad (5.12)$$

with $a_y = \varsigma_y + \gamma_y$, $a_e = \varsigma_e + \gamma_e$, $\bar{A} = \bar{C} + \bar{I} + \delta K$. The aggregate demand function is thus based on income effects (concerning both household consumption[8] and firm investment), state of confidence effects on firm and household goods demand, and self-discipline or enforced discipline of firms with respect to their level of debt. Further, we assume a gradual adjustment of the output level of firms of the form

$$\begin{aligned}\dot{Y} &= \beta_y(Y^d - Y)\\ &= \beta_y(a_y Y + a_e(p_e - p_{eo})E - a_l(\Lambda - \Lambda_o) + \bar{A} - Y).\end{aligned}$$

For the dynamics of the loan rate, after inserting the expressions for i_l and r_e^e into equation (5.4) for new loans, we obtain

$$\begin{aligned}\dot{\Lambda}(Y, i_l(Y, p_e)) &= \lambda_y (Y - Y_o) - \\ &\quad \lambda_i (i_{lo} + \mu_y (Y - Y_o) + \mu_e(r_e^e - r_{eo}^e) - i_{lo})\\ &= (\lambda_y - \lambda_i\mu_y)(Y - Y_o) - \\ &\quad \lambda_i\mu_e \left(\frac{r(Y)}{p_e} + \varepsilon_e - \frac{r(Y_o)}{p_{eo}} - \varepsilon_{eo}\right)\end{aligned}$$

In the following we will consider the interaction of share prices with the credit channel of the economy by keeping capital gains expectations at their steady state value ε_{eo} to keep our analysis as straightforward as possible.[9] Under this assumption the system of differential equations describing the development of the economy is

$$\begin{aligned}\dot{Y} &= \beta_y((a_y - 1)Y + a_e(p_e - p_{eo}) - a_l(\Lambda - \Lambda_o) + \bar{A}),\\ \dot{\Lambda} &= (\lambda_y - \lambda_i\mu_y)(Y - Y_o) - \lambda_i\mu_e\left(\frac{r(Y)}{p_e} - \frac{r(Y_o)}{p_{eo}}\right),\\ \dot{p}_e &= \beta_e\kappa_e\left[f_e\left(\frac{r(Y)}{p_e} + \varepsilon_{eo}\right) - p_e\right],\end{aligned}$$

with $Y_o(= \bar{A}/(1 - a_y))$, Λ_o and $p_{eo}(= r(Y_o)/i_{lo})$ as the steady state levels of the dynamic variables of the system.

Let us however focus first on the dynamic interaction of the real side of the economy by considering the subsystem given by the two laws of motions for Y and Λ keeping p_e at its steady state level p_{eo}. Thus we consider

$$\begin{aligned}\dot{Y} &= \beta_y((a_y-1)Y + a_e(p_e - p_{eo})E - a_l(\Lambda - \Lambda_o) + \bar{A}),\\ \dot{\Lambda} &= (\lambda_y - \lambda_i\mu_y)(Y - Y_o) - \lambda_i\mu_e\left(\frac{r(Y)}{p_e} - \frac{r(Y_o)}{p_{eo}}\right).\end{aligned}$$

The matrix of partial derivatives of the Jacobian of this system at the steady state is given by

$$\begin{aligned}J &= \begin{pmatrix}\beta_y(a_y-1) & -\beta_y a_l\\ \left(\lambda_y - \lambda_i\mu_y - \lambda_i\mu_e\frac{r'(Y_o)}{p_{eo}}\right) & 0\end{pmatrix}\\ &= \begin{pmatrix}- & -\\ \pm & 0\end{pmatrix}\end{aligned}$$

The matrix of partial derivatives shows that the credit channel describing the interaction of firm debt with economic activity determines whether the steady state of the system is stable or of an unstable saddle-point type depending on whether

$$\mu_e < \frac{p_{eo}}{\lambda_i r'(Y_o)}(\lambda_y - \lambda_i\mu_y) \qquad \text{or} \qquad \mu_e > \frac{p_{eo}}{\lambda_i r'(Y_o)}(\lambda_y - \lambda_i\mu_y).$$

The economic rationale of this result is straightforward: because an increase in output leads on the one hand to a higher demand for loans, but on the other hand to an increase in the loan interest rate and in dividends (due to $r'(Y) > 0$), and thus to an increase in r_e^e, the expected rate of return on equities, the final effect on the level of new loans $\dot{\Lambda}$ can be either positive or negative. If the effect is positive ($\partial\dot{\Lambda}/\partial Y > 0$), then the determinant of the Jacobian matrix will be positive and the steady state of the above subsystem will be locally stable. A higher output level will lead to new loans, and thus to a larger debt of the entrepreneurial sector which in turn will negatively affect the output dynamics, acting thus in a stabilising manner. On the contrary, if the partial derivative fulfills $\partial\dot{\Lambda}/\partial Y < 0$, then an increase in output will lead to a lower level of new loans, which in turn will influence the output dynamics in a positive and thus destabilising manner.

It should be clear that the net effect of Y on $\dot{\Lambda}$ depends very much not only on $r'(Y)$, but also on μ_e, the parameter representing the stock market orientation of the commercial banking sector. The larger μ_e the more negative will be the influence of Y on $\dot{\Lambda}$.

Let us now consider the model with the dynamic law of motion for the equity prices p_e included. We thus consider

$$\begin{aligned}
\dot{Y} &= \beta_y((a_y - 1)Y + a_e(p_e - p_{eo}) - a_l(\Lambda - \Lambda_o) + \bar{A}),\\
\dot{\Lambda} &= (\lambda_y - \lambda_i\mu_y)(Y - Y_o) - \lambda_i\mu_e\left(\frac{r(Y)}{p_e} - \frac{r(Y_o)}{p_{eo}}\right),\\
\dot{p}_e &= \beta_e\kappa_e\left[f_e\left(\frac{r(Y)}{p_e} + \varepsilon_{eo}\right) - p_e\right].
\end{aligned}$$

As can be observed, see Chiarella et al. (2011) for details, this Jacobian matrix has the following sign structure

$$J = \begin{bmatrix} - & - & + \\ \pm & 0 & + \\ + & 0 & - \end{bmatrix},$$

under the assumption that $f_e^{'}(\cdot)r(Y_o) > p_{eo}^2$ holds true.

According to the Routh–Hurwitz stability conditions for a 3D dynamical system, the steady state is asymptotic locally stable if and only if

$$\mu_e < \min\{\mu_e^{a_2}, \mu_e^{a_3}\}, \quad \text{where}$$

$$\mu_e^{a_2} = \frac{\beta_e\kappa_e[(1 - a_y)(\frac{f_e' r_o}{p_{eo}} - p_{eo}) - a_e f_e' r']}{a_l\lambda_i r'} + \frac{p_{eo}(\lambda_y - \lambda_i\mu_y)}{\lambda_i r'}$$

$$\mu_e^{a_3} = \frac{\frac{f_e^{'} r_o}{p_{eo}} - p_{eo}}{\lambda_i r'}(\lambda_y - \lambda_i\mu_y) = \frac{\frac{f_e^{'} r_o}{p_{eo}} - p_{eo}}{r'}(\frac{\lambda_y}{\lambda_i} - \mu_y).$$

This is shown in detail in Chiarella et al. (2011) and is thus not repeated here. On the basis of the assumption made above we have that $\mu_e^{a_3}$ will be positive if $\lambda_y > \lambda_i\mu_y$ holds true. In this case we then also get a positive $\mu_e^{a_2}$ if the parameter a_e in the aggregate demand function, representing its reaction to the state of confidence, is made sufficiently small. An increasing parameter λ_i in the credit demand function of firms narrows the range where μ_e is permitting stability (see the second condition). In addition to this, an increasing sensitivity of aggregate demand with respect to the state of confidence as measured by the price of shares also contributes to a broader range of instability scenarios (if the first condition is determining the minimum of the two).

These stability conditions for the original system basically corroborate the results for the two-dimensional system discussed above by way of the financial market orientation parameter μ_e. Within a similar framework the possibilities for the central bank to steer the economy in the context of broad banking were discussed in Flaschel et al. (2011). Since the rate of interest on $t-$deposits does not influence economic activity nor the financial markets in the context of the given model there remains for the central bank only the possibility to conduct open market operations through the purchase or sale of equities on the market for stocks (through trade with the household sector). As shown in Flaschel et al. (2011), however, such open market operations of the central bank do not really improve the stability properties of the dynamical system.

It should be noted that by making the parameter μ_e a function of the long-phased cycle (considered in the preceding chapter), a λ_i which is increasing relative to λ_y, when equity markets become more and more the focus of interest of commercial banks in phases of prosperous economic activity, the occurrence of what we call Minsky (1982, 1986) drifts – where overoptimism introduces sloppy attitudes towards risk management – may make the economy more and more fragile and volatile over time. Minsky type crises, caused by such increasingly sloppy banking habits, can therefore be introduced into the considered dynamics by the modelling of systematic changes in certain parameters of the model. Such instability occurrences are however still very limited in nature compared to what actually happened before and after the subprime crisis in the US economy as the following section will try to sketch.

Exuberant Banking and the Road to Systemic Crises

As already discussed in the general introduction, the basic problem in the broad understanding and the public control of the real-financial market interactions of an advanced capitalist economy like the US economy lies in the widespread disregard of Keynes's (1936) 'General Theory' in mainstream economic theory (and the journals controlled by it).

> *So here's what I think economists have to do. First, they have to face up to the inconvenient reality that financial markets fall far short of perfection, that they are subject to extraordinary delusions and the madness of crowds. Second, they have to admit – and this will be very hard for the people who giggled and whispered over Keynes – that Keynesian economics remains the best framework we have for making sense of recessions and depressions. Third, they'll have to do*

> *their best to incorporate the realities of finance into macroeconomics. Many economists will find these changes deeply disturbing.* (Paul Krugman, *New York Times*, September 6, 2009)

Starting with Sargent and Wallace's (1973) paper, the macro-economy was predominantly modelled by means of the jump-variable technique (marketed under the name of rational expectations). This technique by and large assumes in the deterministic part of the models that there is (if policy makes the economy determinate) a stable manifold of dimension $k < n$ around the steady state of a considered macrodynamics with n state variables and a set of uniquely determined $n - k$ non-predetermined state variables among all state variables which after some economic shock are always reacting (by assumption) such that the economy is placed back on the stable manifold and thus converges back to its steady state position. This happens in the case of unanticipated shocks, while anticipated shocks place the economy in the pre-shock dynamics on an explosive bubble which is chosen such that it passes the stable manifold exactly at the time where the shock will actually occur. The bubble is then switched off (by assumption) and the economy is again converging back to the steady state along its stable manifold. Such 'rational' expectations (represented through the non-predetermined variables) are also part of so-called New Keynesian models, where Walrasian market clearing is married with a theory of monopolistic competition, staggered wage and price setting and financial parity (equilibrium) conditions in their so-called DSGE prototypes.

All this has very little or even nothing to do with Keynes's (1936) General Theory of Employment, Interest and Money.[10] Rational expectation models and in particular Dynamic Stochastic General Equilibrium models generally only become alive as theory of the business cycle when their stochastic component becomes dominant. They are thus strictly based on the Frisch-Slutzky paradigm. In the case of the baseline DSGE model with staggered prices the economy even would not leave the steady state (in the region where it is determinate) if hit by single shocks, since its stable manifold consists of the steady state solely. Reading in particular Keynes's (1936, ch.22) 'Notes on the Trade Cycle' immediately reveals that such approaches are completely at odds with his views of the working of the economy. Business fluctuations are here generated endogenously and are persistent even without exogenous shocks which of course can be added to their deterministic core (the sole source of persistence in the New Keynesian approach).

One cannot, of course, prove on the theoretical level that Keynes was right and that the mainstream was totally misled by its leading representatives in the years following Friedman's (1968) presidential address at the American Economic Association. Ruling macroeconomic theories are disproved by their failure, which – if they are very hegemonic – needs to be massive in order to fulfill this task. And it may well happen that there is just a return to the 'normality' of a market-clearing, representative agent based rational expectations theory when the currently more open-minded discussion on and application of alternative views have done their job and by and large overcome the crisis.[11] Minsky's (1982) question 'Can it happen again?' and his analysis that capitalism tends to systematic instabilities over the longer run may then be superseded again by a return to laissez-faire and deregulation-supportive theories.

The bursting bubble in the US housing market was the point of departure for the current global financial crisis. In the years 2004–2006, subprime lending increased as a proportion of all mortgage lending from under 10% to around 20% by a single leap, supported by an anti-deflationary low interest rate policy (by Alan Greenspan), the homeownership policy of George W. Bush, but primarily caused by widespread credit market liberalisations (even long before George W. Bush came into office), which in the case of subprime lending was subject to circumventive contract practices in addition. This liberalisation of mortgage markets meant a shift from local banks to national and global financial markets and subprime lending became a really important business. Instead of a price volatility moderation by improved credit allocation, markets were swept with liquidity. Cheap finance combined with an illegitimate practice of lending to private clients without sufficient income fired the price rally first and laid the foundation for the following breakdown. Risks were no longer assessed in a reasonable way for the low-income borrowers. This led to a tremendous underestimation of default risk and became later the reason for breaking credit chains and an enduring distrust of banks among themselves.

Problems started when the Fed had to increase interest rates and when adjustable monthly loan rates could no longer be afforded by a large part of the banking clients. Prime and subprime mortgages had meanwhile been bundled and sold in the US and internationally in the form of asset backed securities, creating longer financial chains between the initial borrowers and the final holder of such assets. The asset backed character of securities however disappeared through the dramatic decline in housing prices around the year 2007 and even through rapid physical obsolescence or demolition of whole urban areas in the USA. Securities became toxic papers in large amounts through increasing correlations in their risk structures. In August 2007, Lehman Brothers had to close its subprime lender, BNC Mortgage. In 2008, Lehman then experienced an unprecedented loss due to the continuing subprime crisis. Lehman's loss was the result of holding large positions in subprime and other lower-rated mortgage tranches when securing the underlying mortgages. Huge losses accrued to the bank in lower-rated mortgage-backed securities throughout 2008. Lehman's bankruptcy was the largest failure of an investment bank since Drexel Burnham Lambert collapsed 18 years earlier.

By then it was obvious to policy makers that the housing market collapse could have severe systemic effects on the whole financial system. President Bush asked Congress for a $700 billion bail-out package in order to prevent further bank bankruptcies. Similar measures were taken in the EU where similar building market crashes have occurred, like in Spain or Ireland. By contrast, China's banking system was relatively safe as compared to the trouble in the Western banking system. In addition to bail-out efforts Keynesian stimulus packages were now readily adopted, most successfully in China and in Germany, while the US economy did not perform too well in this regard. In addition, the situation has meanwhile become worse, primarily since the financial crisis revealed the rampant fiscal behaviour, in particular of the Greek government[12] before the start of the crisis, and to a lesser degree in Spain and Portugal and now also Italy. We will come back to this severe increase in the dimension of the crisis in Chapter 8. With respect to commercial banks this meant that not only their practice of securitization has led them into a systemic crisis, but that their holding of government bonds (from the PIGS in Southern Europe in particular) is now contributing to illiquidity and their possible collapse.

As the situation currently is, a huge financial rescue umbrella and a very significant hair-cut regarding Greek debt is now in preparation in the Eurozone, of an amount that may – if things go wrong – endanger the existence of the Euro. We thus have the result that fraudulent subprime lending in the USA and subsequent securitization practices may now endanger the life course perspectives of millions of households, in Europe, in the USA and maybe even more severely in the rest of the world. It is considered as a crime in Germany when 'Gammelfleisch' (spoiled meat) is sold on the markets and those who have done this and are caught, face a charge. In the US, commercial banks have issued spoiled credit contracts and have then shifted the junk coddled up with less risky assets in the form of overrated securities to other banks or households. The simple and compelling obligation that the risk producer should also bear the risk is here completely overthrown, since banks have been allowed to produce financial 'Gammelfleisch' and to sell it in hidden form to other parties. Due to the size of the problems they have caused in this way, this is an urgent task for the law makers and the law courts to prevent or punish such crimes against humanity, much more urgent than the comparably inoffensive crime of the spoiled meat producer. Meanwhile, parts of the population in the USA (and also in Germany) have begun to demonstrate against this bank behaviour, calling these demonstrations 'occupy Wall Street' (respectively the ECB).

Atomic power plants are heavily investigated with respect to their risk (though not in all countries) and will soon be outdated in Germany due to the Fukushima catastrophe. Even small risks matter in this area due to the long-lasting nature of such accidents. With respect to financial markets the risk of destroying the life course perspectives of households on a global scale seems to matter not very much, since individually higher profit margins through the issue of bad credits and their diffusion throughout the world (in order to get rid of the risk again) has not really been an issue neither in the mainstream macroeconomic literature nor for policy makers, and even now the regulation of banks, financial transactions and commercial money creation is not forcefully tackled.

The reader may ask what all this has to do with academic mainstream research the relevance of which we severely questioned at the beginning of this subsection. From the MKS perspective we have sketched in the general introduction and which underlies the present book this can be motivated as follows. There is firstly the conflict between capital and labour, basically about labour productivity in production and income distribution on the labour market (the Marx component). This conflict leads to reoccurring overshooting accumulation and inflation (deflation) processes as shown in the corresponding literature and is not a topic in the mainstream literature (where the balanced growth path is generally attracting). These dynamics need however not endanger the viability of the capitalist system, though it is questionable whether citizenship formation and democracy can flourish under such conditions. There are next the side-effects of unrestricted Schumpeterian competition around process and product innovation which we will discuss in Chapter 7. And from the perspective of the present chapter, Keynes's (1936) observation

> *When the capital development of a country becomes a by-product of the activities of a casino, the job is likely to be ill-done.* (Keynes 1936, 159)

is still characterising the situation we are facing now and which we have to overcome in significant ways.

Neoclassical macroeconomics (including the Keynesian variant of the New Neoclassical Synthesis) has never seriously been investigated whether the macroeconomic feedback structure between the major markets that is in operation in a capitalist economy, is systematically plagued by endogenously reoccurring instabilities (quite independently from the variety of shock that can hit such an economy). Minsky (1982) type questions simply play no role in the currently fashionable market clearing DSGE approaches and – due to this – also played no role in policy recommendations and public opinion. Relevance is replaced by admirable rigour in those types of models. But pursuing such research strategy is either naive or camouflaging.

In the next section we reconsider against the background of this section the implications of Fisher's (1935) 100%-money proposal in the framework of a traditionally oriented banking system as a regulation of our model of a broad commercial banking system that acts on the credit market and the financial markets without any institutional barrier. Separating investment banking from traditional banking and introducing even a 100% reserve ratio on checkable deposits (i.e., eliminating the money creation of commercial banks) may initially reduce the profitability of the resulting type of a narrow banking system, but it increases banks' stability and need not reduce the efficiency of credit supply by such specialised institutions, which moreover are safe against bank runs.

5.4 Dynamics and Macroeconomic Stability under Narrow Banking

The return to the narrow banking idea, based on what Fisher (1935) proposed after the Great Depression in his book '100% Money', has recently been discussed again, for example, by De Grauwe (2008). In the mainstream textbook literature, see, for example, Freixas and Rochet (2008), this idea lives at best a shadowy existence, though of course the topic of bank runs is definitely of importance in the mainstream literature, see for example Rochet (2008) and Sinn (2008). In a recent report by the Independent Commission on Banking (2011, p.9) it is stated however now:

> *A number of UK banks combine domestic retail services with global wholesale and investment banking operations. Both sets of activities are economically valuable while both also entail risks - for example, relating to residential property values in the case of retail banking. Their unstructured combination does, however, give rise to public policy concerns, which structural reform proposals - notably forms of separation between retail banking and wholesale/investment banking - seek to address.*

According to the narrow banking view, commercial banks should not be allowed to endogenously create money out of the central bank money in their balance sheet (where they should simply act as depositary institutions), nor should they be allowed to purchase financial assets through ink stroke money (which would return to them in the form of checkable deposits through the circuit of money). If equities cannot be purchased as substitute for lending (or by money creation), commercial banks proper will no longer engage in speculative behaviour and the rate of return on equities would no longer be of importance for the conduct of banks' activities and would thus be removed from the loan rate policy of these narrowly defined banks. Furthermore, if the $M1$ money supply remains fully under control of the central bank, the main rationale for bank runs on checkable deposits would disappear, as the public would know that all checkable deposits in the hands of the commercial banks are backed up by high-powered money from the central bank. The primary role of the commercial banks – besides being depositary institutions for interest free cash holdings – would then again be confined to the active creation of $t-$deposits through their loan supply decisions via the circuit of credit, possibly supported by an open market money supply rule of the central bank (to be considered later on).

On the basis of what we have modelled and investigated in the case of broad banking, let us therefore begin the discussion of narrow banking by means of the following modifications of the broad banking system previously discussed. We first of all assume that commercial banks are not allowed to trade in financial assets anymore. Moreover, we now assume – to limit such a behaviour from the ideal perspective of Fisher (1935) – that checkable deposits D_c have to be backed up by a reserve requirement of 100% ($\rho_b = 1$) and are thus no longer at the disposal of commercial banks for the provision of loans, reducing commercial banks to purely depository institutions in this regard. We assume instead (as a first example) that an inflow of checkable deposits is reallocated by households in equal portions into such deposit holdings and $t-$deposits. If commercial banks intend to provide loans of amount $\dot{\Lambda}$, this implies a change in the flow account of the commercial banks indicated in Table 5.8.

Table 5.8 Narrow commercial banking

Uses	Resources
$i_t D_t$	$i_l(Y)\Lambda$
$\Pi_{bh} = i_l(Y)\Lambda - i_t D_t$	
Loan Supply $\dot{\Lambda} = \lambda_b(Y - Y_o)$	New $t-$Deposits $\dot{D}_t = \dot{\Lambda}$
Changes in Reserves $\dot{R} = \dot{D}_c$	New $c-$Deposits $\dot{D}_c = \dot{\Lambda}, \rho_b = 1$

By contrast, we assume for the time being no reserve requirements on time-deposits D_t, which are safeguarded by other means (including contract length and withdrawal penalties) against bank runs. Time deposits earn an interest rate that is interrelated with the loan rate on the credit given to firms and manipulated appropriately to ensure that the assumed ratio of 0.5 characterises households' reallocation of received checkable deposits. Though new loans all first reappear as checkable deposits in the money holdings of the household sector, 50% of them are transferred into $t-$deposits. If this process is iterated in virtual time (where loans are not yet fully backed up by $t-$deposits), it will in fact generate through the circuit of money an amount of $t-$deposits which in the limit allows the provision of loans intended by commercial banks (the use of the retained profits of banks as credit supply lead in the same way to an additional credit volume that is twice the size of these funds).

During this process an equally sized amount of $c-$deposits is of course generated. We assume that the described circuit of money works infinitely fast in order to avoid its formal description in dynamic terms. Thus, we now only allow for the endogenous creation of commercial bank money (in the form of time deposits), in contrast to what we considered when the textbook money multiplier was presented (which has now the value one). This money creation, however, concerns only the difference $M2 - M1$, while the creation of $M1$, the narrow measure of money supply, is completely under the control of the central bank. This does therefore not allow commercial banks to get interest income out of those money deposits for which they in fact pay no interest.[13]

To show the viability of narrow banking, we start with a case where the credit demand of firms is rationed by the supply decision ($\dot{\Lambda}$) of banks, in order to move on from this credit rationing situation towards one where the banking system is efficiently supplying the credit that is demanded by firms – and does so in a stable environment where in particular bank runs are excluded by the rules of narrow banking.

Credit Rationing

In this scenario, based on the assumed single determinant (economic activity Y) of the loan supply[14] $\dot{\Lambda}$, gives rise to interaction of the real with the financial markets and the loan supply of commercial banks that can be written as[15]

$$\begin{aligned}
\dot{Y} &= \beta_y((a_y - 1)Y + a_e p_e E - a_l(\Lambda - \Lambda_o) + \dot{\Lambda} + \bar{A}), \\
\dot{\Lambda} &= \lambda_b(Y - Y_o), \\
\hat{p}_e &= \beta_e \kappa_e \left(f_e(\frac{r(Y)}{p_e}) - 1 \right).
\end{aligned}$$

The steady state of this dynamical system is the same as in the case of broad banking and its Jacobian (if we assume that $a_y + \lambda_b < 1$ holds true) has the sign structure

$$J_o = \begin{pmatrix} - & - & + \\ + & 0 & 0 \\ + & 0 & - \end{pmatrix}.$$

The sign structure implies stability of the steady state if the parameter a_e is such that the Routh-Hurwitz condition $a_2 > 0$ holds true (since a_1 and a_3 are obviously positive), since in this case the positive interaction between the state of confidence in the goods market dynamics and the output effect on dividends in the stock market is the only effect that can be destabilising. The term $a_1 a_2 - a_3$ must then be positive too, since the $-a_3$ term is matched by a component in the terms contained in $a_1 a_2$.

The assumed type of narrow banking therefore not only *eliminates* the discontinuities created by the occurrence of *bank runs*, but also makes the economy *a stable one* if the real-financial market interaction between output dynamics and Tobin's q (the product of the coefficients J_{13}, J_{31}) is not allowed to work in such a pronounced way that it overcomes the plus sign of the term $-J_{12}J_{21} + J_{11}J_{33}$. This shows that narrow banking is dynamically much more reliable and robust than the model of broad banking we have considered beforehand. Note that the stated condition is stronger than necessary, since it suffices that to choose a_e such that $a_1a_2 - a_3$ is positive, since a_2 must be positive in this case.

We now add to the above first scenario of narrow banking a role for monetary policy and describe the flow account of the Central Bank as shown in Table 5.9.

Table 5.9 Central bank (flows account)

Uses	Resources
	Open Market Policies $\dot{H} = m_e(p_{eo} - p_e)E$
Equity Demand $p_e\dot{E}_c^d = \dot{H} = -p_e\dot{E}_c^s$	
CB Surplus: $r(Y)E_c$ $\rightarrow$ H-sector	Dividends $r(Y)E_c$

The central bank is thus assumed to know the structure of the model and to pursue a countercyclical money supply rule for the stabilisation of the real-financial market interaction. The central bank therefore expands money supply in a stock market boom by selling equities (the only asset in which it can trade in this model) and by purchasing equities in the bust. Note that the circuit of money induced by the money supply rule of the central bank 'moves' in opposite direction compared to the circuit of money so far considered, since it changes the checkable deposit holdings of asset holders first (by the assumed trade in equities) and – when now a portion s_m of these $c-$deposits is transferred into time deposits by households – provides new opportunities for commercial banks to increase their loan supply.

Note however that, in the case $s_m = 1$, commercial banks get all their loans returned as time-deposits, which they could use then to provide extra loans, leading to an infinite circuit of money. We therefore consider it more realistic (as already done in the special case $s_m = 0.5$ discussed above) to assume that only a portion s_m of the initial result of the new money supply $\dot{H}$ is transformed into time deposits so that $1 - s_m$ remains tied up in the reserves of banks balancing the new demand for checkable deposits $(1 - s_m)\dot{H}$ of the household sector. The circuit of loans therefore creates $s_m s_m \dot{H} = s_m^2 \dot{H}$ time deposits in its next round, leading in the ideal again to the creation of $t_m \dot{H}$ ($t_m = \frac{s_m}{1-s_m}$) new loans and balancing time deposits. The changes implied in the household sector are summarised in the flow account shown by Table 5.11.

Table 5.10 Flow account: households (h, bank and firm owners)

Uses	Resources
$C = \varsigma_y Y + \varsigma_e p_e E + \bar{C}$	wL
	$i_t D_t$
$p_e \dot{E}_h = p_e \dot{E}_c^s$	$rE_h + rE_c$
$c-$deposit change $\dot{D}_c$	
$t-$deposit change $\dot{D}_t$	$\Pi_{bh} = i_l \Lambda - i_t D_t$
Y_h	$wL + rE + i_l \Lambda$

Table 5.12 adjusts the flow account of the commercial banks to what has been assumed as action of the central bank. Note that we assume here that the supply of actual loans $\dot{\Lambda}$ (and not of the loans $\dot{\Lambda}^i = \lambda_b(Y - Y_o)$ intended by the banks) is given by the full use of time deposits that are created by the (infinitely fast) circuit of money that is set into motion by the intended loans $\dot{\Lambda}^i$ of banks.

Table 5.11 Flow account: narrow commercial banking (b, private ownership)

Uses	Resources
$i_t D_t$	$i_l \Lambda$
Loans $t_m(\dot{\Lambda}^i + s_m \dot{H})$	$\dot{D}_t = t_m(\dot{\Lambda}^i + s_m \dot{H})$
Reserve Change $\dot{R} = \dot{D}_c$	$\dot{D}_c = t_m^{-1}(\dot{\Lambda}^i + s_m \dot{H})$
	$\Pi_{bh} = i_l \Lambda - i_t D_t$

Taken together the dynamics of the model we have considered so far is thereby modified to[16]

$$
\begin{aligned}
\dot{Y} &= \beta_y[(a_y-1)Y+a_e p_e E - a_l(\Lambda-\Lambda_o)+t_m(\dot{\Lambda}^i+s_m\dot{H})+\bar{A}]\\
&= \beta_y\left[(a_y+t_m\lambda_b-1)Y+(a_e-t_m s_m m_e)p_e E - a_l(\Lambda-\Lambda_o)+\right.\\
&\quad \left.\bar{A}-\varsigma_b Y_o + t_m s_m m_e p_{eo}E\right],\\
\dot{\Lambda} &= t_m(\lambda_b(Y_o-Y)+s_m m_e(1-p_e)E),\\
\hat{p}_e &= \beta_e\kappa_e\left[f_e\left(\frac{r(Y)}{p_e}\right)-1\right].
\end{aligned}
$$

This gives for the Jacobian of this system at the steady state under the side conditions of the preceding case, $a_y + t_m\lambda_b - 1 < 0$, the sign distribution

$$
J_o = \begin{pmatrix} - & - & \pm \\ + & 0 & - \\ + & 0 & - \end{pmatrix}.
$$

Again, the sign structure in the above Jacobian implies stability of the steady state solution, since a_1, a_2 are obviously positive if a_e is chosen as in the previous case and since $a_1a_2 - a_3$ must be positive then, as the positive term in a_3 is matched by a product in the term a_1a_2 and as the negative one is made positive when a_3 is subtracted from a_1a_2.

It should be further pointed out that the condition $J_{11} < 0$ can be more easily met if a Keynesian countercyclical fiscal policy that reduces the propensity to spend a_y to a sufficient degree is also assumed. Note also that the positive feedback channel created by $a_e p_e$ and $r(Y)$ between the first and the last law of motion needs only be weakened, but not really overthrown, in order to get its possibly destabilising nature fixed. The task of the central bank here is to reduce through its policy parameter m_e the impact of the state of confidence on aggregate demand, as measured by the parameter a_e, by so much that the sum of principal minors of order 2, a_2, becomes positive. As the very least any monetary policy of the assumed type will make the economy less accelerative in nature.

Demand-determined Credit

It should be pointed out that in the just discussed scenario, the firm's loan demand may be rationed, since the loans created by the banks determine the outcome on the credit market. However, a narrow banking system does not need to imply that credit is more rationed than in the case of broad banking and in the end more rationed than is demanded by a proper screening policy of banks. Indeed, a narrow banking system can also handle the case where credit is demand determined, though mathematically determined as in the preceding case of a supply rationed outcome. In such a situation the flow account of the commercial banks is modified as shown in Table 5.12.[17]

Table 5.12 Flow account: narrow commercial banking (b, private ownership)

Uses	Resources
$i_t D_t$	$i_l \Lambda$
Loans $\dot{\Lambda} = \lambda_f (Y - Y_o)$	$\dot{D}_t = t_m \dot{\Lambda}$
Reserve Change $\dot{R} = \dot{D}_c$	$\dot{D}_c = t_m^{-1} \dot{\Lambda}$
	$\Pi_{bh} = i_l \Lambda - i_t D_t$

The task of the banking system is then to manipulate the loan rate and the time-deposit rate such that $s_m \geq 0.5$ is achieved (which in the $>$ case would imply idle time-deposit reserves). An example for this manipulation is the following one. We assume that the parameter s_m, which determines $\dot{D}_t$, is a positive function of the interest rate i_t on time-deposits. The task would then be to choose a deposit rate i_t such that $\frac{s_m(i_t)}{1-s_m(i_t)} > 1$ holds true.

So far we have considered the credit to deposit multipliers as working in virtual time with infinite speed. From the practical point of view this assumption is however not really necessary, since there is a continuous flow of loan-output/deposit-input type in such an economy. In the steady state this flow would balance loans and the creation of deposits in the assumed way in actual time, while for fluctuating loans some further flexibility of the banking system may be needed in order to achieve the result that time-deposits are always created to such a degree that they balance the loan creation of banks.

Such flexibility concerns the practical situation that the reserve ratio on checkable deposits does not need to be 1 as has been assumed so far, but can be adjusted in a downward direction to a certain degree if this is needed in view of the current loan demand. Again the interest rate on time-deposits and the one on loans may be adjusted in such a way as to balance loan demand with loan supply out of time-deposits. Finally, there may exist voluntary time-deposit reserves held by the banking system. A proper management of the banking system may therefore be needed in addition to the ideal constructions we have considered in this section.

It may be easy to maintain a time-deposit ratio $s_m > 0.5$ in times of a normal operation of the economy and its banking system. But in times of financial stress, where liquidity preference is increasing, the ratio s_m may fall below 0.5. This first of all rations credit demand which to a certain degree may be a good thing, if there are firms that are not really viable in such a situation and which only consume financial resources without much change in their default position. Secondly, since this is most likely in a situation with low and falling stock market prices, the central bank may implement a monetary policy as we have considered it above, in order to increase the loan supply and to improve the situation on the stock market simultaneously. Finally, there may also be a quantitative easing policy of the central bank, that is, a supply of central bank money to the banking system at a low rate of interest from which new credits can be generated.

5.5 Conclusions

In this chapter we have considered the implications for macroeconomic stability of a broad banking system where commercial banks are allowed to trade in capital assets (here equities) as a substitute for traditional lending activities. Using a simple dynamic multiplier approach on the market for goods and a simple rate of return driven adjustment rule for stock prices we have shown that such a scenario is likely to be an unstable one. We then considered a narrow banking system defined by a Fisherian 100% reserve ratio for checkable deposits and the exclusion of stock trade for commercial banks. We showed in such a narrow banking system that:

a) the rationale for bank runs no longer exists as all checkable deposits are backed by high-powered central bank money (they therefore provide a form of wealth allocation which is free of risk);

b) speculative behaviour by banks is absent by assumption (or law); while

c) a sufficient loan supply to entrepreneurs (and households) can be guaranteed in such a framework (where in addition there is no resale of credit obligations, so that the risk remains at the bank that grants the loan).

Low and falling stock market prices, increasing liquidity preference and credit rationing are a big problem for any banking system, but in the narrow banking considered here at the very least the exclusion of bank runs (100% reserves) may lead to a more stable real-financial market interaction and presumably also a more efficient credit supply than in the case where the traditional function of commercial banks as credit institutions are mixed up with investment banking and the like. Narrow banking thus can not only provide a much greater systemic stability, but also as much efficiency in the credit creation process as the present banking system. Furthermore while narrow banking appears a too extreme case to be implemented in reality, its features indicate the kind of improvements in macrofinancial stability which can be attained if broad banking is constrained in the direction of a narrow banking system.

We conclude that banking regulation and monetary policy should aim at refining the traditional role of credit-supplying institutions, but not allow it to be distorted by casino-like effects resulting from financial market speculations or even processes like collateralised debt obligations (CDOs) based on toxic assets. Commercial banks should not be allowed to get rid of and pass on their sloppy risk taking attitudes to other financial institutions by way of alleged asset based securities where the extent of risk that is involved in such packages is not made transparent to the potential customers. Credit risk taking should remain in the hands of experienced and responsibly behaving commercial banks and not be spread around the world as collateralised mortgage obligations and the like. This can become even more important now for the case of credit default swaps which can provide a new type of systemic risk in the current situation where whole countries are at risk of defaulting.

The issue here simply is that commercial banking should serve the purpose of financing profitable investment in a way that is as efficient as possible and should therefore not engage in financial activities that are dysfunctional for the central role which dynamic enterprises have to play in a capitalist market economy.

Notes

1 This chapter is partly based on Chiarella, Flaschel, Hartmann and Proaño (2011). We also refer the reader to Charpe, Chiarella, Flaschel and Semmler (2011) and Chiarella, Flaschel and Semmler (2013) for further detailed discussions of financial markets, macroeconomic portfolio choice and banking.

2 The Glass-Steagall Act prohibited any one institution from acting as any combination of an investment bank, a commercial bank, and an insurance

company. The Gramm-Leach-Bliley Act abolished this prohibition by allowing commercial banks, investment banks, securities firms, and insurance companies to consolidate.

[3] Note here that this is a net demand function so that $\dot{A}$ can also be negative if the principal of the currently repaid contracted debt exceeds the new borrowing decisions of firms.

[4] The modelling of the commercial banks' conflict of interest through the loan rate is an implication of the assumption that the actual level of new loans is fully determined by the entrepreneurial sector. See Flaschel et al. (2011) for an alternative specification where banks directly control the amount of loans granted.

[5] Significantly more elaborate versions of the dynamics of the financial sector (and also of the real sector) are provided, for example in Asada, Flaschel, Mouakil and Proaño (2011), there however on the basis of Tobin's portfolio equilibrium approach in place of the delayed disequilibrium adjustment processes we consider in the present section.

[6] This specification implies that when the households observe a stock imbalance in their gross portfolio, they will adjust their equity holdings in a gradual manner, correcting in each (infinitesimal) period only a percentage κ_e of the total imbalance $p_e E^d - p_e E$.

[7] Note here however that such a tax introduces a new type of income into the economy, which might be used to increase the own capital of commercial banks or might be used as a rescue umbrella as it is currently constructed in the Euro area.

[8] Here output is used as a proxy for household income.

[9] This assumption can be justified by means of a Tobin tax on capital gains that is chosen sufficiently high, such that the stability of the 3D dynamics considered here is preserved (see the preceding section).

[10] A more detailed discussion of this can be found among others in Flaschel (2009).

[11] For a counterexample to this prospect see however Chapter 8 where – concerning Greece – insights from Keynes's (1936) GT are again totally ignored.

[12] which was not at all Keynesian in nature.

[13] These money holdings are thus always checkable against central bank money and cannot be subject to bank runs, since they are purely passive in the balance sheet of commercial banks and not at their disposal should they become insolvent.

[14] This is assumed for expositional simplicity and could be replaced by more advanced supply functions or no credit rationing at all in future extensions of the model.

[15] Note that we again assume that the capital gains dynamics is controlled, for example, by a Tobin tax to a sufficient degree so that we need not treat it explicitly here.

[16] Here $\tilde{A}$ is the new constant in the enlarged multiplier dynamics.

[17] We neglect policy actions here.

6. Schumpeterian Innovations Waves from a Classical Perspective

Reiner Franke

In this chapter[1] we finally consider – in addition to the two preceding chapters on Marxian distributive cycles in a dynamic Keynesian framework and the role financial markets play in the Keynesian view of the working of the economy – Schumpeterian long waves in processes of technological innovations and their diffusion as one further big challenge along the way from simple ELR systems of 'full' employment via the generation of institutions of the flexicurity type towards the model of Social Capitalism which we will finally opt for in the next part of the book. We therefore here return to a supply side framework with Classical elements in the theory of income distribution and now focus on long waves in technological change, to be contrasted and combined with the long-phased distributive cycle of Chapter 4 in future research.

6.1 Introduction

Classical and neoclassical theories of growth and income distribution have one thing in common: even in models with technical progress, both theories suppose that all firms have free access to the most efficient technological knowledge, or that the competitive process works so fast as to drive old production methods out of the market immediately when a new and more profitable technique enters the stage. Apart from the wide gap between this idealised world and the industrial structure to be observed in reality, the assumption raises a fundamental problem at the theoretical level, namely, that there would be no one within the system, who has any motivation to change the reached position. Strictly speaking, the long-run equilibrium notion of the classical and neoclassical theory, if it is to apply to a capitalist economy, is a contradiction in terms (Metcalfe 1997, p.6).

With respect to the dynamic character of a capitalist economy, a Schumpeterian view seems more meaningful. What Schumpeter envisaged as 'the essential fact about capitalism' (Schumpeter 1950, p.83) is the process of 'creative destruction', a process that 'incessantly revolutionises the economic structure from within, incessantly destroying the old one, incessantly creating a new one'. According to this view, economic theory should seriously take into account 'the ceaselessly changing pattern of economic activity, expressed over time by the emergence of new activities, the demise of existing ones and the changing relative importance of those that currently compete for markets' (Metcalfe 1997, p.6).

Limiting the discussion to technical change and the introduction of unambiguously more efficient production methods in a one-good world, these features can already be captured by a Schumpeterian prototype model as it has been put forward by Iwai (1984). The basic forces are here technological diffusion and innovation. Their interplay suggests another and more advanced equilibrium notion, which can be described as a balance of the centripetal forces of diffusion with their tendency toward the technological frontier, and the centrifugal forces of a never ceasing inflow of new technological knowledge. Since diffusion is gradual and not instantaneous, the economy has in each period a non-degenerate spectrum of coexisting techniques, a multitude of diverse production methods with different efficiencies. As the dynamic process unfolds, the least productive vintages are wiped out through evolutionary pressure, while at the other end of the spectrum new and more profitable production methods are continuously added.

The present chapter focuses on this equilibrium notion and its direct implications. To make the argument as simple as possible, technical progress and also the rates of diffusion are assumed to be exogenous.[2] If furthermore the innovations improve uniformly and are introduced deterministically at regular intervals of length T, the economy is in long-run equilibrium when the capacity shares of the techniques reproduce themselves over time – only at an increasing technological scale. This means more precisely that the role of technique i at time t is taken over by its more productive successor $i+1$ at time $t+T$. Such a smooth evolution of the economy is called a wave train.[3]

Of course, proponents of classical and neoclassical theories are aware of the methodological criticism mentioned above. They argue that their equilibrium concept is nevertheless a convenient instrument that has proved worthwhile in studying growth and income distribution. The sketchy remarks in the preceding paragraph indicate that alternative modelling devices are available. They can incorporate basic aspects of the Schumpeterian vision and are thus able to overcome (to some extent) the basic methodological problem of the orthodox theories. On the other hand, evolutionary Schumpeterian models usually concentrate on the details of technical change and are not very explicit about income distribution. At this point, the present chapter attempts to build a bridge.

The chapter starts out from the classical notion of income distribution as it is represented by the Sraffian 'degree of freedom', according to which one distributional variable, the real wage or the profit rate, is exogenously given. This treatment of distribution is integrated into the Schumpeterian framework provided by Iwai (1984). An immediate consequence of the new equilibrium concept of a wave train in this model is that the economy's overall profitability can no longer be expressed by a uniform rate of profit. Since there is always a whole spectrum of techniques of different efficiencies, the place of this variable is now taken by the average rate of profit. It is important to note that in this way the otherwise so convenient Sraffian dichotomy between prices and quantities is undermined: whereas in the standard production price systems income distribution can be investigated without recourse to quantities, the determination of the average profit rate involves the capacity shares of different techniques. Since the latter are endogenously determined, the quantity side has to be invoked right from the outset.[4]

From the fact that the equilibrium capacity shares of the techniques are brought about by the interaction of diffusion and innovation, it moreover follows that the parameters that measure the 'strength' of these forces have also a bearing on the characteristics of the wave train. Thus, our approach will be able to identify factors that have an impact on income distribution and growth in long-run equilibrium, which are beyond the scope of the classical analysis. It may be claimed that in this respect the Schumpeterian long-run equilibrium concept here employed, while at a similar level of formalisation, is more fruitful than the classical specification.

In elaborating on these points, the remainder of the chapter is organised as follows. Section 6.2 presents the modelling equations of the evolutionary process of diffusion and innovation. The corresponding long-run equilibrium concept of a wave train is introduced in Section 6.3. Section 6.4 is devoted to the determinants of income distribution, where the exogenous distribution variable is the real wage rate deflated by a measure of labour productivity. A main result is that the average rate of profit on the resulting wave train is influenced by two parameters grounded in the 'quantity side': one is the responsiveness of investors to the profit rate differentials of the existing techniques, the other is related to the initial capacity share at which a new technique is installed. If, on the other hand, these parameters are fixed, it is seen that the inverse relationship of the classical theory between the (deflated) real wage and the (average) rate of profit carries over, though the mechanism is now more complex than in a one-good world with just one technique. The basic arguments are intuitive, while a more careful analysis to confirm this type of reasoning has to resort to numerical simulations. Section 6.5 briefly deals with the Marxian law of the falling rate of profit if technical change is capital-using and labour-saving, and (deflated) real wages remain fixed. In the classical production price systems the profit rate cannot reasonably fall owing to Okishio's theorem, but in the Schumpeterian framework these problems of internal consistency no longer prevail. Section 6.6 concludes. An appendix collects some further details in the formulation of the model.

6.2 Formulation of the Evolutionary Process

The dynamic process begins with $i = 1, 2, \ldots, N_o$ production methods at starting time $t = 0$. Technical progress is exogenous and deterministic. A new technique is introduced into the economy every T years, let us say at dates

$$t \in J \;:=\; \{\, mT\colon\, m = 0, 1, 2, \ldots \,\} \tag{6.1}$$

We consider a one-good world where the same good, besides serving as a consumption good, is installed as a capital good in different production processes. Technical progress is assumed to be Harrod neutral. Correspondingly, the capital coefficient b is the same for all techniques, as well as the rate of depreciation δ. The efficiency of a technique is therefore unambiguously characterised by its labour coefficient. Denote the unit labour requirements of technique i by a_i, and by q_i its labour productivity, $q_i = 1/a_i$. The productivity of the new techniques is supposed to grow exponentially at an annual rate λ. Since the adjustment mechanisms below are specified in continuous time, it is convenient to define λ as the compound rate of growth, so that $q_i/q_{i-1} = \exp(\lambda T)$, or

$$a_i \;=\; e^{-\lambda T}\, a_{i-1}, \qquad i = 1, 2, \ldots \tag{6.2}$$

Let N_t be the index of the best-practice technique (BPT) at time t, the most efficient technique currently in use or just about to be set up. The discontinuous changes in this variable follow from 6.1,

$$\begin{aligned} \dot{N}_t &= 0 && \text{if } t \notin J \\ N_t &= N_{t-T} + 1 && \text{if } t \in J \end{aligned} \tag{6.3}$$

The time index of N_t will be omitted in the running text whenever this seems possible. The capacity share of technique i at time t is denoted by $k_i(t)$. To build up the capacity share k_N of the BPT when it comes into existence at time $(N - N_o)T$, we assume a (short) set-up phase of length T_u. Designate this span of time by

$$U(N_t) \;:=\; [(N_t - N_o)\,T,\; (N_t - N_o)\,T + T_u] \tag{6.4}$$

Within the set-up phase, the capacity share k_N of the BPT is supposed to increase autonomously at a given rate κ,

$$\dot{k}_N(t) \;=\; \kappa \qquad \text{if } t \in U(N)\,, \text{ where } N = N_t \tag{6.5}$$

Certainly, $k_N(t) = 0$ for $t \le (N - N_o)T$. By the end of this transitional stage, at $t = (N - N_o)T + T_u$, the BPT has established a share $k_N(t) = \kappa\, T_u$ in total capacity. From then on, the BPT is treated like any other technique, whose changes are governed by the diffusion equation that is to be derived next.[5]

Given the real wage rate $w = w(t)$, the rate of profit of technique i at time t is

$$r_i(t) \;=\; \frac{1 - w(t)\,a_i}{b} \;-\; \delta \tag{6.6}$$

Average values across techniques are denoted by a bar over the variable. The techniques themselves are weighted by their capacity shares. Thus the average rate of profit at time t is

$$\bar{r}(t) \;=\; \sum_{i=1}^{N_t} r_i(t)\,k_i(t) \tag{6.7}$$

and analogous for average unit labour requirements, $\bar{a} = \sum a_i k_i$, which is equal to L/Y (L total labour, Y aggregate output). An exception is average labour productivity $\bar{q}$, where the coefficients q_i are weighted by the employment shares L_i/L, or directly

$$\bar{q}(t) \;=\; 1\,/\,\bar{a}(t) \tag{6.8}$$

Technological diffusion is a gradual adjustment process such that the more efficient techniques grow faster than the older vintages.[6] In the present context this means that the capital stock growth rates g_i are determined by differential rates of profits. With respect to a propensity to save out of profits, s, we draw on the formulation of investment in classical gravitation processes and specify the growth rate of the capital stock of technique i as

$$g_i(t) \;=\; s\,\bar{r}(t) \,+\, \rho\,[r_i(t) - \bar{r}(t)] \tag{6.9}$$

Eq. (6.9) is an investment function where causality runs from profit rates to growth rates and any problems of effective demand are neglected (an explicit formulation of consumption demand is thus dispensable). The coefficient ρ measures the responsiveness of investors to differential profits. It will be an important factor in the overall speed of diffusion, though not the only one. Obviously, (6.9) directly implies the standard Cambridge equation in the aggregate, that is, $\bar{g}(t) = s\bar{r}(t)$ ($\bar{g}$ the average capital growth rate). If ρ or the differential profits are sufficiently large, net investment may also be negative, $g_i(t) < 0$, for the least productive techniques. Furthermore, some equipment might even be scrapped if a technique is to shrink faster than the capital stock depreciates.[7]

By the assumption of Harrod neutral technical progress, the techniques' capacity shares k_i coincide with their shares in the total stock of fixed capital. It is then easily checked that the changes in k_i are determined by the differential equations $\dot{k}_i = (g_i - \bar{g})k_i = \rho(r_i - \bar{r})k_i$ (there is no implementation lag in this model). These equations also ensure that the identity $\sum_i k_i = 1$ is maintained. It has, however, to be noted that the economy-wide application of eq. (6.9) is limited to the time intervals where the BPT does not expand autonomously according to (6.5). For the set-up phase itself, the growth rates in (6.9) have to be modified in two ways: the BPT $i = N$ is excluded from (6.9), and at the same time the aggregate relationship across all techniques, $\bar{g} = s\bar{r}$, is supposed to be preserved. The variations in the capacity shares k_i may thus be briefly summarised as follows:[8]

$$\begin{aligned} \dot{k}_i(t) &= \rho\,[\,r_i(t) - \bar{r}(t)\,]\,k_i(t) \text{ for } i \leq N_t \;\text{ if } t \notin U(N_t) \\ \dot{k}_i(t) &= \rho\,[\,r_i(t) - \bar{r}(t)\,]\,k_i(t) \text{ for } i \leq N_t - 1 \\ &\quad \text{and subsequent renormalization if } t \in U(N_t). \end{aligned} \tag{6.10}$$

To close the model it remains to specify the time path of the real wage rate $w = w(t)$. If the income shares of wage and profit receivers are not to drift apart over time, the wage rate must grow with labour productivity. Since we will concentrate on the long-run equilibrium evolution of the economy, it may conveniently be assumed that wages grow at a constant rate g_w.[9] Thus, from the specification of the rate of technical progress in eq. (6.2),

$$\dot{w}(t) \;=\; g_w\, w(t)\,, \qquad\qquad \text{where } g_w = \lambda \tag{6.11}$$

Given an initial number of techniques N_o, a frequency distribution of their capacity shares $(k_1, \ldots, k_{N_o})$ at $t = 0$ (with $k_{N_o} = 0$), and also an initial real wage rate $w(0)$, the evolution of these and the newly arriving techniques is now fully described.

6.3 Wave Trains

Equations (6.1) – (6.11) specify an evolutionary process that captures the basic Schumpeterian hypotheses on technological diffusion and innovation. While diffusion constitutes an equilibrating force that tends to steer the economy's state of technology toward an equilibrium in which all firms use the most efficient production method, the function of innovation lies precisely in upsetting this equilibrating tendency. The dynamic interaction between the continuous and equilibrating forces of diffusion, and the discontinuous and disequilibrating forces of innovation, may nevertheless exhibit a certain regularity. In our deterministic setting for the technological innovations, the forces of diffusion and innovation balance if, over regular intervals of time, they reproduce exactly the same spectrum of coexisting techniques, only at a higher scale. This means that the role of technique i at time t is taken over by technique $i{+}1$ at time $t{+}T$. Formally, the capacity shares constitute an equilibrium trajectory, denoted by $\{k_i^\star(t)\}$, if over time and across techniques they are related by

$$k_{i+1}^\star(t+T) \;=\; k_i^\star(t)\,, \qquad\qquad i \in \mathbb{N}\,,\; t \geq 0 \tag{6.12}$$

This time path of capacity shares corresponds to what is known in the literature on partial differential equations (with their continuous state space) as a travelling wave, or a wave train. In the present framework with the discrete unit costs a_i of successive techniques, a solution of system (6.1) – (6.11) is a wave train if there exists a real function $\phi(\cdot)$ such that

$$\phi(\ln a_i + g_w t) \;=\; k_i^\star(t)\,, \qquad i \in \mathbb{N}\,,\; t \geq 0 \qquad (6.13)$$

(see Henkin and Polterovich 1991, p.556). In fact, compatibility of eq.s (6.12) and (6.13) follows from the definition of g_w in (6.11) and reformulation of (6.2) as $\ln a_{i+1} = -\lambda T + \ln a_i = -g_w T + \ln a_i$, and the relationship $k_{i+1}^\star(t+T) = \phi[\ln a_{i+1} + g_w(t+T)] = \phi[-g_w T + \ln a_i + g_w t + g_w T] = \phi[\ln a_i + g_w t] = k_i^\star(t)$.

By introducing the concept of cost gaps, the frequency distributions of techniques can be studied independently of time progressing. The cost gap of technique i is given by its unit cost in relation to the unit cost of the best-practice technique N. Denoting this gap by z_{N-i}, we have

$$z_{N-i} \;=\; a_i \,/\, a_N \qquad (6.14)$$

Clearly, the ratios a_i/a_N remain unaltered if the same number is added to i and N, while the cost gap of a given technique i increases as new techniques are introduced. The frequency distribution of these cost gaps is directly represented by the wave train function $\phi(\cdot)$. To see this suppose a given cost gap $z = z_{N-i}$ is brought about by technique i at a time τ years after the introduction of the most recent technique $N = N_t$. Accordingly, let $0 \leq \tau < T$, $N_t = N_o + m$ for a suitable integer number m, and $t = mT + \tau$. Then it is easily verified that with respect to some constant number C,

$$\phi[\ln z_{N-i} + g_w \tau + C] \;=\; k_i^\star(t)\,, \qquad \text{where } N = N_t \qquad (6.15)$$

(see the appendix). Eq. (6.15) together with (6.12) tells us that it does not matter whether the cost gap z is brought about by technique i at time t, or by technique $i+1$ at time $t+T$: the capacity share will be the same.[10] Hence, the distribution of cost gaps remains invariant over time. More precisely, the distribution of the variable $\ln z$ is slightly shifted between two innovations as the term $g_w \tau$ increases from 0 to $g_w T$, but identical values are assumed if we look at the distribution every T years.

Figure 6.1 presents a typical example of the equilibrium evolution of an economy (the underlying numerical details are given in the next section). The diagram clearly shows how the frequency distribution of the techniques' capacity shares moves regularly over time toward the techniques with lower unit labour requirements (ULR). Correspondingly, as indicated by the bold line on the surface running parallel to the time axis, it is seen how the capacity share of a given technique steadily declines in the later stages of its life-cycle.[11] The wave train function $\phi(\cdot)$ can be read off along the ULR-axis at, for example, $t = 20$.

The unit costs of the active techniques at that date range from a high of $a_{12} = 52.7$ to a low of $a_{12+27} = 12.2$ (see the bold line at $t = 20$). That is, the new techniques are more than four times as productive as the old vintages. Though the only purpose of Figure 6.1 is to illustrate the properties of a highly stylised economic model, these differences in efficiencies might not be too extreme. Thus, to emphasise the economic significance of his general approach, Iwai (1984, p.324) gives a representative example of the frequency distribution of an industry in the USA (the metal stamp industry) where the ratio of payroll to value added covers a range from 0.15 to 0.85.[12]

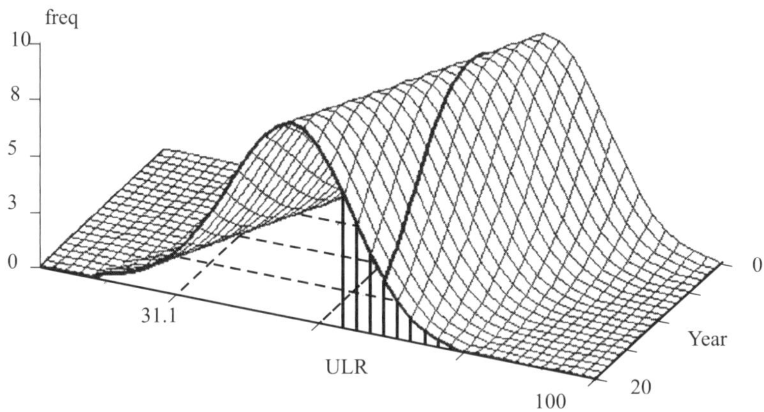

Figure 6.1 Frequency distributions of techniques on a wave train. (Note: Bars indicate frequencies (in %) of techniques with high unit labour requirements (ULR) at time t = 20)

Applying the concept of a wave train to system (6.1) – (6.11) raises three questions: Does a wave train $\{k_i^\star(t)\}$ exist? Is it uniquely determined? Is it globally stable? The latter means that starting from an arbitrary initial frequency distribution $\{k_i(0)\}$, the resulting solution $\{k_i(t)\}$ of (6.1) – (6.11) converges toward the wave train capacity shares $\{k_i^\star(t)\}$ as t gets large.

These problems have been subjected to a rigourous mathematical analysis by Henkin and Polterovich (1991) in another, similarly elementary Schumpeterian model. Under a reasonable set of conditions, the authors prove existence and uniqueness of a wave train as well as its global stability. Unfortunately, the (quite elaborated) analysis cannot be readily carried over since the present model differs in a number of specification details. However, existence and the powerful global stability result were fully confirmed in all our numerical simulations. As we have found no reason to harbour any doubts, we do not pursue the mathematical issue any further.[13]

The property of global stability establishes the economic significance of the long-run equilibrium notion of a wave train. Actually, the global stability was also exploited to compute the wave trains in the numerical investigations below. Accordingly, we initialised the dynamic process (6.1) – (6.11) with an arbitrary distribution of capacity shares $\{k_i(0)\}$ at $t=0$, and let it run for so long until eq. (6.12) was approximately satisfied. Then, setting the wage rate back to $w = w(0)$, the process was rerun with the capacity shares just found as the initial frequency distribution.

Against the background of the classical theory of income distribution, another feature of interest are the wages and profits on a wave train. Since there is now no longer a uniform rate of profit, we refer to the average profit rate in order to characterise the position of profit receivers by a single number. Denoting by v the share of total wages in gross national income ($v = wL/Y$), we have

$$v(t) \quad = \quad w(t)\,\bar{a}(t) \tag{6.16}$$

(see the remark on eq. (6.7)). Using (6.6), the average rate of profit can be written as[14]

$$\bar{r}(t) \quad = \quad \frac{1 - v(t)}{b} \; - \; \delta \quad = \quad \frac{1 - w(t)\,\bar{a}(t)}{b} \; - \; \delta \tag{6.17}$$

Since by hypothesis real wages $w(t)$ grow at the same rate at which the unit labour requirements of the BPT decline, $w(t)\bar{a}(t)$ does not systematically rise or fall in the long-run. That is, $v(t+T) = w(t+T)\,\bar{a}(t+T) = w(t)\,\bar{a}(t) = v(t)$ for all t, while between two innovations $v(t)$ may fluctuate on a small scale (these intermediate fluctuations are neglected in the following discussion). By the same token, it is ensured that the average rate of profit remains constant in the course of the process. Hence, if an initial real wage rate $w(0)$ is exogenously given, it has associated with it a wave train solution $\{k_i^\star(t)\}$ of the evolution of capacity shares, and these in turn determine the average rate of profit $\bar{r}$ as well as the overall growth rate of the economy, $\bar{g} = s\bar{r}$. In this sense, the degree of freedom from the classical theory of income distribution is maintained.

On the other hand, also the average rate of profit $\bar{r}$ may be chosen as the exogenous variable. Observe that, by virtue of eq. (6.17), this is tantamount to fixing the wage share v. In the computation of the corresponding wave train, we can then replace eq. (6.11) with eq. (6.16) and set directly $w(t) = v/\bar{a}(t)$.

Knowledge of the real wage rate $w(0)$ on a wave train is not yet sufficient to assess the position of workers on this long-run equilibrium growth path; we also have to know the general level of technology at that time, $t=0$. To discuss variations of income distribution, it is therefore appropriate to deflate the real wage by an index of labour productivity. However, the weights constituting such an index should be independent of the frequency distribution of techniques, which will generally change from one wave train to another. This requirement rules out average productivity $\bar{q} = 1/\bar{a}$ as a deflator. Instead, it appears natural to employ the labour productivity of the BPT for this purpose. Looking at wages in the middle between two innovations, define

$$\omega = w(T/2)/q_N = w(T/2)a_N, \text{ where } N = N_o = N_{T/2} \qquad (6.18)$$

It will be clear by now that on a wave train we have $w(t_m)/q_{N(m)} = \omega$ for all $m \in \mathbb{N}$, where $t_m := mT+T/2$, $N(m) := N_{mT+T/2}$. This means that if we study changes in income distribution, we exogenously fix the deflated real wage ω and set the initial real wage $w(0)$ such that, on the equilibrium path, $w(T/2) = \omega\, q_N$ comes about $(N=N_o)$. The wave train distribution function $\phi(\cdot)$ is subsequently used to compute the corresponding average rate of profit.[15]

Before we illustrate the construction of a wage-profit frontier in this way, we should stress an important conceptual difference from income distribution in the production price systems of the classical theory. In this type of analysis, the study of income distribution, given the 'book of blueprints' of techniques, requires the computation of relative prices, while at least in single production systems quantities do not interfere. In the present context of a one-good economy, relative prices are no problem (they would reappear if we tried to set up a two-sectoral version of the model). However, given the path of technical progress, the determination of the distributional variables ω and $\bar{r}$ requires the computation of the equilibrium frequencies of the techniques' capacity shares. As already indicated in the introductory section, the 'classical dichotomy' between prices and quantities therefore no longer obtains. Despite the highly simplified assumptions on technology, a study of income distribution in an evolutionary economy has to integrate the quantity side right from the outset.

It has already been noted above that if, instead of the deflated real wage ω, the wage share v is taken as the exogenous variable, the average rate of profit can be directly determined by eq. (6.17) without further knowledge of the capacity shares. However, quantities will then interfere as soon as the assumption of a one-good economy is dropped. More importantly, the interdependence between the price and the quantity side under a given wage share occurs, almost trivially, already at a much more elementary level, in basic (multisectoral) production price systems with a uniform rate of profit and best-practice techniques only (see Franke 1998, 1999). This inconvenience is certainly one of the reasons why classical analysis normally chooses real wages, rather than the wage share, to characterise the position of workers. As we wish to discuss the classical theory within its own preferred setting, we here follow this tradition.

6.4 Determinants of Income Distribution

To study the evolution of the economy on a wave train by means of computer simulations, we now have to specify the numerical parameter values. One set of parameters is given by familiar macroeconomic magnitudes: the capital-output ratio b, the rate of depreciation δ, and the propensity s to save out of profits. On the basis of Simon (1990), they are fixed as follows,[16]

$$b = 1.70 \qquad \delta = 0.0461 \qquad s = 0.2670 \tag{6.19}$$

The other set of parameters governs technological diffusion and innovation: the annual rate of technical progress λ, the innovation time T (the interval between two innovations), the length of the set-up phase T_u, the autonomous rate of change κ at which the capacity share of the BPT increases over this period, and the responsiveness ρ of investors to differential profits. Here we put[17]

$$\lambda = 0.029 \qquad T = 2.00 \qquad T_u = 0.10 \qquad \kappa = 0.02 \qquad \rho = 1.00 \tag{6.20}$$

The innovation parameters T, T_u and κ can be encapsulated in a single parameter ν defined as

$$\nu \;=\; \kappa T_u / T \tag{6.21}$$

The motivation for this definition and its relationship to Iwai's (1984) stochastic innovation hypothesis is discussed in Franke (2000). The remarkable point is that (essentially) the same wave train distribution function $\phi(\cdot)$ is brought about by different combinations of T, T_u and κ that give rise to identical values of ν in eq. (6.21).[18]

Finally, we take the deflated real wage rate ω as the exogenous variable for income distribution and set

$$\omega \;=\; 0.307 \tag{6.22}$$

(Recall $\omega = w(T/2)\,/\,q_N$ from eq. (6.18), with $N = N_o = N_{T/2}$.) Eq.s (6.19, 6.20, 6.22) may serve as a base scenario. In particular, the special choice of $\omega = 0.307$ results in the following values of the wage share, the average profit rate, and the capital growth rate,

$$v(\tau) = 70.02\% \,, \quad \bar{r}(\tau) = 11.22\% \,, \quad \bar{g}(\tau) = s\bar{r}(\tau) = 3.00 \tag{6.23}$$

which prevail on the wave train in the middle between two innovations, at time $\tau = T/2$. Eq. (6.23) shows that the model can be calibrated such as to be roughly compatible with empirical values of the macroeconomic key variables here involved.

The remainder of the chapter is concerned with comparative dynamics. Accordingly, some of the exogenous parameters are varied and the characteristics of the corresponding equilibrium growth paths are studied. In this respect, note first that variations in the exogenous rate of technical progress λ have trivial effects on income distribution, since by construction λ determines directly the growth rate of real wages. In the present setting it is therefore meaningless to compare two economies with different values of λ.

A most important case, however, is a change in the responsiveness ρ of investors to differential profits. Although ρ certainly has its institutional foundations, it is also of a psychological nature. Given the economy's institutions, ρ may be regarded as a psychological coefficient. Now, it is a centrepiece of the classical theory that the long-run equilibrium position is independent of such a reaction intensity. In this theory, the only significance of ρ would be in the disequilibrium adjustment process toward the steady state. For example, a mathematical analysis of a gravitation process might reveal that this parameter must not be too large if stability is to be ensured. By contrast, in the present Schumpeterian framework it turns out that the responsiveness ρ already has a bearing on the long-run equilibrium itself. For example, maintain the other parameter values in equations (6.19, 6.20, 6.22) and increase the responsiveness to, say, $\rho = 1.20$. Income distribution and growth on the new wave train are then given by

$$v(\tau) = 66.31\% \,, \quad \bar{r}(\tau) = 13.40\% \,, \quad \bar{g}(\tau) = 3.58\% \quad (\tau = \frac{T}{2}) \tag{6.24}$$

Comparing these values with eq. (6.23), it is seen that a higher responsiveness of investors, or intensified competition, improves the position of profit earners and also leads to faster growth if workers receive the same real wages.

The qualitative changes in the wage share v and the average profit rate $\bar{r}$ are easily explained. A higher responsiveness ρ means that the more efficient techniques expand more rapidly as before. Average labour productivity $\bar{q}$ is therefore higher, which is tantamount to a lower average cost gap $\bar{z} = \bar{a}/a_N = 1/(\bar{q}\, a_N)$ (see eq.s (6.8) and (6.14)). Recalling eq.s (6.16) and (6.18) and using $w\bar{a} = (w/q_N)\,(\bar{a}/a_N) = \omega\bar{z}$, it remains to note that the wage share is related to the average cost gap by

$$v \;=\; \omega\,\bar{z} \tag{6.25}$$

In the presence of unchanged deflated real wages we therefore have that faster diffusion, which reduces the average cost gap $\bar{z}$, yields a lower wage share and a higher average rate of profit. Again we emphasise that this result and the underlying mechanism have no counterpart in the classical theory of distribution and growth.

In the further discussion of the long-run equilibria it will be useful to refer to the original Iwai (1984) model. Iwai characterises the techniques i by their unit costs c_i and postulates that the motions of the capacity shares are directly governed by these unit costs:

$$\dot{k}_i \;=\; -\,\gamma\,(\ln c_i - \ln \bar{c})\,k_i \tag{6.26}$$

where γ is a constant parameter that measures the general speed of technological diffusion (Iwai 1984, p.328). In Franke (2000) the intuition is confirmed that a higher value of γ indeed reduces the cost gap (analogously defined) on a wave train of this economy.[19] This result is central to the following discussion of the comparative dynamics.

Now, the profit rate differentials in the present model can be expressed as $r_i - \bar{r} = (-v/b)(a_i - \bar{a})/\bar{a}$. With eq. (6.25), the upper part of the diffusion equation (6.10) can thus be rewritten as

$$\dot{k}_i \;=\; \frac{-\,\rho\,\omega\,\bar{z}}{b}\,\frac{a_i - \bar{a}}{\bar{a}}\,k_i \tag{6.27}$$

As the percentage deviations of unit labour requirements a_i in (6.27) correspond to Iwai's log differences in unit costs c_i in (6.26), we have the following approximate relationship between the concept of the technological speed of diffusion and some central parameters in our model,

$$\gamma \;\approx\; \gamma' := \frac{\rho\,\omega\,\bar{z}}{b} \;=\; \frac{\rho\,v}{b} \tag{6.28}$$

Let us also call γ' the speed of technological diffusion.

Before going on, it is worth mentioning that, had the investment function (6.9) been specified as

$$g_i \;=\; s\,[\,\bar{r} + \rho(r_i - \bar{r})\,] \tag{6.9a}$$

eq. (6.28) would become $\gamma \approx s\,\rho\,\omega\,\bar{z}\,/\,b$. In this case, income distribution on the wave trains would also be dependent on the propensity to save out of profits, another result which is alien to the production price systems of the classical theory. Evidently, an increase in s has then the same effect as an increase in ρ. Hence, under eq. (6.9a) a higher savings propensity would lead to a lower wage share and a higher average rate of profit. It is also worth mentioning that the growth rate $\bar{g}$ of the economy would rise more than proportionately.

While in Iwai's model the speed of diffusion is an exogenous parameter, eq. (6.28) reveals that it is endogenous in our setting if the real wage rate ω is chosen as the exogenous income distribution variable.[20] Nevertheless, despite the interference of the average cost gap $\bar{z}$, a ceteris paribus increase in the responsiveness ρ to profit rate differentials will also cause the general speed of technological diffusion γ' to rise. Although, as indicated above, the average cost gap $\bar{z}$ decreases, the direct influence of ρ remains dominant, so that the product $\rho\bar{z}$ in (6.28) increases. (In fact, if $\rho\bar{z}$ were to decrease, the lower value of γ', according to the remark on eq. (6.26), would be associated with a higher value of $\bar{z}$, which would be a contradiction.)

This line of reasoning can be readily carried over to ceteris paribus changes in the deflated real wage rate ω. Just like ρ, a rise in ω speeds up the diffusion of new techniques and thus lowers the average cost gap $\bar{z}$, but again not so much as to diminish γ' in eq. (6.28). Since by (6.25) the higher product $\omega\bar{z}$ means a higher share of wages v, we can conclude that an increase in real wages ω induces a fall of the average rate of profit $\bar{r}$ in the new long-run equilibrium. In this sense, the classical inverse relationship between real wages and profits is re-established.

The income distribution effects just discussed are summarised in Figure 6.2, which shows the response surface of the average rate of profit $\bar{r}$ on the respective wave trains under variations of the deflated real wage rate ω and the responsiveness coefficient ρ. Over the range of parameters considered, the relationship between $\bar{r}$ and ω is nearly linear. On the other hand, $\bar{r}$ is a convex function of ρ, that is, the increments in the profit rate induced by a further rise in ρ become smaller with higher values of ρ.[21]

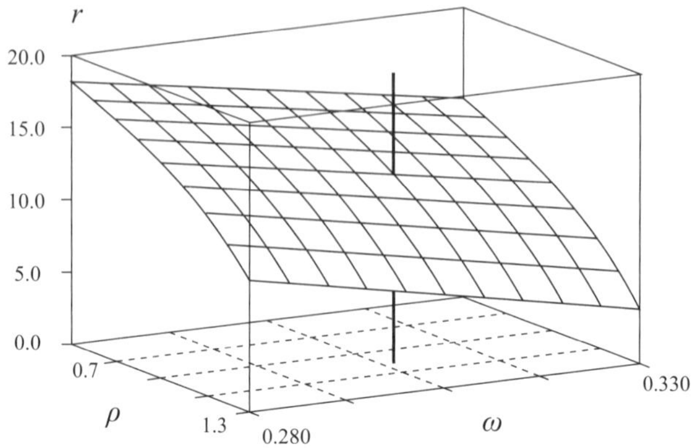

Figure 6.2 Average rate profit ($\tilde{r}$) on a wave train under variations of the deflated real wage rate (ω) and the responsiveness of investors (ρ)

Having discussed the effects of ω and ρ, the parameter ν of eq. (6.21) above, which characterises the introduction of new techniques, should not be neglected. Since a rise in ν corresponds to a faster diffusion of the best-practice techniques in their set-up phase, the effect will be expected to be similar to an increase in ρ. This is certainly true as regards the average profit rate or the wage share. To give an example, raising ν in the base scenario from $\nu = 0.0010$ to $\nu = 0.0030$ increases the average profit rate by about 4%, while reducing ν to $\nu = 0.0003$ lowers $\bar{r}$ by almost 4% (vis-à-vis $\bar{r} = 11.22\%$ and $v = 70.02\%$ in the base scenario, the precise figures are $\bar{r} = 15.23\%$ and $v = 63.21\%$ in the first case, and $\bar{r} = 7.32\%$, $v = 76.66\%$ in the second case).

However, it should also be noted that a change in ν affects the general speed of technological diffusion γ' as it was specified in eq. (6.28). The decrease of the cost gap $\bar{z}$ that is associated with a rise of ν means, perhaps somewhat surprisingly, that a faster introduction of new techniques reduces the overall speed of diffusion γ'. While $\gamma' = 0.412$ in the base scenario, we obtain $\gamma' = 0.372$ for $\nu = 0.0030$, and $\gamma' = 0.451$ for $\nu = 0.0003$.[22]

6.5 The 'Law of the Falling Rate of Profit'

In this section we return to the remaining magnitude b in the specification of the speed of diffusion γ' in (6.28) that has not been varied yet. Formally, a higher capital-output ratio b has the same effect as a ceteris paribus decrease in ρ: it raises the average cost gap $\bar{z}$ on the new wave train distribution. The corresponding average rate of profit therefore declines for two reasons: one is the direct effect of the higher denominator b in the definition of profit rates, the other is the indirect effect of the change in the wage share, which owing to eq. (6.25) is driven up by the rise in $\bar{z}$.[23]

The result is reminiscent of the Marxian law of the falling rate of profit that is attributed to a rising trend in the organic composition of capital. In the Sraffian production price systems, this subject is usually studied in the form of capital-using and labour-saving technical change. It is, however, well-known that here Okishio's theorem holds (Okishio 1961). When a new method of production replaces an existing one because of higher profitability in a given system of production prices, then, if the real wage remains fixed, the uniform rate of profit in the new equilibrium system will inexorably exceed the original profit rate. There is no scope for a falling rate of profit in this setting. While Okishio's theorem highlights the salient point in the discussion on the internal consistency of the Marxian law, that capitalists would avoid any technical change that reduces the profit rate, the problem of coming to terms with 'micro-rational' behaviour is resolved in the present evolutionary framework. At any point in time, the innovation that yields the highest rate of profit will be introduced, irrespective of the kind of technical change it involves. Clearly, an investor who hesitates to invest in such a technique with a higher capital-output ratio because he is afraid of the consequences for the average profit rate in later years, even if he were able to foresee them, would only earn less profits than his competitors. And of course, the average rate of profit is not his concern.[24]

In the above experiment where two economies with the same growth path of labour productivity but different capital-output ratios b are compared, there are two magnitudes that affect the organic composition of capital, x. In Marxian terms, x is the ratio of constant capital to variable capital. Translating this as the capital-wages ratio and decomposing it as $x = (K/wL) = (K/Y)\,(Y/wL) = b/v = b/\omega\bar{z}$, it is seen that the higher average cost gap $\bar{z}$ in the second economy with the higher value of b has a negative impact on x. Nevertheless, the positive effect from b is dominant, so that indeed the organic composition of capital turns out to be higher in the second economy. (The argument is the same as in the previous section for ρ: a higher b reduces $\gamma' = \rho\omega\bar{z}/b$ in (6.28), despite the rise in $\bar{z}$, so that $x = b/\omega\bar{z}$ increases.)

On the other hand, the result that the economy with the higher capital-output ratio exhibits a lower average rate of profit is not particularly exciting. Since labour productivity was assumed to grow at the same rate in this economy, the gains in profitability accruing to an innovation are less than in the economy with the lower value of b, that is, the differences $r_N - r_{N-1}$, and generally $r_i - r_{i-1}$, are smaller. It therefore comes as no surprise that also the average rate of profit is bound to fall.

The discussion so far was based on the ceteris paribus assumption of a fixed value of the responsiveness to differential profits, ρ. This concept may be considered to be too mechanistic. The lower differences $r_i - r_{i-1}$ in eq. (6.10) imply that investors in the profitable techniques wish to expand their market shares less rapidly. By contrast, another basis of comparing two economies with different capital-output ratios may be that one fixes the differences $(\dot{k}_i/k_i) - (\dot{k}_{i-1}/k_{i-1})$ in the growth rates of two successive techniques i and $i-1$ at which they increase their market shares. This hypothesis is captured by variations of ρ proportionally to b. In fact, if the ratio ρ/b remains unaltered in the speed of technological diffusion γ' in (6.28), the average cost gap $\bar{z}$ on the wave train would not be affected either. Since the unit labour requirements a_i are identical, eq. (6.27) shows that in both economies the market shares of the techniques evolve in the same way. Even if the alternative basis of comparison may be felt to be somewhat arbitrary, the few observations may suffice to indicate that a careful investigation into the effects of capital-using technical change has to include more aspects than just the changes of the capital-output ratio in some definitional relationships.[25]

Note also that if, over longer periods, capital-using technical change is associated with higher growth rates of labour productivity while wages continue to increase at the original growth rate, the wage share would systematically fall and (possibly besides unemployment) the economy would sooner or later run into serious conflicts over income distribution. This is only one point where it becomes clear that, if we go beyond the narrow constraints of the present equilibrium setting, the analysis needs to be complemented by a study of additional dynamic mechanisms.

6.6 Conclusions

The model studied in this chapter is an elementary extension of an evolutionary process advanced by Iwai (1984). Translating the Schumpeterian ideas on the dynamic interaction of technological diffusion and innovation into a formal language, Iwai's main goal was to question the appropriateness of the classical and neoclassical concept of long-run equilibrium. He demonstrated that an economy's state of technology will indeed be in a perpetual disequilibrium (from the viewpoint of classical and neoclassical model building). Although the evolutionary pressure on profit-seeking firms constitutes a mechanism that steers the economy toward a classical (or neoclassical) equilibrium in which all firms use the most efficient production method available, the function of innovation lies precisely in upsetting this equilibrating tendency. In the long-run, the opposite forces of diffusion and innovation balance, which implies that a multitude of diverse production methods with a wide range of efficiencies will coexist forever.

This general idea comes most clearly to the fore in a deterministic setting where innovations occur at regular intervals every T years. (Iwai's original hypothesis of stochastic innovations would have complicated our analysis.) While production methods come into existence, run through a life-cycle and eventually die out, the whole spectrum of different techniques reproduces itself, only at an ever increasing scale as time progresses. This means that the role of technique i at some time t is taken over by its more advanced successor at a later point in time, $t+T$. Drawing on Henkin and Polterovich (1991), this smooth evolution of the economy has been called a wave train. Compared to the usual (neo-)classical conception, it may be said that wave trains provide a notion of long-run equilibrium at a higher level.

On the other hand, the balanced growth paths here examined should not be taken too literally. Although they are attractors and, once perturbed, the economy finds its way back to them, the adjustment process would take a long span of time; typically several decades as shown in Franke (2000). There are several parameters in the model that one could not reasonably consider to remain fixed over these periods. So we see our chapter's main contribution, not so much in providing an elaborate equilibrium analysis, but in widening the narrow classical and neoclassical perspective on technical progress. Correspondingly, the main purpose of a highly stylised model such as the present one is to serve as a frame of reference.

On this basis, classical and neoclassical theories may be better aware of significant factors in long-run growth and income distribution for which, as they are presently set up, there is no place in the formal analysis. More specifically, the chapter has made this point for the contemporary classical theory of the wage-profit frontier. Following this approach and employing the (deflated) real wage rate to parameterise the side of wages, we have demonstrated that, in a wave train equilibrium, distribution can no longer be decoupled from the 'quantity side' and is in fact heavily dependent on factors related to the speed of technological diffusion. Thus, it could be seen that distribution depends most prominently on a parameter that measures the general responsiveness of investors to differential rates of profit.

The model has sought to integrate the classical concept of income distribution into the Schumpeterian framework in a straightforward manner. In order to follow the classical tradition and be able to compare directly the level of (deflated) real wages on the growth paths of two distinct economies, it was necessary to treat the rate of technical progress as an exogenous variable, assuming that it is the same in both economies. If one conceives of extensions of the model in the direction of endogenous technical change (which might also fail to be Harrod-neutral), then this type of comparison will have to be replaced with a comparison of the growth rates of real wages, or with a comparison of the wage shares in national income.

Appendix

Generally in the simulations, time is sliced into (arbitrarily) small economic adjustment periods of length h and the discrete time analogues with step size h of the differential equations are used. This device, while simpler than the Runge-Kutta approximations, is not purely technical but has an obvious economic interpretation. Thus, in 'normal' periods where $t \notin U(N_t)$, we take the capital growth rates of eq. (6.9) and determine $\tilde{k}_i(t+h) = k_i(t) + h\,[s\bar{r}(t) + \rho\,(r_i(t) - \bar{r}(t))\,]\,k_i(t)$ for $i \leq N_t$, which corresponds to the level of capital stocks in the next period $t+h$. Subsequent renormalization yields the (capital and) capacity shares, $k_i(t+h) = \tilde{k}_i(t+h) \,/\, \sum_{j \leq N} \tilde{k}_j(t+h)$.

The second part of eq. (6.10), which concerns the set-up phase $t \in U(N_t)$, is a shorthand notation for the following procedure. The growth rates of the capital stocks for techniques $i \leq N_t - 1$ are rescaled such that the growth rate of the total capital stock continues to be equal to $s\bar{r}$. That is, defining $\tilde{g}_i = s\bar{r}(t) + \rho(r_i(t) - \bar{r}(t))$ and $\alpha = (s\bar{r} -$

$\kappa) \,/\, \sum_{j \le N-1} \tilde{g}_j \, k_j(t)$, the growth rates g_i for $i \le N_t{-}1$ are determined by $g_i(t) = \alpha \tilde{g}_i$.[26] For the BPT we put $k_N(t{+}h) = k_N(t) + h\kappa$ by way of eq. (6.5), whereas for the ordinary techniques $i \le N_t{-}1$ we first compute $\tilde{k}_i(t{+}h) = k_i(t) + h\, g_i(t) k_i(t)$ and then $k_i(t{+}h) = \tilde{k}_i(t{+}h) \,/\, [k_N(t{+}h) + \sum_{j \le N-1} \tilde{k}_j(t{+}h)]$.

Another detail is the old vintages, which tend to disappear in the long-run. For practical reasons we reset the capacity share of the least productive technique back to zero in the computer simulations when it declines below a benchmark of 0.1%.

To derive eq. (6.15), note that for a best-practice technique $N = N_{mT}$ one has $\ln a_N + g_w\, mT = \ln a_N + g_w\, mT = \ln a_{N_o} =: C$. Thus, with $t = mT + \tau$, $\ln a_i + g_w t = (\ln a_i - \ln a_N) + \ln a_N + g_w t = \ln(a_i/a_N) + \ln a_N + g_w\, mT + g_w \tau = \ln z_{N-i} + g_w \tau + C$, and eq. (6.15) follows from eq. (6.13).

The numerical parameters in eq. (6.19) are obtained as follows. The capital-output ratio is taken directly from Simon (1990, p.151). Next, in obvious notation, the ratio of gross investment to GNP is equal to $(\dot{K} + \delta K)/Y = \bar{g}b + \delta b$. Adopting Simon's (p.153) ratio of 16% and setting $\bar{g} = 3\%$ yields the value of δ. As for the savings propensity s, we take a wage share $v = 70\%$ (see Simon, p.150), compute the profit rate $\bar{r} = (1-v)/b - \delta$, and thus retrieve s from the Cambridge equation as $s = \bar{g}/\bar{r}$.

Notes

1 This chapter is based on Franke (2000a).

2 Although endogenous rates of diffusion and technical progress are an urgent problem, it is still a useful research strategy to confine the analysis, in a first step, to such an elementary, perhaps even mechanical model. More elaborate versions, for which a great variety of modelling concepts exist, may be subsequently designed in separate steps. In this way it is possible to distinguish basic effects of innovation and diffusion from more special effects that may be associated with different forms of endogenization. A premature endogenization of technical change runs the risk of confusing these effects and their theoretical significance.

3 In Iwai's (1984) model, the introduction of innovations is governed by a random process. The appropriate equilibrium notion is then one of stochastic equilibrium, which is constituted by an invariant probability distribution of 'cost gaps'. (A similar concept of cost gaps is introduced in Section 6.3.)

[4] To be precise, within the chapter's one-good economy (but only here) this holds true if the position of workers is characterised by the (deflated) real wage rate, rather than the share of wages in national income. Our methodological stance on this issue will be made clearer at the end of Section 6.3.

[5] Since (in eq. (6.10) below) the diffusion process yields a growth rate formulation for the changes of the capacity shares, $\dot{k}_i/k_i$ = some functional expression, the BPT can only be subjected to the diffusion equation after a positive capacity share $k_N > 0$ has been erected. The concept of the set-up phase $T_u > 0$ was introduced to make the time path of k_N continuous (rather than assuming a jump from zero up to a certain positive level at times $t \in J$).

[6] Retardation factors that prevent firms from adopting the most productive technique immediately are, in particular, adjustment costs, uncertainty, and the often proprietary nature of the newest technology (see Soete and Turner 1984, p.617).

[7] A referee has pointed out two assumptions implicit in this diffusion model. First, there is no market for used capital goods of older vintages that may be bought at lower prices, so that their prospective profit rate could equal the profit rate on the most productive equipment. Second, the price of the machines used by the older techniques continues to be determined by their production cost, since they are being produced.

[8] The precise details of the renormalization, within the discrete-time framework of the numerical simulations, are given in the appendix.

[9] In more general models demanding less knowledge from the agents, g_w may be plausibly replaced by expectations about future productivity growth, possibly combined with a Phillips curve relationship as in Silverberg and Lehnert (1993). We here neglect these elements since they are mainly a matter of disequilibrium adjustments and the economy's equilibrium evolution would only be marginally affected by such alternative specifications. (Wages would rise less smoothly between two innovations, while their average growth rate over time would remain the same.)

[10] Formally, with $N+1 = N_t + 1 = N_{t+T}$ and $z = z_{N-i} = z_{(N+1)-(i+1)}$, the relationship reads $\phi[\ln z + g_w T + C] = \phi[\ln z_{(N+1)-(i+1)} + g_w T + C] = \phi[\ln z_{N-i} + g_w T + C] = k_i^\star(t) = k_{i+1}^\star(t+T)$.

[11] Its rise in the early stages, when it was still among the most efficient techniques, is hidden by the crest of the distribution surface.

[12] Of course, these differences cannot be directly compared to that of Figure 6.1 since we have no information about the probably varying capital-output ratios in Iwai's example.

[13] Strictly speaking, our results could be compatible with the existence of another, but unstable, wave train, although such a phenomenon would have no practical relevance even if it existed.

[14] In all that follows it will be understood that averages like $\bar{r}$, $\bar{a}$ and $\bar{z}$ (the average cost gap) are based on the capacity shares $k_i^\star$ of a wave train.

[15] Conversely, we may fix $\bar{r}$ (or $v = 1 - b(\bar{r} + \delta)$, respectively), obtain the associated wave train including $\bar{a}(t)$, and then from $w(t) = v/\bar{a}(t)$ compute the deflated real wage as $\omega = w(t_m)/q_{N(m)}$ for some integer number m.

[16] Again, see the appendix for further details.

[17] Actually, λ was derived from a discrete-time rate of growth $\tilde{\lambda} = 3\%$. That is, λ was set such that $\exp(\lambda T) = q_i/q_{i-1} = 1 + \tilde{\lambda}T$, which yields $\lambda = \ln(1 + \tilde{\lambda}T)/T$.

[18] For example, an increase in T together with the corresponding reduction of κ or T_u means a smaller number of 'active' techniques i on the wave train. However, the graph connecting the points $(\ln z_i, \phi(\ln z_i))$ remains (essentially) the same, and so will remain the average rates of profit and growth, etc. That the graphs do not exactly coincide is due to the discrete state space of the technological coefficients.

[19] By using an approximation procedure, Iwai derives an explicit mathematical formula for his (stochastic) economy that produces the same result. In other respects, however, his approximation procedure is problematic; see Franke (2000).

[20] γ' will again be exogenous if instead the average profit rate, or equivalently the wage share v, is chosen as the exogenous distributional variable.

[21] The reference stick indicates the base scenario.

[22] The possible effects from the set-up phase of innovations tends to be underestimated in the literature. For example, Silverberg and Lehnert (1993) and Silverberg and Verspagen (1997) in their stochastic and otherwise more detailed models do not even make ν or a similar parameter explicit. They just mention that the initial capacity share of new techniques is 'small' and do not discuss any variations in this respect.

[23] We may note in passing an interesting phenomenon that occurs if alternatively the wage share v is the distributional variable that is held constant. Then not only does the average profit rate decline by eq. (6.17), but, since $\bar{z}$ rises again, also the deflated real wage rate $\omega = v/\bar{z}$. Incidentally, this cannot possibly happen in a production price framework where, in the presence of a fixed wage share, an increase in some coefficients of the capital stock matrix B decreases the (uniform) rate of profit, but raises the real wage rate; see Figure 1 in Franke (1999).

[24] Note, however, a difference between the problem studied by Okishio and the present framework. Okishio's theorem assumes that the real wage stays constant when the labour productivity increases from one economy to the other, while our discussion allows real wages to rise over time in both economies at the same (unchanged) rate as their labour productivity rises over time.

[25] Thus, the Marxian decomposition (with P = profits) $r = P/K = (P/wL)(wL/K) = (P/wL)/x$, which referring to the wage share v may here be equivalently expressed as $(r+\delta)x = (r+\delta)(b/v) = (1-v)/v$, is only of limited explanatory power.

[26] Of course, this only makes economic sense if $\kappa < s\bar{r}$, which is checked in the simulations.

PART III

Systemic Crises, Policy Responses and the Road to Social Capitalism

7. Capital Accumulation, Environmental Decay and Rehabilitation

> *More than a quarter of the nation's bridges are structurally deficient or functionally obsolete. Leaky pipes lose an estimated seven billion gallons of clean drinking water every day. And aging sewage systems send billions of gallons of untreated wastewater cascading into the nation's waterways each year. These are among the findings of a report to be released Wednesday by the American Society of Civil Engineers, which assigned an overall D grade to the nation's infrastructure and estimated that it would take a $2.2 trillion investment from all levels of government over the next five years to bring it into a state of good repair.* (Michael Cooper, January 27th 2009, The New York Times)

The 'crises' we are going to consider in this chapter are environmental ones. There are early examples where firms started mining, e.g. gold seeking activities which simply destroyed the affected environment, used natural products in new contexts, e.g. water reservoir filling for electricity production, deforesting of the rainforest in order to plant food and so on. Often, the search for natural products in new areas leads to situations where the danger for the environment is still unknown or is underrated (like, e.g. oil production in the sea).

There is a gradual systemic effect here at work, driven by ruthless cost competition which seeks to produce the output as cheaply as possible without concern about environmental effects (which are quite often also affecting human beings – at work as well as at home). It can easily be seen that the whole natural system as well as the economic one are concerned by such crises, since the different actions of environmental misuse can influence each other significantly. We discuss such 'systemic crises' mainly in this chapter with regard to the USA as an example of an industrially developed country with a not really regulated capitalism as far as environmental protection is concerned. Here again, it can be seen how urgent the matter of a regulation of even advanced capitalist economies is. Environmental misbehaviour is of course not only a problem of developed capitalist countries, but is even more a problem for example in the so-called BRIC countries (Brasil, Russia, India, China). One of the main environmental problems in Brasilia is the destruction of the rainforest, while Russia's problems are its nuclear power stations, its air pollution as well as the contamination of rivers and lakes. The latter problems are also well-known from India and China.

7.1 Introduction

In this chapter[1] we expand the model of Chapter 3 which led us from unrestricted capitalism to the ideal of a flexicurity economy. We now consider environmental protection (or if significant damage has already been done, rehabilitation) as a next important matter, investigating first the case of what happens in such a context in a Goodwinian economy of unrestricted capitalism. Thereafter we examine what happens in a flexicurity reformulation of the Goodwin approach in the presence of processes of capital accumulation with negative externalities on the infrastructure of the economy.

Environmental issues have become most relevant topics in the public debate, at least since catastrophes like the Italian dioxin crisis in Seveso 1976, the Three Mile Island near nuclear disaster (Harrisburg, Pennsylvania) in 1979 or the Union Carbide gas leak in Bhopal in 1984 have shocked the world. The list of such events becomes longer each year, the most recent one being the unprecedented nuclear catastrophe at Fukushima in Japan. Meanwhile more worldwide comprehension of the dangers of environmental disasters exists and also many (inter)national programs have been developed in order to reduce the extent of such catastrophes. One reason for such progression is certainly insights (or hindsight?) and growing knowledge about climate change (global warming) and its consequences, but also the reasons which are responsible for them like too much CO^2 emission (see, for example, IEA (2010) in the preparation of the Cancun meeting). It is interesting to remember that pollution already existed long before global warming became a topic, as for example the irresponsible way of industry concerning water pollution due to discharge of liquid waste products shows. Examples are many rivers, like the river Rhine in Europe or the Hudson river in the United States. Partly, the same happens in agriculture. Furthermore it is a remarkable fact that in some cases individual, group or community actions were able to start measures which finally helped to overcome pollution problems. Especially inhabitants of concerned regions in the surroundings of rivers stood up for improvements (see Hudson River Sloop Clearwater, 2011).

The most relevant international agreement is the Kyoto Protocol from 1997, which is an international agreement that has been binding the engaged nations to the United Nations' Framework Convention on Climate Change. An important aim was to reduce greenhouse gas emissions. Unfortunately, subsequent conferences like Copenhagen 2009 or Cancun 2010 have failed to lead to a renewed agreement after the official end of the Kyoto agreement in 2012. Nordhaus (2010) has analysed that the negative climatic and economic consequences could only be stopped with help of 'globally designed environmental policies' which should enhance national and international efforts in overcoming selfish arguments.[2]

There are a variety of further international environmental agreements, but in many cases the cooperation can be afflicted by national demands, as Barrett (1994) demonstrates with two different models. The Year Book 2010 moreover gives an overview of the United Nations Environment Programme (UNEP Year Book, 2010) which points to main environmental problems such as unsustainable use of resources or the growing number of harmful substances which are endangering human health. The report mentions, for example, nanomaterials, brominated flame retardants and toxic waste scandals, and thus gives a detailed overview about environmental problems some of which are only recently erupting because the corresponding production processes have only recently been extended worldwide like nanomaterials (ibid, 23-32). In spite of mostly unsolved problems and the open way of the continuation and development of the Kyoto agreement there are worldwide many international environmental cooperations which are part of the UN's system of international environmental governance, including regional environmental governance as, for example, practiced by the EU (ibid, 1ff.).

Furthermore, in many countries, especially industrial or industrialising nations, organisations have been existing for many years which deal with questions of nature and increasingly also engage in larger environmental questions including the problems of nuclear energy. There are also many international non-governmental organisations such as Greenpeace or WWF (World Wide Fund For Nature) which have national and local organisations as well. In the United States, the

NRDC (Natural Resources Defense Council) deals with all questions of environment, its destruction and rehabilitation. With more than 1.3 million members, it is an effective environmental organisation. It calls for 'preventing pollution, defending endangered wildlife and wild places, curbing global warming and creating a clean energy future' and stresses the priorities as 'reviving the world's oceans, ensuring safe and sufficient water or fostering sustainable communities' (NRDC, 2011). Hence, it is no surprise that the NRDC has intensively dealt with the official American approach to a strict climate and energy legislation.

In 2009, the American Clean Energy and Security Act (ACES) was approved by the Congress after a long time of discussions. The bill is also called Waxman-Markey Bill after its authors. In spite of all positive reactions to Waxman-Markey many arguments are brought forward against it, most of them from an economic perspective about the costs and job losses which Krugman (2009) could easily disprove as being beside the point. An analysis of NRDC even supposes that ACES will boost the economy due to necessary investments and it expects – as stressed in Krugman (2009) – that the costs to American households will be less than a postage stamp per day. The most convincing reasons for the bill are, of course, its enormous environmental implications (Lashof, Wong and Johnson, 2009). In 2010, the Gulf of Mexico oil catastrophe demanded political reactions which – besides other necessary decision taking in the senate – led to decisions different from the ones of the ACES which have been accepted by Congress in 2009 (see, for example, Hulse and Herszenhorn, 2010). There are further developments in 2011, especially dealing with the recommendations of the National Commission on the BP Deepwater Horizon Oil Spill and Offshore Drilling, which delivered its final report in January 2011 (National Commission on the BP Deepwater Horizon Oil Spill and Offshore Drilling, 2011).

These permanent catastrophes show that insights are not yet strong enough to prevent environmental misconduct, wrongdoing and malpractice in spite of national and international decisions. It can easily be shown that international enterprises, like Glencore, large companies and even innovative firms are involved in such behaviour in order to get financial gains and profits by outpacing their business competition. Thus it has to be asked to what extent national and international legal approaches have a chance to impact industrial negotiations on necessary changes in ecological and environmental behaviour. Of course, there are enterprises, companies and firms which agree to such necessities and are willing to organise their industrial projects accordingly but this does not apply to the majority of firms as many case studies show.

The Gulf of Mexico Oil Catastrophe in 2010 is a good example to show such a behaviour since it became obvious after the event that the extreme environmental pollution of the sea and the coasts as well as the death of workers was at least partly due to irresponsible costs savings which led to the explosion and the following spill. This is also the conclusion of the final report of the White House oil spill commission in January 2011 which assumed that many of the taken activities and decisions have increased the risk of the ecological disaster because the companies were mostly interested in saving time and money. In the report, BP was accused of faults, but also the government was blamed for not acting appropriately (National Commission on the BP Deepwater Horizon Oil Spill and Offshore Drilling, 2011). The third part of the final report is called 'lessons learned' which summarises the changes in energy policy that should now be adopted. Here, it is clearly stated that both – industry and state – are responsible for safer actions and thus have to cooperate and underlie stricter controls (ibid, p.216ff.).

This is especially necessary since 'the BP Deepwater Horizon disaster undermined public faith in the oil and gas industry, in government regulators, and even in America's ability to respond to crises' (ibid, p.293), which again points to the double responsibility of the government and industrial companies – here from a different point of view. The commission demands 'that both government and industry must make serious changes to establish the high level of safety in drilling operations on the outer continental shelf' (ibid, p.306). In spite of all critics, there is no doubt in the final report that offshore oil and gas production will be continued, since offshore wells already yield one-third of current U.S. oil production (ibid, p.294). NRDC (2011a, p.3) complains that there is still little information available of such production on the 'biological and ecological impacts'. This also holds true with regard to public health (ibid, p.11ff.). The demand that 'industry must put safety first' (ibid, p.15) is certainly to be underlined, but a look at other drilling down procedures of oil and gas production can raise doubts whether there is a real industrial interest in environmental protection.

'Drilling down' is the common procedure of oil and gas production which holds true for offshore production as well as different forms of production processes on land. The question here is why this method leads to dangerous toxic problems. Mall, Buccino and Nichols (2007, p.4) explain the environmental dangers of these production processes, which always begin with drilling a well, in the following way: First, toxic substances such as pipe dope can be used to reduce frictions, drilling fluids, or hydraulic fluids. Then, those drilling fluids can become waste or have to be kept in a reserve pit in the ground. Other chemicals may be used to inhibit corrosion, scale buildup, or bacteria growth in the employed equipment. A well may begin producing oil, gas, or both after the drilling is completed. This demands for large amounts of a fluid, which can contain oil and toxic substances. To separate the various constituents of the raw product drawn from the well is the next task. Natural gas may need to be separated from other gas items such as carbon dioxide, hydrogen sulfide, propane, and butane as well as oil from dirt or sand. Toxic substances may be used in the resulting separation processes. A strong question here is what happens to the substances separated from the natural gas and other wastes. This short description thus already shows the different toxic dangers which are involved in the drilling procedure (ibid, p.4).

Two of the regions which are strongly concerned with the chosen drilling procedures and the implied pollution are the Rocky Mountains (ibid, p.31) and the Marcellus Shale in Eastern North America, leading from Pennsylvania to New York State (geology.com, 2011; NRDC 2009). Both regions turned out to offer immense resources especially of natural gas so that drilling procedures were started on a large scale. As Mall, Buccino and Nichols (2007, p.v) report there are already many people living in the Rocky Mountains close to oil and gas production places who complain about health problems. This can happen due to the fact that wells can emit toxic materials into the air (ibid, p.5ff). Human health is also in danger when the oil and gas production pollutes drinking water (ibid, p.14ff.). One problem is that many physicians are not yet able to recognise the environmental origin of many kinds of illnesses. And even the people themselves are sometimes hesitating in making their illnesses and its origin public because they fear the loss of workplaces in their communities (ibid, p.v).

Drilling down just refers to the way oil and gas are produced, that is, beginning with drilling a well. In many regions there is moreover the need for a closely related method in the oil and gas industry, which is ecologically very problematic. This so-called hydrofracking or simply fracking – which is officially called horizontal hydraulic fracturing. Fracking works in a way that a fluid is injected into a rock in order to release the gas which raises serious environmental and health problems due to the disposal of radioactive toxins and other dangerous substances. The main danger is the contamination of groundwater resources and thus drinking water, but also the production of smog-forming pollutants, which contribute to air pollution problems (see, for example, Sourcewatch (2011), Kenworthy et al. (2011). Despite the increasing discussions of such problems in the United States, similar methods have been introduced in Germany in order to get access to deeply hidden gas in the earth. In the United States, the demand for this natural gas is very high since it has become an important component of electricity generation and the energy mix as Kenworthy et al. (2011) explain. Furthermore they suspect that the environmental problems are oppressed due to the fact that the provision of a lower carbon future with help of natural gas is desirable, in spite of the ecologically dangerous method of hydraulic fracturing. Kenworthy et al. (2011) formulate the fear that major public health threats could arise while trying to solve other environmental issues. It is also of concern that 'the oil and gas industry enjoys numerous exemptions from the provisions of federal rules intended to protect human health and the environment' (Mall, Buccino and Nichols (2007, iv). Besides an impressive number of such exemptions, there is also the fact that the oil and gas industry can withhold information which of course concerns the working of organisations like NRDC.

There are proposals and attempts to improve fracking with the help of better and more advanced technologies (Kenworthy and Weiss 2011, p.5f.). It is the disposing of wastewater which has most environmental risks so that some companies are developing water purification systems which are regarded as a possible solution (ibid, p.5f.). The Centre of American Progress demands the solution of many questions before 'a massive expansion of natural gas use' can be committed. This includes besides health and environment protection also 'a better understanding of whether switching to natural gas will produce significant reductions in carbon dioxide pollution' (ibid, p.6).

Many further demands and proposals are published which all show the deep concern and uncertainty of the population and the environmental organisations. Mall, Buccino and Nichols (2007, vi; p.28ff.) demand an end to the exemptions from existing laws for the oil and gas industry and require that the industry should develop appropriate technological solutions. Furthermore, they demand more testing for possible pollution and better care with regard to health. More water tests are also demanded in Pennsylvania where problems with wastewater have become a major topic (Urbina, 2011). Water contamination has also turned out as a problem in the Marcellus Shale. The need for more investigation is therefore high. This also holds true with regard to air quality and changes in the landscape (see NRDC, 2009). NRDC asks their readers to become active in participating in environmental activities and demand more activity from elected officials. In many cases of environmental disasters which are produced by companies or firms, the state is not completely innocent since it can be forced in principle by legislation to not allow unexperienced methods or quicker – and thus insecure – procedures, in its cooperation with firms which might otherwise adopt such procedures. The drilling down in oil and gas production in the United States is a good example of this. Furthermore, states often feel the necessity of saving money and are therefore accepting dubious drilling down projects. It should in principle also be taken into account that besides the partly dramatic results of industrially produced pollution, the global climate change and CO^2 emissions are the worldwide and thus general problems which have to be tackled through cooperative international action. The problems discussed here are to be regarded as part of this larger problem.

7.2 Unrestricted Accumulation Dynamics and Environmental Decline

We have seen in Chapters 1 and 2 that generating order and economic viability in market economies through large swings in the unemployment rate, thereby degrading part of the families that make up the society, represent one way to make capitalism work, through the establishment of the distributive cycle, but this way must surely be rejected from the societal point of view because of its social consequences. Such a reproduction mechanism is not compatible with an educated and democratic society in the long-run which is supposed to provide equal opportunity to all of its citizens. In Chapters 2 and 3 we have already discussed modern debates on Employers of Last and First Resort intended to overcome the social decline that is resulting from low income work and a large reserve army of unemployed people.

In this chapter we now turn to the environmental damage that can result from an unrestricted operation of the distributive cycle. To this end we first consider the distributive cycle as it is obtainable from US data by plotting the employment rate e against the wage share v as shown in the phase plot in Figure 7.1. The dots in this phase plot are the data points while the clockwise rotating curve has been obtained by HP filtering.[3] In contrast to the usual use of this filter we have here removed the six business cycles around the HP trend that characterise the considered period of the US economy. This HP trend is in fact a long-phased cycle of the Goodwin (1967) growth cycle type with the same orientation as this baseline model of the distributive cycle.

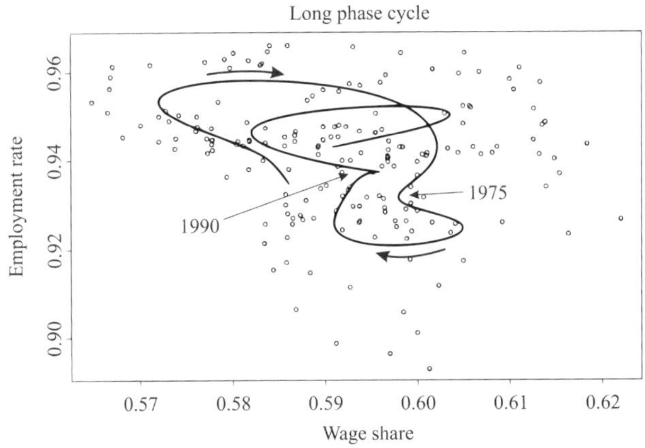

Figure 7.1 The postwar US distributive cycle (1958.0–2004.5)

In Tavani, Flaschel and Taylor (2011), see here chapter 4, we have introduced a variant of the Goodwin (1967) growth cycle model, which besides the cross-dual Marxian dynamics contains a dual dynamics of Keynesian type (based on the Keynesian goods market multiplier dynamics and a real wage barrier in the Chapters 1–3). We have there also used a nonlinearity in the wage Phillips curve (also obtained from the US data set associated with Figure 7.1) which is of the type of a tangens function, that is, relatively flat in the middle and much steeper to the left and the right. Wages are therefore very flexible for fairly large and fairly low unemployment rates with respect to demand pressure on the market for labour and fairly unresponsive around the average value of the employment rate $\bar{e}$ over the business cycle.

One result of this nonlinearity is that the wage share may move into a direction not predicted by the simple Goodwin model, namely when prices are more flexible than wages in an area around $\bar{e}$. For relatively low and falling employment rates this can imply that the wage share goes up since prices in its denominator 'fall' faster than wages, while it can fall when the economy moves into a significant recovery, since prices rise more than wages. This gives rise to the two kinks in Figure 7.1 (around 1975 and 1990) which makes the distributive cycle less regular than is suggested by many other variants of the Goodwin (1967) model. By and large the profit squeeze at the top of the cycle and the wage squeeze at its bottom are clearly visible in Figure 7.1 as well as the recovery on its left side and the downturn of the economy on its right.

The arguments against an acceptance of the reserve army mechanism put forth so far in this book from the social and the political perspective can now be summarised in a very simple statement, namely that what is shown in Figure 7.1 (and Figure 1.3) should not be happening again in this century, since this may give rise to social phenomena, also in the advanced capitalist countries, which further deepens the processes of social segmentation we can observe for example in Germany already in a disturbing way. It could then happen that the evolution of age poverty that is at present predictable from the low income sector in the German society is then augmented by a new sector of low income work of those members in the society that are at present not yet in the labour market.

This problematic situation was therefore contrasted in the preceding chapters with models of an alternative social structure of capital accumulation that allowed for the combination of a highly competitive capitalist market economy with a human rights bill that includes the right (and the obligation) to work, and to get income from this work that at the least supports basic needs and basic happiness. The Danish flexicurity system may provide an example of the path towards such an alternative.

By contrast, a laissez-faire capitalistic society that ruins family structures (and their ethics) to a considerable degree (through alienated work, degrading unemployment and education- and value-decomposing visual media) cannot be made compatible with a democratic society in the long-run, since it produces conflicts ranging from social segmentation to class and race based social clashes. We have argued in this book so far that stable balanced reproduction is possible under a socially responsible regime of flexicurity capitalism that is backed by educational principles conducive to skill formation and citizenship education in a democratic society. These arguments are now carried one step further by considering the environmental externalities of an unrestricted working of capitalism, also in its advanced forms, here by way of a specific Goodwin type model where firms work in a given infrastructure that can de damaged, but also improved depending on the social political forces that surround the forces of production at work in the economy.

7.3 Dissent-driven Capitalism and Infrastructure Decay

> *The oil and gas industry in the United States has expanded rapidly during the last decade, particularly in the Rocky Mountain region. But oil and gas production releases pollution that can have serious impacts on people's health and the surrounding air, water, and land. Although these operations are frequently located near homes, schools, and other community resources, the oil and gas industry enjoys numerous exemptions from provisions of federal laws intended to protect human health and the environment. NRDC's latest report provides a comprehensive assessment of these loopholes, which allow oil and gas companies to continue polluting despite the risks.* (Natural Resources Defense Council, October 31, 2007).[4]

In this section we discuss the implications of a Goodwin (1967) representation of the growth cycle of capitalist economies that is enhanced by the effects of infrastructure consumption and later on its rehabilitation. We are able to treat in this framework two fundamental problems of the process of capital accumulation, namely the partial degradation of workers through recurrent situations of mass unemployment (in the depressed phase) and the partial destruction of the infrastructure through the recurrent overexploitation of 'nature' (in the boom phase). We stress that the Goodwin model does not imply that capitalists are solely responsible for the occurrence of such effects. Instead, the long-phased overshooting nature of the conflict over income distribution between capital and labour drives the results with one group more dominant in the boom and the other one in the bust – where the effects of the boom are removed again to a certain degree, always by way of overshooting wage shares and profit shares on the one hand and overshooting employment or unemployment rates on the other hand.

We will show in later sections that it is by no means necessary to create order in Western type market economies in this way. Instead, structures of economic and social reproduction can be designed where order is created in a way that preserves the flexibility of Western type market economies, yet that is moreover consensus-based through its provision of security in the labour markets. This possibility implies that the crude reserve-army based reproduction mechanism of most current capitalist economies can be overcome by institutional reforms in the labour markets that may lead at least advanced capitalist democracies from the welfare state through workfare arrangements towards flexicurity and maybe beyond.

We begin with a brief formulation of the model. The growth rate $\hat{w}$ of the money wage of workers is assumed to be given by a conventional money wage Phillips curve (where the rate of employment, e, replaces the unemployment rate, $\bar{e}$ the employment rate that corresponds to the NAIRU unemployment rate):

$$\hat{w} = \beta_w(e - \bar{e}) + \hat{p} + \hat{z}, \quad \hat{w} = \dot{w}/w$$

Workers negotiate real wages as in Goodwin (1967), since the inclusion of the actual rate of inflation $\hat{p}$ on the right hand side reduces this nominal wage Phillips curve to a real wage Phillips curve. Moreover, the additional 1-1 pass-through of the growth rate of labour productivity z into nominal wage growth in fact leads immediately to a law of motion for the wage share $v = w/p/z$ given by $\hat{v} = \beta_w(e - \bar{e})$. We consider labour supply as a given magnitude, that is, we abstract from natural growth.

Goodwin's accumulation equation, on the basis of a linear technology with no technical change (that is, given input–output proportions $y = Y/K = \text{const.}$, $z = Y/L^d = \text{const.}$) and classical savings and investment assumptions ($s_c = 1; s_w = 0$), can be stated as follows:

$$\hat{K} = \dot{K}/K = \frac{Y - \delta K - \omega L^d}{K} = y(1 - \omega/z) - \delta, \quad \omega = w/p$$

with δ the depreciation rate of the capital stock. If we add disembodied and exogenous Harrod neutral technical change ($\hat{z} = const$) to this fixed proportions technology, we must replace the variable K (which is now growing over time) with a new state variable K_z, the law of motion of which is given by:

$$\hat{K}_z = \hat{K} - \hat{z} = y(1 - v) - \delta - \hat{z}, \quad K_z = K/z$$

in order to get a trendless magnitude. In what follows, we use g_z in place of $\hat{z}$ to denote the trend growth rate in labour productivity.

We now add a third law of motion for the infrastructure N of the economy to the otherwise standard Goodwin (1967) growth cycle model above. Here we assume the following dynamic equation:

$$\dot{N} = -\alpha_n(y(n) - y(n_o))K, \quad n = N/K, \ y'(n) > 0, \quad i.e.,$$

$$\hat{n} = -\alpha_n(y(n) - y(n_o))/n - \hat{K}_z - g_z$$

We are thus now further modifying the Goodwin model by assuming that the output–capital ratio is no longer constant, but in fact a function of the ratio n of the infrastructure N to the capital stock K. There is a natural level n_o for this ratio and a corresponding output–capital ratio where the existing infrastructure remains intact (unchanged). Higher output capital ratios reduce the existing infrastructure N as shown, while lower ones will lead to its recovery. These output–capital ratios in turn depend on the ratio n between 'nature' N and capital K, with higher n allowing for higher y due to an abundance of 'nature'.

This new feedback structure also modifies the first two laws of motion of the model, since we now have:

$$e = \frac{L^d}{L} = \frac{y(n)K_z}{L}$$

For simplicity we have assumed a given labour supply L (no natural growth) and thus concentrate on productivity growth in this variant of the Goodwin model. From the above we thus get an autonomous 3D system of differential equations in the state variables $v = w/p/z, K_z = K/z, n = N/K$, giving us the dynamics:

$$\dot{v} = \beta_w(y(n)K_z/L - \bar{e})v, \tag{7.1}$$

$$\dot{K}_z = [y(n)(1 - v) - \delta - g_z]K_z, \tag{7.2}$$

$$\dot{n} = -g_z n - \alpha_n(y(n) - y(n_o)) - [y(n)(1 - v) - \delta - g_z]n. \tag{7.3}$$

The uniquely determined interior steady state solution of this system is (if we assume for simplicity that function $y(n)$ is given by γn):

$$v^\star = 1 - \frac{\delta + g_z}{y(n^*)}, \quad K_z^* = \bar{e}L/y(n^*), \quad n^* = \frac{n_o}{1 + g_z/(\gamma\alpha_n)} < n_o$$

Note that the steady state level of n is below its natural level, a result that also holds for all other admissible types of functions $y(n)$. Note also that the steady wage share is lower than it would be at the natural level of the infrastructure. With respect to this steady state position the following holds:

Proposition 1: *The steady state of the dynamics (7.1) – (7.3) with environmental feedback channels is always surrounded by centrifugal forces, that is, this economy is not viable in the long run.*

Proof: The Jacobian matrix of the dynamics we are considering reads at the steady state:

$$J = \begin{pmatrix} J_{11} & J_{12} & J_{13} \\ J_{21} & J_{22} & J_{23} \\ J_{31} & J_{32} & J_{33} \end{pmatrix} = \begin{pmatrix} 0 & + & + \\ - & 0 & + \\ + & 0 & - \end{pmatrix}.$$

Remark: As the distribution of signs in the matrix J shows we have conventional Goodwin type cross-dual dynamics with respect to the state variables v, K_z coupled with a feedback structure between the state variables v and n which is of a cumulative nature.

In order to get convergence of the orbits of the dynamics to the steady state we have to show for the characteristic polynomial $\lambda^3 + a_1\lambda^2 + a_2\lambda + a_3$ of the matrix J that $a_i > 0,\ i = 1, 2, 3$ and $a_1a_2 - a_3 > 0$.[5] Since the term $-[y(n)(1 - v) - \delta - g_z]$ in the third law of motion is proportional to the second law of motion it does not matter for the calculation of the determinant of the Jacobian J. In this calculation of the determinant we can therefore artificially assume $J_{31} = 0$ which gives us:

$$a_3 = -\det J = J_{33}J_{12}J_{21} > 0, \quad i.e., \quad a_1a_2 - a_3 = J_{33}J_{31}J_{13} < 0$$

This simple result is due to the fact that we have only one negative entry in the trace of $J(= -a_1)$ and since the top left principal minor of order 2 of J (when multiplied with a_1) cancels against $\det J(= -a_3)$.

We thus have the result that the positive feedback channel between the wage share v and the nature to capital ratio n through the first and third law of motion always destabilises the growth cycle of this model, leading to fluctuations of income distribution and employment of increasing amplitude. The economy therefore faces the twofold dilemma of partial workforce degradation (in the bust) and partial waste of infrastructure (in the boom). These two problems are not easily overcome in a market economy which is based on overshooting distributional conflicts between capital and labour and an accumulation process that is of a strongly cyclical nature. In a democratic society there is therefore compelling need to find means that transcend such cyclical accumulation dynamics in order to make it sustainable in the long-run.

7.4 Flexicurity Capitalism and Environmental Protection

Technological solutions that reduce environmental contamination and protect the health of communities across the nation are readily available Ů- and often economical. At a minimum, oil and gas exploration and production should be subject to the same environmental measures with which virtually all other industries must already comply. The time for Congress to step into the regulatory void is long overdue. (Natural Resources Defense Council, October 31, 2007).[6]

We now design[7] as an alternative to the Goodwin growth cycle a model of economic growth that rests not on overaccumulation (in the prosperity phase) and mass unemployment (in the stagnant phase), but on a second, public labour market which through its institutional setup guarantees full employment in its interaction with the first labour market, the employment in the industrial sector of the economy, which is modelled as highly flexible and competitive. An excellent introduction into the environmentally oriented literature (with an Employer of Last Resort perspective) with which such a flexicurity modelling approach is compatible can be found in Tcherneva (2007), which also provides the backdrop for Flaschel, Greiner, Luchtenberg and Nell's (2008) discussion of credit, money and Keynesian demand problems. The basic difference is that we interpret the flexicurity model developed below as resting on the concept of an employer of first – not last – resort, where education, skill formation and the principle of equal opportunity allow for a highly educated workforce (see Flaschel (2009, ch.10) on these latter issues).

We first reconsider the corporate sector of the economy:

Table 7.1 Firms: production and income account

Uses	Resources
δK	δK
$\omega_1 L_1^d,\ L_1^d = Y^p/z$	$C_1 + C_2 + C_r$
$\omega_2 L_{2f}^w$	G
Π	$I + g_z N$
$\delta_1 R + \dot{R}$	S_1
Y	Y

This account is a simple one. Firms use their capital stock (at full capacity utilisation as we shall show later on) to employ the amount of labour (in hours): L_1^d, at the real wage ω_1, the law of motion of which is again determined from a model of wage–price interaction in the manufacturing sector. In addition they employ a labour force $L_{2f}^w =$

$\alpha_f L_1^d, \alpha_f = const$ from the second labour market at the wage ω_2, which is a constant fraction α_ω of the market wage in the first labour market. This labour force L_{2f}^w works the normal hours of a standard workday, while the workforce L_1^w from the first labour market may be working overtime or undertime depending on the size of the capital stock in comparison to this 'primary' workforce. The variable $u_w = L_1^d/L_1^w$ is the utilisation rate of the workforce in the first labour market, the industrial workers of the economy (all other employment originates from the work of households occupied in the second labour market, comprising the public sector and the EFR).

Firms produce full capacity output $Y = C_1 + C_2 + C_r - \delta_1 R + I + \delta K + g_z N + G$, that is sold to the two types of consumers (and retired households), sold to investing firms, used for infrastructure rehabilitation, and sold to the government. Note here that part of the consumption of retired persons is backed up through company pension payments. The demand side of the model is thus formulated in a way such that this full capacity output can indeed be sold. Deducting from this output Y, firms' real wage payments to workers from the first and the second labour market and depreciation,[8] we get the profits Π of firms which are here assumed to be invested fully into capital stock growth $\dot{K} = I$ and infrastructure investment $g_z N$. We thus have classical (direct) investment habits in this model with an employer of first resort. We assume again a fixed proportions technology with Harrod neutral technical change, that is, $y = Y/K$ the potential output–capital ratio and with labour productivity $z = Y/L_1^d$, which determines the employment L_1^d of the workforce L_1^w of firms and is growing with the rate g_z.

Compared to Flaschel, Greiner, Luchtenberg and Nell (2008), and Chapter 8, the model here is augmented by efforts to preserve the infrastructure of the economy, a cost that is paid by firms and which therefore appears in the above production account as a deduction from firms' profit. Because of this, the law of motion for N, from the preceding section, is augmented as follows (where again $n = N/K$):

$$\begin{aligned} \dot{N} &= g_z N - \alpha_n(y(n) - y(n_o))K, \; y'(n) > 0, \quad i.e., \\ \hat{n} &= g_z - \alpha_n(y(n) - y(n_o))/n - \hat{K} \end{aligned}$$

Firms therefore introduce in this model of flexicurity capitalism a trend growth term into the reproduction of the infrastructure which is here set equal to the trend in labour productivity g_z, that is, the steady growth rate of the output of firms.

We assume as in the preceding case of unrestricted capitalism that output per unit of capital depends positively on the ratio n. The law of motion of this state variable now takes the form:

$$\dot{n} = -\alpha_n(y(n) - y(n_o)) - [y(n)(1 - (1 + \alpha_\omega \alpha_f)v_1) - \delta - g_z n - g_z]n$$

due to the environmental protection efforts of firms. This removes the trend term in the law of motion for $\hat{K}$, since (with $v_2 = \omega_2/z$):

$$\begin{aligned} \hat{K} =& y(n)(1 - v_1 - \alpha_f v_2) - \delta - g_z n \\ =& y(n)(1 - (1 + \alpha_\omega \alpha_f)v_1) - \delta - g_z n \end{aligned}$$

which – as law of motion – is again to be replaced by the growth rate $\hat{K}_z = \hat{K} - g_z$ of the detrended capital stock.

It might be worthwhile to consider whether the environmental protection efforts of firms should be supervised by the state government so that such a cooperation would lead to a mutual growth of interest in ecology. Environmental efforts are not part of workers' initiatives in our model but there is, of course, an individual responsibility of each person as part of his or her democratic citizenship participation, enforced by lifelong learning especially with regard to civic education. The considered development of the rescue of the river Hudson in the United States from pollution shows that citizens' engagement can be successful (see Section 7.1).

We next consider the household sector, which is composed of worker households working in the first labour market together with those working in the second labour market.

Households of type 1 consume manufacturing goods of amount C_1 and services from the second labour market L_{2h}^w. They pay (all) income taxes T and they pay in addition – via further tax transfers – all workers' income in the labour market that does not come from the services they employ, from firms and in an active way from the government (which is by and large therefore equivalent to an unemployment insurance). Moreover, they pay the pensions of retired households ($\omega_2 L^r$) and accumulate their remaining income S_1 in the form of company pensions into a fund R that is administrated by firms (with inflow S_1 from these households and with outflow $\delta_1 R$ to pensioners).

The transfer $\omega_2(L - (L_1^w + L_{2f}^w + L_{2h}^w + L_{2g}^w)) = \omega_2 L_3^w$ can be interpreted as solidarity payment, since workers from the first labour market who lose their job will automatically be employed in the second or third labour market where full employment is guaranteed by the government

Table 7.2 Households 1 and 2 (primary and secondary labour market): income account

Households 1:

Uses	Resources
$C_1 = c_{h1}(1-\tau_h)\omega_1 L_1^d$	
$\omega_2 L_{2h}^w = c_{h2}(1-\tau_h)\omega_1 L_1^d$	
$T = \tau_h \omega_1 L_1^d$	
$\omega_2(L - (L_1^w + L_{2f}^w + L_{2h}^w + L_{2g}^w))$	
$\omega_2 L^r, L^r = \alpha_r L$	
S_1	$\omega_1 L_1^d$
$Y_1^w = \omega_1 L_1^d$	$Y_1^w = \omega_1 L_1^d$

Households 2:

Uses	Resources
C_2	$\omega_2(L_2^w + L_3^w), L_3^w = L - L_1^w - L_2^w$
Y_2^w	Y_2^w

(as employer of first resort). We consider this employment as skill preserving, since it can be viewed as ordinary office or handicraft work (subject only to learning by doing when such workers return to the first labour market).

The second sector of households is modelled in the simplest way possible: Households employed in the second and third (= EFR) labour market, i.e, $L_2^w = L_{2f}^w + L_{2h}^w + L_{2g}^w, L_3^w$ pay no taxes and totally consume their income. We have classical saving habits in this household sector, while households of type 1 may have positive or negative savings S_1 as residual from their income and expenditures. The law of motion for their pension funds R is:

$$\dot{R} = S_1 - \delta_1 R.$$

where δ_1 is the rate at which these funds are depreciated through company pension payments to the 'officially retired' workers L^r, assumed to be a constant fraction of the 'active' workforce $L^r = \alpha_r L$. These worker households are not really inactive in our model, but offer work according to their still existing capabilities that can be considered as an addition to the supply of work organised by the government

$L_3^w = L - (L_1^w + L_{2f}^w + L_{2h}^w)$ as an EFR. In other words, the working potential of officially retired persons remains a valuable contribution to the total working hours that are supplied by all members of the society. It is obvious that the proper allocation of the work hours under the control of the government needs thorough reflection from both the microeconomic and the social point of view, but this topic is beyond the scope of this chapter.

The income account of retired households shows that they receive pension payments as if they are working in the second labour market and they also get individual transfer income (company pensions) from the accumulated funds R in proportion to the time they have been active in the first labour market, as a portion of $\delta_1 R$ by which the pension funds R are reduced in each period.

Table 7.3 Retired households: income account

Uses	Resources
C_r	$\omega_2 L^r + \delta_1 R, L^r = \alpha_r L$
Y^r	Y^r

Finally there is the government sector, which is also formulated in a very simple fashion:

Table 7.4 The government: income account

Uses	Resources
$G = \alpha_g T$	$T = \tau_h \omega_1 L_1^d$
$\omega_2 L_{g2}^w = (1 - \alpha_g)T$	
$\omega_2(L - (L_1^w + L_{2f}^w + L_{2h}^w + L_{2g}^w))$	$\omega_2 L_r^w$
$\omega_2 L^r$	$\omega_2 \alpha_r L$
Y^g	Y^g

The government receives income taxes, the solidarity payments (unemployment benefits) for the third labour market paid by workers in the first labour market, and old-age pension payments. It uses the taxes to finance government goods demand G and the surplus of taxes over these government expenditures to actively employ workers in the government sector. In addition it employs the workers receiving 'unemployment benefits' and also employs 'retired' persons to the extent they can still contribute to employment activities. The total labour force in the second labour market is thus employed by firms, by type 1 households and the government. The income payments to workers in the second labour market ($\omega_2 L_2^w$) that do not originate from their services to firms, to type 1 households or from an excess of income taxes over government commodity expenditures are thus paid out of transfers from type 1 households to the government, and on the basis of these payments the remaining work in the second labour market is organised by government.

In sum, workers are employed either in the first or second labour market or in the third one by performing auxiliary work within firms, services for type 1 households or services in the government sector associated with public administration, infrastructure services, or other public services. In addition there is the potential labour supply $\alpha_r L$ from retired households, which due to the long-life expectancy in modern societies can remain effective suppliers of specific work over a considerable span of time. In this way the whole workforce is always fully employed in this model of social growth (including retired persons who work according to their capabilities and willingness) and so does not suffer from human degradation through unemployment. Of course, there is a variety of issues concerning state organised work that point to problems with the organisation of such work, but such problems already exist in actual industrialised market economies in one way or another. We thus have a classical growth model of the economy where full employment is not assumed, but actively constructed and where – due to the assumed expenditure structure – Say's law holds true, that is, the capital stock of firms is also always fully utilised.

7.5 Dynamics: Convergence towards Balanced Reproduction

Since the labour market has been redesigned in this approach to flexicurity growth, we assume the adjusted law of motion for the deflated and detrended wage dynamic to be:[9]

$$\hat{v}_1 = \beta_w(u_w - \bar{u}_w),$$

$\bar{u}_w$ the NAIRU utilisation rate of type 1 workers.[10] Wage negotiations are now conducted by type 1 workers (the insider core), according to their utilisation rate $u_w = L_1^d / L_1^w$. Since demand pressure on the external labour market no longer exists in this model, it is simply replaced in the equation above by the extent of over- or under-utilisation of the workers L_1^w.

The growth law of the capital stock moreover reads ($\omega_i = \frac{w_i}{p}, v_i = \frac{\omega_i}{z}$):

$$\begin{aligned}\hat{K} = r &= \frac{Y - \delta K - \omega_1 L_1^d - \omega_2 L_{2f}^w - g_z N}{K} \\ &= y(n)(1 - (1 + \alpha_\omega \alpha_f)v_1) - \delta - g_z n.\end{aligned}$$

The important dynamic innovation in this model is that we now have a law of motion for the stock of type 1 workers employed by firms. This law of motion describes the recruitment policy of firms, that is, their hiring and firing decisions concerning type 1 workers and is given by:

$$\hat{L}_1^w = \beta_u(u_w - \bar{u}_w), \quad i.e.,$$

the growth rate of this part of the workforce depends on the extent to which type 1 the workers are over- or underemployed due to the current state of capital accumulation, that is, the size of the capital stock. Note that type 2 workers are assumed to be skilled enough to enter the type 1 workforce if they are demanded by firms, that is, training costs are neglected for simplicity. This assumes that education and lifelong learning is organised accordingly.

The above three laws of motion can be easily reformulated in terms of the state variables $v_1 = \omega_1/z, l_1^w = zL_1^w/K = L_1^w/K_z$ and $n = N/K$ and give rise to the following autonomous system of differential equations, expressed in growth rate terms:

$$\hat{v}_1 = \beta_w(y/l_1^w - \bar{u}_w) \tag{7.4}$$

$$\hat{l}_1^w = \beta_u(y/l_1^w - \bar{u}_w) - [y(n)(1 - (1 + \alpha_\omega \alpha_f)v_1) - \delta - g_z n - g_z] \tag{7.5}$$

$$\begin{aligned}\dot{n} = &- \alpha_n(y(n) - y(n_o)) - [y(n)(1 - (1 + \alpha_\omega \alpha_f)v_1) - \\ &\delta - g_z n - g_z]n\end{aligned} \tag{7.6}$$

since we have $\omega_2 = \alpha_\omega \omega_1, L_{2f}^w = \alpha_f L_1^d, L_1^d/K = y/z$ and

$$\hat{K}_z = y(n)(1 - (1 + \alpha_\omega \alpha_f)v_1) - \delta - g_z n - g_z.$$

The uniquely determined interior steady state solution of this system is

$$v_1^\star = \frac{y(n_o) - (\delta + g_z + g_z n_o)}{y(n_o)(1 + \alpha_\omega \alpha_f)}, \quad l_1^{w*} = y(n_o)/\bar{u}_w, \quad n^* = n_o$$

Note that the steady state level of n is now at its natural level. Note also that the steady wage share is higher now than it would be under unrestricted capitalism (if $\alpha_\omega \alpha_f = 0$ holds). Under the assumed infrastructure rehabilitation efforts of firms there is therefore an improved steady state solution for the dynamics under consideration. With respect to this steady state position the following holds in addition:

Proposition 2: *Assume that the growth rate of labour productivity g_z is sufficiently small (in order to preserve the condition $J_{33} < 0$). Then: The above 3D flexicurity growth dynamics with environmental protection are convergent to the interior steady state, that is, are viable, if the hiring and firing parameter β_u is chosen sufficiently large, that is, if the employment policy of firms is sufficiently flexible.*

Proof: The Jacobian matrix of the dynamics under consideration reads, at the steady state:

$$J = \begin{pmatrix} J_{11} & J_{12} & J_{13} \\ J_{21} & J_{22} & J_{23} \\ J_{31} & J_{32} & J_{33} \end{pmatrix} = \begin{pmatrix} 0 & - & + \\ + & - & + \\ + & 0 & - \end{pmatrix}.$$

Remark: As the distribution of signs in the matrix J shows we now have conventional Goodwin type cross-dual dynamics with respect to the state variables v, l_1^w, coupled with a feedback structure between the state variables v and n which is of a cumulative nature. In contrast to the preceding section we now however have a negative feedback effect of the size of the type 1 workforce on its rate of growth (through the recruitment policy of firms) and a new slightly positive influence of the ratio n on its time rate of change. This latter effect is however of no importance if the parameter g_z (a growth rate) is chosen sufficiently small.

In order to get convergence of the orbits of the dynamics to the interior steady state we must again show that for the characteristic polynomial $\lambda^3 + a_1\lambda^2 + a_2\lambda + a_3$ of the matrix J the conditions $a_i > 0, \; i = 1, 2, 3$ and $a_1 a_2 - a_3 > 0$. Since the term $\hat{K}_z$ can again be removed from the third law of motion without altering $\det J$, we have $\det J = -J_{33}J_{12}J_{21} < 0$. This makes $a_1 a_2 - a_3$ positive if the parameter β_u is chosen sufficiently large, since this parameter appears with a positive coefficient in a_1, a_2, and a_3, but of course in $a_1 a_2$ in squared form that will dominate a_3 sooner or later. But $a_1 a_2 - a_3, a_1, a_3 > 0$ imply $a_2 > 0$ which proves the asymptotic stability of the interior steady state.

We thus have the result that the positive feedback channel between the wage share v_1 and the nature capital ratio n through the first and the third law of motion is dominated by the central flexibility parameter in our model of flexicurity growth, leading (possibly) to fluctuations of income distribution, but now damped ones, depending on the degree of employment flexibility. The economy therefore no longer faces the twofold dilemma of partial workforce degradation and partial waste of infrastructure as was the case in the model with an active reserve army mechanism. These two problems are overcome in this type of market economy based on employment (not job) security, free entry and exit in the employment of the factors of production, and infrastructure regulation that commits firms to finance a constant rate of growth of infrastructural rehabilitation in order to mitigate the effects of production on the infrastructure of the economy.

7.6 Company Pension Funds

There is a further law of motion in the background of the model that needs to be considered in order to provide a complete statement on the viability of our model of flexicurity capitalism. This law of motion describes the evolution of the pension fund per unit of the capital stock $\rho = \frac{R}{K}$ and is obtained from the defining equation $\dot{R} = S_1 - \delta_1 R$ as follows:

$$\begin{aligned}\hat{\rho} &= \hat{R} - \hat{K} = \frac{S_1 - \delta_1 R}{K}/\rho - r, \quad i.e.: \\ \dot{\rho} &= \frac{S_1}{K} - (\delta_1 + r)\rho = s_1 - (\delta_1 + r)\rho\end{aligned}$$

with savings of households of type 1 and profits of firms per unit of capital being given by:

$$\begin{aligned}s_1 =& (1 - (c_{h1} + c_{h2})(1 - \tau_h) - \tau_h)v_1 y - \alpha_\omega v_1 (l_r^w + l^r) \quad \text{with} \\ & l_x^w = l - (l_1^w + l_{2f}^w + l_{2h}^w + l_{2g}^w) \\ & l^r = \alpha_r l, \ i.e., \text{ due to the financing of } \ l_{2g}^w : \\ s_1 =& (1 - c_{h1}(1 - \tau_h) - \alpha_g \tau_h)v_1 y - ((1 + \alpha_r)l - (l_1^w + l_{2f}^w))\alpha_\omega v_1, \\ & l_{2f}^w = \alpha_f y \\ r =& y[1 - (1 + \alpha_\omega \alpha_f)v_1] - \delta - g_z n, \quad v_1 = \omega_1 / z\end{aligned}$$

For analytical simplicity we assume that all state variables up to ρ have already reached their steady state position. Moreover we also assume for simplicity $\delta_1 = \delta$. This gives us the following law of motion of the pension–capital ratio, ρ:

$$\dot{\rho} = (1 - c_{h1}(1 - \tau_h) - \alpha_g \tau_h) v_1^* y^* - ((1 + \alpha_r) l^* - (l_1^{w*} + \alpha_f y^*) \alpha_\omega v_1^* \\ - (\delta + r^*) \rho$$

This reduced form dynamic is globally asymptotically stable and exhibits the steady state value:

$$\rho_o = \frac{(1 - c_{h1}(1 - \tau_h) - \alpha_g \tau_h) v_1^* y^* - ((1 + \alpha_r) l^* - (1 + \alpha_f) y^*)) \alpha_\omega v_1^*}{\delta + r^*}$$

where r^* denotes the steady state rate of profit of firms. The steady state level of ρ is positive – and the economy is viable – if and only if the full employment labour intensity ratio is such that:

$$l^* < \frac{(1 - c_{h1}(1 - \tau_h) - \alpha_g \tau_h) v_1^* y^* + ((1 + \alpha_f) y^*) \alpha_\omega v_1^*}{(\delta + r^*)(1 + \alpha_r) \alpha_\omega v_1^*}$$

We now augment the model again by credit out of accumulated pension funds and have of course to adjust the accounts in the same way as in Chapter 3, but will not do this here explicitly. We assume that pension funds (maybe also supported by the government) have the ethical position that the infrastructure should be preserved as described in Section 7.4, not only for the retired people, but for the whole workforce they are caring for. They therefore adjust the interest rate i on the loans they give to firms such that the infrastructure investment of firms becomes profitable when financed by the credit received from pension funds. We assume that all infrastructure has been and will be financed in this way. This allows us to identify the amount of real debt D with the amount invested in infrastructure N at all moments in time, as implied by the two conditions $N(0) = D(0)$, $\dot{N} = g_z N = \dot{D}$.

We assume again for simplicity $Y = \gamma N$, that is, $y = \gamma n$. This gives rise to the following definition of the marginal return on infrastructure investment:

$$\iota = \frac{\gamma N - iN}{K} = (\gamma - i) n$$

If the interest rate on loans is chosen such that ι is positive, firms can gain from financing their infrastructure investment through such loans and are thus motivated intrinsically to accept such an offer from pension funds. Moreover, they can now invest all of their profits in real capital formation as shown in the equation below:

$$\hat{K}_z = \gamma n (1 - (1 + \alpha_\omega \alpha_f) v_1) - \delta - in - g_z$$

This expression must now be used in the laws of motion (7.4)-(7.6) in order to investigate again the balanced growth path and its stability. The results are only marginally modified thereby, since one only has to use the term in in place of $g_z n$. Assuming that $g_z > i$ holds, would in addition then give the result that the steady state share of wages of workers of type 1 (and thus also of the remaining workers) is increased as compared to the case considered in Section 7.3.

7.7 Conclusions

We have shown in this chapter that there is a (model) alternative to the classical growth cycle analysis of overshooting income distribution dynamics, which overcomes the degradation of part of the workforce in the depressed part of the growth cycle and which also mitigates workers' overshooting income claims in the prosperity phase of it. In addition, we have seen that the environmental implications of unrestricted capitalist accumulation make the Goodwin growth cycle a (mildly) explosive dynamical process (at an unnaturally low infrastructure level) and thus a nonviable reproduction process in the long-run. However, this can be overcome by an infrastructure rehabilitation policy where firms use part of their profits for environmental reconstruction. A credit financing of infrastructure investment (out of company pension funds) can improve the situation even further.

The overall outcome is not only a better steady state position for the economy, but also a stable dynamics in place of the unstable feedback mechanisms that characterise a reserve army led reproduction process. Combining flexibility in the adjustment of the workforce of firms with employment (but not job) security allows us to formulate a model where stable reproduction can be successfully combined with environmental protection in a consent-driven socio-economic framework, in place of the dissent-driven recurrently overshooting income claims of an unrestricted reserve army mechanism. The approach chosen in this chapter requires further refinement in order to show that it truly represents a viable social structure of accumulation. We refer the reader here to Flaschel, Greiner, Luchtenberg and Nell (2008) and Chapter 3 of this book for generalisations of this model of flexicurity growth to credit relationships and Keynesian demand problems in particular, where the preservation of full employment becomes an even more important issue in an environment where flexibility and social security are to be reconciled with each other. Moreover, speaking of social security should of course include basic rights to be protected against issues as raised in the following quotation from a press release of the NRDC (Natural Resources Defense Council):

> *The pollution associated with oil and gas exploration and production include long-established carcinogens, reproductive toxicants, and other toxic chemicals like arsenic, hydrogen sulfide, mercury and volatile organic compounds (VOCs) including benzene and xylene. Despite the close proximity of these operations to homes, schools, and other community resources, the oil and gas industry enjoys numerous exemptions from provisions of federal laws intended to protect human health and the environment, including the Safe Drinking Water Act, the Clean Water Act, the Clean Air Act, the Comprehensive Environmental Response, Compensation and Liability Act (CERCLA, also known as the Superfund law), waste management laws (RCRA), and public right-to-know provisions of the Emergency Planning and Community Right-to-Know Act.* (Natural Resources Defense Council, October 31, 2007).[11]

Notes

[1] This chapter builds on Flaschel and Greiner (2010).

[2] For a survey on international agreements and their political economy see Carraro and Siniscalco (1998).

[3] Calculated with a smoothing factor of $\lambda = 1600$.

[4] http://www.nrdc.org/land/use/down/contents.asp

[5] See Flaschel (2009, Mathematical Appendix) for details.

[6] http://www.nrdc.org/land/use/down/contents.asp

[7] As an extension of the model considered in Chapter 3.

[8] The term S_1 is equal to $\delta_1 R + \dot{R}$.

[9] Augmenting this Phillips curve by a real wage barrier term would further improve the results obtained in this section, but is left out here for reasons of comparability with the dissent-driven Goodwin (1967) model.

[10] Note that type 2 workers working for firms have a normal working day just as all other workers of this type.

[11] http://www.nrdc.org/media/2007/071031.asp

8. Rampant Fiscal Policy, IMF Intervention and Policy Reforms

8.1 Introduction

In this chapter we consider the conduct of fiscal policy in the context of the distributive cycle. We first investigate a basic case where government expenditures are financed through taxes and bonds (not yet consols, as in Ricardo's times, but fixed-price bonds with a given rate of interest that can be manipulated by the government). Government expenditures are completely unproductive, having no impact on the private sector of the economy whatsoever, that is, in principle the case where the government is acting like a king's court by just extracting taxes from its tributaries and using bonds to finance excess goods demand of the court. We however here still consider a case where this is done in a somewhat disciplined manner, since this government has a debt to capital target towards which it is adjusting its expenditure over time. We therefore start from a distributive cycle model (of Lotka-Volterra prey-predator type) where fiscal policy is just 'harvesting' from this predator-prey (wage share employment rate) interaction.

We therefore start from an extension of the Goodwin growth cycle where government behaves in a way such that Say's Law still holds true, where only wages are taxed and where government bonds are a perfect substitute for asset holders in comparison to their real investment into the capital stock they own. Deficit spending of the government is therefore matched by a reduction of capital stock growth, while wage taxation provides the tax base for government spending. The model provides in a very basic way an extension of the cross-dual dynamics of the distributive cycle which stabilises this cycle further (besides the stability obtained from a real wage barrier mechanism established through some cooperation between capital and labour). We use this baseline fiscal regime in the following as reference for rampant as well as prudent government behaviour.

In the rampant case we investigate first and as an example the Greek way into its current state crisis. The Greek economy and society are plagued by corruption, tax evasion and selfishness. It can therefore be assumed that the corporatist element on the labour market is weak, so that capital is not giving in when real wages are below the real wage barrier, while the opposite happens through workforce behaviour when they are higher than this reference level. Moreover, the debt financing by the government is no longer disciplined, but rampant so that government has to pay more than just the rate of profit as interest rate on its outstanding debt. If this effect becomes sufficiently strong the economy will lose its stability and its balanced growth path becomes a repellent one, and this even more if a positive feedback between outstanding debt and new debt is added.

This process may go on for quite a while in good times (and – in the case of Greece – can lead to an extreme violation of the Maastricht treaty). In bad times, the state of financial embarrassment tends to become obvious and institutions surrounding the Greek economy may intervene. We do not yet consider open economies in this book however. This intervention therefore just becomes imposed on the fiscal authority, imitating the measures that actually have been implemented by the IMF which are discussed in Section 8.4 before these measures are implemented into the model of this chapter. We show that – under certain conditions – the IMF-type interventions can be successful and lead the economy back to a sufficiently low level of the debt to capital ratio and an acceptable deficit to GDP ratio. However this purely economic cure can be accompanied by negative social externalities which may in addition exhibit a tendency to become persistent. In the long-run this negative effect may provide more harm than was gained economically by the cold-turkey intervention of IMF type.

This calls for the need to model an alternative (or addition) to the IMF policy measures, which may mitigate the social consequences of these policies, while they are in force or – when established after the end of the IMF intervention, to give the country a new perspective. The crisis may therefore trigger reforms which in particular improve the socio-economic structure of the considered country. This however may need a widening of the tax base, an increased tax rate and an increase in public sector activities such as education, medicare and other social care. In this model we implement this by assuming that the unproductive consumption of the government can be restructured towards government investment into a stock of social and economic 'infrastructure' (so far assumed to be a given and well developed magnitude), which exhibits positive externalities on labour and capital productivity.

We show in this section that this avoids the repelling forces investigated in the case of a rampant fiscal policy and leads the economy back to a stable balanced growth path. We show moreover that along this growth path the welfare of the society is increased as compared to the case of a 'kinglike government', where welfare is measured by the consumption of the workforce and the size of the level of the infrastructure of the economy per worker.

We conclude from all this that the government should not behave as just an additional consumer that is just imposed on the economy as in the first model of this chapter (as it is often modelled in traditional Keynesian macroeconomics), but should in any case through controlled legislation (like the Maastricht treaty) be hindered to behave in the self-indulgent way the past Greek governments were behaving. If this has happened, as in the Greek case, fiscal policy reforms should however not only be implemented from an economic perspective, but should also reflect how eventually long-lasting social damage can be avoided or at least reduced for the society onto which this economic policy is imposed.

8.2 'Kinglike' Government Behaviour

In this section we want to introduce and investigate the role and the effects of a kinglike type of fiscal policy[1] in a Goodwin growth cycle model where however government is subject to some discipline. The expenditures of the government, financed by taxation and debt, are of a purely consumptive nature (including the consumption of civil servants). There are no externalities induced by government consumption, which in particular does not invest in an improvement of the infrastructure of public goods P, the level of which is a given magnitude in this section (given by $P = \bar{p}L$). An increase of this level would have a positive effect on the output–capital ratio, which is however not an objective of the current government.

In the steady state the budget will be balanced at a value of debt per capital that can be chosen by the government and around which government debt will fluctuate if there is unbalanced growth. The Goodwin part of the model is the same as in Chapter 1, that is, we have a Leontief technology with a constant growth rate of labour productivity (given labour supply L), a real wage Phillips curve with a Marglin (1984) real wage barrier and the assumption of extremely classical savings habits ($s_w = 0, s_c = 1$). The output–capital ratio is however now an increasing function of the ratio $p = P/L$, the amount of public goods per worker. The laws of motion of the state variables v, the wage share and K_z, the capital stock per unit of full employment output, are therefore again the following ones:[2]

$$\hat{v} = \beta_w(y(\bar{p})K_z - \bar{e}) + \alpha(v_o - v), \quad v = \omega/z \tag{8.1}$$

$$\hat{K}_z = y(\bar{p})(1 - v) - \delta - g_z. \quad K_z = K/(zL) \tag{8.2}$$

We now augment this model by a government sector which is described as follows:

$$G = T + \mu(\bar{b} - b)K, \quad b = B/K \tag{8.3}$$

$$T = tvY \tag{8.4}$$

$$G + iB \equiv T + \dot{B}, \quad i.e., \quad \dot{B} = G + iB - T \tag{8.5}$$

The new symbols in these equations and the identity (8.5) denote:

t the tax rate (a fixed parameter),
T taxes,
G government expenditures,
B the stock of government bonds (price = 1, b=B/K),
i the rate of interest,
μ government financing parameter.

Equation (8.3) describes an expenditure policy rule which implies a constant proportion t of government spending of the gross wage income of workers in the steady state.[3] In addition to spending all taxes, the government issues bonds for financing additional consumption if $b = B/K$ is below the target value $\bar{b}$, and it reduces its consumption relative to taxes in the opposite case.

Taxes are only raised on wages, that is, the government is not taxing the profit and interest income of asset holders. Since a portfolio decision of asset holders, which now own the capital stock K and hold government bonds of amount B, is not included in this extension of Goodwin's model it is necessary to assume that bonds and capital goods are characterised by the same rate of return $r = (1-u)Y/K - \delta = i$. This is an admissible assumption, since all bonds are issued by the government, which thus simply has to guarantee that the prevailing rate of profit will always be assumed as point of reference for its current interest payments on the existing stock of bonds. Government debt grows (or falls) according to the difference between consumption/interest expenditures and wage income taxes.

Inserting the equations (8.3) – (8.5) into our model (8.1), (8.2) modifies it in the following way: Equation (8.1) remains unchanged. The rate of change of the capital stock K is then, however, governed by

$$\dot{K} = [y(\bar{p})(1-v) - \delta]K + iB - \dot{B}, \tag{8.6}$$

since it is assumed that asset holders always accept the inflow of new bonds issued by the government. It is thus given by profits (including interest) minus the investment that is going into government bonds instead of real capital formation. We will show below that Say's law holds, that is, there is no goods-market coordination problem in this model, since the aggregation of all components of goods demanded will always be identical to the supply of goods by firms. This follows immediately from the following budget equations of households, firms and the government:

$$\begin{aligned} C &\equiv (1-t)vY \\ I &\equiv (1-v)Y - \delta K + iB - \dot{B} \\ G &\equiv tvY - iB + \dot{B}, \quad i.e. \\ C + I + G &\equiv (1-t)vY + (1-v)Y + tvY \equiv Y - \delta K. \end{aligned}$$

Note again that we are here considering a society where the government acts in a very one-sided way, since only wages are taxed, while profits and interest are not taxed (maybe due to an extreme type of tax evasion).

Equation (8.6) implies by means of (8.3) – (8.5):

$$\begin{aligned} \hat{K}_z &= y(\bar{p})(1-v) - \delta - g_z + ib - \dot{B}/K, \quad \dot{B}/K = ib + \mu(\bar{b} - b) \\ &= y(\bar{p})(1-v) - \delta - g_z - \mu(\bar{b} - b) \end{aligned}$$

Note that the growth rate of the capital stock is reduced, compared to the unrestricted distributive cycle, if $b < \bar{b}$ holds true (since $\mu > 0$ has been assumed).

We define that $p = P/L$ and assume for $\dot{P}$ that it is given by $\tau G/K$, where $\tau = 0$ holds in the present version of the model so that P, denoting the public infrastructure of the economy, is a given magnitude. The complete set of the laws of motion of the economy is given by:

$$\dot{v} = [\beta_w(y(\bar{p})K_z - \bar{e}) + \alpha(v_o - v)]v, \quad v = \omega/z \tag{8.7}$$

$$\dot{K}_z = [y(\bar{p})(1-v) - \delta - g_z - \mu(\bar{b} - b)]K_z, \quad K_z = K/(zL) \tag{8.8}$$

$$\dot{b} = \mu(\bar{b} - b)(1 + b), \quad b = B/K \tag{8.9}$$

since $r(v) = i$ holds and since

$$\hat{b} = \hat{B} - \hat{K} = \frac{\dot{B}/K}{K/B} - \hat{K} = [ib + \mu(\bar{b} - b)]/b - [r(v) - \mu(\bar{b} - b)],$$

The steady state of this dynamical system is given as in the Goodwin model, but now with a steady state value for government debt per unit of capital in addition:

$$v_o = \frac{y(\bar{p}) - (\delta + g_z)}{y(\bar{p})}, \quad K_{zo} = \bar{e}/y(\bar{p}), \quad b_o = \bar{b} > 0.$$

For the Jacobian of these dynamics we get at the steady state:

$$J_o = \begin{pmatrix} -\alpha v_o & \beta_w y(\bar{p}) v_o & 0 \\ -y(\bar{p}) K_z & 0 & \mu K_z \\ 0 & 0 & -\mu \end{pmatrix} = \begin{pmatrix} - & + & 0 \\ - & 0 & + \\ 0 & 0 & - \end{pmatrix}$$

The eigenvalues of this Jacobian are the ones of the Goodwin model with a real wage barrier (which are negative in their real parts) and by $-\mu$, as can be directly obtained from the roots of the characteristic polynomial of the matrix J_o which is determined by $\det(\lambda I - J_o) = 0$. The dynamical system of this section is therefore in a very straightforward way asymptotically stable and, we assert, this also holds from a more than purely local point of view. The balanced growth path of the economy is thus attracting, despite the 'neutral' role played by the government, which does not care about the state of the labour market and which behaves like a wise 'monarchy', with a somewhat regulated debt financing of its purely unproductive consumption (the more moderate, the lower the value of $\bar{b}$ is chosen, and the smaller the adjustment speed μ if adjustment takes place from below).

The dynamical model we have considered so far exhibits some basic parallels to certain countries in the world, though these countries often have significant natural resources which they can exploit, an addition that might provide an interesting extension of the considered model which however will not be pursued here any further. Instead we will consider in the following section an extension of it where the government is no longer as disciplined with respect to its debt financing, as it has been assumed in this section.

8.3 Rampant Financial Conduct: The Greek Case

This section starts from a consideration of the Greek economy in order to describe and understand the present financial and fiscal crises in the Western world from the perspective of this radical misconduct of government behaviour (and also private behaviour) within the realm of the Eurozone and under the stability measures of the Maastricht treaty. We consider this extreme case as providing an example where such deep crisis can be understood as providing the means for a fundamental restructuring of the (Greek) society from the viewpoint of fiscal and social policy, the latter concerning the social capital of the society and the educational system on which it is based.

Greece became a member of the EU in 1981 and entered the Eurozone in 2001. Thus, the country can be regarded as a solid member of the European Union in spite of the fact that Greece only got a democratic constitution in 1975 after the end of the military dictatorship in 1974. There are positive ratings about Greece to be found in international comparisons like the following one: The Greek economy was reported by the World Bank (2011) to be the 27th largest economy in the world (by nominal GPD) in 2009, and furthermore the Greek economy is described as a developed economy with the 22nd highest standard of living in the world (HDR, 2010). Greece had a population of about 11 million in 2010 and is thus among the 10 largest countries of the EU. Between 2003 and 2007 the Greek economy grew by nearly 4.0% per year, which however is partly due to the effects of the 2004 Athens Olympic Games (CIA, 2011).

The Greek workforce is mainly occupied in three sectors: agriculture (with products such as wheat, corn, barley, sugar beets, olives, tomatoes, tobacco, potatoes, beef, dairy products and wine) where about 20% of the workforce is employed; the sector of services with nearly 60% employees, and industry with various sectors, among which maritime industry is of high importance. In industry, about 21% of the workforce find occupation. The most important sectors of the economy are tourism and shipping (Greeka.com 2011). It should also be taken into account that immigrants make up nearly one-fifth of the workforce, who mainly work in agriculture or have unskilled jobs (CIA, 2011). The sectoral output data – as fractions of GDP give in 2010, agriculture: 4%, industry: 17.6% and services: 78.5%. This suggests that the Greek economy is not a very balanced one.

In recent years, the unemployment rate has risen from 6.8 in 2008 to 8.8 in 2009 and 11.8 in 2010 (for 25-64 year old persons with a low level of education). Yet, in Ireland the same group exhibits unemployment figures of 19.5 and in Spain even 24.7 in 2010 (see Eurostat, 2011). From 2009 to 2010 the general unemployment rate in Greece has risen to 14.1, which is among the highest increases in the European Union

(Eurostat 2011a). As Demekas and Kontolemis (1996) have shown, the Greek unemployment rate had already risen from 2 percent in the 1960s to 9–10 percent in the 1990s, despite being accompanied by a rapid expansion of life-time government jobs, which is blamed for the slow economic growth performance of Greece by Greeka.com (2011), due to the increase in wages and reservation wages and the slow adjustment to demand and supply shocks this expansion in particular implied. It is shown there that the Greek economy has a large public sector that accounts for nearly half of GDP.

In 2003, Eurostat reports for Greece as GDP per head 19200 Euro (at market prices) – a number with which Greece is in the second half of the EU countries, similar to Spain with a nearly four times larger population however (GDP per head: 20900), but below Ireland (GDP per head: 29200) with only a third of the Greek population. In 2007, the data were as follows: Greece: 22900, Spain: 26200 and Ireland: 36800. The data for Greece are however from 2004 onwards based on unconfirmed procedures of data collection (Eurostat, 2011). A renewed Eurostat statistics (Eurostat, 2011) about the growth rate of real GDP (percentage change of previous year) gives a clear impression of the economic crisis in 2008 and the following years:

Table 8.1 Growth rate comparisons

	2007	2008	2009	2010
Greece	4.3%	1.0%	-2.0%	-4.5%
Spain	3.6%	0.9%	-3.7%	-0.1%
Ireland	5.6%	-3.5%	-7.6%	-1.0%

Greece exhibited a high inflation rate in the recent past which has increased from 3.5% in 2005, 3.3% in 2006, 3.0% in 2007 to 4.2% in 2008, decreasing to 1.3% in 2009 and now has risen again to 4.7% in 2010, while in the EU there was an inflation rate of 2.1% in 2010, and in the Eurozone of only 1.6% (Eurostat, 2011).

Greeka.com (2011) lists three main problems of the severe economic debt crisis in Greece at the end of 2009: a high rate of unemployment, significant tax invasion, and corruption of the political parties. This can be understood as point of departure for the investigation of Greece-specific reasons for its economic and financial problems, which are indeed significantly stronger than in other EU countries. Tax invasion is there related to widespread tax evasion, as it is characteristic for the Greek economy. While rising unemployment can be regarded as an expected result of increasing private sector difficulties, the Greek unemployment situation is also caused by the conduct of the Greek society, in particular the criminal acts of tax evasion as well as corruption. It is estimated that tax evasion costs the government of Greece about 15 billion Euro a year, but it seems to be very difficult to counteract deep-rooted tax evasion behaviour in Greece, though the government has now proposed strict austerity measures in this regard (The Wall Street Journal, 2011). Tax evasion is related to the 'shadow economy' as a further pillar of unreported income. A high shadow economy in Greece is indeed no surprise. As Schneider (2011, p.20) shows, Greece had the highest shadow economy of the 21 OECD countries for many years (which reached 25.1% of GDP in 2007), followed by Italy and Spain.

While Greece now has developed measures to fight tax evasion, it is unclear how the country will combat corruption. Inefficient government bureaucracy, restrictive labour regulations, corruption and inefficient tax regulations are quoted to be the most problematic factors for doing business in Greece (World Economic Forum, 2009, p.156).

The economic and financial problems in Greece are not only related to the worldwide financial crisis from 2008 onwards. One of the earlier challenges began to show up in 2004 when it became apparent that the Greek government had not given correct data to the Eurozone authorities so that – when corrected – the audit began to reveal financial difficulties (Eurostat, 2004). Especially military expenditures had been stated incorrectly, but also debt data and related other ones were incorrect, so that, between 2000 and 2003, amounts for approximately 5 billion Euro per year were not included in government debt' (ibid, 6). Manolopoulos (2011) ascribes these facts to faults of the Greek government, though his main topic concerns questions about the meaningfulness of lending large sums to the government in order to save the Greek economy from defaulting and in order to stabilise the Euro.

According to the Maastricht criteria of the EU, the public deficit should be less than 3% of GDP and total debt less than 60% of GDP. These requirements are examined and controlled by Eurostat as well as the ECB (see Eurostat, 2010). In 2010, Greece had the third highest deficit in Europe, behind Romania and Hungary, but the amount of indebtedness was even rising to 121 percent of GDP in 2010 from 113.4 percent in 2009 (Reuters, 2010). This is nearly twice as much as allowed by the Maastricht contract. After tedious discussions within the EU and the Eurozone, Greece has received in 2010 significant loans from the IMF and the European Union, also given as a consequence of the perceived menace for the Euro. In 2011, further help has become necessary. In the first quarter of 2011, Greece had a positive percentage change of 0.8 in the debt to GDP ratio compared with the previous quarter, while Portugal is the only country with a negative change of -0.7. Both countries had a negative percentage change compared with the same quarter of the previous year, which was -4.8% for Greece and -0.7% with regard to Portugal (Eurostat, 2011b). Discussions are now beginning that Greece not only needed a strict fiscal consolidation phase, but must also be supported by expansionary growth policies to reanimate the country's economy as the only way to reduce the number of unemployed persons, which has grown up to 16.2% in March 2011 and is extremely high in the age groups 15-24 (42.5%) and 25-34 (22.8%) (Hellenic Statistical Authority, 2011a). The necessity of such measures is to be evaluated in view of the fact that, for example, the production index in industry had declined by 8.0% in the first quarter of 2011 compared with the year before in nearly all sectors (Hellenic Statistical Authority, 2011).

The Greek financial crisis is especially difficult to resolve due to the fact of several causes coming together: A main reason can be seen in the indebtedness which grew in the first decade of the 21st century in spite of the Greek economic growth between 2003 and 2007. The financial problems can also be related to the rules and regulations of the Eurozone to which Greece has belonged since 2001: Greece profited from low real interest rates, but had problems with its significant excess of imports over exports which led to increasing debt especially since Greece could no longer seek help in currency depreciation due to its membership in the Eurozone. Another problem of Greece was the tax evasions and the associated shadow economy which deprives the state of a lot of money. Also corruption in different ways and an unusually high amount of expenses for defense belong to the causes of the evolving severe financial crisis of Greece.

The fact that Eurostat discovered already in 2004 that Greece had given incorrect financial data concerning Greek primary deficit and debt to GDP ratios, gave first indications towards coming financial difficulties. When the international financial crisis began, Greece gave banks large guarantees and new equities so that bank risks became automatically also state risks which had negative results on state securities and government bonds (see Ejsing and Lemke, 2009). The financial crisis also led to increasing interest rates for government bonds as well as the withdrawal of investors. In 2009, the then elected prime minister Papandreou revealed the dramatic situation of the Greek economy which led in 2010 to measures of the EU, which overtook the control of the Greek public household and demanded very strict saving measures that led to more and more protests of the Greek population. It became very difficult for Greece to borrow new money needed to serve its accumulated national debts.

The European Central Bank declared on 3 May, 2010 that the Greek government had approved an economic and financial adjustment program in agreement between the European Commission, the ECB, and the International Monetary Fund which allowed 'a suspension applied to all outstanding and new marketable debt instruments issued or guaranteed by the Greek government' (European Central Bank, 2010). The Greek government decided to implement a variety of strict saving measures together with EU and IMF, including the increase of value-added taxes and a significant reduction in salaries and the hiring of civil servants. These arrangements to end the Greek financial crisis in 2010 were however not as effectual as suggested so that the crisis even expanded in 2011. Again, such concerns grew not only with regard to the Greek economy, the Greek population (who suffer from the saving measures), and the Greek workforce (who suffer under a growing unemployment rate), but again also with regard to the stability of the Euro. This fear existed since the beginning of the Greek financial crisis so that even serious discussions were resumed about a possible withdrawal of Greece from the Eurozone. In May-June 2011 it became obvious that Greece – in order to avoid a threatening national bankruptcy – would need further financial help which the EU is now willing to admit under further restrictions on Greek fiscal policy, and also new topics are now discussed (without a concordance so far) about the possibility to include (voluntarily) private investors, to organise a Greek debt level conversion as well as a seven-year extension on maturing debt (see, for example, The Wall Street Journal, 2011). The discussions about a solution for Greece continue and are meanwhile often related to the situation in the Eurozone. In this context, the countries of the Eurozone have to agree to the expansion of the Euro safety net in autumn 2011.

8.4 Rampant Financial Policy in the Context of the Classical Growth Cycle

In the light of the above discussion, of Greek fiscal policy, we now assume on the basis of the model of Section 8.2 that the target value of the government debt to capital ratio is considerably increased (to a value $\bar{b}$), and that government offers an interest rate that is marked up compared to the rate of profit: $i = (1+m)r, m > 0$, since its situation and its behaviour is judged as much more risky than the situation and conduct of capitalist firms.

The laws of motion of the economy are then given by:

$$\begin{aligned} \dot{v} &= \beta_w(y(\bar{p})K_z - \bar{e})v + \alpha(v_o - v)v & (8.10)\\ \dot{K}_z &= [r(v) - g_z - \mu(\bar{b} - b)]K_z & (8.11)\\ \dot{b} &= \mu(\bar{b} - b)(1+b) + mr(v)b & (8.12) \end{aligned}$$

The steady state of this dynamical system is of course the same as before if $m = 0$ holds. For $m > 0$ we have however to solve the two equations

$$\begin{aligned} 0 &= r(v) - g_z - \mu(\bar{b} - b)\\ 0 &= \mu(\bar{b} - b)(1+b) + mr(v)b \end{aligned}$$

in order to get the steady state values for v, b. Inserting the expression for $r(v)$ obtained from the first equation into the second gives:

$$0 = \mu(\bar{b} - b)(1+b) + m[g_z + \mu(\bar{b} - b)]b$$

It is easy to show that the implicit function theorem, applied to this equation, provides us with a function $b = b(m)$ satisfying $b'(m) > 0$ around $m = 0$.[4] In a neighbourhood of the steady state the steady state value of b is therefore increasing with m and thus in particular larger than $\bar{b}$. The steady state value of v then follows from the equation $r(v) = y(\bar{p})(1-v) - \delta = g_z + \mu(\bar{b} - b_o)$ which provides a smaller value of r as in the original version of the model, see Section 8.2, and thus a larger wage share in the steady state.

For the Jacobian of these dynamics we get at the steady state:

$$J_o = \begin{pmatrix} -\alpha v_o & \beta_w y(\bar{p})v_o & 0\\ -y(\bar{p})K_z & 0 & \mu K_z\\ -my(\bar{p})b_o & 0 & -\mu + mr(v_o) \end{pmatrix} = \begin{pmatrix} - & + & 0\\ - & 0 & +\\ - & 0 & \pm \end{pmatrix}$$

This matrix shows that the balanced growth path of the economy will be definitely repelling if the moderating real wage barrier becomes weak (in a selfish society) and if $mr(v_o) > \mu$ holds true. These are however only sufficient conditions and the stability of the economy is already in question before these conditions are met. Despite such problems the economy is however still fairly robust, since conventional debt-accelerating interest-payment effects are neutralised if $i = r$ holds true. Moreover, the stability of the economy is increased, not decreased, if the government speeds up its debt-financed consumption, since this dampens the Goodwinian profit-squeeze mechanism.

In the case of Greece one may however assume that the debt to capital target itself is increasing in time, depending on the level of the actual ratio that has been achieved. Freezing the wage share at its steady state level, one then gets the following law of motion for the ratio b:

$$\dot{b} = \mu(\bar{b}(b) - b)(1 + b) + mr(v_o)b$$

The right hand side of this equation has a positive derivative, for example if there holds $\bar{b}' \geq 1$ and $\bar{b}(b(0)) > b(0)$ initially (at $t = 0$). The debt to capital ratio will under these conditions rise without limit and this also in the case where the wage share is moving. A weaker dependence of the target ratio on the actual ratio may introduce a ceiling to the evolution of the debt to capital ratio, but this ceiling may be so high that it is far beyond what is demanded as a ceiling by the Maastricht treaty (60%).

If such a process of violating the ceiling condition built into the Maastricht treaty has gone sufficiently far it may well be that also the other ceiling criterion is not at all fulfilled. In our model this ceiling can be represented by

$$ib + \mu(\bar{b} - b) \geq 0.03y$$

which is violated even if b is already close to $\bar{b}$ if $B > Y$ (as in the case of Greece) and $i > \mu$. In the case of a crisis this may well be established, since the government may then be forced to increase the markup m on firms' profitability considerably in order to get its new bond supply placed on the market. The stage is then set for intervention from abroad, here simply by imposing certain rules on the behaviour of the government from the outside, since we have no open economy here under consideration.[5] In the case of Greece, the debt of the government is primarily denoted in Euro which of course provides a firm link to the other countries in the Eurozone.[6]

8.5 IMF Intervention in Practice

The Greek financial problems, which have become more and more of a disaster for Greece, and also for the Eurozone, have been part of the search for solutions not only by the EU but also by the International Monetary Fund (IMF). The acceptance of the IMF surveillance of the Greek economy in April 2010 is described as a humilation for Greece, but also for George Papandreou, just 6 months after he became Greek prime minister (Hope, 2010). To ask for outside help is not only a declaration of failure of one's own fiscal policy, but also a loss of political independence. This is viewed as degradation by many Greeks. When the Greek financial crisis became obvious, the IMF was the institution dedicated to give the country the necessary help – in coordination with the EU and the ECB.

The foundation of the IMF can be traced back to the national reactions to the Great Depression in the 1930s while the official institutional setup was occurring in December 1945 when the Articles of Agreement of the International Monetary Fund were signed by 29 member states. The official work began in 1947 in which year France, as the first country, asked for a loan. Until 1971, the connective rule was a 'par value' system which demanded from the member states 'to keep their exchange rates pegged at rates that could be adjusted only to correct a "fundamental disequilibrium" in the balance of payments, and only with the IMF's agreement' (International Monetary Fund, 2011). This shows that the IMF could influence financial and economic developments from its beginning, and even more when the number of member states increased in the 1960s. In the early 1970s the Bretton Woods system of fixed exchange rates came to an end so that from then on states could decide about their exchange rate arrangements themselves which partially turned out to be a positive decision in the beginning of the oil crisis in particular. Flexible exchange rates here helped to overcome external shocks (ibid, 2011). The IMF reacted to the oil price shock by changing its ways of lending in order to help in particular oil-importing developing countries. The oil crisis finally led to an international debt crisis and in 1982, the IMF also began to coordinate global responses to such crises.

When a debt crisis broke out in Mexico in 1982, engaging commercial banks, the necessity to avoid failures in repaying the debts of countries became obvious. The IMF had grown over the years, but it was the fall of the Iron Curtain which made it 'a (nearly) universal institution' which was also engaged to help the Eastern countries to cope with the needed changes (ibid, 2011). The Asian financial crisis in 1997 led to some further policy changes and a higher attention to the (weak) banking sectors of certain countries. Furthermore, debt relief for poor countries became a topic. In 2007, a new global financial crisis began in the United States and soon became a global one which also needed financial resources from the IMF, as the just considered case of Greece has exemplified. There are however critical considerations with regard to the policy of the IMF, and further international institutions like the World Bank, which refer to the strong neoliberal tendency supported by them (see, for example, Pieper and Taylor, 1998).

The globalisation of financial markets however underlines the importance of IMF and World Bank, as the current financial crisis has shown (ibid, 1998). The original intent to support countries in financial and economic difficulties might therefore gain new importance again. Due to the global financial crisis, the G20 gave the IMF an important role in giving financial assistance (van Waeyenberge, Bargawi and McKinley, 2010). McKinley (2010) asks whether the IMF has abandoned neoliberalism and comes to the opinion that the essentials of the pre-crisis IMF framework will continue to matter. There are however doubts whether the IMF has really changed program and proceedings as announced by this institution. Van Waeyenberge, Bargawi and McKinley (2010, p.4ff.) regard the IMF's institutional dynamics as 'inflexible' since the macroeconomic policy still includes 'low fiscal deficits, low inflation rates, flexible exchange rates and trade and financial liberalisation'. Furthermore, they argue that 'private interests supersede public interests and the role of the state', and that the financial sector is more important than the real and productive one.

As Cohen (2010) reports, there were in 2010 different opinions in the EU whether Greece would need the help of the IMF or could overcome its crisis solely with help of the EU and ECB. A main reason for these discussions was the fact that, for the first time, a Eurozone country would be in need of IMF-help. Even Strauss-Kahn, the then Managing Director of the IMF, signaled understanding when the Eurozone would prefer to solve the crisis by itself, see Cohen (2010) and Elliott (2010). As Elliott (2010) supposed, the IMF would have been involved earlier in the Greek crisis, if the country were not a member of the Eurozone. In February 2010, the Greek population already suffered under the imposed policy measures without differentiating very much whether they were ordered by the EU, their own government or already by the IMF – or all three. There were also discussions whether Greece could – or even should – leave the Eurozone while other arguments dealt with the fact that the Eurozone lacks elements of a fiscal and political union (Elliott, 2010).

The European Union and the IMF as well as the ECB finally agreed with Greece on a joint program which included a € 110 billion financing package, an agreement which is combined with the surveillance of the Greek economy by the International Monetary Fund (Hope, 2010). While the Eurozone contributed two-thirds of the sum and the IMF one-third, the latter also agreed to monitor the implementation of the program through quarterly reviews (International Monetary Fund, 2010). The money is given to Greece in tranches, the last of which is planned for 2013 (European Commission, 2011, p.5). Each tranche is only admitted to Greece when the country has fulfilled the conditions which are imposed by EU/IMF for the next period of time. Since most of the conditions were connected with wage and welfare reductions as well as tax increases, the protests of the population have been growing in Greece.

Strauss-Kahn and the IMF made a common declaration in which they honoured the sacrifices of the Greek people, which they nevertheless regarded as compelling for rebuilding the Greek economy (International Monetary Fund, 2010). Here, the main question is certainly, what can be done to renew the Greek economy? The IMF intended to tackle 'the twin issues of public debt and competitiveness', so that an improvement in the assets and liabilities of the government has to be worked out together with a modernisation of the efficiency and competitiveness of the Greek economy. Most demands referred to fiscal policies which were mostly perceived by the population as severe cuttings (of pensions, wages, social security benefits, etc.) and various tax rises.

As Thomsen, the head of the IMF negotiating mission to Athens, declared when the 2010 arrangement was accepted, 'it will be a multi-year effort' (International Monetary Fund, 2010). Yet, a year later the problem had even grown so that in 2011 new arrangements were needed and will continue to be made in order to avoid a national bankruptcy. This is a special task since a Greek bankruptcy could be an unknown and possibly systemic experience for the Eurozone. Now, not only the provision of more monetary resources is being discussed, but also the German proposal to involve the private creditors in the restructuring of the Greek debt positions (by partial repudiation). This was originally suggested as a compelling demand by the German Minister of Finance Wolfgang Schäuble, but is now primarily discussed as a voluntary contribution of the banking system. According to Paul Krugman, in the New York Times of May 5, 2010,[7] Greece will not only end up in a partial repudiation of its debt, but will in fact be forced to leave the Euro-Zone in addition. He sees the only route to economic expansion, the alternative to a deep slump as the consequence of a strict policy to close the primary, non-interest deficit of the government, in higher exports 'which can only be achieved if Greek costs and prices fall sharply relative to the rest of Europe'. Within Greece this is not going to happen according to Krugman, so higher exports can only be achieved through devaluation and thus by leaving the Euro. But 'this awful outcome is starting to look better than the alternatives.'

In the appendix to this chapter we will investigate the financial costs of Greece leaving the Euro-Zone, while the later sections of Chapter 9 will discuss an alternative to this proposal which is not taken into account by Krugman, namely the potential of the Greek crisis as a chance for restructuring the whole social structure of capital accumulation in Greece, a restructuring of the society which we shall call 'social capitalism'.

Returning to the current state of affairs, the ECB can be described, according to Spiegel and Peel (2011), as the sole source of liquidity for Greek banks in 2011. It is supposed that the banks have posted an estimated €70 billion in bonds at the ECB in return for their refinancing by the ECB, which would have to be replaced if the ECB would stop accepting default rated bonds. This is why the authors believe that not the EU ministers but the ECB will have 'the last word on what form private sector involvement may take place in the Greek programme'.

The new financial amounts needed by Greece in 2011 are supposed to be about €80 – 100 billion. According to a table published in the German faz.net (Nienhaus, 2011), EU, ECB and partly IMF have adopted from 2009 to 2011 Greek debts so that private creditors are relieved. It is predicted that this is a tendency that will continue during the next years. The discussion will now be how a new bailout for Greece can be arranged, again between IMF, ECB and the EU. As Hetzner and Kyriakidou (2011) report, the IMF has warned the EU in May 2011 that Greece will need a second bailout on which the IMF agrees, though the institution also proposes measures for the Greek government itself, such as privatisation of harbours and other state owned firms. The joint European Commission IMF/ECB reviewing group which has made their third Review in January to February 2011 has come to the opinion that the privatisation which might bring about 50 billion Euro could become an important step forward for Greece (European Commission, 2011). While the reports of the joint European Commission IMF/ECB reviewing group (which is also called the Troika) were still rather positive in the beginning of 2011, there is now news about the deepening recession in Greece which prevents the planned saving measures. In autumn 2011, the Troika experienced severe protests from the Greek population which partly hindered them from entering the ministries so that the report was only published later on in October.

Again, most discussions deal with the financial part of the Greek problem. A renewal of the Greek economy is not really discussed, let alone expansionary measures of a recovery program like a Marshall plan[8] which could modernise the Greek economy and bring it back on a sustainable growth path. Yet, the European Commission (2011) raises hope, after its third review, that 'the progressive rebalancing of the economy, supportive external demand and growth-friendly reforms are expected to move the economy back to its potential'. A reason for these beliefs could be that this program for Greece intends to induce a change in growth based on exports and investment. The report acts on the assumption of a 1% growth of the Greek economy in 2012, and even 2% thereafter.

In a speech in June 2011, Bob Traa (IMF Senior Resident Representative in Athens) gave a positive outlook on the economic development of Greece, though he also stated that the 'implementation of the broader real-sector structural reforms has slowed down in 2011'.[9] His recommendations then again refer – besides fiscal reforms – to privatisation and structural reforms in the economy, and liberalisation, efficiency and competitiveness are further keywords in this debate. The role of banks is considered as very important and a banking sector consolidation is seen as a compelling necessity. The IMF controls and assures that the execution of these measures is properly implemented by the Greek government, of course with support by the EU (International Monetary Fund, 2010a). The reforms concern tax administration, the labour market, the health sector, and the management of public finances and are supposed to 'make the economy more competitive, transparent, and efficient'. The aim of these measures is to revitalise the confidence of international investors and the financial markets, which is believed to finally lead to higher and stable growth (ibid, 2010a). In June 2011, the IMF, the European Commission and the ECB have made a statement to underline their demands for privatisation, measures of deficit reduction (including downsizing of public sector employment), by restructuring or closure of public entities. Vulnerable groups shall however be protected in this restructuring process of the public and the private sector of the economy, while tax exemptions shall be reduced, property taxation raised and, tax evasion be fought and sanctioned (International Monetary Fund, 2011a).[10]

The IMF regards Greece and its economic and fiscal problems as part of Europe's and thus underlines that the debt crisis in parts of the

Euro area (PIGS and now possibly also France) might cause trouble in Europe and also the rest of the world. This, of course, means a high necessity to overcome the Greek public sector crisis (IMF Survey online, 2011).

8.6 IMF Intervention in Theory

In view of the above discussion of the IMF policy scenario of a rigourous fiscal adjustment of the Greek economy we now assume for the models of Section 8.2 and Section 8.4 that the tax base of the government can be widened to include all income from production, that is, it is now given by $Y = vY + (1 - v)Y$. On the other hand, the amount of these taxes spent on government consumption is reduced, since income of public servants as well as pensions and social security items are cut down in the public sector. This is achieved in the model by an increase in the adjustment speed μ with which government debt is adjusted in a downward direction towards a lower new target $B = \bar{b}K$. Government expenditure on goods G is therefore given by

$$G = tY + \mu(\bar{b} - b)K,$$

so that the tax base is larger than before, but much less of it is now used as government expenditure. We furthermore assume an accompanying real wage cut in the private sector and a subsequent freeze of its position.

Greek productivity growth has already been weak, but this real wage cut is assumed to lead to a total elimination of increases in labour productivity (due to a totally frustrated labour force). Of course, it is only for reasons of simplicity that we set the parameter g_z now exactly equal to zero. The output–capital ratio may also decline for the same reasons, but this is ignored here as a further negative effect of the IMF regulation of Greek fiscal policy. The implication of all this is however that the wage share is now assumed to be fixed at a value $\bar{v}$ below its former steady state value v_o.

On the financial side we assumed as target value $\bar{b}$ a value very much below the current debt to capital ratio b. Coupled with a higher adjustment speed μ towards this target value will give rise to significant positive effects on capital accumulation (where some profit is however now taxed away). This is happening against the background of an increase in the markup m which already occurred before the IMF policy intervention took place and is in fact inherited from this preceding period of the Greek state crisis.

We thus now also assume as given a situation of the type

$$\dot{B} = G + iB - T = \mu(\bar{B} - B) + iB < 0,$$

so that there is no need to offer further interest rate increases in order to sell a scheduled supply of new bonds (which is no longer happening).

Taken together we thereby arrive at the following modification of the laws of motion characterising the Greek economy after the policy intervention of the IMF.

$$\dot{b} = \mu(\bar{b} - b)(1 + b) + (t + m)r(\bar{v})b \tag{8.13}$$

$$\dot{K} = [(1 - t)r(\bar{v}) - \mu(\bar{b} - b)]K \tag{8.14}$$

These laws of motion are to be viewed as describing a transient situation (in the case of Greece intentionally until 2014). We therefore need not worry about the fact that there is in general no steady state solution for this dynamical system. Moreover, the first equation is independent of the second one and quadratic with the slope (for the right hand side expression):

$$\dot{b}_b = -\mu(1 + 2b) + \bar{b} + (t + m)r(\bar{v}) \gtreqless 0.$$

The graph of the quadratic function is qualitatively of the form shown in Figure 8.1. For $\bar{b} = 0$ we have in particular that one root of the quadratic function defined by $\dot{b} = 0$ is zero, while the other one, the important one, is given by:

$$b_{01} = \frac{(t + m)r(\bar{v})}{\mu} - 1.$$

The figure 8.1 shows (for the case $\bar{b} = 0$) that the speed of adjustment μ of the debt to capital ratio must be chosen with some care such that b_{o1} lies to the left of $b(0)$ and is sufficiently low (from the perspective of the Maastricht treaty). The law of motion for b then implies that the initial debt to capital ratio will be moved towards its steady state value b_{o1}, and this the faster the larger the parameter μ is chosen. This decline in the debt to capital ratio is accompanied by growth of the capital stock at a rate larger than $(1 - t)r(\bar{v}) > 0$, since the second term in its law of motion is positive along the considered path of the state variable b. This situation also applies for positive values of $\bar{b}$, since this shifts the graph shown in Figure 8.1 upwards.

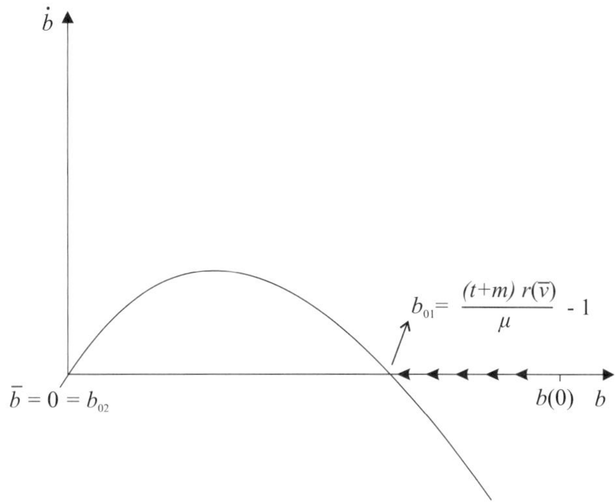

Figure 8.1 The path to lower debt to capital ratios

In Figure 8.2 we show the range where the choice of the adjustment speed μ delivers a positive (attracting) steady state value for $b > 0$, that is, where the chosen fiscal policy provides an attracting point where the debt to capital ratio remains positive.

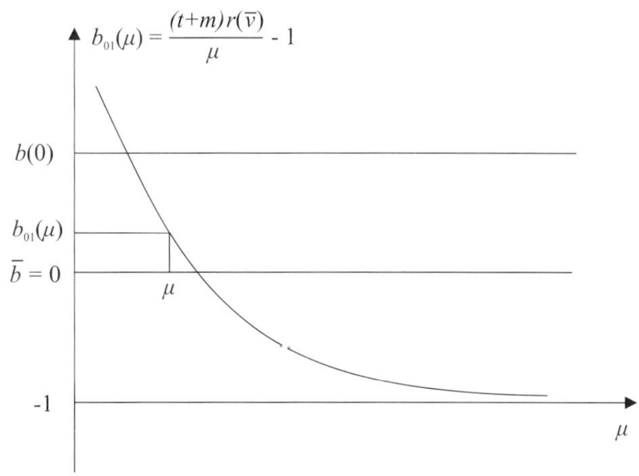

Figure 8.2 Feasibility domains for the parameter μ

The figure shows that there is an upper limit to the choice of μ, a situation which does not hold in the downward direction, where $\mu =$

$(t+m)r(\bar{v})$ separates positive from negative steady state values of the debt to capital ratio.

We thus get the result that the IMF policy intervention successfully reduces government debt (if the speed of adjustment in this process is not chosen too small). In addition this gives extra strength to capital stock growth, since the buying back of government bonds increases the amounts invested in the capital stock of the economy. Note however that the type of bond assumed by the model is a safe asset and that money is still absent from the model. There is thus no capital loss possible and considered by asset holders and also no liquidity trap present. Speculative behaviour is therefore no problem here. Finally, capital is always fully employed by the fact that workers do not save and the goods consumption of firms and the government are mirror images of each other, due to the assumed consumption functions.

Cold turkey policies are therefore effective as far as the model can mirror them. Yet, they may be accompanied by negative economic externalities, such as a decline in capital productivity y. The IMF moreover only assumes that the poorest should be protected against income losses while G may be further decreased (in particular concerning public servants, pensioners and social security, including education).

Such measures can add additional pressures in the further generation of low income work, crime and corruption and thus lead to a further segmentation of the society. Degradation of the workforce is always a problematic issue, since – as Keynes (1936) already observed – workers will not resist by physical actions to decrease in their real wages through commodity price inflation, but will be morally hurt and degraded in their self-esteem when their wages are cut, in particular if the causes for this action lie in the result of the behaviour of the upper class. Social tensions and political disruptions can thus be the result of the discussed policy intervention, with consequences which can last much longer than only up to 2014, the year of recovery from the viewpoint of the IMF.

8.7 Social Reform: The Crisis as a Chance for Social Innovations

We now consider the following modification of the government sector

$$\begin{aligned} G &= (1-\tau)[T+\mu(b_o-b)K]+\gamma(p-\bar{p})K && (8.15)\\ \dot{P} &= \tau[T+\mu(b_o-b)K]+\gamma(\bar{p}-p)K && (8.16)\\ T &= t(Y+iB) && (8.17)\\ \dot{B} &= G+iB-T && (8.18) \end{aligned}$$

We have again increased the tax base for the government, by assuming that also interest income is subject to taxation at the rate t. Besides unproductive consumption government now also invests in a stock of public infrastructure P. For this infrastructure we have already assumed that it has an external benefit on production of the form $Y = y(p)K, p = P/L$ where L is the labour supply. The laws of motion we have investigated so far are thereby modified as follows:

$$\begin{aligned} \dot{v} &= [\beta_w(y(p)K_z-\bar{e})+\alpha(v_o-v)]v\\ \dot{K}_z &= [(1-t)r(v,p)-g_z+(1-t)ib-\mu(b_o-b)-ib]K_z\\ \dot{b} &= \mu(b_o-b)+ib-\hat{K}b \end{aligned}$$

We assume in this section again that $r = i$ holds ($m = 0$) with r being given by $r(v,p) = y(p)(1-v)-\delta$. Rearranging terms we get the dynamical system:

$$\begin{aligned} \dot{v} &= [\beta_w(y(p)K_z-\bar{e})+\alpha(v_o-v)]v && (8.19)\\ \dot{K}_z &= [(1-t-tb)r(v,p)-g_z+\mu(b-b_o)]K_z && (8.20)\\ \dot{b} &= -\mu(b-b_o)(1+b)+t(1+b)r(v,p)b && (8.21) \end{aligned}$$

The steady state of this dynamical system is given by:[11]

$$v_o = 1-\frac{(1-t)\delta+g_z}{(1-t)y(p)}, \quad K_{zo} = \frac{\bar{e}}{y(p)}, \quad b_o = 0.$$

since $(1-t-tb_o)r(v_o) = g_z > 0$ holds. However we now have a further law of motion, for the state variable p which we have assumed to be given by

$$\begin{aligned} \dot{p} &= \tau[t(y(p)+ib)+\mu(b_o-b)]+\gamma(\bar{p}-p)-\hat{K}p\\ &= \tau ty(p)+(\tau+p)\mu(b_o-b)+\gamma(\bar{p}-p)-\\ &\quad [(1-t-tb)p-\tau tb]r(v,p) && (8.22) \end{aligned}$$

On the basis of the other steady state values the steady state value for the public infrastructure is determined by the equation:

$$\tau t y(p) = \gamma(p - \bar{p}) + p g_z = (\gamma + g_z)p - \gamma\bar{p}$$

We assume that there are decreasing returns with respect to public infrastructure increases so that the function is strictly concave and increasing in the state variable p. An example would be given by: $y(p) = \sqrt{p}$. Note that this equation has to be solved first and the obtained result to be inserted in the steady state values for v, K_z from the mathematical point of view. From the economic point of view we then have the result that the steady state wage share and the steady state value of K/z both depend negatively on the state variable p, the amount of infrastructure per worker.

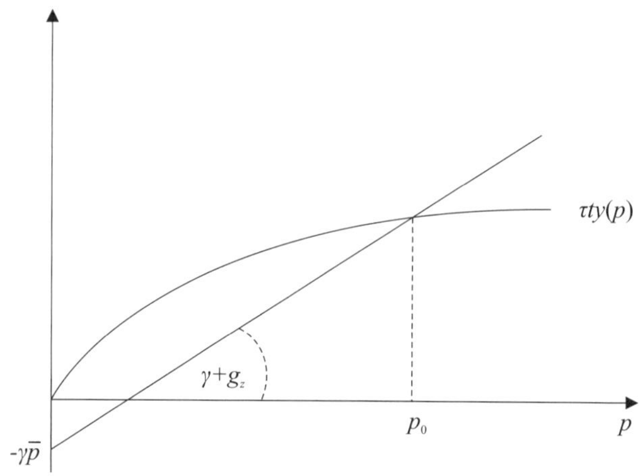

Figure 8.3 Determination of the steady state level of public infrastructure

Figure 8.3 shows that increases in the rates $\tau, t, \gamma, \bar{p}$ will increase the steady state level of p, while increases in g_z will lower it. The comparative dynamics of steady state analysis therefore gives rise to a set of mixed results. Note also that – depending on the function $y(p)$ and the other parameters – the steady state value of the infrastructure P can be smaller or larger than the targeted value $\bar{P}$.

For the investigation of the dynamics around the steady state position let us first consider the system without the new law of motion, by fixing the level of p at its steady state position.

$$\begin{aligned}
\dot{v} &= [\beta_w(y(p_o)K_z - \bar{e}) + \alpha(v_o - v)]v \\
\dot{K}_z &= [(1 - t - tb)r(v, p_o) - g_z + \mu(b - b_o)]K_z \\
\dot{b} &= -\mu(b - b_o)(1 + b) + t(1 + b)r(v, p_o)b
\end{aligned}$$

For the Jacobian of these dynamics we get at the steady state:

$$J_o = \begin{pmatrix} -\alpha v_o & \beta_w y(p_o) v_o & 0 \\ (1-t) r_v K_{zo} & 0 & \mu K_{zo} \\ 0 & 0 & -\mu + t g_z/(1-t) \end{pmatrix}$$
$$= \begin{pmatrix} - & + & 0 \\ - & 0 & + \\ 0 & 0 & - \end{pmatrix}$$

if we assume that $\mu > t g_z/(1-t)$ holds true.

It is easy to see that the trace is negative ($a_1 > 0$), the sum of principal minors of order 2 positive ($a_2 > 0$) and the determinant negative ($a_3 > 0$) as demanded by the Rout-Hurwitz theorem. Moreover, the determinant cancels against one of the expressions in the product $a_1 a_2 > 0$ so that also the remaining condition of the theorem ($a_1 a_2 - a_3 > 0$) is fulfilled. The steady state is therefore an attractor of the considered subdynamics.

If we now enlarge the dynamics by the new law of motion (for the infrastructure of the economy) we get as Jacobian at the steady state:

$$J_o = \begin{pmatrix} -\alpha v_o & \beta_w y(p_o) v_o & 0 & \beta_w y' K_{zo} v_o \\ (1-t) r_v K_{zo} & 0 & \mu K_{zo} & (1-t) r_p K_{zo} \\ 0 & 0 & -\mu + t g_z/(1-t) & 0 \\ -(1-t) r_v p_o & 0 & -(\tau + p_o)\mu + (t p_o + \tau t) g_z/(1-t) & -\gamma - [g_z + p_o(1-t) r_p] + \tau t y' \end{pmatrix}$$
$$= \begin{pmatrix} - & + & 0 & + \\ - & 0 & + & + \\ 0 & 0 & - & 0 \\ + & 0 & \pm & - \end{pmatrix}$$

if we assume that $\gamma + [g_z + p_o(1-t)r_p] > \tau t y'$ holds true, that is, if the parameter τ is chosen sufficiently small. Since there is only the entry J_{33} in the third row of this Jacobian matrix non-zero, we know that one eigenvalue must be equal to this entry and is therefore negative. The third row and column can then be deleted from the matrix J_o in order to determine from the resulting 3D matrix the remaining three eigenvalues of the full Jacobian. This gives:

$$J_o = \begin{pmatrix} -\alpha v_o & \beta_w y(p_o)v_o & \beta_w y' K_{zo} v_o \\ (1-t)r_v K_{zo} & 0 & (1-t)r_p K_{zo} \\ -(1-t)r_v p_o & 0 & -(1-t)p_o r_p - \gamma - g_z + \tau t y' \end{pmatrix}$$

$$= \begin{pmatrix} - & + & + \\ - & 0 & + \\ + & 0 & - \end{pmatrix}$$

For the determinant of this matrix we get (since some r_v, r_p expressions cancel against each other)

$$\det J_o = \beta_w y(p_o) v_o (1-t) r_v K_{zo} [\gamma + g_z - \tau t y']$$

For stability ($a_3 = -\det J_o > 0$) we therefore need the less generous condition

$$\gamma + g_z > \tau t y', \quad i.e., \quad \tau < \frac{\gamma + g_z}{t y'}.$$

It is obvious that $a_1 = -tr\ J_o > 0$ holds and that the determinant is dominated by the subexpression $J_{12}J_{21}J_{33}$ contained in the product $a_1 a_2$, i.e., $a_1 a_2 - a_3$ must be positive. This is however only possible if a_2 is positive. This gives that the assumptions of the Routh-Hurwitz theorem are all fulfilled. The balanced growth path of the dynamics is therefore attracting.

Summarising the results of this section we can state that active infrastructure investment can improve the situation considered in Sections 8.2 and 8.4.[12] The stationary state of Section 8.2 is given by

$$(1-t)v_o y(\bar{p}) = (1-t)[y(\bar{p}) - (\delta + g_z)], \quad K_{zo} = \frac{\bar{e}}{y(\bar{p})}, \quad b_o = \bar{b} > 0$$

and it is clearly inferior to the one we have in the present section

$$(1-t)v_o y(p_o) = (1-t)[y(p_o) - (\delta + g_z) - \frac{t g_z}{1-t}], \quad K_{zo} = \frac{\bar{e}}{y(p)}, \quad b_o = 0$$

if we measure the welfare of both societies by the net wage income per unit of capital and the level of their infrastructures (which includes schooling) and if the following weak conditions hold true as compared to the 'kinglike' government case:

$$p_o > \bar{p}, \qquad y(p_o) - \frac{tg_z}{1-t} > \bar{y}.$$

The measured increase in the welfare of worker households and public infrastructure is of course just given by assumption, but these assumptions are quite plausible if the assumed 'kinglike' behaviour of the government of model 1 of Section 8.2 is taken into account and interpreted. This in particular holds with respect to a proper choice of the parameters τ, t. Moreover, the consensus that may have been reached in the society considered in this section may increase the parameter α, which measures the moderation in wage negotiation and thus a type of corporatist behaviour. This type of economy may therefore be considerably more stable than the one considered in Section 8.2, which adds security to the achieved levels of income, infrastructure and GDP per unit of capital.

The transient dynamics of Section 8.4 may be a necessary one in countries like Greece in its current situation (as of September 2011), but may be subject to considerable social conflict, degradation of workforce and social segmentation. It may therefore be that the sooner a social consensus can be reached regarding the tax base (by lowering tax evasion, leading to more social justice), that puts considerable effort to the improvement of the social infrastructure (in particular education) and that brings the economy back onto a stable growth path with improving labour and 'capital' productivity, the less strangulations by IMF type interventions are needed to ensure a sound fiscal policy regarding deficits and debt accumulation.

8.8 Conclusions

We have shown in this chapter that prudent fiscal policy and public investment can tame the repelling forces as they were shown to be implied in the case of a rampant fiscal policy. They can thus lead the economy back onto a stable and sustainable balanced growth path. We have moreover shown that along this growth path the welfare of the society is increased as compared to the case of the 'kinglike government' we introduced in Section 8.2, when welfare is measured by the consumption of the workforce and the size of the infrastructure of the economy per worker. We conclude from all this that the government should not behave as just an additional consumer, being imposed onto the economy as in the model of Section 8.2 (a case often assumed in traditional Keynesian macroeconomics), and should in any case be hindered – through controlled legislation (like the Maastricht treaty) – to behave in the self-indulgent way as the past Greek governments were behaving.

If this has happened, as in the recent past of the Greek economy, fiscal policy reforms should however not only be implemented from an economic perspective as in Section 8.4, but should also reflect how eventually long-lasting social damage can be avoided or at least reduced for the society onto which this economic policy is imposed. We therefore will reconsider and extend the proposed reforms of this chapter in Chapter 9 by way of the design of a new social structure for capital accumulation for the Greek society which not only introduces new types of fiscal authorities to cope with budget deficits in a responsible way, new types of bank regulation as modelled in Chapter 5 in this book, but also – and most importantly (temporarily to be based on some kind of Marshall plan) – a restructuring of essential pillars for the future evolution of the Greek society, which are

1. safe life-course perspectives of working households,
2. a lifelong learning system of education and skill formation and
3. restructured property rights to be coupled with the formation of economic and political elites who are conducting the society in socially responsible and democratically controlled ways.

Before we come to such a radically extended perspective let us close this chapter with a brief view on what has been achieved by the IMF type policy which was forced onto the Greek society and what needs to be done from a Keynesian perspective given the situation in Greece as it now is at the end of January 2012. We view the result of the IMF austerity measures[13] by and large as a failure, since they have undermined fiscal consolidation by their contractive implications for output as well as labour productivity, the latter also through the creation of social conflicts in many areas of the society. After all stimulating economic growth is the best strategy to balance the budget, in particular when it is combined with a financial hair-cut as it seems to be accepted by European policy at last. Greek debt increased dramatically since 2008 so that this step appears to be unavoidable now. But why not combine such a step with the construction of a new institution, an independent fiscal authority like the central bank that gets some starting capital for running stimulus packages and that is allowed to use debt financing in the recession (to be repaid in the boom) and thus is acting strictly in a Keynesian anti-cyclical way.

Governments have too often proved that they are unable to properly manage the economy with respect to the business cycle and the German debt break is but the recognition of this, though totally inappropriate from a Keynesian perspective, since it may prevent fiscal action when it is urgently needed. Rampant kinglike monetary policy has led to the idea of independent central banks, first implemented institutionally in the UK as the Bank of England, and kinglike fiscal policy should be reflected in the same way and lead to the creation of an independent fiscal policy authority, which is responsible for the control of the business cycle and which can use debt instruments besides raising some funds. The government proper is then reduced in its spending activities to infrastructure investment which is only allowed to be debt financed if this investment creates profits (net of interest payments). All other government activities must be tax financed. Such a clear-cut situation would no longer allow for what has happened in Greece before 2008 and is much easier to control than the present situation.

The current Greek government could be committed to create such an institution and thus to hand over part of its current sovereignty to it, if it wants the financial hair-cut and a sequence of stimulus packages. In our view this would be a much more promising route out of the current crisis than any IMF-oriented strategy which will still be polluted by too much orthodox thinking instead of having a truly Keynesian orientation. It was reported earlier by the IMF that the primary deficit of Greece could already become a surplus in 2012, but this seems no longer to be possible now. A financial hair-cut and a sequence of stimulus packages could therefore bring the Greek economy back on a growth path and the Greek society back to an acceptance of foreign intervention. The problem for Europe is the banking crisis which a financial hair-cut may imply, but here too the situation may be easier to handle if such a hair-cut is not conducted in isolation, but combined with a strategy that is expansionary and institution improving in its core. It is not at all obvious that Greece is not a larger problem for Europe than East-Germany was (and to a certain extent still is) for West-Germany. This holds in particular since labour and capital will stay in Greece and even expand in amount and income and since the Euro is already there and working. The complaint about Greek competitiveness is here only partly relevant, since tourism and merchandise shipping are Greek specialities and since other sectors can be expanded and diversified through appropriate infrastructure investment and stimulus packages.

In the appendix to this chapter we show possible dramatic consequences should the Greek government decide to leave the Eurozone and to reintroduce the Drachma. Yet, even if this radical step is not made, the financial and real situation described in the appendix may be enforced to Greece through IMF-type policies and the public discussion about it. We view IMF austerity measures as being by and large responsible for the real decline of the GDP of the Greek economy over the last years. Due to this output and the implied tax revenue loss the Greek debt situation has worsened and is now taken more and more often in the public as an argument that Greece should indeed leave the Eurozone. This however induces credit rationing even for firms which are quite 'healthy', since also their balance sheets would worsen dramatically if potential creditors expect a return to the Drachma sooner or later. In the current situation IMF-type policies not only damage government's and households' consumption demand, but – due to a worsening in the Greek solvency situation and its perception – also investment demand of firms.

It is very questionable that any increase in Greek competitiveness can cope with these negative tendencies. A debt haircut and a 'Marshall plan' plan for Greece therefor seems to us the only way to bring Greece back on track in a sound and socially acceptable way. It has to be recalled here that the banking system, see Chapter 5, was the point of departure for the mess the world economy is now in. Discrediting Keynesian regulation proposals for the financial markets and thus allowing (subprime) credit to become a commodity (packed into securities) so that unresponsible risk-taking behaviour could be transferred to other private and public agencies and discrediting the Keynesian view of a strictly anti-cyclical behaviour of debt-financed fiscal policies here worked together and created the dramatic fiscal crisis the Eurozone is now facing. The European discussion on 'debt breaks' may still be an insufficient solution to this question of economic and social survival.

Appendix: Reintroducing the Drachma: A Greek Tragedy

In the classification of Section 9.2 of the next chapter, Greece could be considered from the political perspective as an extremely ugly example among the ugly welfare states of Esping-Andersen, with devastating implications for the international competitiveness of the Greek economy. Krugman's suggestion, see Section 8.3, that Greece must therefore leave the Euro area is in our view however by far the worst among the alternatives we have discussed in the present (and will discuss in the next) chapter with respect to Greece. To demonstrate this, this appendix briefly presents a basic modelling scenario underlying such a conclusion. For simplicity we do this in graphical terms solely.

We denote in Figure 8.4 by $\Delta\rho$ the Drachma and by Y GDP. Greece being in the Eurozone is represented by the horizontal line (at $\Delta\rho = 1$) in Figure 8.4. This line cuts a Krugman (2000) type of IS-curve, caused by the Euro debt of Greek firms and augmented now by Euro-financed government expenditures (that significantly enhance the negative Krugman balance sheet effect of increasing exchange rates). These investment and government expenditures depend negatively on the exchange rate (representing the case where Greece has returned to the Drachma), since firms' and the government's balance sheet worsens significantly with a depreciation of the Drachma and since interest payments are also denoted in Euros.

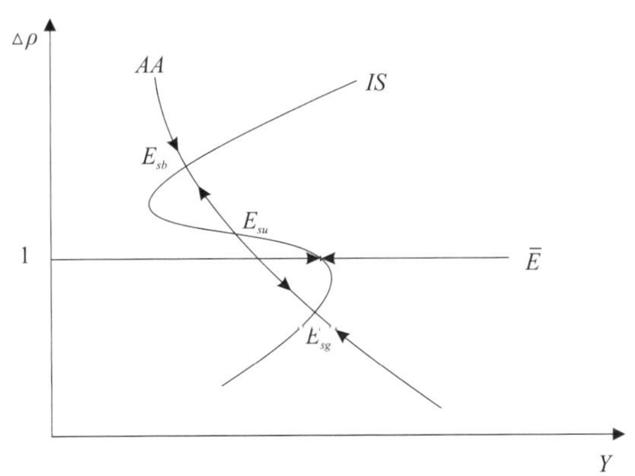

Figure 8.4 Krugman type balance sheet effects for the case of an exit from a monetary union

These effects at the least dominate the competitiveness effect of currency devaluations in a midrange interval for the Drachma and peter out for very large devaluations, since investment and government expenditure adjustments have reached their floor (while there may be supply bottlenecks for very low levels of the Drachma, where domestic demand for domestic goods is strong and again the competitiveness effect the dominant one). This explains the shape of the IS-curve shown in Figure 8.4.

Concerning capital and foreign exchange markets we use as in Krugman and Obstfeld (2003) the UIP condition: $i* = i + (\Delta\rho^e - \epsilon)/\epsilon$ which – when coupled with an LM-curve or a conventional type of Taylor rule – implies a negatively sloped strictly convex financial markets equilibrium curve, with the future expected exchange rate as a shift parameter. This financial markets equilibrium relationship is denoted by AA in Figure 8.4.

We have drawn the curves such that three equilibria exist, a good and stable one (sg) and a bad and stable one (sb), while the equilibrium in the middle is saddle-point unstable (su), all backed up by the assumption that the dynamic multiplier process, that is, output adjustment is stable, leading as a partial mechanism horizontally towards the IS-curve from the left and from the right and in a flexible exchange rate system with adjusting $\Delta\rho$ along the AA-curve towards either E_{sg} or E_{sb}. All this holds after a return of the Greek economy to the Drachma, while the situation where Greece stays in the Eurozone is depicted as the horizontal line at $\Delta\rho = 1$ with $\bar{E}$ as IS-equilibrium and point of rest of the Keynesian dynamic multiplier.

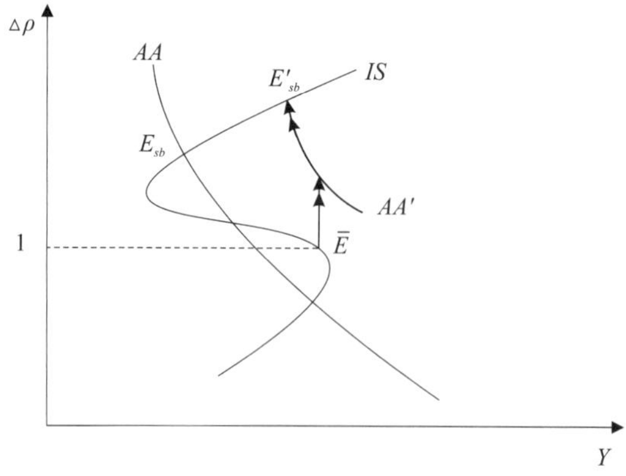

Figure 8.5 A return to a flexible Drachma

In all cases where $\bar{E}$ lies below E_{su}, flexible exchange rates will lead to an output adjustment towards E_{sg}, that is, an appreciation of the currency. The corridor between E_{su} and $\bar{E}$ may however be small, but nevertheless there is the possibility that a return to the flexible Drachma will not lead to currency devaluations, but instead to an improvement of the domestic balance sheets of firms and the government. Yet speculation (the expectation of devaluations of the Drachma) may shift the AA-curve by so much to the right such that only the upper equilibrium is in existence and is then self-confirming.

If the situation in Figure 8.5 applies, a Greek return to a flexible domestic exchange rate will lead to a strong devaluation of the Drachma and a total breakdown of investment and of government expenditures. Moreover, the expectations of further devaluations of the newly introduced currency will shift the AA-curve further to the right and thus continue to worsen the situation dramatically. Since Greece is indebted in (now foreign) Euro-bonds, the result of such a spiral may be a disaster for the Greek economy. It is completely open here how and when such a depreciation spiral can be stopped.

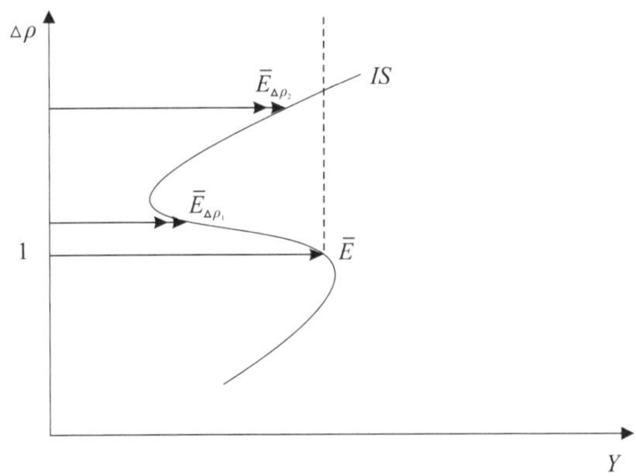

Figure 8.6 Leaving the Eurozone via a pegged Drachma

Figure 8.6 finally shows the case of a return to the Drachma that is pegged against the Euro. The figure indicates that this may resemble a blind flight, since it very much depends on the level to which the new Greek exchange rate is pegged. Moreover if the Greek economy as part of the Eurozone is already in the backward bending part of the IS-curve it is very likely that the Drachma is fixed at a level where there is large output loss and where therefore the exchange rate is not devalued by so much that the competitiveness effect outweighs the balance sheet effect.

And even if this would happen this would mean that investment and government expenditure have reached their bottom level, a situation that is also of a highly problematic nature.

Summing up we get the result that a return to the Drachma – whether flexible or fixed – will almost certainly damage investment behaviour and the budget of the government to such a degree that the gain in competitiveness through a strong devaluation of the Greek currency – when decoupled from the Euro – will lead to large GDP losses, and possibly then also massive defaults of firms and drastic increases in government indebtedness.

It can be objected that Argentina went the same way without too much harm (away from dollarization back to the Peso) and managed its default in 2002 quite well, in particular concerning the length of the contraction period (where increasing exports helped a lot) and the rapid growth nearly from 2003 onwards (preceded by an inflationary outburst and a -6% inflation adjusted growth rate).

When approaching the crisis, Argentina's Public Debt/GDP ratio rose significantly, from about 35% in 1998 to about 45% in 2001. The country abandoned in January 2002 the fixed 1-to-1 Peso-Dollar parity that had been in place for ten years.[14] Greece had a steeper increase from 105% in 2008 to an expected 150% in 2011. It thus started from a much higher percentage than Argentina and also a much higher level (since GDP levels were of comparable size in 1998 and 2008, respectively).

If Greece would return to the Drachma, the debt of all of its sectors (including commercial banks) would be in foreign currency and an economywide default nearly unavoidable. In the case of the defaulting Argentina its debt was to a significant degree held outside the banking sector, while the Greek debt is largely held by the European banking sector (with France and Germany – and Greece – as the most involved countries). A defaulting Greece would therefore cause significant contagion effects in particular within the Eurozone, with the other Southern countries as top candidates for the further spread of the Greek insolvency situation. We conclude that the Argentine way is not a recommendable solution for the Greek situation, due to the fact that all of its public and private debt would become foreign debt if Greece would leave the Eurozone.

Notes

[1] The term 'kinglike government behaviour' has been chosen to indicate that selfish government behaviour is nothing new, but was a common attitude in the case of absolute rulers of nation states. Of course, such a type of behaviour is not acceptable in a democracy where government should serve the welfare of the country and not vice versa.

[2] We have used the definition $K_z = K/z$ in Chapter 4 which however makes no difference with respect to mathematical implications.

[3] Later on we will change the tax base to $Y + iB$.

[4] The slope of this function is given by $\frac{g_z \bar{b}}{\mu(1+\bar{b})}$.

[5] See however the appendix to this chapter for the compact treatment of the huge problems should Greece return to the Drachma and thus to an autonomous exchange rate policy.

[6] And which already indicates the financial turmoil in the balance sheets of the public as well as the private sector should Greece attempt to increase its competitiveness by reintroducing the Drachma and by its devaluation against the Euro.

[7] http://krugman.blogs.nytimes.com/2010/05/05/Greek-end-game/?pagemode=print

[8] A Marshall plan in the sense that this cannot be seen as the task of Greece alone, but as an economic stimulus package for Greece that is in the interest of the EU and should be supported by the EU and the IMF financially and with regard to planning.

[9] See Traa (2011).

[10] See also Manolopoulos (2011) for further reflections on practical and 'non-practical' recommendations.

[11] Note that the steady state value of b implies that government is also temporarily a creditor to the owners of firms, a situation that can be avoided if the government sets a target $\bar{b} > 0$ in place of 0 in its debt adjustment rule. The steady state level b_o is in such a case positive and lower than this exogenous target.

[12] Note here that the models of Sections 8.2 and 8.4 cannot really be considered as viable ones from a long-run perspective.

[13] An austerity program is a program in which a government drastically reduces spending and increases taxes or other revenue sources.

[14] See http://www.tradingeconomics.com/argentina for further details.

9. Social Capitalism: A New Social Structure for Capital Accumulation

9.1 Introduction

In this chapter[1] we start from a Keynesian macroeconomic model of advanced capitalist societies, Section 9.2, and briefly summarise on this basis the functional chains and their stability properties that characterise the working of such economies from the Keynesian perspective. We do so in order to provide a theoretical description of the status quo of such societies, which will then be contrasted with an ideal model of a flexicurity economy, in Section 9.5, as one central result of the European debate on the welfare state. This type of economy we then extend towards our conceptualisation of a society which is built on the principles of what we shall call 'social capitalism' and its three pillars, flexible and socially oriented labour market institutions, a coherent educational system and on this basis the formation of democratic elites and the change in property rights this implies, see Section 9.6. The current crisis and its impact in particular on the Eurozone indeed provides an important opportunity in this regard, where central institutions are in question and where therefore openness for new ideas can be expected.

An ideal construction of 'social capitalism' as in Section 9.6 is indeed needed before compromises with the actual status quo of given capitalist economies should be sought and investigated, as it is suggested by the word 'compromise'. Without an ideal, against which potential and actual reforms in countries like Denmark can be investigated, there is a lack of a coherent theoretical structure against which one can evaluate the sustainability of such reforms in isolation and in their interaction and also the 'progress path' to a further development of capitalist societies. The same applies to the evaluation of current welfare and workfare systems which we shall briefly consider in Section 9.4.

Our first model of a flexicurity economy is summarised in Section 9.5. It combines flexibility (a strictly competitive form of capitalism) with social security (concerning employment and income) into a coherent and sustainable whole, suggested to overcome forms of capitalism which are founded on the Marxian reserve army mechanism (which is therefore based on flexibility solely) as well as forms of regulated socialism (which is based on rigid 'security' features primarily). It preserves room for the deconvolution of the capitalist forces of production within a widely acceptable social system of relations of production, a synthesis which we believe is not only possible on the stage of development advanced capitalism has now reached (in contrast to the times of Marx), but is also necessary when contrasted with the current severe economic and social imbalances in the world economy (under the worldwide dominant regime of unleashed capitalism). The chapter however does not yet approach in detail factual analysis of the variety of current forms of capitalism, that is, their status quo, which one has to consider when possible steps along a progress path towards 'social capitalism' are to be formulated and discussed and when history and hysteresis effects (path-dependent evolutions) have to be taken into account. In Section 9.7 it will however present a variety of proposals for a restructuring of an especially critical case, the Greek economy, against the background of what has been discussed in Chapter 8 with respect to this economy and the IMF based policies it is now subject to. Section 9.8 concludes.

9.2 The Point of Departure: Unleashed Financialized Capitalism and its Regulation

Macroeconomic Feedback Channels

We start the discussion of the functional chains acting under the surface of the current forms of capitalism from the perspective of Keynes's (1936) summary of the 'causal nexus' that is characteristic for such economies. In the 'General Theory', Keynes based his analysis of the interaction of the financial markets with the goods markets (based on the concepts of liquidity preference and effective demand) on a strictly hierarchical ordering of the markets in an advanced capitalist economy, where financial markets are at the top of the hierarchy, with goods markets depending on the outcomes on financial markets and with labour markets at the bottom, depending in their behaviour on the outcome on the market for goods. This hierarchy is shown in the middle of Figure 9.1, but is already augmented there by a variety of repercussions from the lower markets to the higher ones which are to be added to the hierarchical perspective and of importance in the full dynamic evolution that is implied by this macroeconomic model.

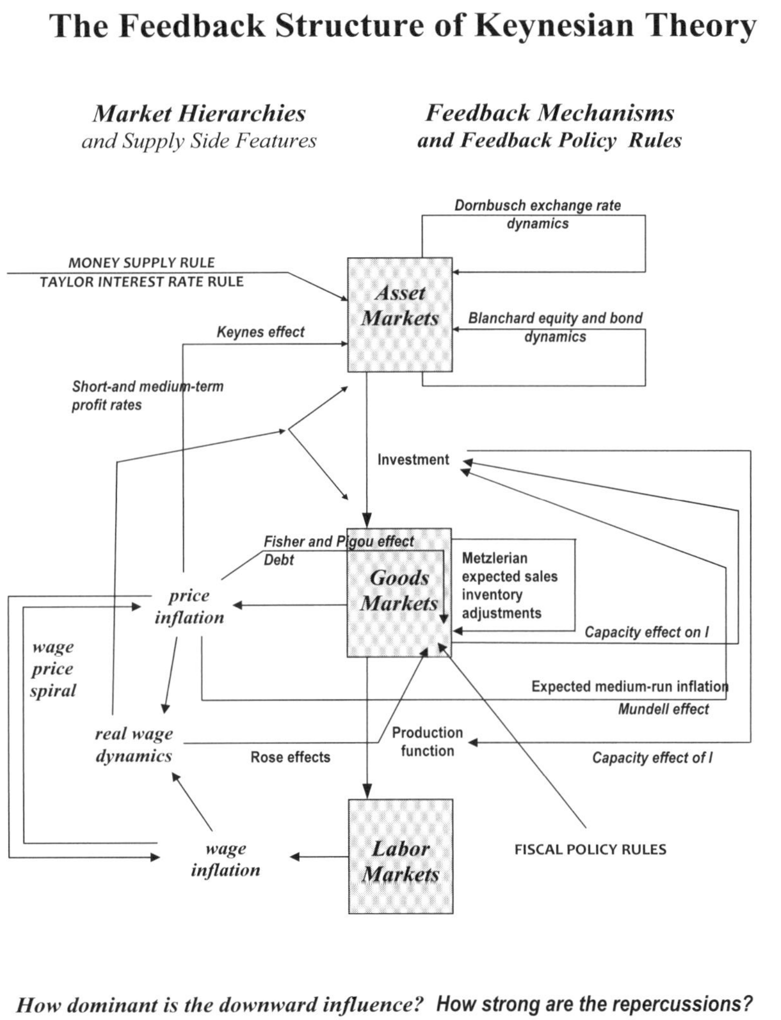

Figure 9.1 The Keynesian view of the real-financial market interaction

They do not really question the downward chain, leading from a short-sighted 'casino-type' behaviour on the financial markets to the long-sighted tasks of the debt financed investment strategies of firms and from there – via directly and indirectly induced income streams – to further investment and consumption expenditures on the market for goods, the so-called dynamic multiplier process. The employment on the labour market is then by and large a result of this multiplier process and thus the weakest element in this downward dependency.

Monetary policy is impacting the financial markets via short-term interest rate steering and generally suggested to be responsible for the control of price inflation, but – as it has become obvious now – should be much more oriented towards and responsible for the behaviour of financial markets, since inflation can (to a certain degree) be controlled by a well-designed anti-cyclical fiscal policy as well as through a corporatist (wage) income policy. We will return to the question of the appropriate choice of fiscal and monetary policy measures below, but will first provide a brief summary of the feedback structures that characterise the working of the private sector of the economy.

We start with the financial markets in their internal interaction which is generally characterised by centrifugal forces, since increasing capital gain expectations generate – at least on an average and for some time – rising asset prices creating thereby the room for actual rises in capital gains which in turn stimulate the expectations of further capital gains. This type of a primarily backward-looking chartist behaviour can – in certain cases – be of a very naive type, but can also be – in other segments of the market – as technical as modern computer algorithms allow for this. The accelerating forces of such positive feedback mechanisms are of course subject to sudden turning points which however (when predictable) would make the predictors very rich. They are however very hard to explain even in qualitative terms since their occurrence may be very much dependent on actual news and other shocks that hit the financial markets. It can however be shown by means of macroeconomic portfolio approaches that financial markets with static expectations are exhibiting a stable adjustment behaviour of asset prices towards their equilibrium positions implying that the formation of capital gain expectations is (but not always) the 'villain' in these asset markets.

There is next an across-market feedback structure, concerning the interaction of the financial with the goods markets, which is also of a destabilising nature. We explain this cumulative process by using Tobin's q, defined as the total value of equities divided by the value of the capital stock of firms, as measure of the state of confidence characterising the economy. If this ratio increases, firms are evaluated in more positive terms which improves their financing position and on this basis their actual investment. Increases in investment in turn stimulate national income and output by the Keynesian income multiplier process, which in turn raises the profitability of firms. Firms are then evaluated by the stock market through a further increase in Tobin's q which is a self-feeding, cumulative process of a real-financial market interaction.

Such an accelerating mechanism is also characterising the goods market in itself where increases in the capacity utilisation rate of firms stimulate their propensity to invest which via the Keynesian multiplier process increases income and output and thus leads to further rises in the capacity utilisation of firms. Moreover, a similar mechanism is characterising inventory adjustment processes in the manufacturing sector which become destabilising when inventories are adjusted by firms with a sufficient speed.

Of more importance – in particular in the public debate – are however the forces that generate price inflation in the goods market in isolation as well as through a wage–price spiral relating the goods with the labour market. Price inflation can adjust in an explosive way by an accelerating mechanism that works in the market for goods solely (known as Mundell effect in the literature). This effect starts from the observation that rises in expected inflation reduce the expected real rate of interest which stimulates investment demand as well as the demand for consumer durables which in turn lead to increases in the rate of capacity utilisation of firms. This stimulates in turn current price inflation and thus leads – under appropriate circumstances – to increases in the expected rate of inflation and so on.

However, also the interaction of price and wage inflation can lead to an accelerating inflationary climate. One situation where this can occur is the case where overall goods demand depends positively on the real wage, that is, the wage level divided by the price level, and where wages adjust faster than prices when increases in goods demand and the output of firms occur. Real wage increases then stimulate goods demand and thus in turn increase the real wage further, since the numerator in this expression increases faster than the denominator. The same upward spiral is also occurring when aggregate demand depends negatively on real wages and when prices are responding more strongly than wages to increases in goods demand and output. The reader is referred to Chapter 4 for a modelling of such situations.

These mechanisms of course also work in a downward direction leading to deflationary spirals then, a situation which is much more dangerous than that of inflationary spirals. This is due to the fact that inflation can be stopped by sufficient increases in the nominal interest rate, but since this interest rate is bounded from below by zero, monetary policy may be totally ineffective in stopping a deflationary process. In such a case falling prices increase the real debt of firms which pushes their bankruptcy rate up and this all the more the stronger deflation becomes.

This so-called Fisher debt effect can indeed lead to a complete collapse of the economy. One may argue that falling prices also increase the real wealth of households and thus stimulate goods demand (the so-called Pigou effect), but this effect will be dominated by the Fisher effect if deflation becomes an issue. Moreover Keynesian liquidity preference (money hoarding) may lead to rising nominal rates of interest and may thus imply in the case of deflation that the real interest rate – the difference between the nominal rate and price inflation – rises due to two forces, as real interest rates are the sum of the nominal rate and the deflation rate in the case of negative inflation rates.

There is finally a 'Minsky effect' in the evolution of financial markets (including banking and the credit market), a scenario which not only makes the economic agents in good times less and less risk-aware, but also more and more careless in their choices of new financial instruments (an example is securities) as the recent worldwide mortgage crisis and the resulting banking crisis have shown in a dramatic way. In addition, commercial banking and investment banking became more and more intertwined, leading to a situation where credit risks were significantly increased through the joint financial market operations of commercial banks, see Chapter 5.

Policy Issues

One may ask in view of the above why capitalism has been so successful at all, instead of being always on the run into uncontrolled booms or busts. There are however inbuilt bounding mechanisms for bounding accelerating tendencies in the private sector, increasing interest rates and increasing real wages in the boom (if investment decreases in a stronger way than consumption is increased in such a situation). Falling interest rates may do the same in the bust, while a floor to the downward adjustment of money wages (based on workers' resistance to falling wages) and a similar floor to price level adjustment (based on cost-plus pricing of firms) can avoid the dangers of debt deflation.

Moreover, one may argue that the absence of any fiscal or monetary policy after World War II would indeed have led to accelerating booms or busts in the private sector of the economy (Nixon's wage–price stop is one example and Japan's fight against deflation is another one).

We conclude that unleashed capitalism – accompanied by more or less conventional macro-policies – may work for some time, but will in these good times undergo a development which more and more endangers its stability through 'innovations' in the financial sector in particular, on the basis of which a casino-type behaviour in this sector becomes more and more dominant. Ideal (radical) macro-policies which could stop and reverse such an evolution are here briefly enumerated and given by the following list of policy measures:[2]

1. A 100% Tobin-type tax on capital gains which makes speculation meaningless and supports the social obligation of financial markets to serve the real economy and not vice versa.
2. A 100% Fisherian type reserve ratio for commercial banks which allows credit creation only out of time deposits and not out of checkable deposits, serving the social function of channelling interest-bearing savings of households into investment decisions of firms without the possibility of bank runs (on immediately checkable deposits).
3. An independent fiscal authority besides an independent central bank which pursues a strictly anti-cyclical demand management out of funds it can raise independently from the government. This would reduce business fluctuations to a certain degree and thus also contribute to price stability.
4. A corporatist regime in the labour market (wage management) whereby wages are made independent from employment and utilisation rate fluctuations by way of a scala mobile endorsement. This would further reduce inflationary processes and would also help to avoid time-consuming wage negotiations between capital and labour (and the possibility of strikes when such negotiations fail).
5. Anti-cyclical open market policies of central banks in risky assets (treasury bonds or even equities) in place of the current orientation of monetary policy towards the short end of the financial markets. This would stabilise financial markets even further and also contribute to a reduction in business fluctuations and inflation, in addition to the above fiscal policy measure.

One can show for the above Keynesian representation of the working of the macroeconomy, see Asada, Flaschel, Mouakil and Proaño (2011) for example, that this will make its business cycles damped and its financial markets and the banking system stable and this in a way that does not significantly encumber the savings-investment channel. Here rates of interest play an important role, but without interference from speculation about capital gains into such a lending–borrowing relationship. The current discussions in Europe about Tobin transaction taxes on financial trade, about the fiscal mess in Greece, about the return of the narrow banking idea, of the corporatist regimes in the Nordic countries and of Keynes's (1936) suggestion that the central bank must be prepared to trade on long end of financial markets show that all of these reform agendas are currently of a topical nature. We stress however again that the above proposals are still ideal ones which have to be compromised with the actual status quo, but which represent a coherent whole on the basis of which these compromises have to be and can be found.

All these reforms are however only (though surely important) first steps in the improvement of already existing institutions and regulations – which are indeed discussed in the political debate, with the exception maybe of the construction of an independent business-oriented fiscal institution. From the perspective of Marx's (1954) *Capital*, Vol. I one might however argue (or be faced with the argument) that the fundamental conflict in capitalism is the one between capital and labour about income distribution and within production which can only temporarily be overcome by corporatist regimes and welfare state regulations, as Kalecki (1943) has argued.

The Road Ahead

Against this argument, the main focus of the chapter therefore finally becomes to what extent we can establish a system of labour market reforms that goes much beyond processes of wage management in that they remove from an efficient functioning of capitalism the recurrent need for a substantial reserve army of unemployed, the creation of a substantial low income work sector, and the existence of pauperism in a dead segment in the labour market, see Chapter 2 in this regard. Capitalism, it may be claimed by many researches, not only with a Marxist background and using a different language, cannot remain profitable in the long-run without the existence of the disciplining devices of low income work and pauperism for the fluid part of the labour market.

However, due to processes of social segmentation, resulting social conflicts and more, these disciplining devices will create in the long-run, a form of capitalism that is not a sustainable one, in view of its social degradation processes. The present chapter will however argue that a competitive type of capitalism can work under full employment (guaranteed by an employer of first resort) in a society with no unskilled workers and an educational system that counteracts processes of social segmentation. Its three pillars, adequate labour market institutions, a well-designed educational system and responsibly behaving elites, are the pillars which we will investigate one by one in the sections on 'social capitalism' (SC) in the second part of the chapter.

Pillar I, which by and large is already present in our conceptualisation of an economy of flexicurity type, concerns labour market institutions and the implied life course perspectives of workers, which considerably transcend those of an Employer of Last Resort as discussed in the Anglo-Saxon literature, see Chapter 2. Pillar II of an SC world concerns the modelling of an educational system that allows it to support all students as much as possible in order to give them a chance to develop their competencies and skills as well as their abilities to organise their learning processes and finally to train social skills. It is not by chance that our basic model of the underlying educational system is similar to the Scandinavian one, especially the Finnish school system, since we here find some characteristics which are also relevant in our model of 'social capitalism' such as an all-day comprehensive school until the age of 15/16 with no grading in the first years and no class repeating. Furthermore all students get a chance to attend a secondary school for 2–4 years which is either technically or academically oriented. The main aspect is, however, the individual support given to each student to develop his/her competencies. This is also related to equal opportunity which plays an important role in our model. The third essential pillar of an SC society concerns the characteristics and the influence of economic and political elites, in contrast to the role elites play in most of the current forms of capitalism, which includes the question of property rights as well as control rights. In both cases, elites (properly defined) are a crucial component of the societal development processes, since they by and large determine decision rules, actual decision making as well as sanctions in the case of failure. Their formation, selection and reproduction, that is, how the elite status is attained and transmitted to others, their leadership role, that is, how their power is exercised and controlled, and their ethics, that is, how consistency between the goals of elites and national objectives can be achieved, indeed needs detailed discussion within democratic societies (which is however by and large lacking in the current literature, in particular in economic theorising).

The chapter is closed by a consideration of the current state crisis in Greece and the opportunities this situation gives rise to, concerning a fundamental reshaping of the economic and social institutions of this member of the Eurozone. The current IMF–EU–ECB program may to a certain degree be a necessary step in the reshaping of the Greek society, but it is far too limited and contractive in nature. It may need to be augmented by a partial repudiation of Greek government debt, not however by a return to the drachma, as it is currently suggested even by prominent economists (see Chapter 8). The proposal that Greece should leave the Eurozone in order to increase its competitiveness would be a disaster in the current situation as was shown in the appendix of Chapter 8. Instead strongly expansionary Keynesian growth and anti-cyclical policies should be implemented, that is, economic stimuli should be created, together with new fiscal and monetary institutions, in order to prevent severe economic, financial and social crises within the Greek society.

9.3 The Crisis as Chance: Rebuilding Socio-economic Institutions in a Democratic Society

> *Greece – and, not to underestimate the importance of international politics, Europe too – is at a sort of crossroads. The time frame within which to imagine, contemplate and put into action a different future for it is closing rapidly. We must not squander this unprecedented opportunity and end up with a short-sighted and short-lived solution. We must soberly examine all possible alternatives, radical or not. We must consider the long-term effects of our decisions. We must instigate debate and actively engage, following ideological convictions and visions without merely carving out an escape route from an uncomfortable situation that might turn out to be a dead end. There is work to be done from the ground up, and we will have to do it.* (Alexandros Stavrakas, May 13 2010, www.guardian.co.uk)

In view of this quotation, the approach chosen in this chapter is of the following kind. Our primary objective in the provision of a radical alternative to the presently discussed proposals to deal with the crisis of unleashed capitalism in general and the state crisis in Greece in particular is to formulate an ideal, that is, an abstract model of a new social structure for capital accumulation, similar to an architect who designs a new type of building on the purely mental level first. Of course, detailed knowledge of the actual status quo of a given society is needed if the ideal model is to be used to find a workable compromise, a tentative roadmap, intended to transform the considered society in the direction of such an ideal. Yet, without the ideal construction, the formulation of a compromise model is a contradiction in itself. Reforming a society by providing solely a list of more or less related purely economic instructions, runs the danger of providing patchwork politics instead of a reflected interlinked set of socio-economic policy measures. This however does not mean that such patchwork policy is inferior with respect to its realisation chances to an ideal model-guided proposal. Quite the contrary: Quesnay's famous Tableau Economique for the French economy of the 18th century provides an impressive counterexample to this, since his maxims for the reconstruction of the French society which his ideal Tableau implied were never seriously considered by King Louis XV and his courtly environment. It is a matter of speculation to suggest that the French revolution would not have happened if his contribution to the Age of Enlightenment had been taken seriously by the monarch to a sufficient degree. Be this as it may, the ideal he formulated has survived, but the French royal dynasty did not.

In this chapter we are therefore primarily concerned with considering the origins and in formulating the basic principles of an ideal construction of what we will call 'social capitalism'. The stress here is on the cohesion of these two words by which we attempt to express that the productive forces of capitalism are (currently) unrivaled, but are to be enframed by sound social relations of production to guarantee the proper working of these forces in the longer run in Western type democracies. The profit-seeking motive and the innovative powers of capitalist firms that are based on this motive (when properly regulated) in our view provide the central instruments to warrant urgently needed innovations (in environmental protection for example), see Chapter 7. Needless to say that this does not mean that any profitable innovation is commensurable. On the contrary, unregulated capitalism is in fact not (and has never been) a viable economic structure, but needs a comprehensive body of legislation to realise its potentials for the progress of democratic societies.

From this perspective, the chapter will however find that the various actual approaches to 'socialise' capitalism:

- by variants of the welfare state,
- by their neoliberal transformation into workfare states, and

- by the construction of an Employer of Last Resort system,

are premature, since these approaches are either too one-sided, or too unregulated or too much status-quo oriented, respectively.

The ideal model of a new social structure for capital accumulation we are proposing in this chapter builds on the detailed modelling of a flexicurity economy of Flaschel, Greiner and Luchtenberg (2009), see here Chapter 3. We presume knowledge of this model, its detailed system of transfers between the sectors of the economy and its stability features concerning labour market flexibilities and income cum employment (not job) security. We regard this ideal of a flexi(bility-se)curity reform of primarily the labour market institutions of the economy as underlying the arguments of this chapter. From the viewpoint of the current EU-debate on 'flexicurity' we however will argue here that this concept is too much focused on the labour market and indeed needs to be embedded in a wider concept – which we have done already in Chapter 3 to a certain degree. It integrates the Marx-Keynes-Schumpeter analysis of the productive forces of capitalism with a reflection of the social relations of production within which capitalism should be operating in a democratic society and its human-rights oriented constitution. This enlarged concept of a 'social capitalism' essentially rests on three pillars, life course perspectives of the households of the considered society, the educational system and 'social' property rights[3] as well as the formation of 'socially oriented' elites. If these pillars are present in a comprehensive way we would then speak of 'social capitalism' instead of just a Flexicurity Economy. We stress here that the German concept of a 'Social Market Economy' is in this respect too vague, since markets have existed in slavery systems, in feudalism and also in Ancient Greece.

This chapter then uses our ideal design of a society we characterise as 'social capitalism' and applies it in a first tentative step to the current state crisis of the Greek economy. This is not the most promising status quo situation to which our ideal model of social capitalism can be applied. It is obvious, in view of the Finnish educational system, the Danish flexicurity status and maybe the solidarity structure in Sweden, that other countries are more advanced regarding the directions we are here proposing as ideal guiding principles. Yet, the enduring crisis in Greece can be understood as providing a chance on the basis of which broader and far-reaching concepts of societal reform can provide new aspects in the political debate in Greece, in particular for the longer run. This holds the stronger the more the IMF rescue plan becomes a failure from a socio-economic perspective.

Subdividing welfare states into 'good' (by and large the Nordic countries), 'bad' (by and large the Anglo-Saxon world) and 'ugly' (Germany, France, Austria, Belgium and Luxembourg: GFABL, as the continental cluster and Portugal, Italy, Greece and Spain: PIGS, as the Mediterranean cluster, see Ioannidis (2011) for a brief discussion of these country clusters, we consequently apply our model of social capitalism to the Southern ugly end of this characterisation of welfare states and Greece in particular. There is definitely a chance in the crisis the Greek society is currently experiencing, in particular if the orthodox cure of the IMF, the ECB and the EU is not able to put the Greek economy on a sound path from the societal point of view.

There is a long tradition in economic thinking that suggests the cleansing effects of (great) depressions as main mechanism to generate a new long-lasting boom period with new institutions, strong growth and higher employment. The late Robert Heilbroner, a student of Joseph Schumpeter and himself an eminent economist, teaching at the New School for Social Research in New York, always used to cite remarks that Schumpeter made in his lectures: A recession is like a cold shower. This expresses what in particular Schumpeterians believe: significant busts have cleansing effects in removing disproportions in industrial development, in income distribution (where labour has become too self-confident and demanding), imbalances in the number of firms in an industry, imbalances in the relationship between real and financial development and imbalances in international economic relationships, such as the trade account. Moreover, significant institutional change may come about in the attempt to solve the contradictions in the observed crisis of the financial–industrial structure of the economy.

Indeed, the notion of a 'cleansing effect of busts' is known since the 19th century in business cycle theory and is also not far from how Karl Marx has viewed the dynamics of capitalist economies which correct themselves through large swings in unemployment and through economic crisis, generating long-phased distributive cycles from today's perspective, see Tavani et al. (2010) and here Chapter 4 for the case of the US-economy after World War II. In this chapter we argue in this respect that the current worldwide crisis in the financial–industrial structure is of such a significance that the chance is indeed given, at least for some countries, to reshape their socio-economic structure to such an extent that the deregulations in labour markets (atypical or low income work and their consequences for the life course perspectives of households), systemic instabilities in financial markets (where a casino-type of behaviour has become established) and the deformations in the political system of a country can all (be attempted to) be replaced by a coherent new social structure of capital accumulation, namely 'social capitalism'.

Chances are that one may be able to create now a 'progress path' towards such a socio-economic structure that is much more promising than the standard IMF-policies to put such countries back on track, a track without much innovative potential that therefore does not really solve the societal problems of such countries. Social capitalism by contrast embeds Schumpeterian creative destruction into a regulated river bed of Schumpeterian process and product innovations and creates a social surrounding that allows for proper life course perspectives of the households of the society, based on citizenship education, skill formation and processes of lifelong learning, as well as well educated and responsibly behaving elites (elected executive persons in the economic, social and political structure of the considered society). The social capitalism project is certainly a very ambitious one, some might say utopian, but we view a progress path to such a society as inevitable for, in particular, the larger countries in the world, since the alternative of sticking to the current financialized capitalist mode of production will only lead the world into further economic, financial, ecological and political crises (and to the dissolution of the current form of Western democracies) in the longer run. There is urgent need for radical change, encompassing all types of capital (real, financial, human, social and cultural) and the possibility of such far-reaching change is within reach when the current crisis of capitalism and the political climate this has generated is grasped as a 'cleansing' opportunity.

9.4 Continental Welfare and UK Workfare: Too One-sided, too Neoliberal?

After WWII the idea of a welfare state arose, visible first in the Beveridge plan and then later on pushed forward by many forces, mainly social democratic ones, but also by some Christian democratic parties. In more recent times, academics, having seen many variants of the welfare state, have started classifying the welfare states in various ways. By now, a classic work in this area is Esping-Andersen's (1990) study of the three worlds of welfare capitalism where he distinguishes between, firstly, the 'social-democratic' welfare state (the Nordic countries and the Netherlands, with a Keynesian understanding of the economy), deriving from the relative stability of social-democratic regimes in these countries, secondly, the neoliberal welfare state (the US, Canada, UK, Ireland and partly Australia, with a broadly speaking 'Walrasian' understanding of the economy), and thirdly the conservative and strongly 'corporatist' welfare states (the GFABL and the PIGS, as explained above, partly based on a Schumpeterian understanding of the working of the markets of the economy), in short: the good, the bad and the ugly ones,[4] the latter in the case of Germany for example, a mixture of neoliberal and social market economy ideas.

The concept of the welfare states primarily suggests that it is a giving, but not taking, but since it is based on the capitalist mode of production and its dynamic evolution of the forces of production it has to face the dilemma that it flourishes – and leads to strong regulations in favour of the workforce of the economy – in the prosperity phase of Goodwin's (1967) model of long-phased distributive cycle, while it becomes deregulated again in the depressed phase of this distributive cycle where mass unemployment puts workers and their unions back into a weak position. What political and other proponents of the welfare state have given to the workers' employment and income perspectives in the prosperity phase is then again taken away from them to a possibly larger degree, depending on the political structure of the country under consideration.

This is obviously not a very attractive way of shaping the life course perspectives of the majority of the population in a democratic society, with its long swings in the social ascent and descent of a part of the families comprising it. The Goodwinian approach to the overshooting interaction of employment and income distribution, as a modelling of the Marxian reserve army mechanism, clearly suggests that political regimes may just mirror its four typical regimes (boom, stagflation, bust and recovery) in a very unreflected way as can for example be observed for the UK and Germany, but not so much for the Nordic countries of Europe.

We view this course of events as not being a coherent one. Flaschel and Greiner (2009) for example argue in view of such long swings in the institutional evolution of capitalist economies that already an agreement between unions and firms on minimum as well as maximum real wages – if properly tailored – would have helped to reduce the amplitude of the distributive cycle and thus the evolution of mass unemployment considerably. This shows that a giving and taking is the proper foundation in the construction of welfare states, which however implies that welfare is too one-sided a word to represent this basic idea for a road towards 'social capitalism'. We briefly stress that the type of voting system and the change in actual political government has to be taken into account when specific countries are investigated. In particular, the weaknesses of coalitions in the multi-party systems under proportional voting – which become more and more a fact of life – may be responsible for the evolution of ambiguous types of welfare state situations as we have observed it in the recent past.

After the fall of the Iron Curtain, which reduced the pressure for supporting welfare systems, additional elements were added to the economic and social reproduction process of Western type economies, by going on to so-called workfare systems with their distinctive (Scandinavian or neoliberal) labour market activation policies, where the state was assumed of no longer being only in a giving, but also in a taking position in its relationships to the workforce of the economy. In the Scandinavian countries this was based on high tax contributions from the working population and thus became more of the flexicurity type considered in the next section. By contrast, in the USA – and later on also in the UK – workfare started with the introduction of the Personal Responsibility and Work Opportunity Reconciliation Act (PROWRA) in 1996 under the presidency of Bill Clinton. In the UK, Blair's New Labour policy and the New Deal project (welfare to work) stressed personal responsibility and the role of activating labour market policies (the enabling state) from the microeconomic perspective. However, in contrast to the Nordic countries and the Netherlands, the tax base for such programs was a very limited one, implying that the implemented ability to withdraw benefits from those who refused 'reasonable' employment did only partly become a success story, in particular due to the fact that the New Deal in the UK intended to induce in particular young people to work full time for about only £ 60 a week.

Moreover, to the extent the New Deal has been a success story, the widespread introduction of atypical or low income work of various kinds in the 1990s weakened the security net of the welfare state in the downward direction, and – for example in Germany – has led to wage regimes where a significant part of the population is now endangered by poverty, whether in the workforce or not (especially children and more and more retired people). The breakdown of Eastern socialism has significantly alleviated this neoliberal deregulation of the benefits of the welfare state for the working as well as the retired part of the population.

Workfare may represent an approach where capable adults are required to perform work, often in quasi-public services and with atypical profiles, as a condition of receiving aid. Benefits thus become conditional, which is a step into a right direction, but the conditions of workfare systems, in particular in the USA and the UK economy are not of the kind yet, where aid and obligations can be considered to be sufficient and balanced from the social point of view. The extent of the riots in England's larger cities in summer 2011 are very telling in this respect: *So yes, the broken society is back at the top of my agenda.* (David Cameron, on August 15, 2011). In contrast to the current situation in England, the possibilities for a social network of civic work, not necessarily to be organised by the state, at least in its entirety, are not at all exhausted as the blighted areas of many advanced capitalist economies, not only in the UK, clearly exemplify. Categories such as the 'layabouts' and the 'workshy' do however not really get to the root of the problem of the precarious lives of the many people in the dismantled sectors of workfare-based advanced capitalist economies.

Against this background, the flexicurity concept, see Chapter 3, which attempts to find an appropriate mix between workplace flexibility and normal employment security seems to be a significant step forward in the evolution of the social structure of capital accumulation in Western democracies (maybe already applied successfully – in a more authoritarian way than suggested by our model – in the Japanese society from quite a different perspective). The next section will present a brief summary of such an economic framework from the viewpoint of its architecture, not however from one of its actual working in some of the countries of the European Union.

9.5 The 'Good'?: Flexicurity Capitalism

This section provides the fundament for our subsequent discussion of 'social capitalism' which is built around the labour market institutions of the here envisaged flexicurity economy. We consider briefly some basic features, but also problems, which have to be solved in such a flexicurity economy, the next step in our discussion of the varieties of capitalist welfare states. We do this through appropriate combinations of aspects of economic flexibility as well as social security, by building on the modelling proposals provided for the flexicurity debate in the European Union in Flaschel, Greiner and Luchtenberg (2009), see also Flaschel and Greiner (2011, 2012) for detailed discussions of the origins, the problems and the perspectives of the flexicurity models of these books.

As already shown in Section 3.1, flexicurity has been seriously discussed in the European Union since some years which led – among others – to a briefing in relation to the Lisbon Strategy. Here, statements about flexicurity include:

> *Flexicurity aims at ensuring that EU citizens can enjoy a high level of employment security, that is the possibility to easily find a job at every stage of active life and have a good prospect for career development in a quickly changing economic environment. It also aims at helping employees and employers alike to fully reap the opportunities presented by globalisation. It therefore creates a situation in which security and flexibility can reinforce each other. … Flexicurity can be defined as an integrated strategy to enhance, at the same time, flexibility and security in the labour market. … Thus, enterprises and workers can both benefit from flexibility and from security, …, from the upward mobility resulting from increased skills, from investment in training that pay off for enterprises while helping workers adapt to and accept change. … flexicurity policies can be designed and implemented across four policy components: – Flexible and reliable contractual arrangements, …, – Comprehensive lifelong learning (LLL) strategies. … – Effective active labour market policies (ALMP), … . – Modern social security systems* (COM 2007).

'Flexicurity' was originally developed in Denmark where this concept was first brought into politics by the social democratic prime minister Poul Nyrup Rasmussen in the early 1990s.[5] It soon became a topic in the academic literature as we already discussed in Section 3.1 so that we here only shortly refer to Ton Wilthagen (1998) on the Dutch origins of the flexicurity model. The role of the flexicurity approach in the performance of the Danish economy is not always positively judged as the approach by Andersen and Svarer (2007) shows. Funk (2008) and Viebrock and Clasen (2009) are further critical discussions of the flexicurity approach. We stress in this context that our following approach to flexicurity is a purely macroeconomic one that neglects the difficulties of how to implement flexicurity on the microlevel from the economic, the social and the legal point of view.

The flexicurity concept – primarily discussed with respect to the Nordic economies – intends to combine two labour market components which – as many economists might argue – cannot be reconciled with each other, namely workplace flexibility in a very competitive environment with income and employment (but not job) security for workers in this economy. The problem here is to find the appropriate mix between these two aspects of labour market institutions, intended to overcome both the case of flexibility without much security (free hiring and firing capitalism) as well as the case of security without much flexibility (past Eastern socialism). We consider the suggested labour market reforms as representing one central pillar for a flexicurity society, to be supplemented however by three further essential pillars: the life course perspectives of worker households, the schooling system, and the role of political and economic elites, which we will investigate in detail in the later part of the chapter.

There are many basic aspects, questions and problems with regard to an acceptable combination of flexibility with security, see ch.3 for details, which lead to many conceivable though alternative ways of solving this task. The main aspect is always how much flexibility respectively security can be accepted. So it has to be asked how much flexibility will be allowed in hiring and firing and in job discontinuities as well as in wage and price setting? This can be put in contrast to the question how much security in base income payments and employment protection is allowed? Flexibility and security are furthermore of importance with regard to workplace mobility, that is choice of the location of the working places. It becomes obvious that nearly all work related aspects are relevant with regard to flexibility and security, not only regular work, but also the gestation of atypical employment and skill preservation. Yet, also further economic aspects are to be considered such as the forces of globalisation and financialization or technical change due to creative destruction.

If we regard pillar II (educational questions) and III (elites), it is quite distinguishable that flexibility and security play here also a role concerning, for example, education and lifelong learning, education and equal opportunity at primary and secondary schools as well as skill differentiation and the selection of elites.

In Flaschel, Greiner and Luchtenberg (2009) we have designed an ideal, that is, mathematical model of a flexicurity economy by describing the flow identities or the social accounting matrix of such an economy, basically by considering a triple of labour markets, in the private sector of the economy, in its public sector and in the sector where the government acts as an Employer of First Resort (EFR), not of Last Resort (ELR), see Chapter 2. The basic idea behind the EFR principle is that instead of an unemployment benefit scheme we have transfer payments of those working in the industrial sector of the economy (where Keynesian business cycles and Schumpeterian creative destruction are at work and shape the entry or exit of workers into or from this sector), and the EFR sector where public sector wages apply and where government organises meaningful employment, just as in the public sector of the economy, see Section 3.4 for further details. This is a very direct substitution of the current unemployment schemes, where benefits are provided without essentially making use of the unemployed workforce (for which many useful types of employment in the provision of public goods indeed exist, if existing skills are not endangered by long-term unemployment). Employees in the first labour market (the private sector) are moreover transferring base pension payment contributions into the public sector and are gaining advantage in addition to base pensions through company pension funds to which they contribute through their savings. This scenario is based on the assumption that wages in the private sector are sufficiently above the ones in the public sector (based on a sufficient degree of labour productivity in industry).

It can be shown for such an economy, where wage changes are represented by way of a standard Phillips curve and employment policies of firms described by some sort of Okun's law, that such an economy exhibits not only an attracting balanced growth path. It indeed converges to it the better the more flexible the hiring and firing system in the private sector of the economy is. Of course, the choice of this degree of flexibility by firms can be expected in such an economy to be of a kind that does not disrupt the ongoing production process in a short-sided manner.

There exist many approaches to improve the situation of the working population, and especially of the underprivileged workers which partly have similar aims as we have discussed in our approach to labour market institutions of the flexicurity type, see, for example Basic Income Guarantee (BIG) and Employer of Last Resort (ELR) (see Tcherneva and Wray, 2005). Yet, there is a significant difference since in our view it is not possible to find an acceptable compromise from the status quo, but we think it to be necessary to find a compromise by looking at an ideal and the status quo. Comparing the ideal with the present capitalist economies will then allow us to develop compromises between the status quo and the ideal. Therefore, our approach is – to a certain degree – similar in spirit to the Tableau Economique of Quesnay.

The conclusion may however still be that there may be more flexibility than security that characterises the evolution of the flexicurity model at least when applied to larger economies and in particular in cases where social cohesion is low. And even if this is not the case, flexicurity is maybe too much focused on the labour market and its activation and not so much on the social structure surrounding it, where life course perspectives, (citizenship) education, and social elite formation may be of crucial importance.

This chapter will therefore in its second part go beyond the formal consideration of flexicurity economies towards the introduction of the concept of 'social capitalism' where the just named three pillars are integrated into the flexicurity project with an emphasis on a socially oriented democracy. This includes reflections on social property rights. We consider social capitalism as on the one hand accepting the productive forces of capitalism, that is, the Schumpeterian process of creative destruction and postulating on the other hand that it is now possible to combine this process with relationships of production that can be considered social in nature.

To our knowledge the concept of 'social capitalism' was first used in Kersbergen (1995) for the Christian-democratic view of the (in Germany) social market economy. It has recently been used by the former Australian prime minister Kevin Rudd (2009) to describe the return of a Social-democratic regime after the neoliberal deregulation phase under Prime Minister John Howard. Compared to the introduction of flexicurity in Denmark in the early 1990s by its Prime Minister Poul Nyrup Rasmussen, Kevin Rudd has not been able to implement such a concept in Australia. But in contrast to the flexicurity concept, the concept of 'social capitalism' can be considered as being more to the point, since it has roots in Christian- as well as Social-democratic thinking and is honest with respect to the economic basis on which this social framework is to be based: the profit-seeking process of creative destruction by the Schumpeterian dynamic entrepreneurs.

We believe that future discussions should concentrate on social capitalism as a significant enlargement of the economic concept of flexicurity. We view this scenario also as building a bridge between Social- and Christian-democratic parties and thus as capable of reaching the majority of voters in many democratic countries.

With respect to the situation in Germany we would however emphasise that the concept of a 'Social Market Economy' is too vague as a concept, since markets have existed in many pre-capitalist societies and in past Eastern socialism. Rather, one has to acknowledge that the world is dominated by a variety of capitalistic systems, with various degrees of Schumpeterian creative innovations and destructions. The problem –

at least for a longer run – is to design a new social structure around these profit-seeking forces of production which makes them compatible with social relations of production that are based on human rights, democratic principles, equal opportunity and environmental protection. At present even advanced capitalist economies seem generally not to realise their full potentials towards the inclusion of such fundamental objectives.

Moreover, the 'truncation' of the entity 'social capitalism' to just 'socialism' is not a proper alternative on the theoretical and the empirical level, since the Walrasian conceptualisation of socialism of Lange-Lerner type, and – to a certain degree, also of Schumpeterian competitive socialism type – is a very hypothetical construction, while Eastern socialism was just a 'regulated' one, but not one where the notion of 'planning' was in fact successfully applied.

As Roemer (1994, pp.11/125), in his book *A Future for Socialism*, states:

> *I believe that socialists want equality of opportunity for:*
>
> - *self-realisation and welfare,*
> - *political influence, and*
> - *social status.*
>
> *I am saying, in other words, that property relations must be evaluated by socialists with respect to their ability to deliver that kind of egalitarianism. ... The second idea is that modern capitalism provides us with many fertile possibilities for designing the next wave of socialist experiments.*

In our view, these statements provide strict arguments in favour of 'social capitalism' as we define this concept in this chapter. Or as Schumpeter (1942, p.134) has stated it:

> *The true pacemakers of socialism were not the intellectuals or agitators who preached it but the Vanderbilts, Carnegies and Rockefellers.*

The flexicurity scenario may be a viable one under certain side conditions, but it is still of an imperfect nature from the social point of view, since it neglects the role of education not only of skill formation, but also citizenship education, the education and formation of responsibly behaving elites, and the proper life course perspective of households which form the society. In short, an educated society is needed for the proper evolution of citizens who understand and accept their worklife environment – with its job discontinuities and the resulting lifelong learning processes – and who altogether create the social environment or the social capital in which a thereby significantly regulated, but nevertheless very flexible type of capitalism can operate. These topics will be discussed in more detail in the following section.

9.6 A New Social Structure for Capital Accumulation: Social Capitalism

> *Others have argued that we are seeing a more fundamental regime change: the third in postwar history, starting with the Keynesian model, from the 1940s to the 1970s; the neoliberal ascendancy, from 1978 to 2008; followed by a new regime, which is currently being shaped. Perhaps this new regime will come to be called 'social capitalism' or 'social democratic capitalism', or simply the term 'social democracy' itself. Whatever the nomenclature, the concept is clear: a system of open markets, unambiguously regulated by an activist state, and one in which the state intervenes to reduce the greater inequalities that competitive markets will inevitably generate.* (Kevin Rudd, former Australian Prime Minister, February 2009, The Monthly)

Neoliberalism has indeed – in the form of workfare systems (like Hartz IV in Germany) – led to decline of the welfare state in such countries, maybe justified by its earlier one-sided nature to provide welfare without taking something from the welfare receivers. Flexicurity is improving this situation in our view, since it is also demanding something (by activating labour market policies) from the receivers of welfare provisions (though there may be elements of flexploitation in the actual implementations of the flexicurity idea). From our perspective it is a step forward from the concept of an 'Employer of Last Resort', since it is not so close to the status quo of actual economies, but more ideal and due to this also more coherent in nature (but maybe due to this also further apart from the status quo, see Wray (2008) on the manageability aspects of the ELR concept).

In the following we augment our abstract model of a flexicurity economy by designing the architecture, or the ideal model, of what we define as 'social capitalism',[6] which we have developed from Schumpeter's (1942) vision of a Western type of democratic socialism. We would consider a Marx-Keynes-Schumpeter (M-K-S) framework here as the most appropriate one for the study of the concept of social capitalism, that is as point of departure for a proper understanding of this composed entity. By contrast, the use of the concept of 'social capitalism' in Offe (2003) and Lošonc (2006) is, by far, too vague and too backward looking to be of use.

The notion of 'social capitalism' (SC) is also from a microeconomic perspective (concerning social entrepreneurship) which can be embedded into the structure we are investigating in this chapter, but which is not as a central component from our macrodynamic MKS perspective. We define this type of capitalism as the project of regulating in appropriate ways the Schumpeterian type of dynamic entrepreneur (and its large-scale analogues) and the processes of (credit-financed) creative destruction he/she is pushing forward. In Marx's view, capitalism is dominated by the restless circulation of money $M \rightarrow C \rightarrow M'$ using commodities (factors of production) to realise more money. Such a circulation form of money need not imperil people's health, societal cohesion or nature if appropriately administered, and is much more innovative than the very limited circulation form $C \rightarrow M \rightarrow C'$ characterising the concept of a market economy. The latter applies to the theoretical Lange-Lerner type of discussions of socialism in the literature and provides a further argument why such a socialist market economy cannot compete with advanced forms of capitalism, whether sufficiently regulated from a social and political perspective or not.

The profit-seeking innovation, diffusion and death of new types of production processes and the birth of new types of products is therefore at the heart of our understanding of the word capitalism, where however a first type of socialisation and ethical orientation has to be introduced by way of limitations to the type of processes and products that are available for innovation. These limits are found through proper societal awareness, are to be rooted in secure life course perspectives of workers and also call for a well educated and responsibly behaving elite on the economic, the social and on the political level. This defines in broad terms our understanding of the entity 'social capitalism', a concept that in these broad terms should be acceptable to both Social- as well as Christian-democrats.

This assumes that the former are acknowledging that Schumpeterian capitalism is by far the most efficient way to create income and wealth for the citizens of market economies and that the latter are realising that neoliberal laissez-faire policy is not in accordance with social obligations. Flexicurity may be considered as a first and politically already debated step into such a direction, but is in our view a too limited one against the background of the industrial, financial and ecological problems the world is now facing. A corporatist regime that avoids the Marxian distributive cycle and reserve army mechanism is therefore only an (important) first step for a social modernisation of capitalism.

In this section we therefore consider the concept of a flexicurity economy from an enlarged social perspective which extends the security aspect to the whole life course perspective of the household sector (which includes besides employment and income security also the aspects of medicare over the life course of the individual families and the form of pensions on the basis of which they live and contribute to the evolution of the social economy when retired). A second pillar for the extension of flexicurity to a truly social form of competitive capitalism is the educational system that underlies its occupational structure of skilled, high-skilled workers and also professional elites. We therefore now extend the flexicurity model towards the integration of an educational sector that is adequately structured concerning the objectives of such a society. A third pillar of the flexicurity based form of social capitalism we are portraying is the formation and conduct of the economic and political elites of the considered society which must be thoroughly based on the educational system, must be democratic in nature and must solve coordination problems as well as incentives problems on all levels of the considered society. We stress here that the three pillars are not to be considered as only providing 'welfare' to the household sector, but also expecting contributions from its various components, through participation in activating labour market policies (where necessary), through active engagement in the process of lifelong learning and through adequate contributions to the solution of economic and social coordination problems as well as incentive formation.

Pillar I (Accepting SC): Households' Life Course Perspectives: Employment, Income, Medicare, Pensions and Care for the Elderly

Under a flexicurity regime, we have considered in Flaschel, Greiner and Luchtenberg (2009) that the households working in the private sector of the economy are supplying the payments to those employed on the basis of an Employer of First Resort principle (a quasi unemployment insurance for this sector) and moreover also the base pensions of the retired households. Under social capitalism we would assume instead that the latter transfer is made out of the budget of the government (out of ordinary tax payments) as are the now added medicare expenses (including the care for the elderly). Taxes in the government sector can be netted out, so that taxes in the private sector must be sufficiently high to cover all these expenses.

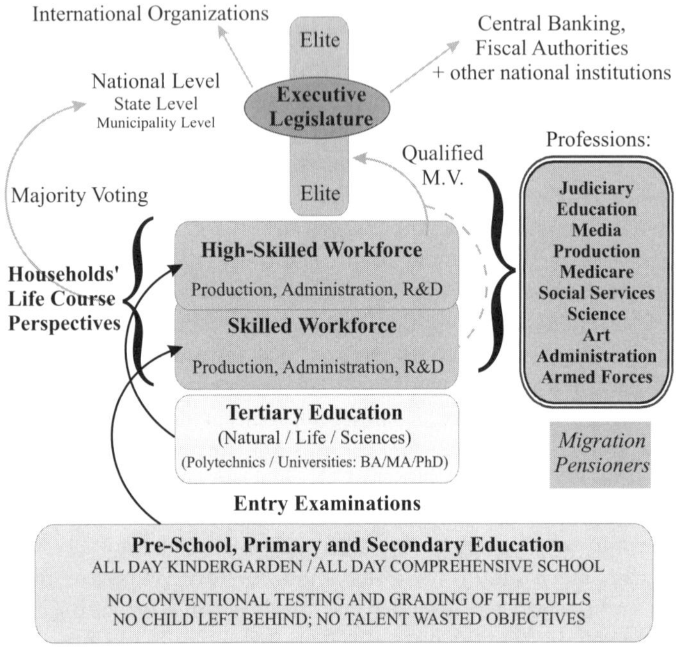

Figure 9.2 The social structure of the society and households life course perspectives: Employment, income, medicare and pensions

There has to be a ministry for health services as well as a ministry for pension issues (including company pension fund regulations) who are in charge of organising these fundamental sectors for the life course of the citizens of the society. 'Pay as you go' and related characterisations are thus no longer relevant in these central components of life course security since these ministries will have a budget like any other ministry in the government, where efficiency issues as well as equity issues have to be solved on the microeconomic level in addition. The provision of medicare can thus in principle (ignoring actual deficiencies) be organised as in countries like Sweden, where sufficiently high taxes are accepted for solving the problems of health insurance. In contrast to the EFR transfers which depend on the state of the business cycle, these government provisions are of a fairly regular nature and based on health requirement conditions and life expectancy statistics. We do not yet discuss the accumulation of funds of the three transfer payments for the life course structure of the household sector, but assume a sufficient flow of funds in this respect.

We view the provision of such a life course perspective for the household sector[7] as laying the proper foundations for the acceptance of the capitalist conduct in the private sector of the economy that is indispensable for a proper functioning of the considered new social structure of capital accumulation. It is also our belief that secure life course perspectives contribute not only to economic efficiency (similar to efficiency wages), but also to the creation of social and cultural capital and the networks based on them which enhances the working environment and the skills of the working population in significant ways (note that we are implicitly here assuming a stationary population for reasons of simplicity).

Life course perspectives for the household sector include the rules of retirement as an important topic. In most European countries the official retirement age, that is the age when full pension is paid, is 65, but only few people are able to do full-time work until this age. In Germany, for example, the present average age to retire is between 63.8 (men) and 63.3 (women). This is about 1 year later than in 2008 though it still means a reduction of pension payments due to early retirement. While this can be positively evaluated, it has nevertheless to be related to the fact that in Germany in 2010 only about 60% of those aged between 55 and 64 were employed (Eurostat, 2011d). In the present working situation, many full-time jobs are no longer conducted by elderly people, for example in mining, construction, etc., but also in supermarkets and the like. These problems have, of course, to be taken into account, since in Germany the retirement age will be gradually increased up to 67 years until 2024. Unemployment of the elderly would not represent a problem under 'social capitalism', however, since on the one hand there is no discrimination allowed by law concerning sex or ethnicity, but it is assumed in this model that there can be age discrimination (due to the varying employment conditions in the private sector, concerning work-conditions and significant overtime work in particular). The EFR principle however guarantees that people who are approaching retirement are occupied in meaningful ways in the official public or EFR sector of the economy. It therefore becomes natural to consider such job changes from say age 55 onwards.

Pillar II (Understanding SC): The Educational Systems: Equal Opportunity, Skill Formation, Lifelong Learning and Citizenship Education

We assume in our model only two types of workers: skilled and high-skilled ones which demands that all students will pass a secondary school certificate like the Abitur or A-levels. Therefore, a strict concept of demand and support is necessary as well as the rules of equal opportunity in order to eliminate all hindrances for children to participate in an education that fits their abilities and allows them to meet the requirements of the schools. It is the task of education to provide students in (pre)schools not only with the necessary skills to become adequate workers in their later professions and jobs but also to help them to understand this system and to integrate themselves into it which does not exclude – as all kinds of good socialisation – a critical and reflecting approach.

Our educational system[8] begins for children at the age of 2, though nursery schools may be available for younger children if parents prefer this. All forms of schooling are thought to be all-day institutions though families may have a choice of lesser schooling until the child is 3 years old. Following the Scandinavian model of schooling, all children will be together in a general school at least until grade 8 or 9 when they are about 15 or 16 years old after a common kindergarten from 3-6. There will be no grading or repeating of classes but students will get individual reports at least at the end of each school year. When students have to opt for different types of secondary (or high) school types thereafter they can be aware that all types will lead them to a matriculation certificate though with different focuses (either more academic or more technical) and a different length of schooling (between 2 and 4 years depending on the preferences of a student) so that they are able to plan their secondary school time with the help of their teachers, following their individual abilities and interests.

This school system needs to bring to life all abilities and interests a child may have, since otherwise the ambitious aim of a final certificate for all cannot be reached. Education has to improve its didactics and methods, so that each child can be supported in its special competencies, and furthermore that each child can be supported individually so that he/she will be able to pass school successfully. This strong focus on individual support in relation with the common aim of reaching the final certificate demands not only a well equipped school with regard to teaching personnel, further personnel such as social workers, psychologists, librarians, medical helpers and close relationships with professionals from outside such as sport trainers, artists etc., but it also demands a well equipped school with attractive rooms and more. All teachers from Nursery School onwards will have to be a university graduate.

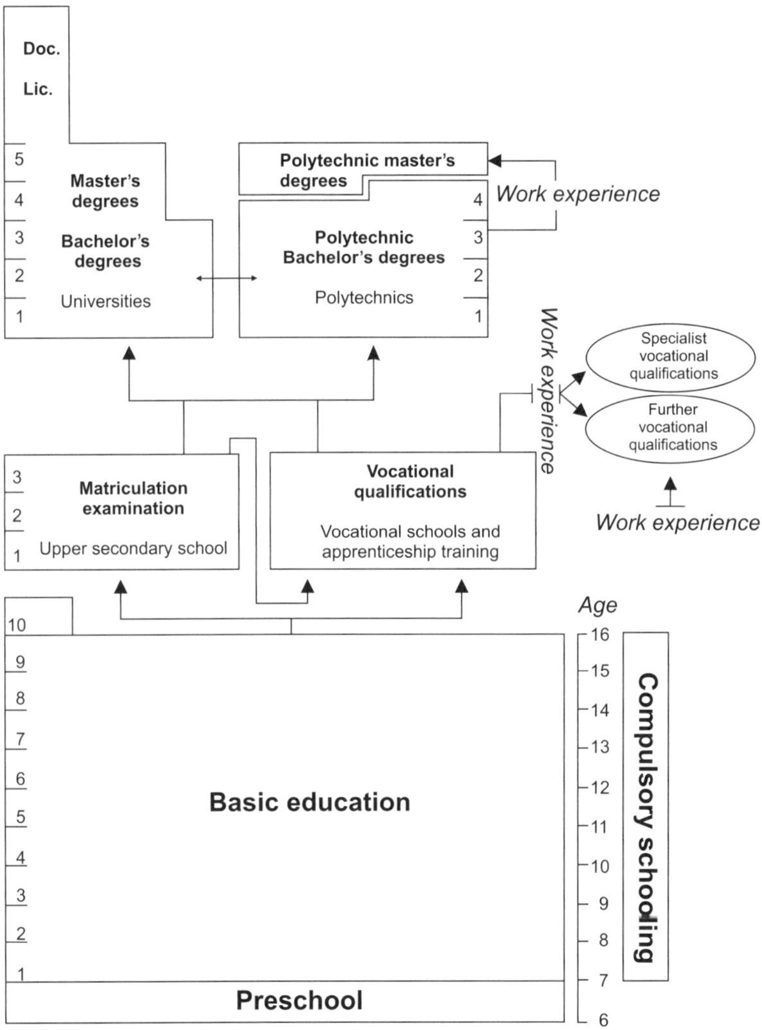

Figure 9.3 The structure of the schooling system: The Finnish example (Source: http://www.edu.fi/english/SubPage.asp?path=500, 4699)

Equal opportunity is thus an important aim of the school system, but also the way in which the ambitious objective of a final certificate for all students is to be reached. About half of the students with the final certificate are supposed to become high skilled workers in our model. Of course, there are exceptions to these rules to be allowed for, such as for example given by open universities for the skilled segment of the labour market (based on the possibility of only part time occupation or simply by a voluntary utilisation of leisure time of the accordingly motivated members of the skilled workforce).

Students who finish school with the final certificate and enter the workforce as well as those who do so after having obtained a University degree are already well trained in organising their learning processes so that lifelong learning will be no problem for them, the aim of which is not restricted to skills and competencies with regard to later employment, but is regarded as important for a personal, civic or social perspective as well. The idea of lifelong learning adds to the concept of equal opportunity, since the personal access to knowledge and competencies is increased by the possibilities of learning independently of age or position.

Political learning plays an important role in education, especially in a model where the state has a major role as employer and provider of social services. Political learning, which is often referred to as citizenship (civic) education, is of high relevance in a system that depends on individual skills and knowledge of its workforce, and that at the same time calls for a high degree of social commitment and acceptance of different work places (though not of unemployment). Furthermore, the principles of equal opportunity, on which we have commented above, have to be integrated in more general political concepts such as human rights, which again underlines the necessity of political learning. Political learning will be part of school education as well as of lifelong learning.

Besides the acceptance of the considered social structure of capital accumulation, this second pillar thus has to provide the foundations for an understanding of the socio-economic structure within which the citizens of the country are constructing their life course pattern.

Pillar III (Coordinating SC): Elected Executive Persons (Elites): Microeconomic and Political Conduct, Democratic Competition and Elite Formation

Following Higley (2006) we define, for our brief discussion of the role of elites under social capitalism, members of elites:

as persons, who by virtue of their strategic location in large or otherwise pivotal organisations and movements, are able to affect political outcomes regularly and substantially.

This is a functional definition of elite members (not a factual one and not one that analyses the current and past power elites, their habitus and their formation rules). It must be made more concrete by considering the formation of elites, their areas of operation, their conduct and remuneration as well as their failures and democratic control for our envisaged new social structure of capital accumulation, in clear distinction from the status quo of actual developed capitalist economies. Note also that elites in this sense must be distinguished from prominence (such as artists, philosophers and entertainers).

A main question when dealing with the role of elites is the question of their tasks. Determining decision rules, decision making as well as decision evaluation can be regarded as the main tasks of elites in economics as well as in politics. Here it is visible that elites are directly involved in economic (and political) decisions which underlines their importance, but also their responsibility. Elites in a given society should be well-educated, well-trained and also well aware of their obligations as citizens as well as of their role as top decision makers, moral institutions and leading representatives of the political and cultural system they belong to.

Such an importance of elites might give cause for questioning the necessity of elites in social capitalism. This leads to the discussion on property rights as Figure 9.4 explains: While small firms may be private property, midsize and large firms need a board of elected managing leaders who conduct investment and employment decisions, since the responsibility for firms of this size in globalised societies needs to be transferred to responsible engaged persons with very high knowledge and efficiency – elites who are capable to act in a decisive manner. To a certain degree, running the economy is similar to politics where elected persons – elites – are responsible for the best way of leading the country. The necessity of the election of elites not only in political activities but as well in economic ones is a demand of democracy so that elites may be better called EEPs (not CEOs), that is, Elected Executive Persons.

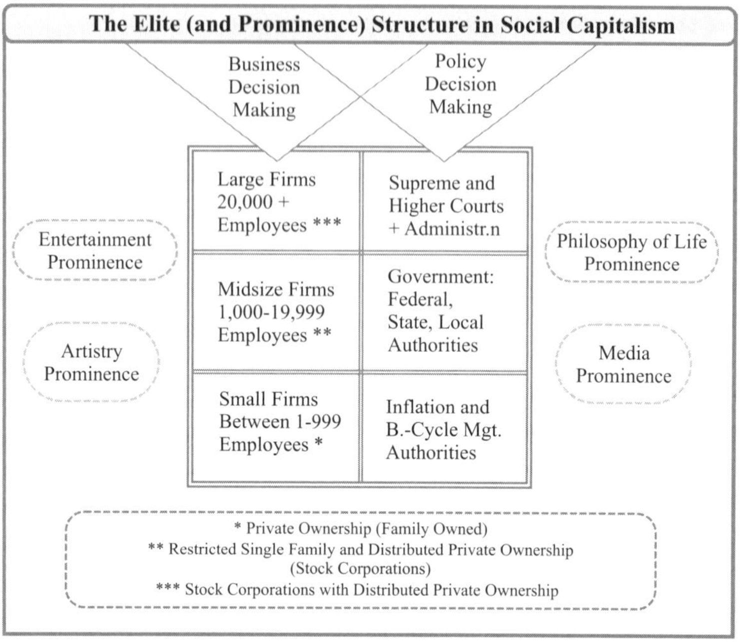

Figure 9.4 Property rights, stock distribution, decision making elites (vs. prominence) and the conduct of small, medium-sized and large companies

Elites are not only elected but they are also controlled and supervised in their conduct of the board of managers. In politics, this procedure is easier to follow due to the division of power in democracies, where not the parliament but also a Supreme Court helps control political elites (due to executive, legislative and judiciary power divisions). It is important that the supervisory boards in firms are fully aware of their responsibility for the conduct of the enterprises and also the result of democratic choice processes within the firms as well as from outside.

Elites have to fulfill very important tasks and to accept high managerial responsibility. Therefore they have to be appropriately paid, significantly above the income of high-skilled workers, but – from the viewpoint of proper incentives – there is no need for paying millions of Euros to the top management of firms. Here, it is helpful to discuss possible incentives which are relevant for elites. The preferences of elites are not necessarily exogenously determined but quite often endogenous so that incentives to get a higher level of exclusiveness may be of great interest as Schumpeter (1942) has already noted. We believe that Schumpeter's following statement on the integration of the ex-bourgeoisie into his Western type of competitive socialism, intended by him also as a design of a new structure of capital accumulation, can be meaningfully extended to our concept of social capitalism in place of his model of competitive socialism.

> *This prestige or distinction value of private wealth has of course always been recognised by economists. ... And it is clear that among the incentives to supernormal performance this is one of the most important. ... Moreover the prestige motive, more than any other, can be molded by simple reconditioning: Successful performers may conceivably be satisfied nearly as well with the privilege – if granted with judicious economy – of being allowed to stick a penny stamp on their trousers as they are by receiving a million a year.* (Schumpeter 1942, p.208)

We consider Schumpeter's formulation of the role and the behaviour of elites under his type of a competitive socialist society as 'socialist elites' as being in stark contrast to the discussion of 'power elites' (Pareto, 1935 and Mills, 1959) or 'habitus elites' (Bourdieu, 1979 and Hartmann, 2007). Our understanding of the formation, role and behaviour of elites under social capitalism builds on Schumpeter's conceptualisation of 'elites' which provides the reason why we would denote them as 'socialist elites' as well. Hartmann (2007) provides a detailed discussion of 'the sociology of elites' with a strong focus on the formation and reproduction of actual elites, the antecessors of our concept of 'socialist elites'.

Referring to the above quotation from Schumpeter's *Capitalism, Socialism and Democracy* we expect that economic elites when remunerated in a similar way to political elites will not become underperformers, but contribute to economic and social decision making in similar ways as before, if not even better (from the viewpoint of responsibility). We note however that remuneration in the business sector of not only elites, but also sub-elites, may be partly profit (and loss) based, since this sector represents the capitalist part under social capitalism.

We expect that elites will be giving their best to fulfill the highly important task for which they have been elected. The recent years have shown, however, that – in the present western capitalist societies – the performances of elites have not at all been adequate or even acceptable. On the contrary, the recent financial crisis has shown massive failures in elite behaviour, regarding risk-taking decisions in particular (at least at the end point of so-called securitization chains). How should we react to failures of elites in social capitalism? Of course, there exist many different forms of failures which can be unconsciously, but also in some cases consciously, made such as misuse of elite positions or different forms of corruption, unallowed enrichment sometimes even by gambling or accepting too high a risk, for example, in banking. Then, of course, all kinds of mismanagement are possible, be it, for example, inadequate human resource management or inadequate environmental resource management. Partly, such failures may be traced back to malfunctions or incompetence, but in many cases there is a lack of responsibility that leads to such failures as the recent financial crisis has shown. We think a system of sanctions must apply in the case of failures or misconduct which may include a reduction of the income (down to the level of high-skilled wages), but also personal responsibilities may be designed. Furthermore, there need to be rules for status removal.

While rules on how to act in cases of failure are necessary it is also useful to reflect on ways of how to avoid failures. Here we have to underline the importance of the control institutions and the way in which elections of elites take place but furthermore, the role of education and the development of career paths turn out to be fundamental. Elites should be high-skilled persons (with an appropriate university degree), of course with the exception of political elite formation which should be open to all adult citizens of the country. Since we expect that elites must be well-educated and well-trained as well as aware of their citizen obligation, education is of high importance with regard to the later occupations with their different demands, but also with regard to their ethical obligation in a democratic society where they have to understand themselves not only as elites but also as citizens.

In democratic states, it cannot be predicted whether a child will join the group of elites after education and training since children of elite families do not automatically become elites themselves, but children of all backgrounds may become elites later on. Therefore it has to be taken into consideration here that in (pre)school it cannot be found out whether a child will become a member of elites as an adult even if the social and intellectual background of his/her family may give reason for such an assumption. Therefore, it is absolutely necessary to support each child in his/her progress so that he/she can develop all his/her skills, competencies and talents. This demands an education with the strict aim of not only 'no child left behind' but furthermore to develop hidden talents, skills and competencies, which starts early and is capable of supporting each child in his/her individual progress. The necessity of an early support of the development of children is one of the reasons why not only teachers, but all educators need a university degree. In tertiary education, quite generally, students will get a chance to deepen their skills and competencies so that they may become trained for later top executive or managerial tasks – as elites. Most of them will finish their university education with a PhD.

The career paths of elites may begin in school and may be formally accomplished in tertiary education, with the exception of political elites, however, who instead often have to pass through career paths in their respective parties. This shows that career paths of elites are very much depending on the elite category, even more when further elites like public administration or supreme courts are included. As Hartmann (2007) has shown there exist quite different career paths not only with regard to the elite category but also with regard to different countries. There is a further aspect to be discussed: While we expect schools to bring forward all children even to the possibility of becoming a member of the elite group as an adult, there is still a tradition that the social background may affect the chances of a student becoming a member of the elite, especially if the family already belongs to the elite since he/she then grows up in gaining an elite habitus. Here, education – in (pre)school as well as in university – has to underline reflections about the social power students may gain later and about civil responsibility and commitment which has to be related with it. There is a hope that the fact that in social capitalism, all workers will at least be skilled, and many will be high skilled, may lead to a higher social awareness of community issues on one hand and a more similar social habitus across families on the other hand.

There exist well-established elite schools and elite universities in many Western countries which provide in general a very good education but also give students access to a network which will be helpful for their later career, in particular as leading elites. Especially those who come from a 'elite family' may develop an elite habitus which again demands tertiary education as well as schools to teach reflected citizenship awareness, ethical norms in the conduct of social power as well as in reflections about a proper elite habitus. The individual support of all children in preschool and school is mainly due to the underlying concept of equal opportunity, which also includes the support of gifted and highly gifted children. It belongs to the tasks of schools to keep in mind that some children will develop their skills, behaviour and responsible commitment such that they will belong to elite or sub-elite groups in their later adult life. Therefore all children have to understand the democratic basis of their status and their responsibility as a citizen, independently of their later profession.

Education of elites is a crucial element in any society, not only from the point of view of preparing such talented persons for their later occupations, but also with respect to their ethical conduct in a pluralistic democratic society and their role as citizens of such a society. This includes not only the reflection of the factual origins of elite formation, their habitus and their full participation in a multi-faceted democratic society, but also the reflection of elite failures, in particular in their professional conduct, in the misuse of their power and the violation of human rights.

People's Capitalism and the Redesign of Property Rights

Against this background or the processes of elite formation and elite conduct, social capitalism also calls for new, or better: further developed property and control rights, on the level of small firms (primarily private ownership), medium-sized firms (mixed ownership) and large firms (equity owned, with upper limits to individual ownership) as Figure 9.4 illustrates, where on the last level professional business decision makers will be leading these larger firms as (top-) managers. Furthermore, a democratic election of supervisory boards in the latter two cases (composed of representatives of the still existing owners, the representatives of workers and of the government) will be demanded, and on this basis the implementation of a board of managers (with an elected executive person at the top).

The basic principle here is that firms become more and more equity owned when they increase in size (with credit-financing of course in addition) and that share holdings by single households or institutions is limited (to say 10 percent), while the original founder of the firm may hold up to 25 percent on the medium-sized level of the firms that make up the economy. Moreover, while the board of managers is selected and approved by the owners of the firms solely, the supervisory board (which has the right to veto in matters of employment, workplace safety, production ethics and the like) basically controls that the board of managers is behaving professionally with respect to competitive pressure and responsibly with respect to issues of social importance. We do not consider this a break with the existing conduct of capitalist firms, but simply a – admittedly far-reaching – further regulation of its existing array of property rights arrangements, away from the behaviour of firms that risk the life of their employees in an unjustifiable way, in order to cut costs and make profits on the basis of a 'press on regardless' strategy, like BP in the deepwater horizon accident.

The basic problems that rearranged property rights have to solve under a regime of social capitalism is on the one hand to allow for the conduct of firms which incorporates and makes flexible and appropriate use of the accumulated knowledge of Western type business administration on all levels and scales of operation. This includes what we have discussed under the heading of flexibility for flexicurity economies, with security as an important side condition for such flexibility. On the other hand, the management and control of small, medium-sized and large companies, though subject to satisfying profit-seeking routines, must be organised in a way where property remains widespread, subject to legal ownership restrictions which prevent that single families or persons, like Joseph P. Kennedy or Rupert Murdoch, gain too much power over the employees of certain sectors in the economy. Of course, the further development of business ethics, on the theoretical as well as the practical level, is also essential. But all this is already part of the social capital of modern capitalism, though of course always discredited by firms and single individuals that do not shy away from the gray or even dark sides in the conduct of the profit-seeking motive.

In the political sphere we propose – following Schumpeter (1942) – majority voting, in the interest of the formation of governments that are capable of acting in a decisive way, in contrast to the clumsy and cumbersome coalition formation processes that can happen under proportional voting in the case when a larger number of parties is elected into parliament. Yet, majority voting must be tailored such that it cannot drift too far away from the percentages that underlie its outcomes and it must be organised as a form of Schumpeterian political competition where individuals, not only parties, compete with each other. This means that majority voting systems need reform as for example it was attempted in the UK in 2011: The United Kingdom alternative vote referendum was a nationwide vote held on Thursday 5 May 2011 to choose the method of electing MPs at subsequent general elections. The referendum concerned whether to replace the present 'first-past-the-post' (simple plurality) system with the 'alternative vote' method. The proposal to introduce an Alternative Vote was however rejected by the voters. We believe nevertheless that a redesigned majority voting system is to be preferred over a proportional voting system, since it tends to make politicians professionals in their constituency and not just party followers and since it avoids the formation of coalitions with minimal commonalities.

The basic aim of a democracy is not to represent the will of the citizens (which is not possible both from the theoretical as well as from the practical point of view), but to change governments – within the frame of a democratic constitution and division of powers – in a civilised way towards a government that is capable of acting (by its sufficient majority in the parliament). Of course, elected governments have the ethical obligation – to be supported by the educational system – to improve the social cohesion in its country in the many aspects that this may call for. Majority voting is largely Anglo-Saxon in origin (including the former British colonies). And looking at the current status of the political system in the US, it does not look too convincing compared to what we have stated above, This however is there due to the fact that the power of the president of the USA can be very limited, since he is not the prime minister of the party which holds the majority of the seats in parliament. The USA constituency is therefore not a good example of the superiority of an advanced majority system over one with proportional representation. In this respect the British system represents a much more coherent one, though the closeness to laissez-faire ideologies and related low-scaled workfare reforms may have segmented the British society much more than is acceptable. It may therefore well be that countries like Australia – see the quotation of Kevin Rudd at the beginning of this section – are among the closest towards a way to social capitalism in the world of majority voting systems.

Parallel to his figure of a dynamic entrepreneur, Schumpeter (1942) also formulated political competition in the democratic type of competitive socialism he envisaged and the architecture of which he was designing in his book. In our view there could be a further change in majority voting which might help to overcome the often very traditional way in which candidates of a party are chosen – in addition to what exists in current majority voting systems. Assume that there are always two candidates for the same party in the same constituency, one of whom should be a newcomer or an outsider. This might provide opportunities to avoid the situation that parties control their seats in parliament solely from the top, as actually also happens under majority voting (and even more under proportional voting). In the age of the internet, it is no longer a problem to design rules such that the voters of an electoral district can choose from possible new candidates one who then competes with established candidates to be the party's elected one for this voting district.

Christian-Democratic and Social-Democratic Ethics and Beyond

Summing up we stress that the considered flexicurity systems (though much less biased than welfare states) still concentrate too much on the economic aspects of societal evolution and ignore more or less its social aspects, which are however needed in order to provide sustainability for the evolution of Western capitalist democracies, the point of departure of this chapter. Besides the acceptance of social capitalism being based on a sound gestation of pillar I and the understanding of it created in pillar II, the considered society must also solve the coordination and incentive problems inherent in its reliance on a strictly competitive form of capitalism, in particular through its economic and political elites. However, this may not be a perspective for the future evolution of capitalism that can be considered as being in line with the following characterisation of capitalism by Marx:

> *A rise in the price of labour, as a consequence of accumulation of capital, only means, in fact, that the length and weight of the golden chain the wage-worker has already forged for himself, allow of a relaxation of the tension of it.* (Marx 1867 (1954), p.579-80)

In a rare contribution on Social Capitalism in its relationship to Christian Democratic political parties one finds instead in Kersbergen (1995, p.177) the view:

> *The conclusion is that there is – despite variations – a core of social policies that is distinctively Christian democratic. This core will be defined as social capitalism. [...] This model of social capitalism significantly and systematically differs from both the liberal and the social democratic conceptions of social citizenship, although real differences between social democratic and Christian democratic welfare state regimes are concealed behind a veil of comparable levels of social spending.*

From today's perspective we would however conclude here that both the Christian as well as the Social democratic political parties can accept that we are living in a world where the productive forces are of a very dynamic, lifestyle changing profit seeking and thus creative destruction type à la Schumpeter, though – as discussed – subject to political regulation concerning the choice of products and production techniques. Such productive forces are without comparable (socialist) alternative at present, but have to be embedded into a social regime that allows its citizens the development of a sufficiently reliable life course perspective, based on high-level education and well educated elites in particular. This may not yet be so in the Anglo-Saxon world,[9] but in our view is within reach at least in the welfare states we classified as 'good'.

9.7 Greece: A Mediterranean Roadmap towards Social Capitalism?

Points of Departure

> *You cannot fix a problem with the kind of thinking that created it. (Albert Einstein)* (Ioannidis, 2011, p.127)

In this section we return to the statement of Alexandros Stavrakas: 'We must soberly examine all possible alternatives, radical or not' this chapter started from. We do not however discuss here the status quo of the Greek economy in detail, before and after the imposition of the IMF's recovery plan for the Greek economy. We also do not go into a detailed discussion of the adequacy of the IMF measures any more (see the preceding chapter) intended to bring the Greek economy back on track. Instead, we use our concept of 'social capitalism' to formulate a strategy for the evolution of the Greek society in the longer run where the three pillars (for accepting, understanding and coordinating a socially oriented advanced type of capitalist democracy) are the compass for the intended radical socio-economic evolution.

In view of what we surveyed in the general introduction of the book we believe that we have reached a state of the evolution of capitalism now where significant segments of it are periled by failure, in particular regarding the economic and political status of the USA, while a Schumpeterian type of authoritarian competitive socialism is on the rise. Europe is in between these two developments and is open enough in its political sphere for reflected socio-economic change as for example expressed in the Lisbon Agenda where the aim is formulated to make the EU 'the most competitive and dynamic knowledge-based economy in the world capable of sustainable economic growth with more and better jobs and greater social cohesion' (European Union Parliament Website, Lisbon European Council 23 and 24 March Presidency Conclusion). The Agenda may not have been successful between 2000 and 2010, but it surely is compatible with the suggestion that making Greece a showcase for such evolution – in particular from the viewpoint of its current status quo – cannot be underestimated from the political point of view. Such a policy would be guided by a vision and not primarily be interpreted as sanction, in particular by the Greek population, as it is the danger of the case of IMF type recovery plans.

Applying aspects of a long-run strategy towards the evolution of social capitalism to the Greek situation does not however imply that Greece should adopt a strategy that may work for some Nordic countries without reflection of its 'Southern' environment. Instead we only intend to show in the following what can be formulated on an abstract level as a tentative roadmap to social capitalism, a roadmap that definitely needs further discussion and modification from the perspective of Greek history, and Greek economic, social and political institutions, that is, its actual status quo in short. The important issue however is that there must be a general perspective for those willing to support a deep-rooted reform of the Greek society without which the proposed steps – higher taxes and a larger public sector with more public duties – may appear questionable. The central aspect here is that such an all-embracing policy must be strongly expansionary on all levels of the economy, an aspect that is totally missing in the IMF austerity measures for Greece, but is not so hard to shoulder in this case.

The danger however is that Kalecki's (1943) political business cycle analysis may apply again, where a coalition of 'industrial leaders' and clientelistic politicians may be formed in order to undermine the chosen policy frame, arguing that the Greek structure of free markets and a free society is in danger and on the way towards socialism with all its historical failures, if the direction and the important objectives of this new agenda for Greece are not well presented and understood. There is moreover the need that existing democracies, in this case Greece, move away from short-term patchwork decisions towards coherent longer-term projects. This may in fact also demand a redesign of democratic decision making, where Schumpeter's (1942) analysis of the advantages of reformed majority voting systems may provide a good point of departure, towards the figure of a dynamic political entrepreneur. In contrast to that, a debate on a broad media basis has taken place during the recent months about quite different strategies out of the Greek state crisis. Given the severity of the situation, unusual and indeed quite radical measures have been seriously discussed both at the academic and at the more policy-oriented level. Probably the most radical policy suggestion has been the voluntarily (or involuntary) exit of Greece from the Euro Area. Indeed, among others, Arghyrou and Tsoukalas (2010) have recently investigated such a possibility as an option of last resort by proposing the introduction of a weak Euro for Greece in a two currency EMU setup and a devaluation of the weak Euro sufficiently strongly to give rise to a competitive boost in Greece.

Though conceived in a constructive way, such proposals seem however to underestimate the catastrophic consequences that such a measure would have on the Greek economy (leaving all implications for the Euro itself aside), due to the resulting currency-mismatch between the denomination of liabilities (in euros or another non-domestic currency) and the foreign-currency value of profits and assets in the newly introduced 'weak Euro'. The quite likely short-run reaction of the international financial markets to such a measure has been vividly described by Paul Krugman as follows:

> *What can be done? ... Greece could alleviate some of its problems by leaving the euro, and devaluing. But it's hard to see how Greece could do that without triggering a catastrophic run on its banking system. Indeed, worried depositors have already begun pulling cash out of Greek banks. There are no good answers here — actually, no nonterrible answers.* (Paul Krugman, April 8 2010, New York Times)[10]

As we have discussed in Section 8.4, Krugman changed his opinion a month later so that, in May 2010, he suggested that there is no way to bring Greece back to the drachma currency, though his arguments in April 2010, based on Krugman (2000) are quite convincing from our point of view, see the appendix of Chapter 8. Indeed, as much research on previous episodes of financial turmoil such as the Mexican and East Asian financial crises of the 1990s have shown, see for example Krugman (2000), Aghion et al. (2001) and Goldstein and Turner (2004), when an economy has a significant share of liabilities denominated in foreign currency, a devaluation of its domestic currency often leads to a severe slowdown in aggregate investment due to a strongly adverse balance sheet effect and the subsequent credit line shortages by both the domestic and international financial sectors in the short run. As Joseph Stiglitz points out:

> *One proposed solution is for these countries to engineer the equivalent of a devaluation – a uniform decrease in wages. This, I believe, is unachievable, and its distributive consequences are unacceptable. The social tensions would be enormous. It is a fantasy. There is a second solution: the exit of Germany from the Eurozone or the division of the Eurozone into two sub-regions. The euro was an interesting experiment, but, like the almost forgotten exchange rate mechanism that preceded it and fell apart when speculators attacked*

> *sterling in 1992, it lacks the institutional support required to make it work.* (Joseph Stiglitz, May 5 2010, www.guardian.co.uk)

In sum, the introduction of a 'weak euro', or a return to the Drachma will almost certainly lead to a disruption of the domestic financial system, affect aggregate investment behaviour as well the budget of the government to such an extent that the improvement in competitiveness through a devaluation of the Greek currency will quite likely lead to large GDP losses and to large defaults of firms and government debt. We therefore very strongly opt for the alternative solution proposed above by Joseph Stiglitz, the details of which may not be the ones he was thinking of when making this proposal.

> *There is an alternative solution, which Europe may come to realise is the most promising for all: implement the institutional reforms, including the necessary fiscal framework, that should have been made when the euro was launched. It is not too late for Europe to implement these reforms and thus live up to the ideals, based on solidarity, that underlay the euro's creation.* (Joseph Stiglitz, May 5 2010, www.guardian.co.uk)

So far, according to views expressed by the IMF, Greece's reform program seems to be broadly on track. The Greek government has started reducing spending significantly and has implemented austerity measures aimed at reducing the deficit by more than 10 billion Euros. It has hiked taxes on fuel, tobacco and alcohol, raised the retirement age by two years, imposed public sector pay cuts and applied tough new tax evasion regulations. But is this sufficient in view of the longer run evolution of the Greek economy and its social structure of capital accumulation?

In the following we will enumerate various policy measures which taken together go significantly beyond and away from the IMF agenda. They indicate the direction towards which a 'progress path' to a social type of capitalism can be established, where in particular Schumpeterian creative destruction in a competitive environment is coupled in a sustainable way with secure life course perspectives of the household sector as described in Section 9.6. We believe that only multi-level expansionary policy measures, in a socio-economic sense, and in addition to the austerity measures which have now passed Greek parliament, will gradually give rise to the needed acceptance of these measures in the Greek society.

At present Greece is however still part of the Southern types of 'ugly' welfare states according to our extended classification of Esping-

Andersen type briefly discussed in Sections 9.3 and 9.4. It may still be, despite the recent acceptance of the second stage of the unpopular austerity measures required by the EU, the ECB and the IMF before the release of the next segment of financial aid, that the Panhellenic Socialist Movement and its majority of 155 to 145 seats in the parliament is too heterogeneous to really conduct part of the proposed radical reforms of the social structure of capital accumulation in Greece from the unifying perspective of a social capitalism project, also because the New Democracy Party is not at all cooperatively behaving, despite being at least partly responsible for the mess in which Greece finds itself with its systematic tax evasion, corruption and irresponsible government budget policies.

The Creation of New Institutions in the Public Sector and in Banking

We assume in the following discussion of the current Greek situation, where the new package of austerity measures has just passed parliament (June 29, 2011), that the past and the new measures of the IMF, the EU and the ECB will work with some success from the economic point of view, not necessarily however from the social point of view. We also assume that the restructuring of Greek debt and also cautious partial repudiation will take place in the future, in addition to what has already been done by the ECB, and will work with some success. Against this background we are now adding further institutional changes and expansionary policy measures that should not only be supporting the Greek economy and bring it back on track, but that can also be understood by those who primarily suffer from the adopted austerity as strategies that will improve again their lot and lead the Greek society out of its deep socio-economic crisis.

We start the discussion of additional socio-economic policy measures from the assertion that the largely unregulated (international) banking and the rampant fiscal mismanagement and riotously debt-based behaviour of the past Greek governments are at the root of the problems that Greece has now to face. The remedies for the future avoidance of these types of behaviour are on the one hand the erection of credit institutions that are based on the principles of narrow banking we discussed in Chapter 5 of the book. This need not exclude further banking activities from the banking sector, like investment banking, but these financial activities should be kept separate from the ones that link the deposit holdings of households with credit-financing of firms (or of the household sector). Since these narrowly defined banks cannot sell the risk they are taking when they connect savings with investment decisions, they will not create Minsky-type effects (in good times) by not screening thoroughly enough the creditors before credit is given, and then by just exporting their uncontrolled risk-taking activities to other institutions in the financial sector. The US subprime crisis would not have happened under such a system of narrow banking (Ch. 5). We however do not want to underestimate here the effects that also such a primarily credit-oriented banking sector, just as all other financial activities, is continually subject to financial innovations which may also reintroduce bad commercial banking habits into a Narrow Banking System (NBS). When a NBS has been established it must necessarily be supervised and maybe regulated further if Minskyian sloppiness effects are penetrating again the NBS.

Concerning rampant fiscal policy behaviour, the case of Germany is a telling one. In 2009, under the Christian/Social-democratic government, the German parliament decided to put something called the debt brake into the German constitution. This means that both the federal government and the states will no longer be allowed to run deficits from 2016 (federal government) and 2020 (states) onwards, subject to certain exceptions however. Such details are here of no importance, but what is important simply is the fact that policy makers do not trust in the ability of the parliament to properly manage government debt. Moreover, in the past, the German supreme court was often acting as an independent fiscal authority, judging and preventing some fiscal actions that had passed parliament. Our view here is that debt-financed fiscal policy is by and large only admissible in the area of a counter-cyclical steering of the macroeconomy, that is, in the area of Keynesian macro-policy and that this policy should be the subject of an independent fiscal authority, besides the monetary authority, while the government should care about the socio-economic infrastructure of the country and should do this largely in a tax-based way. The current agreements between Merkel and Sarkozy about a Euro-wide tax brake, by contrast, is the wrong solution to the problem of bad conduct in debt-financed government activities as it may prevent needed fiscal policy stimuli when urgently needed, instead of establishing a professional Keynesian fiscal policy that saves in the boom and spends in the bust.

The creation of an independent fiscal agency, concerning the control of business fluctuations, is already a topic in the literature. Hemming and Kell (2001) provide a review of the literature and discuss key issues concerning independent fiscal authorities. A more recent contribution to the discussion of independent fiscal agencies is Debrun, Hauner and Kumar (2009) where proposals for 'independent fiscal authorities' are also surveyed to a certain extent. Against this background our proposal would thus here be to institutionalise a Business Cycle Agency (BCA) on the national level of Eurozone member states which would run a debt and tax financed anti-cyclical Keynesian expenditure policy on the national level in order to reduce the size of national business fluctuations. Of course, there may be a similar institution on the ECB level and cooperation between these agencies as well as the National Bank of a country is to be recommended and to be investigated in its pros and cons.

The budget equation of the BCA and the fiscal policy pursued by it could in a first approach be formulated as follows:

$$pI_{bca} + i_\lambda \Lambda \equiv pt_{bca}Y + \dot{\Lambda}, \quad \dot{\Lambda} = -\beta_\lambda(u - \bar{u})\Lambda + n\Lambda.$$

We here assume that the expenditures I_{bca} by the BCA are investment oriented (creating infrastructure improvements, in addition to the ones planned by the government). This infrastructure investment is financed by some taxes (out of National Income Y) and by credit where credit grows on the one hand at the natural rate and is expanded respectively reduced in an anti-cyclical fashion by reacting negatively to the deviation of the rate of capacity utilisation of firms, from its normal rate $\bar{u}$. We assume that the creditworthiness of the BCA is out of question and assume here also for simplicity that it can get credit at a loan rate i_λ that is set equal to the natural rate of growth of the economy. This implies in the steady state, where $\dot{\Lambda} = n\Lambda$ must hold, that the rate of BCA investment in national income is given by the tax rate t_{bca}. The assumption on the interest rate guarantees that interest rate payments are just financed by the trend term in new loans. Further loans are made in view of the severity of the recession or bust, while loans are reduced below their trend growth n in the boom, depending on its strength. There may be assumed in addition a negative dependence of the parameter β_λ on the deviation of the debt to GDP ratio from a certain target level. However, even then, the expenditure policy rule here considered is only a baseline rule which can and should be modified if circumstances demand or which can be supplemented by discretionary actions if this is needed.

The essential thing is however that this agency acts independently of the government, in a way that is assumed to be the case for Central Banks. Since its tasks are fairly transparent, control of such an agency can be designed in well-known ways. Of course, the existence of this fiscal authority reduces the scope of actions of the ruling government. This is however just as necessary as the creation of an independent central bank, since the past has repeatedly shown that governments are neither behaving wisely in the control of the monetary side of the economy, nor are they reliable in the proper conduct of fiscal (debt-financed) stimuli to the real economy.

The role of government is then reduced towards supporting the quantitative or qualitative growth of the private sector of the economy through the expansion of the infrastructure of the country, ranging from schooling on the one hand to public administration on the other hand. This implies that these infrastructure investments (or just public consumption) are to be financed primarily by taxes (and are often concerning the big issues of the country about which party competition should be conducted) and can then be subject to a debt-brake in addition as we have discussed it above for the case of Germany. Such an institutional scenario could have helped to avoid the Greek fiscal crisis. We thus should not only take monetary policy out of the hands of the politicians, but also anti-cyclical fiscal policy, as the next step to a proper conduct of the economy on the macro level. Since inflation is generally following economic activity, and not leading it, the BCA would also contribute to the anti-inflationary policy of the Central Bank, which in addition has to care about the behaviour of the financial markets and in this regard to impact inflationary processes also through quantitative easing procedures aimed at reducing financial market volatilities and therefore larger fluctuations in investment behaviour.

Equality, Efficiency and Elementariness of Tax Collection

The basic point in the following enumeration is that taxes must be increased significantly and in various ways in order to properly finance the set of government expenditures needed for infrastructure evolution under social capitalism even in the initial phase and along its 'progress path'. In 2010/11, the Greek population has massively demonstrated against the heavily rising taxes, money wage reductions, growing unemployment etc. Yet, tax increases are absolutely necessary for a growth oriented investment policy of the government and need to be explained to the population in detail. However, in a country where the top 20% income receivers get 41% of GDP and the same percentage at the bottom is only 6.6% of GDP there is definitely room for tax increases. The same conclusion holds if one compares average gross wages in gas-electricity and water production (3117 Euro, tax rate 35%) as against 853 Euro (tax rate 17%) in hotel and restaurant services. Average working hours in these sectors are 38.7h and 47.8h, respectively.[11] The main aim is to make the people understand the meaning and intent of taxation in general, and of raising taxes now in particular, where however it is clear that the main burden must be put on the higher income groups, which therefore must understand this as a solidarity contribution for the evolution of the public infrastructure of the Greek society (from which they will definitely gain). Increasing the tax base can be done in Greece in particular in the following more detailed ways:

1. Public access to (basic aspects) of the tax declarations of households as in Sweden,[12] in order to fight tax evasion
2. Severe sanctions when tax evasion is discovered (penalties in proportion to the size of corresponding income streams)
3. A significant increase in income taxes in order to start the financing of a modern educational system and the framework requirements of sound life course perspectives for all citizens
4. Economic elites (in a system with profit-sharing) are confronted with income losses in the case of negative profits (operated as transfers to the government) down to the reservation wage level of high-skilled work, in proportion to the realised losses in the sector where they are acting as responsible executives.
5. A step by step reduction in payroll taxation in order to make firms internationally more competitive
6. Stepwise value added tax increases on domestic consumption up to a level of 25%
7. Tobin taxation of domestic capital gains as considered in Asada et al. (2010, 2011) as an income source and a means to calm down speculation.

Reducing tax evasion in Greece to a sufficient degree may already be a big step forward in increasing the tax base of the government. Moreover, we have seen that trillions of dollars or Euros are in fact available for the banking sector in the case of a systemic banking crisis. The question then is why not at least a small portion of this amount of money can be invested in the future of a country in a publically controlled and accepted way, such that the road to social capitalism can be opened as a showcase. The Nordic countries show from a different perspective that this possibility is not out of reach.

Tax Financed Socio-economic Infrastructure Investment

We have discussed the banking system, and the need for independent monetary and fiscal authorities as far as macro-policies are concerned, and have opted for a radical institutional change where the role of the government is restricted to basically tax-financed growth policies concerning the socio-economic infrastructure of the economy. We have already discussed the ways by which the tax base can be significantly increased for the Greek government and will now further justify the need for such increases by the expansionary effects this has on the Greek economy (since flagging private consumption and investment is thereby replaced by strong and focused government investment, and then subject to stimulating dynamic multiplier effects, instead of the contractionary effects caused by the measures of the IMF policy). Such an expansionary program is absolutely necessary for the Greek society to recover properly from its political and economic crisis and the creation of enough social capital to make the economy not only internationally competitive, but also robust in its socio-economic foundations.

It is of course necessary for such a package to be acceptable to the voting population and that its benefits, the intended changes in the structure of government expenditures/transfers towards a stable system of life course perspectives for the household sector, are clearly visible and understood, by the voters, in their contribution to the core evolution of social structure in Greece. This in particular holds for the adoption of an EFR transfer system, see Chapter 3, if a flexicurity type labour market reform is introduced, which on the one hand replaces the proliferation of unemployment costs characteristic for today's unemployment benefit payments of various kinds and degrees and which, on the other hand, must be coupled with social employment schedules, including lifelong learning, activating labour market policies and civic work in the wider sense of the word, among others. Of course, there is continual learning by doing involved along the 'progress path' towards the erection of such an expenditure and transfer system and significant new perspectives and resulting changes may become necessary along this path. In any event, such a system is and must be characterised by giving as well as by taking to its participants.

The enumeration below summarises components and implications of such an EFR program for the restructuring of government expenditures in the goods markets, for labour market reforms and the income transfers they imply, and more:

1. A comprehensive all day pre-school, school, high-school system with enough resources to allow for highly educated teaching in an adequate schooling infrastructure as in Finland for example, building on and improving significantly the three level schooling system that already exists in Greece.
2. An advanced public health sector with qualified medical care on all levels within a sound infrastructure (augmented by private health insurances)
3. A care of the elderly system with educated personnel operating in an adequate social environment
4. The government as an Employer of First Resort, based on transfer payments originating in the financial–industrial sector of the economy
5. A baseline pension fund system for pensioners partly financed on a 'pay as you go' basis by contributions from the households working in the private sector of the economy (augmented by company-pension payments based on the savings of households in this sector) plus balancing government contributions to the baseline pension payments.

We are fully aware that this is a very demanding selection for government expenditures, which can only be realised step by step. However, taking properly into account the many hidden (social) costs caused by the operation of current structures of the above range makes more plausible the argument that such a system can be financed, in particular when the size of the Greek economy is taken into account from the perspective of the EU and its possibilities. Moreover sound and safe life course perspectives of households tend to increase labour productivity as compared to situations where there is unskilled low-income work in a low productivity environment. The above education system would eliminate such unskilled work in the course of time, though of course it would not eliminate the need for simple work to be organised by a skilled/high-skilled workforce in a cooperative way.

As discussed in Flaschel, Greiner and Luchtenberg (2009), see here Chapter 3, the base income of workers in the public sector (and pension payments) can reach an adequate level if labour productivity (based on modern technologies) in the private sector has reached a sufficiently high level, while the significantly higher wages paid in the private sector on the basis of its productivity fluctuate with economic activity in this sector (as does employment and also overtime/undertime work). On the basis of this, the government as an EFR must organise the work in this third labour market and it is also conceivable then that all pensioners (and their skills) remain available within the social work structure of the economy as long as they wish to contribute to social activities on the basis of their work experiences acquired during their remunerated working-life. There is thus an array of work profiles available in such an economy that can significantly contribute to the input and output of socially oriented activities in all sectors of the economy.

We stress with respect to the above enumeration that part of it may be shaped (though not in its basic ingredients, which are an issue of national perspective) on the basis of municipal taxes and their expenditure in the form of laboratories as they are publically discussed in these areas and whose success is critically evaluated. 'Learning by doing' is an important element on such a path to better education, health care and care for the elderly. It is very important to rely on such communal activities when the infrastructure of a country is to be rebuilt in a fundamental way. It is of course also obvious that all governmental activities must allow for exceptions when specific cases are given or minorities of socially disadvantaged households are impacted. Moreover, communities with a weak tax generation may be subsidised in a balancing way by the central government. We also stress that workforce is definitely available from the EFR sector as well as from (properly addressed and motivated) pensioners to support the social activities in the public sector.

Schumpeterian Creative Destruction, Flexicurity-type Labour Market Reforms and Productivity Increase in Place of Wage Dumping

Process and product innovations (when based on social values like workplace safety and ethical product norms) should be easily possible in the business sector of the flexicurity type, including very flexible employment policies of firms. We have shown in Flaschel, Greiner and Luchtenberg (2009) that the latter does not create stability problems around the balanced growth path of a model economy, but is indeed improving stability if firms adjust their workforce with a higher speed, as long as this is reasonable from the viewpoint of a long-run profit-seeking motive. Of course, there is in addition a public sector of the conventional type plus an Employer of First Resort where the workers dismissed from the private sector get meaningful employment and sufficient income to maintain their life course perspectives. We do not believe that the conventional concept of the disutility of labour is applicable under social capitalism (with such a flexicurity component), since it primarily characterises the sector of alienated work, which is not really present within the social capital and cultural capital of a social capitalism society. To give a simple example, the private or commercial activity of 'cooking' is work and pleasure at one and the same time. We believe therefore that work can be organised in a way that most people will enjoy their work as a significant part of their life even if this work contains components which they would not include if they had the choice to disentangle them from their work effort.

As in a flexicurity economy, there must of course exist an activating labour market policy under social capitalism wherever necessary and a corporatist regime that by and large allows fluctuating wages to increase with labour productivity, which makes aggressive wage negotiations superfluous. Trade unions are necessary institutions also under flexicurity, but their role is primarily related to microeconomic issues within the firms, than to wage negotiations on a sectoral or even global level. There is of course – under the full employment regime of a flexicurity economy – the question whether overall price stability is guaranteed by it. Our view here is that this stability will be guaranteed if the Goodwinian distributive cycle, the role of a reserve army of unemployed within the conflict over income distribution, characterising current advanced capitalist economies, is well understood (from a Goodwinian perspective), so that wages by and large guarantee a fair participation in the annual growth of labour productivity, that is, GDP per work hour. Such an understanding, supplemented by minimum as well as maximum real wages, guarantees stability and also the viability of Social Capitalism, as investigated in Flaschel and Greiner (2009) in the case of flexicurity already.

We believe that properly designed education and safe life course perspectives of households will create a social understanding as well as social acceptance of the social work to be done when households become (temporarily) part of the EFR sector or when they are asked (as pensioners) to continue to contribute social work to the needs of the society. Educated (not habitus) elites moreover have to solve the coordination as well as the incentive problems in these areas as well as in business or politics. The social and ethical climate that is generated in this way will definitely enhance the performance of social capitalism. We note that such fruitful possibilities already exist under current capitalism in the form of social, intellectual and other networks.

Turning now to the competitiveness of the Greek economy, we note that the subdivision of the Greek GDP into agricultural products, manufacturing merchandise and services is approximately given by the percentages 4%, 26% and 70%. The share of exports in GDP was about 23% during 2006 and 2008 and fell to 19% in 2009. The share of tourism related exports in total exports has been about 24% over the recent past.[13] These numbers suggest that policies aimed at increasing the international competitiveness of the Greek economy need not only be directed at a reduction of internal components of such competitiveness (wage levels) which can be a very long and painful way to solve for Greek productivity problems. We have moreover argued in the appendix of Chapter 8 that an external reduction of Greek export prices, demanding that Greece leaves the Euro area, returns to the Drachma and accomplishes its devaluation in one way or another would create severe problems for the balance sheets of firms and the government which may also turn out to be much too costly for the Greek society.

In view of low productivity sectors in the Greek economy, we would argue that the way out (a longer run strategy) is to increase the attractiveness of the commodities making up the Greek exports. Besides agriculture, there are two fields about which discussion has begun in different organisations, politics and media in order to improve the Greek economy: Tourism and Renewable Energy Sources. As Chaini (2011) reports German firms are very much interested in Greek solar energy generation, though there is still a lack of an appropriate infrastructure. Alternative energy, especially solar energy, could on the one hand attract foreign investment to a significant degree, and also induce the erection of a corresponding infrastructure with many new jobs on the other hand.

Increasing the attractiveness of 'export commodities' is probably possible in tourism by investing in modernisation or by subsidising it appropriately for some time, since the Greek supply of tourism goods has characteristics which make it somewhat unique in the international supply of such goods. Especially the high number of partly very small islands seems to be attractive for tourists so that it is necessary on the one hand to invest to improve hotels, traffic connections and bathing possibilities, and on the other hand to develop the present form of tourism on Greek islands in its individual offers which are far from mass tourism and should not open up to it. Besides the islands, there are also further possibilities to intensify tourism in the Greek countryside. In 2011, Greece undergoes a tourism boom in spite of the strikes and political disturbances. There is of course a danger that this hinders the Greek economy to improve tourism in the mentioned way, which would be problematic, since the tourism boom is probably partly due to the situation in North Arabic countries like Egypt or Tunisia. Of course, it is a chance for Greece to win new tourists (see Bawden, 2011).

Infrastructure investment in the tourism sector also concerns vessels, harbours, airports and more. The case in this sector of the Greek economy is that it is not so much a matter of productivity disadvantages, but poor performance, which can relatively easily be changed through appropriate and sufficiently large investment expenditures. Decreases of value added taxes may also be of help in this part of the economy and are much easier to be achieved than decreases in the money wages of the workers who work in this sector (which are already incredibly low as we have noted above).

But also in agriculture qualitative improvements in products or their marketing may be a way out of the competitiveness trap. Greek local wines, neglecting the trivial brands Greece was well known for, have a very high quality, but are fairly overlooked on the world markets for wine. Agriculture is a small sector of the Greek economy, but is fairly labour intensive and would therefore have a larger impact on employment if its products are improved in quality and better marketed. Cultivated land in Greece is not a very large proportion in the landscape of this country, but can surely be used more widely and intensively than done so far. EU subsidies, quite a lot in the case of Greece, are here of a somewhat erratic nature, and could surely be more focused on those commodities which need a Southern climate to really flourish and thus contribute to a positive development of the Greek agriculture.

From the above three sectors of the Greek economy, there remains the manufacturing sector to be considered. Here, and primarily only here, real unit labour costs matter in a direct way, since these products compete with the manufacturing products within the EU and the US economy in terms of production costs (but also quality). Again however we would think that policies aiming at modernisation (Schumpeterian creative destruction) are the better strategy than reductions in money wages, though wages in manufacturing are fairly high in general as compared to those in tourism for example. One may therefore here in addition propose wage freezes for some time, by arguments that call for such a national consensus in those cases where wage differentials are of a pronounced size.

Taken together it is not at all clear therefore that the only remedy for the Greek economy is to leave the Eurozone by reintroducing the drachma and to push up exports through a strong devaluation of the drachma. Instead the strong Business Cycle Authority (BCA) policy discussed earlier, a tax-based innovation policy of the Greek government and a Marshall plan from the EU could push Greece back into growth and on this basis growing tax revenues. The reason for all this is not, of course, to do the Greek economy a great favour, but to avoid a systemic crisis for the whole EU area which might endanger its further existence and the political stability this existence has guaranteed. The development in Europe has now passed a stage where primarily economic reasons are of importance. It must be considered now a political project to create a viable union of multilayered countries which can significantly contribute to the political evolution of the world between the two polar cases, the USA and China, we considered in the general introduction to this book. Viewed from this perspective, a successful steering of the Greek case out of its economic and political crisis will therefore have great importance for the future evolution of the European Union.

9.8 Conclusions and Outlook

We have described in this chapter the progress from welfare states of Christian- or Social-democratic type (as the relations of production) via the concept of a flexicurity economy towards social capitalism built around the forces of production of an economy characterised by profit-seeking creative destruction, but without the Marxian reserve army mechanism (conceived however by many to be needed for maintaining economic and social stability through the threat of unemployment). We by contrast believe that insight into the working of this mechanism under past and current forms of capitalism can establish a cooperative regime between the elites who control the private enterprises and the representatives of the employees that overcomes the role of unemployment as a disciplining device in the establishment of social capitalism. Moreover, such a new social structure of capital accumulation can be based in the political spectrum on the parties in the middle of it, like Christian- and Social-democrats. It thus allows the overcoming in the further evolution of Western type capitalist societies the extreme views of neoliberals (laissez-faire) as well as the views of the new left (socialist). The first believe that a largely unregulated form of capitalism is not only a viable, but also a desirable construction, while the latter believe in societies that do not internalise the productive forces of capitalism, but which are subject to some sort of social planning in all of its sectors of the economy, without need of capitalist techniques of quantity as well as price determination.

We however support the view that modern societies will continue to be mixed ones, where the planning experience of small, medium-sized and large capitalistic firms operates in a strictly competitive private sector, surrounded by a public sector built on the pillars we have described in Section 9.6. The central idea therefore is that the fertile possibilities of capitalism (its forces of production) can be embedded into a social structure of capital accumulation (the relations of production) which makes this type of capitalism a social one in the sense we have discussed it in this chapter.

We have applied these ideas to the situation as it is currently given in the Greek economy and society. Among other things we argued that the possibility of Greece abandoning the Euro Area would give rise to a Greek tragedy, and that expansionary growth and cycle policies, based on appropriate tax reforms (inducing tax base increases) could provide the basis for a sound restructuring of the Greek economy and society that could put it on a 'progress path' to social capitalism. Since we have removed Keynesian fiscal policy from government activities in this chapter, this condition of a balanced budget is a reasonable one, since debt should be used primarily in the anticyclical policies that attempt to reduce such business fluctuations and the accompanying processes of price inflation (or deflation).

It may not be likely that our preceding proposals will convince policy makers in Greece without a further deep crisis in the financial–industrial structure of that country. Indeed, the crisis management in Greece may already be in a state that a truly cleansing effect will not be taken into consideration anymore, due to the power distribution in the Greek parliament and the status and insights of its leading elites. In the end it may therefore well happen that the political decision makers will only implement the IMF–EU reform package in the attempt to bring the Greek society economically back on track, considered by many as sufficient to handle the state crisis in Greece. But this IMF-type of a recovery exhibits no real prospect for the future evolution of the Greek as well as other Western democracies, since it only brings back the train on the (previous) track with less public 'bulk' than before.

However, we believe that the social topics of this chapter will continue to impact the minds of people in advanced capitalist democracies and this again latest when the instabilities of the deregulated financial-industrial market interactions, the social segmentation processes resulting from deregulated labour markets, and the extent of ecological disasters towards which we are moving, come to surface again in a pronounced way. This will then show again that there is at present no alternative to the establishment of a socially-oriented type of capitalism. This debate is – under the name of flexicurity – to a certain degree already conducted within the European Union, but needs the wider perspective of 'social capitalism' as a coherent vision and architecture for the future evolution of, in particular, advanced Western capitalist economies and their democratic decision-making processes.

Our fear however is that political parties in Western type capitalist economies gradually lose their power to shape effective policy through the formation of more and smaller parties under proportional voting schemes and – under majority voting – through the influence of big business in particular in the USA, where features of a media-driven plutocracy are becoming more and more pronounced. The generation of sufficient tax flows and their expenditure as needed under social capitalism may therefore not become the focus of interest under proportional as well as under majority voting. Glasnost and Perestroika concerning the type of capitalism we are living in may therefore not really work in many of the current types of capitalist democracies. It may therefore also happen under 'capitalism' that there holds: They who come too late will be punished by life. But:

> *Crises can homogenise risks, even when citizens are not so similar as the Swedes are (or were in the post-war era) to each other. To the extent that we believe that capitalism's problems can be solved without going through this dynamic process of social insurance followed by changing preferences - that is the social ethos - we ignore history at our peril.*(J. Roemer 2009)

From our perspective, the task to be solved is that parties in the middle of the political spectrum of a country must be convinced that there is urgent need for joint political action towards a modern and healthy public sector, surrounding a private sector of flexicurity type, that is, in particular strictly competitive in orientation and innovation-driven in a Schumpeterian way. How to adjust current forms of capitalism to the sort of social capitalism we have designed in this chapter is of course a huge problem, since institutional changes tend to be slow and contradictory in the patchwork normally generated by the ruling political parties. Like firms, public institutions should however be subject to Darwinian selection processes. Capitalism is fairly successful on the level of firms and clearly outperformed past Eastern Socialism in this, but Western type multi-party democracies still fall too much apart from the successful solution of the problems of socio-political 'creative institutional destruction'.

Notes

[1] This chapter builds on and extends the article of P. Flaschel, S. Luchtenberg and C. Proaño (2011).

[2] See Asada et al. (2010, 2011) for a detailed discussion and proof of these propositions.

[3] See Flaschel, Greiner and Luchtenberg (2012) for their first presentation.

[4] Borrowed from the title of a famous so-called italo-western: '*Il buono, il brutto, il cattivo*.'

[5] http://www.eurofound.europa.eu/areas/industrialrelations/dictionary/definitions/flexicurity.htm

[6] Variants of social capitalism are discussed in detail in Kersbergen (1995), Corfe (2008) and Chan (2002) from a variety of perspectives. We add to these approaches our view that 'social capitalism' has to be rooted in Schumpeter's work on the dynamics of capitalism and its way into a competitive form of socialism (augmented by contributions of Marx as well as Keynes), see Flaschel (2009) with respect to a synthesis of (part of) the work of these three authors.

[7] We stress however that this does not mean that 'private initiative' is dispensable in this matter.

[8] We here refer to 'schools' from age 2 on, but of course nursery schools, kindergarten and schools proper follow different educational aims and practices.

[9] The Australian development is however partly different from the other Anglo–Saxon countries. In 1972–1975, the Australian Labour Party introduced major changes in Australia's social and economic policy agenda and especially extensive reforms in health, education, social security, industrial relations as well as in foreign affairs.

[10] http://www.nytimes.com/2010/04/09/opinion/09krugman.html

[11] http://www.worldsalaries.org/greece.shtml

[12] Once the tax authorities have decided how much tax one must pay it also becomes an official document in Sweden, so that it is free and open for everyone else to see. This is in accordance to the press law from 1949. So you can write to the tax authorities asking them to get basic information about your neighbours' income and tax declaration. ... Historically there has been a tendency towards general publicity when it comes to authorities in Sweden. That's why so many Swedes criticise the lack of openness about decisions in the EU and also complain about it. Swedes are used to having access to protocols and minutes when an authority has made a decision,

such as deciding about the taxes, for example (private communication with Tore Otterup, 2010). In this matter it in fact just happened that the new Greek government published a list of the countryŠs 4152 worst tax evaders, on January 22, 2012, after months of warning those same evaders to pay up or risk being named and shamed.

[13] See the data set of the World Bank: http://data.worldbank.org/indicator/st.int.rcpt.xp.zs.

References

Adrian, T., E. Moench and S.S. Shin (2010), 'Macro risk premium and intermediary balance sheet quantities', Federal Reserve Bank of New York Staff Reports, No. 428.

Aghion, P., P. Bacchetta and A. Banerjee (2001), 'Currency crises and monetary policy in an economy with credit constraints', *European Economic Review*, **45**, pp. 1121–1150.

Alesina, A. and F. Giavazzi (2006), *T*he Future of Europe: Reform or Decline. Cambridge, MA: The MIT Press.

Alonso, S., J. Keane and W. Merkel with the collaboration of M. Fotou (eds)(2011), *The Future of Representative Democracy*, Cambridge: Cambridge University Press.

Andersen, S.K and M. Mailand (2006), *The Danish Flexicurity Model. The Role of the Collective Bargaining System*, Copenhagen: FAOS.

Andersen, T.M. and M. Svarer (2007), 'Flexicurity - Labour Market Performance in Denmark', CESIFO Working Paper 2108.

Arghyrou, M. and J. Tsoukalas (2010), 'The option of last resort. A two-currency EMU', A Roubini Global Economics Project, Europe EconoMonitor, February 7, 2010 (http://www.economonitor.com/blog/2010/02/the-option-of-last-resort-a-two-currency-emu/).

Asada, T., C. Chiarella, P. Flaschel and R. Franke (2010), *Monetary Macrodynamics*, New York: Routledge.

Asada, T., P. Flaschel, T. Mouakil and C.R. Proaño (2011), *Asset Markets, Portfolio Choice and Macroeconomic Activity: A Keynesian Perspective*, Basingstoke, Hampshire: Palgrave Macmillan.

Barbosa-Filho, N. and L. Taylor (2006), 'Distributive and demand cycles in the US economy - A structuralist Goodwin model', *Metroeconomica*, **57**, pp. 389–411.

Barrett, S. (1994), 'Self-Enforcing International Environmental Agreements', *Oxford Economic Papers*, **46**, pp. 878–894.

Barth, J.R., R.D. Jr. Brumbaugh and J.A. Wilcox (2000), 'The repeal of Glass-Steagall and the advent of broad banking', *Journal of Economic Perspectives*, **14**(2), pp. 191–204.

Bawden, T. (2011), 'Arab unrest puts spring in Greece's tourism step', Guardian.co.uk, June 15, 2011 (http://www.guardian.co.uk/world/2011/jun/15/greece-tourism-med-arab-spring).

Bekker, S. and T. Wilthagen (2008), 'Europe's pathways to flexicurity: Lessons presented from and to the Netherlands', *Intereconomics, Review of European Economic Policy*, **43**(2), pp. 68–73.

Bernanke, B. and M. Gertler (1989), 'Agency Costs, Net Worth, and Business Fluctuations', *American Economic Review*, **79**(1), pp. 14–31.

Beveridge, W. (1942), *Social insurance and allied services: Report by Sir William Beveridge*, London: Her Majesty's Stationery Office (HMSO).

Beveridge, W. (1945), *Full employment in a free society*, New York: WW Norton & Co.

Blanchard, O. and L. Katz (1999), 'Wage dynamics: Reconciling theory and evidence', *American Economic Review*, Papers and Proceedings, **89**, pp. 69–74.

Blaschke, B. (2010), 'Basic income and a free activity society. Thoughts on an alternative society' (http://www.archiv-grundeinkommen.de/blaschke/20100129-Basic-Income-and-free-activity-society.pdf).

Blien, U., U. Walwei and H. Werner (2002), 'Labour market policy in Germany. Job placement, unemployment insurance and active labour market policy in Germany', in: K.- S. Yoo and J. Chang (ed.), *Active labor market policies and unemployment insurance in selected countries*, Seoul, pp. 225–285.

BMAS (2010), *Das Arbeitszeitgesetz*, Bundesministerium für Arbeit und Soziales (http://www.bmas.de/portal/9804/arbeitszeitgesetz_a_120.html).

Bordo, M. (2007), 'The crisis of 2007: The same old story, only the players have changed', Remarks prepared for the Federal Reserve Bank of Chicago and International Monetary Fund conference; Globalization and Systemic Risk. Chicago, Illinois September 28, 2007.

Bosch, G. and T. Kalina (2008), 'Low-wage work in Germany: An overview', in: Bosch, G. and Weinkopf, C. (eds), *Low-Wage Work in Germany*, New York: Russel Sage Foundation, pp. 19-112.

Bosch, G. and C. Weinkopf (2008a), 'Preface', in: Bosch, G. and C. Weinkopf (eds), *Low-Wage Work in Germany*, New York: Russel Sage Foundation, pp. 15–18.

Bourdieu, P. (1979), *La distinction. Critique sociale du jugement*, Paris: Edition de Minuit.

Boyer, R. (2006), 'Employment and decent work in the era of flexicurity', United Nations Department of Economic and Social Affairs, Working Paper No. 32.

Bredgaard, T., F. Larsen and P.K. Madsen (2006), 'Opportunities and challenges for flexicurity – The Danish Example', *Transfer: European Review of Labour and Research*, **12**(1), 61–82.

Bredgaard, T., F. Larsen, P.K. Madsen and S. Rasmussen (2009), 'Flexicurity and atypical employment in Denmark', Centre for Labour Market Research, Aalborg University, CARMA Research Paper 2009:01.

Brooker, P. (2010), *Leadership in Democracy*, Second Edition, Houndsmill and New York: Palgrave Macmillan.

Brunnermeier, M. and Y. Sannikov (2010), 'A macroeconomic model with a financial sector', Working Paper, Princeton University.

Bundesagentur für Arbeit (2010), *Monatsbericht Dezember und Jahr 2010* (http://statistik.arbeitsagentur.de/cae/servlet/contentblob/240798/publicationFile/115650/Monatsbericht-201012.pdf).

Busch, M. (1898), *Bismarck. Some Secret Pages of his History being a Diary kept by Dr. Moritz Busch during Twenty-five Years' Official and Private Intercourse with the Great Chancellor in Three Volumes*, Vol. III, London: Macmillan.

Carraro, C. and D. Siniscalco (1998), 'International environmental agreements: Incentives and political economy', *European Economic Review*, **42**, pp. 561 – 572.

Chaini, A. (2011), 'Germans give emphasis on Greece's solar energy', Greek Europe Reporter, July 10 (http://eu.greekreporter.com/2011/07/10/germans-give-emphasis-on-greeces-solar-energy/).

Chan, S.K. (2002), *Social Capitalism*, New York: Vantage Press.

Charpe, M., C. Chiarella, P. Flaschel and W. Semmler (2011), *Financial Assets, Debt and Liquidity Crises. A Keynesian Approach*, Cambridge, UK: Cambridge University Press.

Chiarella, C. and P. Flaschel (2000), *The Dynamics of Keynesian Monetary Growth: Macrofoundations*, Cambridge, UK: Cambridge University Press.

Chiarella, C., P. Flaschel and R. Franke (2005), *Foundations for a Disequilibrium Theory of the Business Cycle. Quantitative Analysis and Qualitative Assessment*, Cambridge, UK: Cambridge University Press.

Chiarella, C., P. Flaschel and W. Semmler (2012a), *Reconstructing Keynesian Macroeconomics. Volume I. Partial Perspectives*, New York: Routledge.

Chiarella, C., P. Flaschel and W. Semmler (2012b), *Reconstructing Keynesian Macroeconomics. Volume II: Integrated Approaches*, New York: Routledge.

Chiarella, C., P. Flaschel and W. Semmler (2013), *Reconstructing Keynesian Macroeconomics. Volume III: Financial Markets and Banking*, New York: Routledge.

Chiarella, C., P. Flaschel, R. Franke and W. Semmler (2009), *Financial Markets and the Macroeconomy. A Keynesian Perspective*, New York: Routledge.

Chiarella, C., P. Flaschel, F. Hartmann and C. Proaño (2012), 'Stock market booms, endogenous credit creation and the implications of broad and narrow banking for macroeconomic stability', Bielefeld University: CEMM working paper.

CIA (2011), *The World Factbook*, Greece (https://www.cia.gov/library/publications/the-world-factbook/geos/gr.html).

Cockshott, P., A. Cottrell and H. Dieterich (2010), 'Transition to 21st century socialism in the European Union', in: puk e.V. (ed.), *Sozialismus XXI. Übergangsprogramm zum Demokratischen Sozialismus des 21. Jahrhunderts in Europa*, Göttingen: AktivDruck & Verlag, pp. 55–74.

Cohen, A. (2010), 'EU debates IMF role for Greece', *The Wall Street*, Journal February 10, 2010.

COM (2007), 'Communication from the commission to the european parliament, the council, the european economic and social committee and the committee of the regions', Commission of the European communities, Brussels (http://eur-lex.europa.eu/LexUriServ/LexUriServ.do?uri=COM:2007:0359:FIN:EN:PDF).

Corfe, R. (2008), *Social Capitalism in Theory and in Practice. Volume I, II, III*, Bury St. Edmunds: Arena Books.

Cornish, W.R. and G. de N. Clark (1989), *Law and Society in England 1750-1950*, London: Sweet and Maxwell.

Dahrendorf, R. (1990), *The Modern Social Conflict: An Essay on the Politics of Liberty*, Berkeley: University of California Press.

Debrun, X., D. Hauner and M. Kumar (2009), 'Independent fiscal agencies', *Journal of Economic Surveys*, **23**(1), pp. 44–81.

Demekas, D.G. and Z.G. Kontolemis (1996), 'Unemployment in Greece: A survey of the issues', IMF Working Paper 96/91, pp. 1–72.

Ejsing, J.W. and W. Lemke (2009), 'The Janus-headed salvation. Sovereign and bank credit risk premia during 2008-09', European Central Bank, Working Paper Series No. 1127.

Elliott, L. (2010), 'Greece's financial crisis puts the future of the Euro in question', *The Observer*, February 7, 2010 (http://www.guardian.co.uk/business/2010/feb/07/greece-fiscal-crisis-european-union-euro).

Esping-Andersen, G. (1990), *The Three Worlds of Welfare Capitalism*, Cambridge, UK: Cambridge University Press.

Eurofound (2009), *Bismarck's Social Security Legislation* (http://www.eurofound.europa.eu/emire/germany/bismarckssocialsecuritylegislation-de.htm).

Eurofound (2010), *Austria: Flexible forms of work: 'very atypical' contractual arrangements* (http://www.eurofound.europa.eu/ewco/studies/tn0812019s/at0812019q.htm).

European Central Bank (2010), 'Press Release', May 3, 2010 (http://www.ecb.int/press/pr/date/2010/html/pr100503.en.html).

European Commission (2007), 'Towards Common Principles of Flexicurity: More and better jobs through flexibility and security', Directorate-General for Employment, Social Affairs and Equal Opportunities, Luxembourg: Office for Official Publications of the European Communities.

European Commission (2008), 'Final report by the Flexicurity Mission', Dec. 2008 (http://ec.europa.eu/social/BlobServlet?docId=1515&langId=en).

European Commission (2008a), 'Towards Common Principles of Flexicurity: More and better jobs through flexibility and security', Brussels (http://eur-lex.europa.eu/LexUriServ/LexUriServ.do?uri=CELEX:52007DC0359:EN:NOT).

European Commission (2010), *Tackling unemployment in Austria* (http://ec.europa.eu/financial-crisis/pdf/tackling_unemployment_at_en.pdf).

European Commission (2011), 'The Economic Adjustment Programme for Greece. Third Review', European Economy, Occasional Papers 77 (http://ec.europa.eu/economy_finance/publications/occasional_paper/2011/pdf/ocp77_en.pdf).

Eurostat (2004), 'Report by Eurostat on the revision of the Greek government deficit and debt figures' (http://epp.eurostat.ec.europa.eu/cache/ity_public/greece/en/greece-en.pdf).

Eurostat (2010), 'Eurostat - Watchdog of European public finances' (http://epp.eurostat.ec.europa.eu/statistics_explained/index.php/Eurostat_-_Watchdog_of_European_public_finances).

Eurostat (2011), 'Statistics' (http://epp.eurostat.ec.europa.eu/portal/page/portal/eurostat/home/).

Eurostat (2011a), 'Unemployment' (http://epp.eurostat.ec.europa.eu/statistics_explained/index.php/Unemployment_statistics#Recent_developments_in_unemployment_at_a_European_and_Member_State_level).

Eurostat (2011b), 'Eurostat newsrelease euroindicators', 69/2011, May 13, 2011 (http://epp.eurostat.ec.europa.eu/cache/ity_public/2-13052011-ap/en/2-13052011-ap-en.pdf).

Eurostat (2011c), *Eurostat Tables, Graph and Maps - Interface TGM Table* (http://epp.eurostat.ec.europa.eu/tgm/table.do?tab=table&language=en&pcode=teilm020&tableSelection=1&footnotes=yes&labeling=labels&plugin=1).

Eurostat (2011d), 'Employment rate of the group 55-64 years, by NUTS 2 regions' (http://epp.eurostat.ec.europa.eu/tgm/table.do?tab=table&init=1&plugin=1&language=en&pcode=tgs00054).

Federal Statistical Office (2011), *Eckzahlen zum Arbeitsmarkt* (http://www.destatis.de/jetspeed/portal/cms/Sites/destatis/Internet/de/Content/Statistiken/Arbeitsmarkt/content75/Eckwertetabelle,templateId=renderPrint.psml).

Fisher, I. (1935), *100% - Money*, New York: Adelphi.

Flaschel, P.(2009), *The Macrodynamics of Capitalism. Elements for a Synthesis of Marx, Keynes and Schumpeter*, Heidelberg: Springer Verlag.

Flaschel, P. (2010), *Topics in Classical Micro- and Macroeconomics*, Heidelberg: Springer Verlag.

Flaschel, P. and A. Greiner (2009), 'Employment cycles and minimum wages: A macro view', *Structural Change and Economic Dynamics*, **20**(4), 279–287.

Flaschel, P. and A. Greiner (2010), 'Dissent-driven capitalism, flexicurity growth and environmental rehabilitation', in: M. Setterfield (ed.), *Handbook of Alternative Theories of Economic Growth*, pp. 331–343, Cheltenham, UK and Northampton, MA, USA: Edward Elgar.

Flaschel, P. and A. Greiner (2011), *A Future for Capitalism. Classical, Neoclassical and Keynesian Perspectives*, Cheltenham, UK and Northampton, MA, USA: Edward Elgar.

Flaschel, P. and A. Greiner (2012), *Flexicurity Capitalism. Foundations, Problems and Perspectives*, Oxford: Oxford University Press.

Flaschel, P. and H.-M. Krolzig (2006), 'Wage-price Phillips curves and macroeconomic stability: Basic structural form, estimation and analysis', in: C. Chiarella, P. Flaschel, R. Franke and W. Semmler (eds), *Quantitative and Empirical Analysis of Nonlinear Dynamic Macromodels. Contributions to Economic Analysis*, Series Editors: B. Baltagi, E. Sadka and D. Wildasin, Amsterdam: Elsevier, pp. 4–48.

Flaschel, P. and M. Landesmann (2006), 'Richard Murphey Goodwin (1993 – 1996). His legacy continued', in: P. Flaschel and M. Landesmann (eds) *Structural Change and Economic Dynamics (Special Issue)*, **17**, pp.379–381.

Flaschel, P. and M. Landesmann (2008), *Mathematical Economics and the Dynamics of Capitalism. The Legacy of Richard Goodwin Continued*, New York: Routledge Frontiers of Political Economy.

Flaschel, P. and C. Malikane (2011), 'Segmented Labor Markets, Distributive Cycles and an Employer of Last Resort', Bielefeld University: CEMM working paper.

Flaschel, P., R. Franke and R. Veneziani (2011), *Value and Competition from the Classical Perspective*, Bielefeld University: Unpublished book manuscript.

Flaschel, P., A. Greiner and S. Luchtenberg (2009), 'Flexicurity capitalism in small Euro-area economies', *Bulletin of Political Economy*, **3**, pp. 107–149.

Flaschel, P., A. Greiner and S. Luchtenberg (2012), 'Flexicurity societies, educational foundations and the formation of elites', *Review of Political Economy*, **24**, pp. 85–111.

Flaschel, P., G. Kauermann and W. Semmler (2007), 'Testing wage and price Phillips curves for the United States', *Metroeconomica*, **58**, pp. 550–581.

Flaschel, P., S. Luchtenberg and C. Proaño (2011), Crisis as Opportunity: Roads towards Social Capitalism. *Bulletin of Political Economy*, 5, 1–40.

Flaschel, P., A. Greiner, S. Luchtenberg and E. Nell (2008), 'Varieties of capitalism. The flexicurity model', in: Flaschel, P. and M. Landesmann (eds.), *Mathematical Economics and the Dynamics of Capitalism*, London, Routledge.

Flaschel, P., F. Hartmann, C. Malikane and W. Semmler (2011), 'Broad banking, financial markets and the return of the narrow banking idea', *Journal of Economic Asymmetries*, **7**(2), pp. 105–138.

Flaschel, P., D. Tavani, L. Taylor and T. Teuber (2008), 'Demand Driven Goodwin Growth Cycles with a Three-Regimes Wage Phillips Curve', Bielefeld University: CEMM working paper No.153.

Franke, R. (1998), 'Quantities and prices', in: Kurz, H.-D. and N. Salvadori (eds), *The Elgar Companion to Classical Economics; L–Z*, Cheltenham, UK and Northampton, MA, USA: Edward Elgar, pp. 236–238.

Franke, R. (1999), 'Technical change and a falling wage share if profits are maintained', *Metroeconomica*, **50**, pp. 35–53.

Franke, R. (2000), 'Wave trains and long waves: a reconsideration of Professor Iwai's Schumpeterian dynamics', in: Delli Gatti, D., M. Gallegati and A.P. Kirman (eds), *Interaction and Market Structure: Essays on Heterogeneity in Economics*, Berlin: Springer Verlag, pp. 89–131.

Franke, R. (2000a), 'An integration of Schumpeterian and classical theories of growth and distribution', *Structural Change and Economic Dynamics*, **11**(3), pp. 317–336.

Franke, R., P. Flaschel and C. Proaño (2006), 'Wage-price dynamics and income distribution in a semi-structural Keynes-Goodwin model', *Structural Change and Economic Dynamics*, **17**, pp. 452–465.

Fredman, S. (2004), 'Women at work: The broken promise of flexicurity', *Industrial Law Journal*, **33**(4), pp. 299–319.

Freixas, X. and J.-C. Rochet (2008), *Microeconomics of Banking*, Cambridge, MA: The MIT Press.

Friedman, M. (1968), 'The role of monetary policy', *American Economic Review*, **58**, pp. 1–17.

Funk, L. (2008), 'European flexicurity policies: A critical assessment', *The International Journal of Comparative Labour Law and Industrial Relations*, **24**(3), pp. 349–384.

Garfinkel, I., L. Rainwater and T. Smeeding (2010), *Wealth and Welfare States. Is America a Laggard or Leader?*, Oxford: Oxford University Press.

Geology.com (2011), 'Marcellus Shale – Appalachian Basin Natural Gas Play' (http://geology.com/articles/marcellus-shale.shtml).

Goldstein, M. and P. Turner (2004), *Controlling Currency Mismatches in Emerging Markets*, Washington D.C.: Institute for International Economics.

Gomez, P.-Y. and H. Korine (2010), *Entrepreneurs and Democracy. A Political Theory of Corporate Governance*, Cambridge: Cambridge University Press.

Goodwin, R. (1967), 'A growth cycle', in: C.H. Feinstein (ed.), *Socialism, Capitalism and Economic Growth*, Cambridge: Cambridge University Press, pp. 54–58.

Goodwin, R. (1972), 'A growth cycle', in: E.K. Hunt and J.G. Schwartz (eds), *A Critique of Economic Theory*, Harmondsworth: Penguin Books, pp. 442–449.

Goodwin, R. M. (1989), *Essays in Nonlinear Economic Dynamics. Collected Papers 1980-1987*, Frankfurt am Main: Peter Lang.

Gorton, G.B. (2009), *Slapped in the Face by the Invisible Hand: Banking and the Panic of 2007*, New York: Oxford University Press.

Gorton, G.B. (2010), 'Questions and answers about the financial crisis', NBER Working Paper No. 15787.

de Grauwe, P. (2008), 'Returning to narrow banking', Center for European Policy Studies: CEPS Commentary (http://www.ceps.be/book/returning-narrow-banking).

Greeka.com (2011), 'Greece economy: Information about the economy of Greece and the Greek Islands'.

Grofman, B., A. Blais and S. Bowler (eds) (2009), *Duverger's Law of Plurality Voting. The Logic of Party Competition in Canada, India, the United Kingdom and the United States*, New York: Springer.

Hanusch, H. and A. Pyka (2007), *The Elgar Companion to Neo-Schumpeterian Economics*, Cheltenham, UK and Northampton, MA, USA: Edward Elgar.

Hanusch, H. and A. Pyka (2007a), 'Applying a comprehensive neo-Schumpeterian approach to Europe and its Lisbon Agenda', in: Tilly R., Welfens, P.J.J. and M. Heise (eds), *50 Years of EU Economics. Integration, Financial Markets and Innovations*, Berlin-Heidelberg, New York: Springer Verlag, pp. 275–299.

Hartmann, M. (2007), *The Sociology of Elites*, Studies in Social and Political Thought, London: Routledge.

Hartmann, D. (2007a), 'Understanding the Lisbon Strategy and policies from a neo-Schumpeterian point of view', *Revista Universitaria Europea*, **7**, pp. 15–40.

Harvie, D. (2000), 'Testing Goodwin: growth cycles in ten OECD countries', *Cambridge Journal of Economics*, **24**, pp. 349–376.

HDR (2010), 'Human Development Index and its components', Human Development Report (http://hdr.undp.org/en/reports/global/hdr2010/chapters/en).

Hellenic Statistical Authority (2011), 'Press Release' (http://www.statistics.gr/portal/page/portal/esye/bucket/a0503/pressreleases/a0503_dkt21_dt_mm_03_2011_01_p_en.pdf).

Hellenic Statistical Authority (2011a), 'Press Release. Unemployment rate' (http://www.statistics.gr/portal/page/portal/esye/bucket/a0101/pressreleases/a0101_sjo02_dt_mm_03_2011_01_f_en.pdf).

Hemming, R. and M. Kell (2001), 'Promoting Fiscal Responsibility: Transparency, Rules and Independent Fiscal Authorities', Paper presented at the Bank of Italy third workshop on 'Fiscal rules' held in Perugia, February 1–3, pp. 433–460 (http://www.bancaditalia.it/studiricerche/convegni/atti/fisc_rules/session3/433\discretionary-460_hemming_and_kell.pdf).

Henkin, G.M. and V.M. Polterovich (1991), 'Schumpeterian dynamics as a non-linear wave theory', *Journal of Mathematical Economics*, **20**, pp. 551–590.

Hetzner, C. and D. Kyriakidou (2011), 'IMF warns EU debt crisis may still spread to core', Reuters May 13, 2011 (http://www.reuters.com/article/2011/05/13/us-eurozone-iduslde7490un20110513).

Higley, J. (2006), 'Elite theory in political sociology', University of Texas (http://theoriesofsocialchange.files.wordpress.com/2010/02/higley_elite_theory_ipsa_2008.pdf).

Hirsch, M. and S. Smale (1974), *Differential Equations, Dynamical Systems and Linear Algebra*, London: Academic Press.

Historyhome.co.uk (2010), 'Factory Legislation 1802–1878' (http://www.historyhome.co.uk/peel/factmine/factleg.htm).

Holborn, H. (1969), *A History of Modern Germany, Volume III*, Princeton, NJ: Princeton University Press.

Hope, K. (2010), 'Humiliation as Papandreou accepts IMF terms', *Financial Times*, April 23 2010 (http://www.ft.com/cms/s/0/762db152-4efb-11df-b8f4-00144feab49a.html#axzz1PZRo76vV).

Hudson River Sloop Clearwater (2011), 'Latest News' (http://www.clearwater.org/category/latest-news).

Hulse, C. and D.M. Herszenhorn (2010), 'Democrats call cff Climate Bill effort', *The New York Times*, July 22, 2010.

IEA (2010), CO_2 emissions from fuel combustion. Highlights', International Energy Agency, Paris.

International Monetary Fund (2010), 'Europe and IMF Agree €110 billion financing plan with Greece', IMF Survey online (http://www.imf.org/external/pubs/ft/survey/so/2010/car050210a.htm).

International Monetary Fund (2010a), 'Frequently Asked Questions Greece' (http://www.imf.org/external/np/exr/faq/greecefaqs.htm).

International Monetary Fund (2011), 'About the IMF' (http://www.imf.org/external/).

International Monetary Fund (2011a), 'Statement by the European Commission, the ECB and IMF on the Fourth Review Mission to Greece', Press Release, No. 11/212, June 3, 2011 (http://www.imf.org/external/np/sec/pr/2011/pr11212.htm).

IMF survey online (2011), 'Recovery continues but crisis risk remains, says IMF', June 21, 2011 (http://www.imf.org/external/pubs/ft/survey/so/2011/car062111a.htm).

Independent Commission on Banking (2011), 'Final Report. Recommendations', September 2011 (http://bankingcommission.independent.gov.uk/).

Ioannidis, A. (2011), 'The social market economy: A cure for all ills?', in: K.E. Botsiou and A. Klapsis (eds) *The Konstantinos Karamanlis Institute for Democracy, Yearbook 2011. The Global Economic Crisis and the Case of Greece*, Heidelberg: Springer Verlag, pp.121–129.

Iwai, K. (1984), 'Schumpeterian dynamics, part II: Technological progress, firm growth and 'economic selection'', *Journal of Economic Behavior and Organization*, **5**, pp. 321–351.

Kalecki, M. (1943), 'Political aspects of full employment', Reprinted in M. Kalecki (ed.) (1971), *Selected Essays on the Dynamics of the Capitalist Economy*, Cambridge: Cambridge University Press.

Kauermann, G., T. Teuber and P. Flaschel (2007), 'Exploring US business cycles with bivariate loops using penalized spline regression', Working Paper, No. 148, Bielefeld University: Center for Empirical Macro- and Microeconomics (CEMM).

Kenworthy, T., D.J. Weiss, L. Kaufman and C.C. DiPasquale (2011), 'Drilling down on fracking concerns. The potential and peril of hydraulic fracturing to drill for natural gas', Center for American Progress (http://www.americanprogress.org/issues/2011/03/pdf/fracking.pdf).

Kersbergen, K. van (1995), *Social Capitalism. A Study of Christian Democracy and the Welfare State*, London: Routledge.

Keune, M. and M. Jepsen (2007), 'Not balanced and hardly new: The European Commission's quest for flexicurity', ETUI-REHS (European Trade Union Institute for Research, Education and Health and Safety), Working Paper 1/2007.

Keynes, J.M. (1936), *The General Theory of Employment, Interest and Money*, New York: Macmillan.

Khoudour-Casteras, D. (2008), 'Welfare state and labor mobility: The impact of Bismarck's social legislation on German emigration before World War I', *Journal of Economic History*, **68**, pp. 211–243.

Kindleberger, C.P. and R.Z. Aliber (2005), *Manias, Panics and Crashes: A History of Financial Crises*, Hoboken, New Jersey: Jon Wiley & Sons.

Kissinger, H. (2011), *On China*, New York: The Penguin Press.

Klammer, U. (2004), 'Flexicurity in a life-course perspective', *Transfer: European Review of Labour and Research*, **10**, pp.282–299.

Krugman, P. (2000), 'Crises: The price of globalization?', *Global Economic Integration: Opportunities and Challenges*, Federal Reserve Bank of Kansas City, pp. 75–105.

Krugman, P. (2009), 'It's easy being green', *The New York Times*, September 25, 2009.

Krugman, P. and M. Obstfeld (2003), *International Economics. Theory and Policy*, , 6th edition, London: Addison-Wesley.

Lashof, D., J. Wong and L. Johnson (2009), 'A clean energy bargain: More jobs, less global warming, pollution, and greater security for less than the cost of a postage stamp', NRDC (Natural Resources Defense Council) (http://www.nrdc.org/globalwarming/cap2.0/files/ebargain.pdf).

Lawn, P. (ed.) (2009), *Environment and Employment: A Reconciliation. (Routledge Studies in Ecological Economics)*, Abingdon, New York: Routledge Chapman & Hall.

Lloyd, C., G. Mason and K. Mayhew (2008), *Low-Wage Work in the United Kingdom (The Russell Sage Foundation Case Studies of Job Quality in Advanced Economies)*, New York: Russell Sage Foundation.

Lošonc, A. (2006), 'Is there an opportunity to establish the social capitalism in the post-socialist tradition?', *Panoeconomicus*, **4**, pp. 407–425.

Mall, A., S. Buccino and J. Nichols (2007), 'Drilling down. Protecting western communities from the health and environmental effects of oil and gas production', NRDC (Natural Resources Defense Council) (http://www.nrdc.org/land/use/down/down.pdf).

McGregor, R. (2010), *The Party. The Secret World of China's Communist Rulers*, New York: HarperCollins Publishers.

McKinley, T. (2010), 'Has the IMF abandoned neoliberalism?', London: Centre for Development Policy and Research SOAS, University of London, Development Viewpoint 51 (http://www.soas.ac.uk/cdpr/publications/dv/file58920.pdf).

Manolopoulos, J. (2011), *Greece's 'Odious' Debt: The Looting of the Hellenic Republic by the Euro, the Political Elite and the Investment Community*, London: Anthem Press.

Marglin, S. (1984), *Growth, Distribution, and Prices*, Cambridge, MA: Harvard University Press.

Marx, K. (1954), *Capital. A Critique of Political Economy, Vol. I*, New York: Lawrence and Wishart.

van Meerhaeghe, M. (2006), 'Bismarck and the social question', *Journal of Economic Studies*, **33**, pp. 284–301.

Melinz, G. (2006), 'Zwischen Vision und Wirklichkeit – ÖKSA eine Plattform im Wandel der Zeit' (http://www.oeksa.at/files/melinz_textbeilage.pdf).

Metcalfe, J.S. (1997), *Evolutionary Economics and Creative Destruction*, London: Routledge.

Mills, C.W. (1959), *The Power Elite*, Oxford: Oxford University Press.

Minsky, H.P. (1982), *Can it Happen Again? Essays on Instability and Finance*, New York: M.E. Sharpe.

Minsky, H.P. (1986), *Stabilizing an unstable economy*, New Haven: Yale University Press.

Mohun, S. and R. Veneziani (2008), 'Goodwin cycles and the US economy, 1948–2004', in: Flaschel, P. and M. Landesmann (2008), *Mathematical Economics and the Dynamics of Capitalism. The Legacy of Richard Goodwin Continued*, London: Routledge Frontiers of Political Economy, pp. 107–130.

Naastepad, C.W.M. (2006), 'Technology, demand and distribution: A cumulative growth model with an application to the dutch productivity slowdown', *Cambridge Journal of Economics*, **30**, pp. 403–434.

National Commission on the BP Deepwater Horizon Oil Spill and Offshore Drilling (2011), Final Report (http://www.oilspillcommission.gov/final-report).

Neck, R. (2009), 'Was ist aus der Berufsständischen Ordnung geworden?', Referat zur Tagung des Ausschusses 'Wirtschaftswissenschaften und Ethik' des Vereins für Socialpolitik, February 26–28, 2009.

Nienhaus, L. (2011), 'Umschuldung. Was kosten uns die Griechen?', *Frankfurter Allgemeine Zeitung*, June, 14, 2011 (http://www.

faz.net/artikel/S30638/umschuldung-was-kosten-uns-die-griechen-30337827.html).

Nordhaus, W.D. (2010),'Economic aspects of global warming in a post-Copenhagen environment', *Proceedings of the National Academy of Sciences of the United States of America*, **107**(26), pp. 11721–11726.

NRDC (2009), 'Protecting New Yorkers' health and the environment by regulating drilling in the Marcellus shale', Natural Resources Defense Council (http://www.nrdc.org/land/files/marcellus.pdf).

NRDC (2011), 'About NRDC', Natural Resources Defense Council (http://www.nrdc.org/about/priorities.asp).

NRDC (2011a), 'The BP oil disaster at one year: A straightforward assessment of what we know, what we don't, and what questions need to be answered', April 2011, Natural Resources Defense Council (http://www.nrdc.org/energy/files/bpoildisasteroneyear.pdf).

Offe, C. (2003), 'The European model of 'social' capitalism: Can it survive European integration?', *The Journal of Political Philosophy*, **11**, pp. 437–469.

Okishio, N. (1961), 'Technical change and the rate of profit', *Kobe University Economic Review*, **7**, pp. 86–99.

Okun, A.M. (1970), *The Political Economy of Prosperity*, Washington, D.C.: The Brookings Institution.

Pareto, V. (1935), *The Mind and Society*, London: Harcourt Brace.

Pieper, U. and L. Taylor (1998), 'The revival of the liberal creed: The IMF, the World Bank, and inequality in a globalized economy', Schwartz Center for Economic Policy Analysis, No. 96/05.

Pissarides, C.A. (1990), *Equilibrium Unemployment Theory*. Cambridge, MA: The MIT Press.

Proaño, C., P. Flaschel, E. Ernst and W. Semmler (2006), 'Gradual wage-price adjustments and Keynesian macrodynamics: Evidence from the U.S. and the Euro Area', Available online under the title: *Disequilibrium Macroeconomic Dynamics, Income Distribution and Wage-Price Phillips Curves: Evidence from the U.S. and the euro area*, Macroeconomic Policy Institute (IMK), IMK Working Paper 04/2006.

Proaño, C., P. Flaschel, H.-M. Krolzig and B. Diallo (2011), 'Reconsidering the dynamic interaction between real wages and macroeconomic activity', *Research in World Economy*, **2**, pp. 77–93.

Pryor, F.L. (2010), *Capitalism Reassessed*, Cambridge: Cambridge University Press.

Public Employment Service Austria (AMS)(2011), *Unemployment Insurance* (http://www.ams.or.at/english/14609.html).

Quirk, V. et al. (2006), 'The job guarantee in practice', University of Newcastle, Australia, Center of Full Employment and Equity, CofFEE Working Paper No. 06-15.

Reuters (2010), 'Timeline: Greece's economic crisis' (http://www.reuters.com/article/2010/02/03/us-greece-economy-events-idUSTRE6124EL20100203).

Rochet, J.-C. (2008), *Why are there so many Banking Crises. The Politics and Policy of Bank Regulation*, Princeton: Princeton University Press.

Roemer, J. (1994), *A Future for Socialism*, Cambridge, MA: Harvard University Press.

Roemer, J. (2009), 'Changing the social ethos is the key', *The Economists Voice*, Berkeley Electronic Press, **6**(7).

Rose, H. (1967), 'On the non-linear theory of the employment cycle', *Review of Economic Studies*, **34**, pp. 153–173.

Rudd, K. (2009), 'The global financial crisis', *The Monthly Essays*, 20–29 February 2009 (http://www.themonthly.com.au/monthly-essays-kevin-rudd-global-financial-crisis--1421).

Sargent, T. and N. Wallace (1973), 'The stability of models of money and growth with perfect foresight', *Econometrica*, **41**, pp. 1043–1048.

Sawyer, M. (2005), 'Employer of last resort: An extended response to my critics' (http://129.11.89.221/MKB/MalcolmSawyer/elra.pdf).

Schneider, F. (2011), 'The shadow economy and shadow economy labor force: What do we (not) know?' (http://www.iza.org/conference_files/InfoETE2011/schneider_f206.pdf).

Schumpeter, J.A. (1934), *The Theory of Economic Development*, Oxford: Oxford University Press.

Schumpeter, J.A. (1939), *Business Cycles*, Vols. I and II, Philadelphia: Porcupine Press.

Schumpeter, J.A. (1942), *Capitalism, Socialism and Democracy*, 3rd edition, New York: Harper and Row.

Schumpeter, J.A. (1950), *Kapitalismus, Sozialismus und Demokratie*, 2nd edition, Bern: Francke.

Siaroff, A. (1999), 'Corporatism in 24 industrial democracies: Meaning and measurement', *European Journal of Political Research*, **36**, pp. 175–205.

Silverberg, G. and D. Lehnert (1993), 'Long waves and "evolutionary chaos" in a simple Schumpeterian model of embodied technical change', *Structural Change and Economic Dynamics*, **4**, pp. 9–37.

Silverberg, G. and B. Verspagen (1997), 'Of artificial and real worlds, or from modeling to econometric metaphor', Maastricht Economic Research Institute on Innovation and Technology, *mimeo*.

Simon, J.L. (1990), 'Great and almost-great magnitudes in economics', *Journal of Economic Perspectives*, **4**, pp. 149–156.

Sinn, H.-W. (2008), *Risk-Taking, Limited Liability and the Banking Crisis*, Munich: Ifo Institute.

Soete, L. and R. Turner (1984), 'Technology diffusion and the rate of technical change', *Economic Journal*, **94**, pp. 612–623.

Solow, R. (1956), 'A contribution to the theory of economic growth', *Quarterly Journal of Economics*, **70**, pp. 65–94.

Solow, R. (1990), 'Goodwin's growth cycle: Reminiscence and rumination', in: K. Velupillai (ed.), *Nonlinear and Multisectoral Macrodynamics*, London: Macmillan, pp. 31–41.

Solow, R. (2008), 'The German Story (Introduction)', in: Bosch, G. and C. Weinkopf (eds), *Low-Wage Work in Germany*, New York: Russel Sage Foundation, pp. 1–18.

Solow, R. (2008a), 'Introduction. The Danish Story', in: N. Westergaard-Nielsen (eds), *Low-Wage Work in Denmark*, New York: Russell Sage Foundation, pp. 1–15.

Sourcewatch (2011), 'Fracking', Sourcewatch/Center for Media and Democracy (CMD) (http://www.sourcewatch.org/index.php?title=Fracking).

Spiegel, P. and Q. Peel (2011), 'Proposal raises Greek downgrade fears', *The Economist*, June 14, 2011 (http://www.ft.com/cms/s/0/943db9b2-96b7-11e0-baca-00144feab49a.html#axzz1PZRo76vV).

Statistics Denmark (2011), 'Net unemployment seasonally adjusted' (http://www.dst.dk/HomeUK/Statistics/Key_indicators/Labour_market/Unemployment.aspx).

Statistik Austria (2009), Arbeitsmarktstatistik 3. Quartal 2009, Mikrozensus-Arbeitskräfteerhebung, Schnellbericht 5.8, Wien: Statistik Austria.

Swedberg, R. (1991), *Schumpeter. A Biography*, Princeton: Princeton University Press.

Tangian, A. (2007), 'European flexicurity: concept, methodology and policies', *Transfer: European Review of Labour and Research*, **4**, pp. 551–573.

Tavani, D., P. Flaschel and L. Taylor (2011), 'Estimated non-linearities and multiple equilibria in a model of distributive-demand cycles', *International Review of Applied Economics*, **255**, pp. 519–538.

Tavani, D., P. Flaschel, L. Taylor and T. Teuber (2010), 'Estimated non-linearities and multiple equilibria in a model of distributive-demand cycles', Working Paper, No. 141, Bielefeld University: Center for Empirical Macro- and Microeconomics (CEMM).

Taylor, L. (2004), *Reconstructing Macroeconomics. Structuralist Proposals and Critique of the Mainstream*, Cambridge, MA: Harvard University Press.

Tcherneva, P. (2007), 'What are the relative macroeconomic merits and environmental impacts of direct job creation and basic income guarantees?', The Levy Economics Institute of Bard College, Working Paper No. 517.

Tcherneva, P. and L.R. Wray (2005), 'Common goals – different solutions: Can basic income and job guarantees deliver their own promises?', *Rutgers Journal of Law and Urban Policy*, **2**(1), pp. 125–166.

Tobin, J. (1980), *Asset Accumulation and Economic Activity. Reflections on Contemporary Macroeconomic Theory*, Oxford: Basil Blackwell

Tompson, W. (2009), 'The political economy of reform: Lessons from pensions, product markets and labour markets in ten OECD countries', OECD Publishing.

Traa, B. (2011), 'Achieving sustainable economic reforms in Greece in 2011 and beyond', IMF External Relations Department, June 7, 2011 (http://www.imf.org/external/np/speeches/2011/060711.htm).

UNEP Year Book (2010), 'United Nations Environment Programme: New Science and Developments in pour changing environment' (http://www.unep.org/yearbook/2010).

Urbina, I. (2011), 'Pennsylvania calls for more water tests', *The New York Times*, April 7, 2011.

Vandaele, K. (2006), 'Special focus on the Ghent system. A report from the homeland of the Ghent system: The relationship between unemployment and trade union membership in Belgium', *Transfer: European Review of Labour and Research*, **4**, pp. 647–657.

Van Waeyenberge, E., H. Bargawi, H. and T. McKinley (2010), 'Standing in the way of development? A critical survey of the IMF's crisis response in low income countries', A Eurodad and Third World Network report in cooperation with the Heinrich Böll Foundation (http://www.eurodad.org/whatsnew/reports.aspx?id=4083).

Vielle, P. and J.-M. Bonvin (2008), 'Putting security at the heart of the European social pact - proposals to make flexicurity more balanced', *Transfer: European Review of Labour and Research*, **3**, pp. 419–433.

Viebrock, E. (2004), 'Coping with corporatism's legitimacy deficit: Recent attempts at reforming the Austrian chamber system', Annual Meeting of the American Political Science Association 2–5 September, 2004.

Viebrock, E. and J. Clasen (2009), 'Flexicurity and welfare reform: a review', *Socio-economic Review*, **7**, pp. 305–331.

The Wall Street Journal (2011), 'Plan focuses on rescheduling of Greek debt', Europe News – June 6, 2011 (http://online.wsj.com/article/SB10001424052702304474804576367563185441814.html).

Westergaard-Nielsen, N. (ed.) (2008), *Low-Wage Work in Denmark (The Russell Sage Foundation Case Studies of Job Quality in Advanced Economies)*, New York: Russell Sage Foundation.

Wilthagen, T. (1998), 'Flexicurity: A new paradigm for labour market policy reform?', Social Science Research Center Berlin, Discussion Paper No. FS I 98-202.

Wilthagen , T. and F. Tros (2004), 'The concept of 'flexicurity': A new approach to regulating employment and labour markets', *European Review of Labour and Research*, **10**(2), pp. 166–186.

Wörgötter, A. (1986), 'Who's who in Goodwin's growth cycle', *Jahrbuch für Nationalökonomie und Statistik*, **201**, pp. 222–228.

Wolff, J. (2002), *Why Read Marx Today?*, Oxford: Oxford University Press.

Wolfstetter, E. (1977), *Wert, Profitrate und Beschäftigung*, Frankfurt a.M.: Campus Verlag.

Wong, J. and Z. Bo (2010), *China's Reform in Global Perspective*, Series on Contemporary China - Vol. 24, Singapore et al.: World Scientific Publishing.

World Bank (2011), World Development Indicators database, April 14, 2011 (http://siteresources.worldbank.org/DATASTATISTICS/Resources/GDP_PPP.pdf.)

World Economic Forum (2009), 'The Global Competitiveness Report 2009–2010', Geneva (https://members.weforum.org/pdf/GCR09/GCR20092010fullreport.pdf).

Wray, L.R. (2008), 'Macroeconomic stability, affordability and manageability of employer of last resort programmes', in: Arestis, P. and J. McCombie (eds), *Missing Links in the Unemployment Relationship*, Basingstoke, UK: Palgrave Macmillan, pp. 95–112.

Wray, L.R. and P. Tcherneva (2005), 'Basic Income Guarantees Versus Employers of Last Resort: Responses to Questions and Comments', *Rutgers Journal of Law & Urban Policy*, **2**(1), pp. 248–256.

Notations

Steady state or trend values are indicated by a sub(super)script 'o'. A dot over a variable $x = x(t)$ denotes the time derivative, a caret its growth rate; $\dot{x} = dx/dt$, $\hat{x} = \dot{x}/x$. As far as possible, the notation tries to follow the logic of using capital letters for level variables and lower case letters for variables in intensive form, or for constant (steady state) ratios. Greek letters are most often constant coefficients in behavioral equations (with, however, the notable exceptions being the π's, and ω). Moreover there is some 'local' notation which only applies to certain chapters of the book.

B	outstanding government fixed-price bonds (priced at $p_b = 1$)
C	real private consumption (demand is generally realized)
E	number of equities
G	real government expenditure (demand is always realized)
I	real net investment of fixed capital (demand is always realized)
J	Jacobian matrix in the mathematical analysis
K	stock of fixed capital
L^d	employment, i.e., total working hours per year (labor demand is always realized)
L^w	employed workforce, i.e., number of employed people
L	labor supply, i.e., supply of total working hours per year
M	stock of money supply
S_f	real saving of firms
S_g	real government saving
S_p	real saving of private households
S	total real saving; $S = S_f + S_g + S_h$
T	total real tax collections
Λ_f, Λ_g	debt of firms, government
D_c, D_t	checkable and time deposits
W^n	nominal wealth of private households

Y	real output
Y^d	real aggregate demand
c	marginal propensity to consume
e	employment rate
$U = 1 - e$	unemployment rate
$f_x = f_1$ *etc.*	partial derivative
i	nominal rate of interest on government bonds
r	short-run rate of profit of firms (or dividend rate)
p	price level
n	natural growth rate of the labor force
p_e	price of equities
s_c	propensity to save out of capital income on the part of asset owners
s_w	workers' propensity to save out of their income
u	rate of capacity utilization; $u = Y/Y^n = y/y^n$
v	wage share (in gross product); $v = wL/pY$
w	nominal wage rate per hour
y	output–capital ratio; $y = Y/K$;
l	labor intensity
k	capital intensity K/L
z or x	labor productivity, i.e., output per worker; $z = Y/L^d$
$n = N/K$	infrastructure (per unit of capital), ch.7
β_x	generically, reaction coefficient in an equation determining x, $\dot{x}$ or $\hat{x}$
β_{xy}	generically, reaction coefficient related to the determination of variable x, $\dot{x}$ or $\hat{x}$ with respect to changes in the exogenous variable y
δ	rate of depreciation of fixed capital (a constant)
$\eta_{m,i}$	interest elasticity of money demand (expressed as a positive number)
κ_p	parameter weighting $\hat{w}$ vs. π^c in price Phillips curve
κ_w	parameter weighting $\hat{p}$ vs. π^c in wage Phillips curve
κ	coefficient in reduced-form wage–price equations; $\kappa = 1/(1 - \kappa_p\kappa_w)$
ω	real wage rate w/p
g_z	growth rate of labor productivity

Author Index

Subject Index